COLLECTED VERSE
OF
EDGAR A. GUEST

COLLECTED VERSE

OF

EDGAR A. GUEST

I'd like to think when life is done
That I had filled a needed post,
That here and there I'd paid my fare
With more than idle talk and boast;
That I had taken gifts divine,
The breath of life and manhood fine,
And tried to use them now and then
In service for my fellow men.

EDGAR A. GUEST

August 20, 1881 — August 5, 1959

THE REILLY & LEE CO.
PUBLISHERS—CHICAGO

Copyright © 1934 by Contemporary Books, Inc.
All rights reserved
Published by Contemporary Books, Inc.
180 North Michigan Avenue, Chicago, Illinois 60601
Manufactured in the United States of America
Library of Congress Catalog Card Number: 77-92070
International Standard Book Number: 0-8092-8828-1

Published simultaneously in Canada by
Beaverbooks
953 Dillingham Road
Pickering, Ontario L1W 1Z7
Canada

TO NELLIE

Whose devotion through the years deserves a greater tribute.

FOREWORD

I am grateful to my publishers for deciding to make this single volume collection of my verse and even more grateful to the many friends who have urged that it be done. I know that there will be bits omitted which some will think should have been included, for that has always been the way. However here they are—gathered together into a single book—the old ones and many of the new and my hope is that I have chosen well.

Edgar A. Guest

CONTENTS

CONTENTS *(Continued)*

CONTENTS *(Continued)*

CONTENTS *(Continued)*

CONTENTS *(Continued)*

CONTENTS *(Continued)*

CONTENTS *(Continued)*

WHEN YOU KNOW A FELLOW

When you get to know a fellow, know his joys
 and know his cares,
When you've come to understand him and the
 burdens that he bears,
When you've learned the fight he's making and
 the troubles in his way,
Then you find that he is different than you
 thought him yesterday.
You find his faults are trivial and there's not so
 much to blame
In the brother that you jeered at when you only
 knew his name.

You are quick to see the blemish in the distant
 neighbor's style,
You can point to all his errors and may sneer
 at him the while,
And your prejudices fatten and your hates
 more violent grow
As you talk about the failures of the man you
 do not know,
But when drawn a little closer, and your hands
 and shoulders touch,
You find the traits you hated really don't
 amount to much.

When you get to know a fellow, know his every
    mood and whim,
You begin to find the texture of the splendid
    side of him;
You begin to understand him, and you cease to
    scoff and sneer,
For with understanding always prejudices dis-
    appear.
You begin to find his virtues and his faults you
    cease to tell,
For you seldom hate a fellow when you know
    him very well.

When next you start in sneering and your
    phrases turn to blame,
Know more of him you censure than his business
    and his name;
For it's likely that acquaintance would your
    prejudice dispel
And you'd really come to like him if you
    knew him very well.
When you get to know a fellow and you under-
    stand his ways,
Then his faults won't really matter, for you'll
    find a lot to praise.

THE ROUGH LITTLE RASCAL

A smudge on his nose and a smear on his cheek
And knees that might not have been washed in
    a week;
A bump on his forehead, a scar on his lip,
A relic of many a tumble and trip:
A rough little, tough little rascal, but sweet,
Is he that each evening I'm eager to meet.

A brow that is beady with jewels of sweat;
A face that's as black as a visage can get;
A suit that at noon was a garment of white,
Now one that his mother declares is a fright:
A fun-loving, sun-loving rascal, and fine,
Is he that comes placing his black fist in mine.

A crop of brown hair that is tousled and tossed;
A waist from which two of the buttons are lost;
A smile that shines out through the dirt and the
    grime,
And eyes that are flashing delight all the time:
All these are the joys that I'm eager to meet
And look for the moment I get to my street

MY CREED

To live as gently as I can;
To be, no matter where, a man;
To take what comes of good or ill
And cling to faith and honor still;
To do my best, and let that stand
The record of my brain and hand;
And then, should failure come to me,
Still work and hope for victory.

To have no secret place wherein
I stoop unseen to shame or sin;
To be the same when I'm alone
As when my every deed is known;
To live undaunted, unafraid
Of any step that I have made;
To be without pretense or sham
Exactly what men think I am.

To leave some simple mark behind
To keep my having lived in mind;
If enmity to aught I show,
To be an honest, generous foe,
To play my little part, nor whine
That greater honors are not mine.
This, I believe, is all I need
For my philosophy and creed.

WHAT A BABY COSTS

"How much do babies cost?" said he
The other night upon my knee;
And then I said: "They cost a lot;
A lot of watching by a cot,
A lot of sleepless hours and care,
A lot of heart-ache and despair,
A lot of fear and trying dread,
And sometimes many tears are shed
In payment for our babies small,
But every one is worth it all.

"For babies people have to pay
A heavy price from day to day —
There is no way to get one cheap.
Why, sometimes when they're fast asleep
You have to get up in the night
And go and see that they're all right.
But what they cost in constant care
And worry, does not half compare
With what they bring of joy and bliss —
You'd pay much more for just a kiss.

"Who buys a baby has to pay
A portion of the bill each day;
He has to give his time and thought
Unto the little one he's bought.
He has to stand a lot of pain
Inside his heart and not complain;

And pay with lonely days and sad
For all the happy hours he's had.
All this a baby costs, and yet
His smile is worth it all, you bet."

MOTHER

Never a sigh for the cares that she bore for me,
   Never a thought of the joys that flew by;
Her one regret that she couldn't do more for me,
   Thoughtless and selfish, her Master was I.

Oh, the long nights that she came at my call to
      me!
   Oh, the soft touch of her hands on my brow!
Oh, the long years that she gave up her all to
      me!
   Oh, how I yearn for her gentleness now!

Slave to her baby! Yes, that was the way of
      her,
   Counting her greatest of services small;
Words cannot tell what this old heart would
      say of her,
   Mother -— the sweetest and fairest of all.

SELFISH

I am selfish in my wishin' every sort o' joy for
    you;
I am selfish when I tell you that I'm wishin'
    skies o' blue
Bending o'er you every minute, and a pocketful
    of gold,
An' as much of love an' gladness as a human
    heart can hold.
Coz I know beyond all question that if such a
    thing could be
As you cornerin' life's riches you would share
    'em all with me.

I am selfish in my wishin' every sorrow from
    your way,
With no trouble thoughts to fret you at the
    closin' o' the day;
An' it's selfishness that bids me wish you com-
    forts by the score,
An' all the joys you long for, an' on top o'
    them, some more;
Coz I know, old tried an' faithful, that if such
    a thing could be
As you cornerin' life's riches you would share
    'em all with me.

MA AND THE AUTO

Before we take an auto ride Pa says to Ma: "My dear,
Now just remember I don't need suggestions from the rear.
If you will just sit still back there and hold in check your fright,
I'll take you where you want to go and get you back all right.
Remember that my hearing's good and also I'm not blind,
And I can drive this car without suggestions from behind."

Ma promises that she'll keep still, then off we gayly start,
But soon she notices ahead a peddler and his cart.
"You'd better toot your horn," says she, "to let him know we're near;
He might turn out!" and Pa replies: "Just shriek at him, my dear."
And then he adds: "Some day, some guy will make a lot of dough
By putting horns on tonneau seats for women-folks to blow!"

A little farther on Ma cries: "He signaled for
 a turn!"
And Pa says: "Did he?" in a tone that's hot
 enough to burn.
"Oh, there's a boy on roller skates!" cries Ma.
 "Now do go slow.
I'm sure he doesn't see our car." And Pa says:
 "I dunno,
I think I don't need glasses yet, but really it
 may be
That I am blind and cannot see what's right
 in front of me."

If Pa should speed the car a bit some rigs to
 hurry past
Ma whispers: "Do be careful now. You're
 driving much too fast."
And all the time she's pointing out the dangers
 of the street
And keeps him posted on the roads where
 trolley cars he'll meet.
Last night when we got safely home, Pa sighed
 and said: "My dear,
I'm sure we've all enjoyed the drive you gave
 us from the rear!"

ON GOING HOME FOR CHRISTMAS

He little knew the sorrow that was in his vacant
      chair;
He never guessed they'd miss him, or he'd
      surely have been there;
He couldn't see his mother or the lump that
      filled her throat,
Or the tears that started falling as she read
      his hasty note;
And he couldn't see his father, sitting sor-
      rowful and dumb,
Or he never would have written that he thought
      he couldn't come.

He little knew the gladness that his presence
      would have made,
And the joy it would have given, or he never
      would have stayed.
He didn't know how hungry had the little
      mother grown
Once again to see her baby and to claim him
      for her own.
He didn't guess the meaning of his visit
      Christmas Day
Or he never would have written that he
      couldn't get away.

He couldn't see the fading of the cheeks that
     once were pink,
And the silver in the tresses; and he didn't
     stop to think
How the years are passing swiftly, and next
     Christmas it might be
There would be no home to visit and no mother
     dear to see.
He didn't think about it — I'll not say he didn't
     care.
He was heedless and forgetful or he'd surely
     have been there.

Are you going home for Christmas? Have you
     written you'll be there?
Going home to kiss the mother and to show
     her that you care?
Going home to greet the father in a way to
     make him glad?
If you're not I hope there'll never come a time
     you'll wish you had.
Just sit down and write a letter — it will make
     their heart strings hum
With a tune of perfect gladness — if you'll tell
     them that you'll come.

HOME

It takes a heap o' livin' in a house t' make it
 home,
A heap o' sun an' shadder, an' ye sometimes
 have t' roam
Afore ye really 'preciate the things ye lef'
 behind,
An' hunger fer 'em somehow, with 'em allus
 on yer mind.
It don't make any differunce how rich ye get
 t' be,
How much yer chairs an' tables cost, how great
 yer luxury;
It ain't home t' ye, though it be the palace of a
 king,
Until somehow yer soul is sort o' wrapped round
 everything.

Home ain't a place that gold can buy or get up
 in a minute;
Afore it's home there's got t' be a heap o' livin'
 in it;
Within the walls there's got t' be some babies
 born, and then
Right there ye've got t' bring 'em up t' women
 good, an' men;
And gradjerly, as time goes on, ye find ye
 wouldn't part

With anything they ever used — they've grown
    into yer heart:
The old high chairs, the playthings, too, the
    little shoes they wore
Ye hoard; an' if ye could ye'd keep the thumb-
    marks on the door.

Ye've got t' weep t' make it home, ye've got t'
    sit an' sigh
An' watch beside a loved one's bed, an' know
    that Death is nigh;
An' in the stillness o' the night t' see Death's
    angel come,
An' close the eyes o' her that smiled, an' leave
    her sweet voice dumb.
Fer these are scenes that grip the heart, an'
    when yer tears are dried,
Ye find the home is dearer than it was, an'
    sanctified;
An' tuggin' at ye always are the pleasant
    memories
O' her that was an' is no more — ye can't escape
    from these.

Ye've got t' sing an' dance fer years, ye've got
    t' romp an' play,
An' learn t' love the things ye have by usin' 'em
    each day;
Even the roses 'round the porch must blossom
    year by year

Afore they 'come a part o' ye, suggestin'
    someone dear
Who used t' love 'em long ago, an' trained 'em
    jes' t' run
The way they do, so's they would get the early
    mornin' sun;
Ye've got t' love each brick an' stone from
    cellar up t' dome:
It takes a heap o' livin' in a house t' make it
    home.

THE PATH THAT LEADS TO HOME

The little path that leads to home,
    That is the road for me,
I know no finer path to roam,
    With finer sights to see.
With thoroughfares the world is lined
    That lead to wonders new,
But he who treads them leaves behind
    The tender things and true.

Oh, north and south and east and west
    The crowded roadways go,
And sweating brow and weary breast
    Are all they seem to know.
And mad for pleasure some are bent,
    And some are seeking fame,

And some are sick with discontent,
 And some are bruised and lame.

Across the world the gleaming steel
 Holds out its lure for men,
But no one finds his comfort real
 Till he comes home again.
And charted lanes now line the sea
 For weary hearts to roam,
But, Oh, the finest path to me
 Is that which leads to home.

'Tis there I come to laughing eyes
 And find a welcome true;
'Tis there all care behind me lies
 And joy is ever new.
And, Oh, when every day is done
 Upon that little street,
A pair of rosy youngsters run
 To me with flying feet.

The world with myriad paths is lined
 But one alone for me,
One little road where I may find
 The charms I want to see.
Though thoroughfares majestic call
 The multitude to roam,
I would not leave, to know them all,
 The path that leads to home.

A FRIEND'S GREETING

I'd like to be the sort of friend that you have
been to me;
I'd like to be the help that you've been always
glad to be;
I'd like to mean as much to you each minute
of the day
As you have meant, old friend of mine, to me
along the way.

I'd like to do the big things and the splendid
things for you,
To brush the gray from out your skies and
leave them only blue;
I'd like to say the kindly things that I so oft
have heard,
And feel that I could rouse your soul the way
that mine you've stirred.

I'd like to give you back the joy that you have
given me,
Yet that were wishing you a need I hope will
never be;
I'd like to make you feel as rich as I, who
travel on
Undaunted in the darkest hours with you to
lean upon.

I'm wishing at this Christmas time that I could
    but repay
A portion of the gladness that you've strewn
    along my way;
And could I have one wish this year, this only
    would it be:
I'd like to be the sort of friend that you have
    been to me.

A SONG

None knows the day that friends must part
    None knows how near is sorrow;
If there be laughter in your heart,
    Don't hold it for to-morrow.
Smile all the smiles you can to-day;
Grief waits for all along the way.

To-day is ours for joy and mirth;
    We may be sad to-morrow;
Then let us sing for all we're worth,
    Nor give a thought to sorrow.
None knows what lies along the way;
Let's smile what smiles we can to-day.

OLD FRIENDS

I do not say new friends are not considerate and
    true,
Or that their smiles ain't genuine, but still I'm
    tellin' you
That when a feller's heart is crushed and achin'
    with the pain,
And teardrops come a-splashin' down his cheeks
    like summer rain,
Becoz his grief an' loneliness are more than
    he can bear,
Somehow it's only old friends, then, that really
    seem to care.
The friends who've stuck through thick an'
    thin, who've known you, good an' bad,
Your faults an' virtues, an' have seen the strug-
    gles you have had,
When they come to you gentle-like an' take
    your hand an' say:
" Cheer up! we're with you still," it counts, for
    that's the old friends' way.

The new friends may be fond of you for what
    you are to-day;
They've only known you rich, perhaps, an' only
    seen you gay;
You can't tell what's attracted them; your
    station may appeal;

Perhaps they smile on you because you're doin'
     something real;
But old friends who have seen you fail, an' also
     seen you win,
Who've loved you either up or down, stuck
     to you, thick or thin,
Who knew you as a budding youth, an' watched
     you start to climb,
Through weal an' woe, still friends of yours
     an' constant all the time,
When trouble comes an' things go wrong, I
     don't care what you say,
They are the friends you'll turn to, for you
     want the old friends' way.

The new friends may be richer, an' more stylish,
     too, but when
Your heart is achin' an' you think your sun
     won't shine again,
It's not the riches of new friends you want, it's
     not their style,
It's not the airs of grandeur then, it's just the
     old friend's smile,
The old hand that has helped before, stretched
     out once more to you,
The old words ringin' in your ears, so sweet an',
     Oh, so true!
The tenderness of folks who know just what
     your sorrow means,

These are the things on which, somehow, your
    spirit always leans.
When grief is poundin' at your breast — the
    new friends disappear
An' to the old ones tried an' true, you turn for
    aid an' cheer.

FOLKS

We was speakin' of folks, jes' common folks,
    An' we come to this conclusion,
That wherever they be, on land or sea,
    They warm to a home allusion;
That under the skin an' under the hide
    There's a spark that starts a-glowin'
Whenever they look at a scene or book
    That something of home is showin'.

They may differ in creeds an' politics,
    They may argue an' even quarrel,
But their throats grip tight, if they catch a
    sight
    Of their favorite elm or laurel.
An' the winding lane that they used to tread
    With never a care to fret 'em,
Or the pasture gate where they used to wait,
    Right under the skin will get 'em.

Now folks is folks on their different ways,
　　With their different griefs an' pleasures,
But the home they knew, when their years were
　　　　few,
　　Is the dearest of all their treasures.
An' the richest man to the poorest waif
　　Right under the skin is brother
When they stand an' sigh, with a tear-dimmed
　　　　eye,
　　At a thought of the dear old mother.

It makes no difference where it may be,
　　Nor the fortunes that years may alter,
Be they simple or wise, the old home ties
　　Make all of 'em often falter.
Time may robe 'em in sackcloth coarse
　　Or garb 'em in gorgeous splendor,
But whatever their lot, they keep one spot
　　Down deep that is sweet an' tender.

We was speakin' of folks, jes' common folks,
　　An' we come to this conclusion,
That one an' all, be they great or small,
　　Will warm to a home allusion;
That under the skin an' the beaten hide
　　They're kin in a real affection
For the joys they knew, when their years were
　　　　few,
　　An' the home of their recollection.

LITTLE MASTER MISCHIEVOUS

Little Master Mischievous, that's the name for
    you;
There's no better title that describes the things
    you do:
Into something all the while where you
    shouldn't be,
Prying into matters that are not for you to see;
Little Master Mischievous, order's overthrown
If your mother leaves you for a minute all
    alone.

Little Master Mischievous, opening every door,
Spilling books and papers round about the parlor
    floor,
Scratching all the tables and marring all the
    chairs,
Climbing where you shouldn't climb and tum-
    bling down the stairs.
How'd you get the ink well? We can never
    guess.
Now the rug is ruined; so's your little dress.

Little Master Mischievous, in the cookie jar,
Who has ever told you where the cookies are?
Now your sticky fingers smear the curtains
    white;
You have finger-printed everything in sight.

There's no use in scolding; when you smile that
     way
You can rob of terror every word we say.

Little Master Mischievous, that's the name for
     you;
There's no better title that describes the things
     you do:
Prying into corners, peering into nooks,
Tugging table covers, tearing costly books.
Little Master Mischievous, have your roguish
     way;
Time, I know, will stop you, soon enough some
     day.

OPPORTUNITY

So long as men shall be on earth
    There will be tasks for them to do,
Some way for them to show their worth;
    Each day shall bring its problems new.

And men shall dream of mightier deeds
    Than ever have been done before:
There always shall be human needs
    For men to work and struggle for.

THE SORROW TUGS

There's a lot of joy in the smiling world,
there's plenty of morning sun,
And laughter and songs and dances, too, when-
ever the day's work's done;
Full many an hour is a shining one, when
viewed by itself apart,
But the golden threads in the warp of life are
the sorrow tugs at your heart.

Oh, the fun is froth and it blows away, and
many a joy's forgot,
And the pleasures come and the pleasures go,
and memory holds them not;
But treasured ever you keep the pain that causes
your tears to start,
For the sweetest hours are the ones that bring
the sorrow tugs at your heart.

The lump in your throat and the little sigh when
your baby trudged away
The very first time to the big red school — how
long will their memory stay?
The fever days and the long black nights you
watched as she troubled, slept,
And the joy you felt when she smiled once
more — how long will that all be kept?

The glad hours live in a feeble way, but the sad
    ones never die.
His first long trousers caused a pang and you
    saw them with a sigh.
And the big still house when the boy and girl,
    unto youth and beauty grown,
To college went; will you e'er forget that first
    grim hour alone?

It seems as you look back over things, that all
    that you treasure dear
Is somehow blent in a wondrous way with a
    heart pang and a tear.
Though many a day is a joyous one when
    viewed by itself apart,
The golden threads in the warp of life are the
    sorrow tugs at your heart.

ONLY A DAD

Only a dad with a tired face,
Coming home from the daily race,
Bringing little of gold or fame
To show how well he has played the game;
But glad in his heart that his own rejoice
To see him come and to hear his voice.

Only a dad with a brood of four,
One of ten million men or more
Plodding along in the daily strife,
Bearing the whips and the scorns of life,
With never a whimper of pain or hate,
For the sake of those who at home await.

Only a dad, neither rich nor proud,
Merely one of the surging crowd,
Toiling, striving from day to day,
Facing whatever may come his way,
Silent whenever the harsh condemn,
And bearing it all for the love of them.

Only a dad but he gives his all,
To smooth the way for his children small,
Doing with courage stern and grim
The deeds that his father did for him.
This is the line that for him I pen:
Only a dad, but the best of men.

HARD KNOCKS

I'm not the man to say that failure's sweet,
  Nor tell a chap to laugh when things go
      wrong;
I know it hurts to have to take defeat
  An' no one likes to lose before a throng;
It isn't very pleasant not to win
  When you have done the very best you could;
But if you're down, get up an' buckle in —
  A lickin' often does a fellow good.

I've seen some chaps who never knew their
      power
  Until somebody knocked 'em to the floor;
I've known men who discovered in an hour
  A courage they had never shown before.
I've seen 'em rise from failure to the top
  By doin' things they hadn't understood
Before the day disaster made 'em drop —
  A lickin' often does a fellow good.

Success is not the teacher, wise an' true,
  That gruff old failure is, remember that;
She's much too apt to make a fool of you,
  Which isn't true of blows that knock you flat.
Hard knocks are painful things an' hard to bear,
  An' most of us would dodge 'em if we could;
There's something mighty broadening in care —
  A lickin' often does a fellow good.

FATHER

Used to wonder just why father
   Never had much time for play,
Used to wonder why he'd rather
   Work each minute of the day.
Used to wonder why he never
   Loafed along the road an' shirked;
Can't recall a time whenever
   Father played while others worked.

Father didn't dress in fashion,
   Sort of hated clothing new;
Style with him was not a passion;
   He had other things in view.
Boys are blind to much that's going
   On about 'em day by day,
And I had no way of knowing
   What became of father's pay.

All I knew was when I needed
   Shoes I got 'em on the spot;
Everything for which I pleaded,
   Somehow, father always got.
Wondered, season after season,
   Why he never took a rest,
And that *I* might be the reason
   Then I never even guessed.

Father set a store on knowledge;
   If he'd lived to have his way
He'd have sent me off to college
   And the bills been glad to pay.
That, I know, was his ambition:
   Now and then he used to say
He'd have done his earthly mission
   On my graduation day.

Saw his cheeks were getting paler,
   Didn't understand just why;
Saw his body growing frailer,
   Then at last I saw him die.
Rest had come! His tasks were ended,
   Calm was written on his brow;
Father's life was big and splendid,
   And I understand it now.

AT BREAKFAST TIME

My Pa he eats his breakfast in a funny sort of
      way:
We hardly ever see him at the first meal of the
      day.
Ma puts his food before him and he settles in
      his place
An' then he props the paper up and we can't
      see his face;
We hear him blow his coffee and we hear him
      chew his toast,
But it's for the morning paper that he seems
      to care the most.

Ma says that little children mighty grateful
      ought to be
To the folks that fixed the evening as the proper
      time for tea.
She says if meals were only served to people
      once a day,
An' that was in the morning just before Pa goes
      away,
We'd never know how father looked when he
      was in his place,
Coz he'd always have the morning paper stuck
      before his face.

He drinks his coffee steamin' hot, an' passes
    Ma his cup
To have it filled a second time, an' never once
    looks up.
He never has a word to say, but just sits there
    an' reads,
An' when she sees his hand stuck out Ma gives
    him what he needs.
She guesses what it is he wants, coz it's no use
    to ask:
Pa's got to read his paper an' sometimes that's
    quite a task.

One morning we had breakfast an' his features
    we could see,
But his face was long an' solemn an' he didn't
    speak to me,
An' we couldn't get him laughin' an' we couldn't
    make him smile,
An' he said the toast was soggy an' the coffee
    simply vile.
Then Ma said: "What's the matter? Why are
    you so cross an' glum?"
An' Pa 'most took her head off coz the paper
    didn't come.

JAMES WHITCOMB RILEY

*Written July 22, 1916, when the
world lost its "Poet of Childhood."*

There must be great rejoicin' on the Golden
    Shore to-day,
An' the big an' little angels must be feelin'
    mighty gay:
Could we look beyond the curtain now I fancy
    we should see
Old Aunt Mary waitin', smilin', for the coming
    that's to be,
An' Little Orphant Annie an' the whole excited
    pack
Dancin' up an' down an' shoutin': "Mr. Riley's
    comin' back!"

There's a heap o' real sadness in this good old
    world to-day;
There are lumpy throats this morning now that
    Riley's gone away;
There's a voice now stilled forever that in
    sweetness only spoke
An' whispered words of courage with a faith that
    never broke.
There is much of joy and laughter that we
    mortals here will lack,
But the angels must be happy now that Riley's
    comin' back.

The world was gettin' dreary, there was too
     much sigh an' frown
In this vale o' mortal strivin', so God sent Jim
     Riley down,
An' He said: "Go there an' cheer 'em in your
     good old-fashioned way,
With your songs of tender sweetness, but don't
     make your plans to stay,
Coz you're needed up in Heaven. I am lendin'
     you to men
Just to help 'em with your music, but I'll want
     you back again."

An' Riley came, an' mortals heard the music of
     his voice
An' they caught his songs o' beauty an' they
     started to rejoice;
An' they leaned on him in sorrow, an' they
     shared with him their joys,
An' they walked with him the pathways that
     they knew when they were boys.
But the heavenly angels missed him, missed his
     tender, gentle knack
Of makin' people happy, an' they wanted Riley
     back.

There must be great rejoicin' on the streets of
     Heaven to-day
An' all the angel children must be troopin'
     down the way,

Singin' heavenly songs of welcome an' pre-
   parin' now to greet
The soul that God had tinctured with an ever-
   lasting sweet;
The world is robed in sadness an' is draped in
   sombre black;
But joy must reign in Heaven now that Riley's
   comin' back.

RESULTS AND ROSES

The man who wants a garden fair,
   Or small or very big,
With flowers growing here and there,
   Must bend his back and dig.

The things are mighty few on earth
   That wishes can attain.
Whate'er we want of any worth
   We've got to work to gain.

It matters not what goal you seek
   Its secret here reposes:
You've got to dig from week to week
   To get Results or Roses.

IT'S SEPTEMBER

It's September, and the orchards are afire with
 red and gold,
And the nights with dew are heavy, and the
 morning's sharp with cold;
Now the garden's at its gayest with the salvia
 blazing red
And the good old-fashioned asters laughing
 at us from their bed;
Once again in shoes and stockings are the chil-
 dren's little feet,
And the dog now does his snoozing on the
 bright side of the street.

It's September, and the cornstalks are as high
 as they will go,
And the red cheeks of the apples everywhere
 begin to show;
Now the supper's scarcely over ere the dark-
 ness settles down
And the moon looms big and yellow at the
 edges of the town;
Oh, it's good to see the children, when their
 little prayers are said,
Duck beneath the patchwork covers when they
 tumble into bed.

It's September, and a calmness and a sweetness
    seem to fall
Over everything that's living, just as though it
    hears the call
Of Old Winter, trudging slowly, with his pack
    of ice and snow,
In the distance over yonder, and it somehow
    seems as though
Every tiny little blossom wants to look its very
    best
When the frost shall bite its petals and it droops
    away to rest.

It's September! It's the fullness and the ripe-
    ness of the year;
All the work of earth is finished, or the final
    tasks are near,
But there is no doleful wailing; every living
    thing that grows,
For the end that is approaching wears the
    finest garb it knows.
And I pray that I may proudly hold my head
    up high and smile
When I come to my September in the golden
    afterwhile.

HOW DO YOU TACKLE YOUR WORK?

How do you tackle your work each day?
 Are you scared of the job you find?
Do you grapple the task that comes your way
 With a confident, easy mind?
Do you stand right up to the work ahead
 Or fearfully pause to view it?
Do you start to toil with a sense of dread
 Or feel that you're going to do it?

You can do as much as you think you can,
 But you'll never accomplish more;
If you're afraid of yourself, young man,
 There's little for you in store.
For failure comes from the inside first,
 It's there if we only knew it,
And you can win, though you face the worst,
 If you feel that you're going to do it.

Success! It's found in the soul of you,
 And not in the realm of luck!
The world will furnish the work to do,
 But you must provide the pluck.
You can do whatever you think you can,
 It's all in the way you view it.
It's all in the start that you make, young man:
 You must feel that you're going to do it.

How do you tackle your work each day?
　　With confidence clear, or dread?
What to yourself do you stop and say
　　When a new task lies ahead?
What is the thought that is in your mind?
　　Is fear ever running through it?
If so, just tackle the next you find
　　By thinking you're going to do it.

LIFE

Life is a gift to be used every day,
Not to be smothered and hidden away;
It isn't a thing to be stored in the chest
Where you gather your keepsakes and treasure
　　　　your best;
It isn't a joy to be sipped now and then
And promptly put back in a dark place again.

Life is a gift that the humblest may boast of
And one that the humblest may well make the
　　　　most of.
Get out and live it each hour of the day,
Wear it and use it as much as you may;
Don't keep it in niches and corners and grooves,
You'll find that in service its beauty improves.

CANNING TIME

There's a wondrous smell of spices
     In the kitchen,
     Most bewitchin';
There are fruits cut into slices
That just set the palate itchin';
There's the sound of spoon on platter
And the rattle and the clatter;
And a bunch of kids are hastin'
To the splendid joy of tastin':
It's the fragrant time of year
When fruit-cannin' days are here.

There's a good wife gayly smilin'
     And perspirin'
     Some, and tirin';
And while jar on jar she's pilin'
And the necks o' them she's wirin'
I'm a-sittin' here an' dreamin'
Of the kettles that are steamin',
And the cares that have been troublin'
All have vanished in the bubblin'.
I am happy that I'm here
At the cannin' time of year.

Lord, I'm sorry for the feller
     That is missin'
     All the hissin'
Of the juices, red and yeller,

And can never sit and listen
To the rattle and the clatter
Of the sound of spoon on platter.
I am sorry for the single,
For they miss the thrill and tingle
Of the splendid time of year
When the cannin' days are here.

THE DULL ROAD

It's the dull road that leads to the gay road;
  The practice that leads to success;
The work road that leads to the play road;
  It is trouble that breeds happiness.

It's the hard work and merciless grinding
  That purchases glory and fame;
It's repeatedly doing, nor minding
  The drudgery drear of the game.

It's the passing up glamor or pleasure
  For the sake of the skill we may gain,
And in giving up comfort or leisure
  For the joy that we hope to attain.

It's the hard road of trying and learning,
  Of toiling, uncheered and alone,
That wins us the prizes worth earning,
  And leads us to goals we would own.

THE APPLE TREE

When an apple tree is ready for the world to
     come and eat,
There isn't any structure in the land that's
     " got it beat."
There's nothing man has builded with the
     beauty or the charm
That can touch the simple grandeur of the
     monarch of the farm.
There's never any picture from a human
     being's brush
That has ever caught the redness of a single
     apple's blush.

When an apple tree's in blossom it is glorious
     to see,
But that's just a hint, at springtime, of the
     better things to be;
That is just a fairy promise from the Great
     Magician's wand
Of the wonders and the splendors that are
     waiting just beyond
The distant edge of summer; just a forecast
     of the treat
When the apple tree is ready for the world
     to come and eat.

Architects of splendid vision long have labored
    on the earth,
And have raised their dreams in marble and
    we've marveled at their worth;
Long the spires of costly churches have looked
    upward at the sky;
Rich in promise and in the beauty, they have
    cheered the passer-by.
But I'm sure there's nothing finer for the eye
    of man to meet
Than an apple tree that's ready for the world
    to come and eat.

There's the promise of the apples, red and
    gleaming in the sun,
Like the medals worn by mortals as rewards
    for labors done;
And the big arms stretched wide open, with a
    welcome warm and true
In a way that sets you thinking it's intended
    just for you.
There is nothing with a beauty so entrancing,
    so complete,
As an apple tree that's ready for the world to
    come and eat.

COURAGE

Courage isn't a brilliant dash,
A daring deed in a moment's flash;
It isn't an instantaneous thing
Born of despair with a sudden spring
It isn't a creature of flickered hope
Or the final tug at a slipping rope;
But it's something deep in the soul of man
That is working always to serve some plan.

Courage isn't the last resort
In the work of life or the game of sport;
It isn't a thing that a man can call
At some future time when he's apt to fall;
If he hasn't it now, he will have it not
When the strain is great and the pace is hot.
For who would strive for a distant goal
Must always have courage within his soul.

Courage isn't a dazzling light
That flashes and passes away from sight;
It's a slow, unwavering, ingrained trait
With the patience to work and the strength to
                wait.
It's part of a man when his skies are blue,
It's part of him when he has work to do.
The brave man never is freed of it.
He has it when there is no need of it.

Courage was never designed for show;
It isn't a thing that can come and go;
It's written in victory and defeat
And every trial a man may meet.
It's part of his hours, his days and his years,
Back of his smiles and behind his tears.
Courage is more than a daring deed:
It's the breath of life and a strong man's creed.

GREATNESS

We can be great by helping one another;
  We can be loved for very simple deeds:
Who has the grateful mention of a brother
  Has really all the honor that he needs.

We can be famous for our works of kindness —
  Fame is not born alone of strength or skill;
It sometimes comes from deafness and from
      blindness
  To petty words and faults, and loving still.

We can be rich in gentle smiles and sunny:
  A jeweled soul exceeds a royal crown.
The richest men sometimes have little money,
  And Croesus oft's the poorest man in town.

THE EPICURE

I've sipped a rich man's sparkling wine,
   His silverware I've handled.
I've placed these battered legs of mine
   'Neath tables gayly candled.
I dine on rare and costly fare
   Whene'er good fortune lets me,
But there's no meal that can compare
   With those the missus gets me.

I've had your steaks three inches thick
   With all your Sam Ward trimming,
I've had the breast of milk-fed chick
   In luscious gravy swimming.
To dine in swell café or club
   But irritates and frets me;
Give me the plain and wholesome grub—
   The grub the missus gets me.

Two kiddies smiling at the board,
   The cook right at the table,
The four of us, a hungry horde,
   To beat that none is able.
A big meat pie, with flaky crust!
   'Tis then that joy besets me;
Oh, I could eat until I " bust,"
   Those meals the missus gets me.

THE GENTLE GARDENER

I'd like to leave but daffodills to mark my little
way,
To leave but tulips red and white behind me as
I stray;
I'd like to pass away from earth and feel I'd
left behind
But roses and forget-me-nots for all who come
to find.

I'd like to sow the barren spots with all the
flowers of earth,
To leave a path where those who come should
find but gentle mirth;
And when at last I'm called upon to join the
heavenly throng
I'd like to feel along my way I'd left no sign
of wrong.

And yet the cares are many and the hours of
toil are few;
There is not time enough on earth for all I'd
like to do;
But, having lived and having toiled, I'd like the
world to find
Some little touch of beauty that my soul had
left behind.

THE PEACEFUL WARRIORS

Let others sing their songs of war
  And chant their hymns of splendid death,
Let others praise the soldiers' ways
  And hail the cannon's flaming breath.
Let others sing of Glory's fields
  Where blood for Victory is paid,
I choose to sing some simple thing
  To those who wield not gun or blade —
  The peaceful warriors of trade.

Let others choose the deeds of war
  For symbols of our nation's skill,
The blood-red coat, the rattling throat,
  The regiment that charged the hill,
The boy who died to serve the flag,
  Who heard the order and obeyed,
But leave to me the gallantry
  Of those who labor unafraid —
  The peaceful warriors of trade.

Aye, let me sing the splendid deeds
  Of those who toil to serve mankind,
The men who break old ways and make
  New paths for those who come behind.
The young who war with customs old
  And face their problems, unafraid,
Who think and plan to lift for man
  The burden that on him is laid —
  The splendid warriors of trade.

I sing of battles with disease
   And victories o'er death and pain,
Of ships that fly the summer sky,
   And glorious deeds of strength and brain.
The call for help that rings through space
   By which a vessel's course is stayed,
Thrills me far more than fields of gore,
   Or heroes decked in golden braid —
   I sing the warriors of trade.

FAILURES

'Tis better to have tried in vain,
   Sincerely striving for a goal,
Than to have lived upon the plain
   An idle and a timid soul.

'Tis better to have fought and spent
   Your courage, missing all applause,
Than to have lived in smug content
   And never ventured for a cause.

For he who tries and fails may be
   The founder of a better day;
Though never his the victory,
   From him shall others learn the way.

RAISIN PIE

There's a heap of pent-up goodness in the yellow
    bantam corn,
And I sort o' like to linger round a berry patch
    at morn;
Oh, the Lord has set our table with a stock o'
    things to eat
An' there's just enough o' bitter in the blend
    to cut the sweet,
But I run the whole list over, an' it seems
    somehow that I
Find the keenest sort o' pleasure in a chunk
    o' raisin pie.

There are pies that start the water circulatin' in
    the mouth;
There are pies that wear the flavor of the warm
    an' sunny south;
Some with oriental spices spur the drowsy appe-
    tite
An' just fill a fellow's being with a thrill o'
    real delight;
But for downright solid goodness that comes
    drippin' from the sky
There is nothing quite the equal of a chunk o'
    raisin pie.

I'm admittin' tastes are diff'runt, I'm not settin'
    up myself

As the judge an' final critic of the good things
    on the shelf.
I'm just sort o' payin' tribute to a simple joy on
    earth,
Sort o' feebly testifyin' to its lasting charm an'
    worth,
An' I'll hold to this conclusion till it comes my
    time to die,
That there's no dessert that's finer than a chunk
    o' raisin pie.

PREPAREDNESS

Right must not live in idleness,
    Nor dwell in smug content;
It must be strong, against the throng
    Of foes, on evil bent.

Justice must not a weakling be
    But it must guard its own,
And live each day, that none can say
    Justice is overthrown.

Peace, the sweet glory of the world,
    Faces a duty, too;
Death is her fate, leaves she one gate
    For war to enter through.

THE READY ARTISTS

The green is in the meadow and the blue is in
the sky,
And all of Nature's artists have their colors
handy by;
With a few days bright with sunshine and a
few nights free from frost
They will start to splash their colors quite
regardless of the cost.
There's an artist waiting ready at each bleak
and dismal spot
To paint the flashing tulip or the meek forget-
me-not.

May is lurking in the distance and her lap is
filled with flowers,
And the choicest of her blossoms very shortly
will be ours.
There is not a lane so dreary or a field so dark
with gloom
But that soon will be resplendent with its little
touch of bloom.
There's an artist keen and eager to make beau-
tiful each scene
And remove with colors gorgeous every trace of
of what has been.

Oh, the world is now in mourning; round about
       us all are spread
The ruins and the symbols of the winter that
       is dead.
But the bleak and barren picture very shortly
       now will pass,
For the halls of life are ready for their velvet
       rugs of grass;
And the painters now are waiting with their
       magic to replace
This dullness with a beauty that no mortal hand
       can trace.

The green is in the meadow and the blue is in
       the sky;
The chill of death is passing, life will shortly
       greet the eye.
We shall revel soon in colors only Nature's
       artists make
And the humblest plant that's sleeping unto
       beauty shall awake.
For there's not a leaf forgotten, not a twig
       neglected there,
And the tiniest of pansies shall the royal purple
       wear.

MOTHER'S GLASSES

I've told about the times that Ma can't find
　　her pocketbook,
And how we have to hustle round for it to help
　　her look,
But there's another care we know that often
　　comes our way,
I guess it happens easily a dozen times a day.
It starts when first the postman through the
　　door a letter passes,
And Ma says: "Goodness gracious me! Wher-
　　ever are my glasses?"

We hunt 'em on the mantelpiece an' by the
　　kitchen sink,
Until Ma says: "Now, children, stop, an' give
　　me time to think
Just when it was I used 'em last an' just
　　exactly where.
Yes, now I know — the dining room.　I'm sure
　　you'll find 'em there."
We even look behind the clock, we busy boys
　　an' lasses,
Until somebody runs across Ma's missing pair of
　　glasses.

We've found 'em in the Bible, an' we've found
      'em in the flour,
We've found 'em in the sugar bowl, an' once
      we looked an hour
Before we came across 'em in the padding of
      her chair;
An' many a time we've found 'em in the topknot
      of her hair.
It's a search that ruins order an' the home com-
      pletely wrecks,
For there's no place where you may not find
      poor Ma's elusive specs.

But we're mighty glad, I tell you, that the
      duty's ours to do,
An' we hope to hunt those glasses till our time
      of life is through;
It's a little bit of service that is joyous in its
      thrill,
It's a task that calls us daily an' we hope it
      always will.
Rich or poor, the saddest mortals of all the
      joyless masses
Are the ones who have no mother dear to lose
      her reading glasses.

THE PRINCESS PAT'S

Written when the Canadian regiment, known as the "Princess Pat's," left for the front.

A touch of the plain and the prairie,
  A bit of the Motherland, too;
A strain of the fur-trapper wary,
  A blend of the old and the new;
A bit of the pioneer splendor
  That opened the wilderness' flats,
A touch of the home-lover, tender,
  You'll find in the boys they call Pat's.

The glory and grace of the maple,
  The strength that is born of the wheat,
The pride of a stock that is staple,
  The bronze of a midsummer heat;
A blending of wisdom and daring,
  The best of a new land, and that's
The regiment gallantly bearing
  The neat little title of Pat's.

A bit of the man who has neighbored
  With mountains and forests and streams,
A touch of the man who has labored
  To model and fashion his dreams;
The strength of an age of clean living,
  Of right-minded fatherly chats,
The best that a land could be giving
  Is there in the breasts of the Pat's.

BE A FRIEND

Be a friend. You don't need money:
Just a disposition sunny;
Just the wish to help another
Get along some way or other;
Just a kindly hand extended
Out to one who's unbefriended;
Just the will to give or lend,
This will make you someone's friend.

Be a friend. You don't need glory.
Friendship is a simple story.
Pass by trifling errors blindly,
Gaze on honest effort kindly,
Cheer the youth who's bravely trying,
Pity him who's sadly sighing;
Just a little labor spend
On the duties of a friend.

Be a friend. The pay is bigger
(Though not written by a figure)
Than is earned by people clever
In what's merely self-endeavor.
You'll have friends instead of neighbors
For the profits of your labors;
You'll be richer in the end
Than a prince, if you're a friend.

THANKSGIVING

Thankful for the glory of the old Red, White
    and Blue,
For the spirit of America that still is staunch
    and true,
For the laughter of our children and the sun-
    light in their eyes,
And the joy of radiant mothers and their even-
    ing lullabies;
And thankful that our harvests wear no taint
    of blood to-day,
But were sown and reaped by toilers who were
    light of heart and gay.

Thankful for the riches that are ours to claim
    and keep,
The joy of honest labor and the boon of happy
    sleep,
For each little family circle where there is no
    empty chair
Save where God has sent the sorrow for the
    loving hearts to bear;
And thankful for the loyal souls and brave
    hearts of the past
Who builded that contentment should be with
    us to the last.

Thankful for the plenty that our peaceful land
  has blessed,
For the rising sun that beckons every man to
  do his best,
For the goal that lies before him and the promise
  when he sows
That his hand shall reap the harvest, undisturbed
  by cruel foes;
For the flaming torch of justice, symbolizing
  as it burns:
Here none may rob the toiler of the prize he
  fairly earns.

To-day our thanks we're giving for the riches
  that are ours,
For the red fruits of the orchards and the per-
  fume of the flowers,
For our homes with laughter ringing and our
  hearthfires blazing bright,
For our land of peace and plenty and our land
  of truth and right;
And we're thankful for the glory of the old
  Red, White and Blue,
For the spirit of our fathers and a manhood
  that is true.

MA AND HER CHECK BOOK

Ma has a dandy little book that's full of narrow
    slips,
An' when she wants to pay a bill a page from
    it she rips;
She just writes in the dollars and the cents and
    signs her name
An' that's as good as money, though it doesn't
    lock the same.
When she wants another bonnet or some
    feathers for her neck,
She promptly goes an' gets 'em, an' she writes
    another check.
I don't just understand it, but I know she
    sputters when
Pa says to her at supper: "Well! You're
    overdrawn again!"

Ma's not a business woman, she is much too
    kind of heart
To squabble over pennies or to play a selfish
    part,
An' when someone asks for money, she's not
    one to stop an' think
Of a little piece of paper an' the cost of pen
    an' ink.

She just tells him very sweetly if he'll only
    wait a bit
An' be seated in the parlor, she will write a
    check for it.
She can write one out for twenty just as easily
    as ten,
An' forgets that Pa may grumble: "Well,
    you're overdrawn again!"

Pa says it looks as though he'll have to start in
    workin' nights
To gather in the money for the checks that
    mother writes.
He says that every morning when he's sum-
    moned to the phone,
He's afraid the bank is calling to make mother's
    shortage known.
He tells his friends if ever anything our fortune
    wrecks
They can trace it to the moment mother started
    writing checks.
He's got so that he trembles when he sees her
    fountain pen
An' he mutters: "Do be careful! You'll be
    overdrawn again!"

REAL SINGING

You can talk about your music, and your
    operatic airs,
And your phonographic record that Caruso's
    tenor bears;
But there isn't any music that such wondrous
    joy can bring
Like the concert when the kiddies and their
    mother start to sing.

When the supper time is over, then the mother
    starts to play
Some simple little ditty, and our concert's under
    way.
And I'm happier and richer than a millionaire
    or king
When I listen to the kiddies and their mother
    as they sing.

There's a sweetness most appealing in the trill-
    ing of their notes:
It is innocence that's pouring from their little
    baby throats;
And I gaze at them enraptured, for my joy's
    a real thing
Every evening when the kiddies and their mother
    start to sing.

WHEN PA COUNTS

Pa's not so very big or brave; he can't lift
weights like Uncle Jim;
His hands are soft like little girls'; most anyone
could wallop him.
Ma weighs a whole lot more than Pa. When
they go swimming, she could stay
Out in the river all day long, but Pa gets frozen
right away.
But when the thunder starts to roll, an' lightnin'
spits, Ma says, " Oh, dear,
I'm sure we'll all of us be killed. I only wish
your Pa was here."

Pa's cheeks are thin an' kinder pale; he couldn't
rough it worth a cent.
He couldn't stand the hike we had the day the
Boy Scouts camping went.
He has to hire a man to dig the garden, coz his
back gets lame,
An' he'd be crippled for a week, if he should
play a baseball game.
But when a thunder storm comes up, Ma sits an'
shivers in the gloam
An' every time the thunder rolls, she says: " I
wish your Pa was home."

I don't know just what Pa could do if he were
       home, he seems so frail,
But every time the skies grow black I notice Ma
       gets rather pale.
An' when she's called us children in, an' locked
       the windows an' the doors,
She jumps at every lightnin' flash an' trembles
       when the thunder roars.
An' when the baby starts to cry, she wrings her
       hands an' says: " Oh, dear!
It's terrible! It's terrible! I only wish your
       Pa was here."

PEACE

A man must earn his hour of peace,
  Must pay for it with hours of strife and care,
Must win by toil the evening's sweet release,
  The rest that may be portioned for his share;
The idler never knows it, never can.
  Peace is the glory ever of a man.

A man must win contentment for his soul,
  Must battle for it bravely day by day;
The peace he seeks is not a near-by goal;
  To claim it he must tread a rugged way.
The shirker never knows a tranquil breast;
  Peace but rewards the man who does his best.

NO PLACE TO GO

The happiest nights
   I ever know
Are those when I've
   No place to go,
And the missus says
   When the day is through:
" To-night we haven't
   A thing to do."

Oh, the joy of it,
   And the peace untold
Of sitting 'round
   In my slippers old,
With my pipe and book
   In my easy chair,
Knowing I needn't
   Go anywhere.

Needn't hurry
   My evening meal
Nor force the smiles
   That I do not feel,
But can grab a book
   From a near-by shelf,
And drop all sham
   And be myself.

Oh, the charm of it
    And the comfort rare;
Nothing on earth
    With it can compare;
And I'm sorry for him
    Who doesn't know
The joy of having
    No place to go.

GROWTH

This is man's utmost hope: that he can be
    Friend to another in his hour of need;
Can find someone in doubt and set him free
    And gain the growth of one unselfish deed.

Nor pomp nor power nor luxury's lavish show
    Improves so much the man as to be kind.
Who stops to help another, fallen low,
    Shall find himself by that one act refined.

High place and low this common splendor share!
    'Tis generous giving makes the larger growth.
Who turns his hand to ease another's care
    Though rich or poor achieves the goal of both.

THE THINGS THAT MAKE A SOLDIER GREAT

The things that make a soldier great and send
    him out to die,
To face the flaming cannon's mouth nor ever
    question why,
Are lilacs by a little porch, the row of tulips
    red,
The peonies and pansies, too, the old petunia bed,
The grass plot where his children play, the roses
    on the wall:
'Tis these that make a soldier great. He's fight-
    ing for them all.

'Tis not the pomp and pride of kings that make
    a soldier brave;
'Tis not allegiance to the flag that over him may
    wave;
For soldiers never fight so well on land or on
    the foam
As when behind the cause they see the little
    place called home.
Endanger but that humble street whereon his
    children run,
You make a soldier of the man who never bore
    a gun.

What is it through the battle smoke the valiant
soldier sees?
The little garden far away, the budding apple
trees,
The little patch of ground back there, the chil-
dren at their play,
Perhaps a tiny mound behind the simple church
of gray.
The golden thread of courage isn't linked to
castle dome
But to the spot, where'er it be — the humble spot
called home.

And now the lilacs bud again and all is lovely
there
And homesick soldiers far away know spring
is in the air;
The tulips come to bloom again, the grass
once more is green,
And every man can see the spot where all his
joys have been.
He sees his children smile at him, he hears the
bugle call,
And only death can stop him now — he's fight-
ing for them all.

THE JOY OF A DOG

Ma says no, it's too much care
An' it will scatter germs an' hair,
An' it's a nuisance through and through,
An' barks when you don't want it to;
An' carries dirt from off the street,
An' tracks the carpets with its feet.
But it's a sign he's growin' up
When he is longin' for a pup.

Most every night he comes to me
An' climbs a-straddle of my knee
An' starts to fondle me an' pet,
Then asks me if I've found one yet.
An' ma says: " Now don't tell him yes;
You know they make an awful mess,"
An' starts their faults to catalogue.
But every boy should have a dog.

An' some night when he comes to me,
Deep in my pocket there will be
The pup he's hungry to possess
Or else I sadly miss my guess.
For I remember all the joy
A dog meant to a little boy
Who loved it in the long ago,
The joy that's now his right to know.

HOMESICK

It's tough when you are homesick in a strange
   and distant place;
It's anguish when you're hungry for an old-
   familiar face.
And yearning for the good folks and the joys
   you used to know,
When you're miles away from friendship, is a
   bitter sort of woe.
But it's tougher, let me tell you, and a stiffer
   discipline
To see them through the window, and to know
   you can't go in.

Oh, I never knew the meaning of that red sign
   on the door,
Never really understood it, never thought of it
   before;
But I'll never see another since they've tacked
   one up on mine
But I'll think about the father that is barred
   from all that's fine.
And I'll think about the mother who is prisoner
   in there
So her little son or daughter shall not miss a
   mother's care.
And I'll share a fellow feeling with the saddest
   of my kin,
The dad beside the gateway of the home he
   can't go in.

Oh, we laugh and joke together and the mother
    tries to be
Brave and sunny in her prison, and she thinks
    she's fooling me;
And I do my bravest smiling and I feign a
    merry air
In the hope she won't discover that I'm bur-
    dened down with care.
But it's only empty laughter, and there's nothing
    in the grin
When you're talking through the window of the
    home you can't go in.

THE PERFECT DINNER TABLE

A table cloth that's slightly soiled
Where greasy little hands have toiled;
The napkins kept in silver rings,
And only ordinary things
From which to eat, a simple fare,
And just the wife and kiddies there,
And while I serve, the clatter glad
Of little girl and little lad
Who have so very much to say
About the happenings of the day.

Four big round eyes that dance with glee,
Forever flashing joys at me,
Two little tongues that race and run
To tell of troubles and of fun;

The mother with a patient smile
Who knows that she must wait awhile
Before she'll get a chance to say
What she's discovered through the day.
She steps aside for girl and lad
Who have so much to tell their dad.

Our manners may not be the best;
Perhaps our elbows often rest
Upon the table, and at times
That very worst of dinner crimes,
That very shameful act and rude
Of speaking ere you've downed your food,
Too frequently, I fear, is done,
So fast the little voices run.
Yet why should table manners stay
Those tongues that have so much to say?

At many a table I have been
Where wealth and luxury were seen,
And I have dined in halls of pride
Where all the guests were dignified;
But when it comes to pleasure rare
The perfect dinner table's where
No stranger's face is ever known:
The dinner hour we spend alone,
When little girl and little lad
Run riot telling things to dad,

TO-MORROW

He was going to be all that a mortal should be
      To-morrow.
No one should be kinder or braver than he
      To-morrow.
A friend who was troubled and weary he knew,
Who'd be glad of a lift and who needed it, too;
On him he would call and see what he could do
      To-morrow.

Each morning he stacked up the letters he'd
    write
      To-morrow.
And thought of the folks he would fill with
    delight
      To-morrow.
It was too bad, indeed, he was busy to-day,
And hadn't a minute to stop on his way;
More time he would have to give others, he'd
    say,
      To-morrow.

The greatest of workers this man would have
    been
      To-morrow.
The world would have known him, had he ever
    seen
      To-morrow.

But the fact is he died and he faded from view,
And all that he left here when living was
    through
Was a mountain of things he intended to do
      To-morrow.

A PRAYER

God grant me kindly thought
    And patience through the day,
And in the things I've wrought
    Let no man living say
That hate's grim mark has stained
What little joy I've gained.

God keep my nature sweet,
    Teach me to bear a blow,
Disaster and defeat,
    And no resentment show.
If failure must be mine
Sustain this soul of mine.

God grant me strength to face
    Undaunted day or night;
To stoop to no disgrace
    To win my little fight;
Let me be, when it is o'er,
As manly as before.

THE MAN WHO COULDN'T SAVE

He spent what he made, or he gave it away,
Tried to save money, and would for a day,
Started a bank-account time an' again,
Got a hundred or so for a nest egg, an' then
Some fellow that needed it more than he did,
Who was down on his luck, with a sick wife
    or kid,
Came along an' he wasted no time till he went
An' drew out the coin that for saving was
    meant.

They say he died poor, and I guess that is so:
To pile up a fortune he hadn't a show;
He worked all the time and good money he made,
Was known as an excellent man at his trade,
But he saw too much, heard too much, felt too
    much here
To save anything by the end of the year,
An' the shabbiest wreck the Lord ever let live
Could get money from him if he had it to give.

I've seen him slip dimes to the bums on the street
Who told him they hungered for something to
    eat,
An' though I remarked they were going for
    drink
He'd say: " Mebbe so. But I'd just hate to
    think

That fellow was hungry an' I'd passed him by;
I'd rather be fooled twenty times by a lie
Than wonder if one of 'em I wouldn't feed
Had told me the truth an' was really in need."

Never stinted his family out of a thing:
They had everything that his money could bring;
Said he'd rather be broke and just know they
   were glad,
Than rich, with them pining an' wishing they had
Some of the pleasures his money would buy;
Said he never could look a bank book in the eye
If he knew it had grown on the pleasures and
   joys
That he'd robbed from his wife and his girls
   and his boys.

Queer sort of notion he had, I confess,
Yet many a rich man on earth is mourned less.
All who had known him came back to his side
To honor his name on the day that he died.
Didn't leave much in the bank, it is true,
But did leave a fortune in people who knew
The big heart of him, an' I'm willing to swear
That to-day he is one of the richest up there.

FATHER AND SON

Be more than his dad,
Be a chum to the lad;
Be a part of his life
Every hour of the day;
Find time to talk with him,
Take time to walk with him,
Share in his studies
And share in his play;
Take him to places,
To ball games and races,
Teach him the things
That you want him to know;
Don't live apart from him,
Don't keep your heart from him,
Be his best comrade,
He's needing you so!

Never neglect him,
Though young, still respect him,
Hear his opinions
With patience and pride;
Show him his error,
But be not a terror,
Grim-visaged and fearful,
When he's at your side.

Know what his thoughts are,
Know what his sports are,
Know all his playmates,
It's easy to learn to;
Be such a father
That when troubles gather
You'll be the first one
For counsel, he'll turn to.

You can inspire him
With courage, and fire him
Hot with ambition
For deeds that are good;
He'll not betray you
Nor illy repay you,
If you have taught him
The things that you should.
Father and son
Must in all things be one —
Partners in trouble
And comrades in joy.
More than a dad
Was the best pal you had;
Be such a chum
As you knew, to your boy.

THE JUNE COUPLE

She is fair to see and sweet,
Dainty from her head to feet,
Modest, as her blushing shows,
Happy, as her smiles disclose,
And the young man at her side
Nervously attempts to hide
Underneath a visage grim
That the fuss is bothering him.

Pause a moment, happy pair!
This is not the station where
Romance ends, and wooing stops
And the charm from courtship drops;
This is but the outward gate
Where the souls of mortals mate,
But the border of the land
You must travel hand in hand.

You who come to marriage, bring
All your tenderness, and cling
Steadfastly to all the ways
That have marked your wooing days.
You are only starting out
On life's roadways, hedged about
Thick with roses and with tares,
Sweet delights and bitter cares.

Heretofore you've only played
At love's game, young man and maid;
Only known it at its best;
Now you'll have to face its test.
You must prove your love worth while,
Something time cannot defile,
Something neither care nor pain
Can destroy or mar or stain.

You are now about to show
Whether love is real or no;
Yonder down the lane of life
You will find, as man and wife,
Sorrows, disappointments, doubt,
Hope will almost flicker out;
But if rightly you are wed
Love will linger where you tread.

There are joys that you will share,
Joys to balance every care;
Arm in arm remain, and you
Will not fear the storms that brew,
If when you are sorest tried
You face your trials, side by side.
Now your wooing days are done,
And your loving years begun.

AT THE DOOR

He wiped his shoes before his door,
But ere he entered he did more:
'Twas not enough to cleanse his feet
Of dirt they'd gathered in the street;
He stood and dusted off his mind
And left all trace of care behind.
"In here I will not take," said he,
"The stains the day has brought to me.

"Beyond this door shall never go
The burdens that are mine to know;
The day is done, and here I leave
The petty things that vex and grieve;
What clings to me of hate and sin
To them I will not carry in;
Only the good shall go with me
For their devoted eyes to see.

"I will not burden them with cares,
Nor track the home with grim affairs;
I will not at my table sit
With soul unclean, and mind unfit;
Beyond this door I will not take
The outward signs of inward ache;
I will not take a dreary mind
Into this house for them to find."

He wiped his shoes before his door,
But paused to do a little more.

He dusted off the stains of strife,
The mud that's incident to life,
The blemishes of careless thought,
The traces of the fight he'd fought,
The selfish humors and the mean,
And when he entered he was clean.

DUTY

To do your little bit of toil,
  To play life's game with head erect;
To stoop to nothing that would soil
  Your honor or your self-respect;
To win what gold and fame you can,
But first of all to be a man.

To know the bitter and the sweet,
  The sunshine and the days of rain;
To meet both victory and defeat,
  Nor boast too loudly nor complain;
To face whatever fates befall
And be a man throughout it all.

To seek success in honest strife,
  But not to value it so much
That, winning it, you go through life
  Stained by dishonor's scarlet touch.
What goal or dream you choose, pursue,
But be a man whate'er you do!

A BEAR STORY

There was a bear — his name was Jim,
An' children weren't askeered of him,
An' he lived in a cave, where he
Was confortubbul as could be,
An' in that cave, so my Pa said,
Jim always kept a stock of bread
An' honey, so that he could treat
The boys an' girls along his street.

An' all that Jim could say was " Woof!"
An' give a grunt that went like " Soof!"
An' Pa says when his grunt went off
It sounded jus' like Grandpa's cough,
Or like our Jerry when he's mad
An' growls at peddler men that's bad.
While grown-ups were afraid of Jim,
Kids could do anything with him.

One day a little boy like me
That had a sister Marjorie,
Was walking through the woods, an' they
Heard something " woofing " down that way,
An' they was scared an' stood stock still
An' wished they had a gun to kill
Whatever 'twas, but little boys
Don't have no guns that make a noise.

An' soon the " woofing " closer grew,
An' then a bear came into view,
The biggest bear you ever saw —
Ma's muff was smaller than his paw.
He saw the children an' he said:
" I ain't a-goin' to kill you dead;
You needn't turn away an' run;
I'm only scarin' you for fun."

An' then he stood up just like those
Big bears in circuses an' shows,
An' danced a jig, an' rolled about
An' said " Woof! Woof!" which meant " Look
      out!"
An' turned a somersault as slick
As any boy can do the trick.
Those children had been told of Jim
An' they decided it was him.

They stroked his nose when they got brave,
An' followed him into his cave,
An' Jim asked them if they liked honey,
They said they did. Said Jim: " That's funny.
I've asked a thousand boys or so
That question, an' not one's said no."
What happened then I cannot say
'Cause next I knew 'twas light as day.

AUTUMN AT THE ORCHARD

The sumac's flaming scarlet on the edges o' the
       lake,
An' the pear trees are invitin' everyone t' come
       an' shake.
Now the gorgeous tints of autumn are appearin'
       everywhere
Till it seems that you can almost see the Master
       Painter there.
There's a solemn sort o' stillness that's pervadin'
       every thing,
Save the farewell songs to summer that the
       feathered tenors sing,
An' you quite forget the city where disgruntled
       folks are kickin'
Off yonder with the Pelletiers, when spies are
       ripe fer pickin'.

The Holsteins are a-posin' in a clearin' near a
       wood,
Very dignified an' stately, just as though they
       understood
That they're lending to life's pictures just the
       touch the Master needs,
An' they're preachin' more refinement than a lot
       o' printed creeds.
The orchard's fairly groanin' with the gifts o'
       God to man,
Just as though they meant to shame us who
       have doubted once His plan.

Oh, there's somethin' most inspirin' to a soul in
    need o' prickin'
Off yonder with the Pelletiers when spies are
    ripe fer pickin'.

The frisky little Shetlands now are growin'
    shaggy coats
An' acquirin' silken mufflers of their own to
    guard their throats;
An' a Russian wolf-hound puppy left its mother
    yesterday,
An' a tinge o' sorrow touched us as we saw it
    go away.
For the sight was full o' meanin', an' we knew,
    when it had gone,
'Twas a symbol of the partin's that the years are
    bringin' on.
Oh, a feller must be better — to his faith he can't
    help stickin'
Off yonder with the Pelletiers when spies are ripe
    fer pickin'.

The year is almost over, now at dusk the valleys
    glow
With the misty mantle chillin', that is hangin'
    very low.
An' each mornin' sees the maples just a little
    redder turned
Than they were the night we left 'em, an' the
    elms are browner burned.

An' a feller can't help feelin', an' I don't care
    who it is,
That the mind that works such wonders has a
    greater power than his.
Oh, I know that I'll remember till life's last few
    sparks are flickin'
The lessons out at Pelletiers when spies were ripe
    for pickin'.

WHEN PA COMES HOME

When Pa comes home, I'm at the door,
An' then he grabs me off the floor
An' throws me up an' catches me.
When I come down, an' then, says he:
"Well, how'd you get along to-day?
An' were you good, an' did you play,
An' keep right out of mamma's way?
An' how'd you get that awful bump
Above your eye? My, what a lump!
An' who spilled jelly on your shirt?
An' where'd you ever find the dirt
That's on your hands? And my! Oh, my!
I guess those eyes have had a cry,
They look so red. What was it, pray?
What has been happening here to-day?"

An' then he drops his coat an' hat
Upon a chair, an' says: "What's that?

Who knocked that engine on its back
An' stepped upon that piece of track?"
An' then he takes me on his knee
An' says: "What's this that now I see?
Whatever can the matter be?
Who strewed those toys upon the floor,
An' left those things behind the door?
Who upset all those parlor chairs
An' threw those blocks upon the stairs?
I guess a cyclone called to-day
While I was workin' far away.
Who was it worried mamma so?
It can't be anyone I know."

An' then I laugh an' say: "It's me!
Me did most ever'thing you see.
Me got this bump the time me tripped.
An' here is where the jelly slipped
Right off my bread upon my shirt,
An' when me tumbled down it hurt.
That's how me got all over dirt.
Me threw those building blocks downstairs,
An' me upset the parlor chairs,
Coz when you're playin' train you've got
To move things 'round an awful lot."
An' then my Pa he kisses me
An' bounces me upon his knee
An' says: "Well, well, my little lad,
What glorious fun you must have had!"

MOTHER'S DAY

Gentle hands that never weary toiling in love's
vineyard sweet,
Eyes that seem forever cheery when our eyes
they chance to meet,
Tender, patient, brave, devoted, this is always
mother's way.
Could her worth in gold be quoted as you think
of her to-day?

There shall never be another quite so tender,
quite so kind
As the patient little mother; nowhere on this
earth you'll find
Her affection duplicated; none so proud if you
are fine.
Could her worth be overstated? Not by any
words of mine.

Death stood near the hour she bore us, agony
was hers to know,
Yet she bravely faced it for us, smiling in her
time of woe;
Down the years how oft we've tried her, often
selfish, heedless, blind,
Yet with love alone to guide her she was never
once unkind.

Vain are all our tributes to her if in words
    alone they dwell.
We must live the praises due her; there's no
    other way to tell
Gentle mother that we love her. Would you say,
    as you recall
All the patient service of her, you've been
    worthy of it all?

DIVISION

You cannot gather every rose,
    Nor every pleasure claim,
Nor bask in every breeze that blows,
    Nor play in every game.

No millionaire could ever own
    The world's supply of pearls,
And no man here has ever known
    All of the pretty girls.

So take what joy may come your way,
    And envy not your brothers;
Enjoy your share of fun each day,
    And leave the rest for others.

A MAN

A man doesn't whine at his losses.
    A man doesn't whimper and fret,
Or rail at the weight of his crosses
    And ask life to rear him a pet.
A man doesn't grudgingly labor
    Or look upon toil as a blight;
A man doesn't sneer at his neighbor
    Or sneak from a cause that is right.

A man doesn't sulk when another
    Succeeds where his efforts have failed;
Doesn't keep all his praise for the brother
    Whose glory is publicly hailed;
And pass by the weak and the humble
    As though they were not of his clay;
A man doesn't ceaselessly grumble
    When things are not going his way.

A man looks on woman as tender
    And gentle, and stands at her side
At all times to guard and defend her,
    And never to scorn or deride.
A man looks on life as a mission.
    To serve, just so far as he can;
A man holds his noblest ambition
    On earth is to live as a man.

A VOW

I might not ever scale the mountain heights
　　Where all the great men stand in glory now;
I may not ever gain the world's delights
　　Or win a wreath of laurel for my brow;
I may not gain the victories that men
　　Are fighting for, nor do a thing to boast of;
I may not get a fortune here, but then,
　　The little that I have I'll make the most of.

I'll make my little home a palace fine,
　　My little patch of green a garden fair,
And I shall know each humble plant and vine
　　As rich men know their orchid blossoms rare.
My little home may not be much to see;
　　Its chimneys may not tower far above;
But it will be a mansion great to me,
　　For in its walls I'll keep a hoard of love.

I will not pass my modest pleasures by
　　To grasp at shadows of more splendid things,
Disdaining what of joyousness is nigh
　　Because I am denied the joy of kings.
But I will laugh and sing my way along,
　　I'll make the most of what is mine to-day,
And if I never rise above the throng,
　　I shall have lived a full life anyway.

GUESSING TIME

It's guessing time at our house; every evening
    after tea
We start guessing what old Santa's going to
    leave us on our tree.
Everyone of us holds secrets that the others try
    to steal,
And that eyes and lips are plainly having trouble
    to conceal.
And a little lip that quivered just a bit the other
    night
Was a sad and startling warning that I mustn't
    guess it right.

" Guess what you will get for Christmas! " is the
    cry that starts the fun.
And I answer: " Give the letter with which the
    name's begun."
Oh, the eyes that dance around me and the joy-
    ous faces there
Keep me nightly guessing wildly: " Is it some-
    thing I can wear? "
I implore them all to tell me in a frantic sort
    of way
And pretend that I am puzzled, just to keep them
    feeling gay.

Oh, the wise and knowing glances that across the
    table fly
And the winks exchanged with mother, that they
    think I never spy;
Oh, the whispered confidences that are poured
    into her ear,
And the laughter gay that follows when I try
    my best to hear!
Oh, the shouts of glad derision when I bet that
    it's a cane,
And the merry answering chorus: "No, it's
    not. Just guess again!"

It's guessing time at our house, and the fun is
    running fast,
And I wish somehow this contest of delight
    could always last,
For the love that's in their faces and their laugh-
    ter ringing clear
Is their dad's most precious present when the
    Christmas time is near.
And soon as it is over, when the tree is bare
    and plain,
I shall start in looking forward to the time to
    guess again.

UNDERSTANDING

When I was young and frivolous and never
    stopped to think,
When I was always doing wrong, or just upon
    the brink;
When I was just a lad of seven and eight and
    nine and ten,
It seemed to me that every day I got in trouble
    then,
And strangers used to shake their heads and say
    I was no good,
But father always stuck to me — it seems he
    understood.

I used to have to go to him 'most every night
    and say
The dreadful things that I had done to worry
    folks that day.
I know I didn't mean to be a turmoil round the
    place,
And with the womenfolks about forever in dis-
    grace;
To do the way they said I should, I tried the
    best I could,
But though they scolded me a lot — my father
    understood.

He never seemed to think it queer that I should
    risk my bones,
Or fight with other boys at times, or pelt a cat
    with stones;
An' when I'd break a window pane, it used to
    make him sad,
But though the neighbors said I was, he never
    thought me bad;
He never whipped me, as they used to say to me
    he should;
That boys can't always do what's right — it
    seemed he understood.

Now there's that little chap of mine, just full of
    life and fun,
Comes up to me with solemn face to tell the
    bad he's done.
It's natural for any boy to be a roguish elf,
He hasn't time to stop and think and figure for
    himself,
And though the womenfolks insist that I should
    take a hand,
They've never been a boy themselves, and they
    don't understand.

Some day I've got to go up there, and make a
    sad report

And tell the Father of us all where I have fallen
     short;
And there will be a lot of wrong I never meant
     to do,
A lot of smudges on my sheet that He will have
     to view.
And little chance for heavenly bliss, up there,
     will I command,
Unless the Father smiles and says: " My boy,
     I understand."

PEOPLE LIKED HIM

People liked him, not because
    He was rich or known to fame;
He had never won applause
    As a star in any game.
His was not a brilliant style,
    His was not a forceful way,
But he had a gentle smile
    And a kindly word to say.

Never arrogant or proud,
    On he went with manner mild;
Never quarrelsome or loud,
    Just as simple as a child;
Honest, patient, brave and true:
    Thus he lived from day to day,
Doing what he found to do
    In a cheerful sort of way.

Wasn't one to boast of gold
  Or belittle it with sneers,
Didn't change from hot to cold,
  Kept his friends throughout the years,
Sort of man you like to meet
  Any time or any place.
There was always something sweet
  And refreshing in his face.

Sort of man you'd like to be:
  Balanced well and truly square;
Patient in adversity,
  Generous when his skies were fair.
Never lied to friend or foe,
  Never rash in word or deed,
Quick to come and slow to go
  In a neighbor's time of need.

Never rose to wealth or fame,
  Simply lived, and simply died,
But the passing of his name
  Left a sorrow, far and wide.
Not for glory he'd attained,
  Nor for what he had of pelf,
Were the friends that he had gained,
  But for what he was himself.

WHEN FATHER SHOOK THE STOVE

'Twas not so many years ago,
  Say, twenty-two or three,
When zero weather or below
  Held many a thrill for me.
Then in my icy room I slept
  A youngster's sweet repose,
And always on my form I kept
  My flannel underclothes.
Then I was roused by sudden shock
  Though still to sleep I strove,
I knew that it was seven o'clock
  When father shook the stove.

I never heard him quit his bed
  Or his alarm clock ring;
I never heard his gentle tread,
  Or his attempts to sing;
The sun that found my window pane
  On me was wholly lost,
Though many a sunbeam tried in vain
  To penetrate the frost.
To human voice I never stirred,
  But deeper down I dove
Beneath the covers, when I heard
  My father shake the stove.

To-day it all comes back to me
    And I can hear it still;
He seemed to take a special glee
    In shaking with a will.
He flung the noisy dampers back,
    Then rattled steel on steel,
Until the force of his attack
    The building seemed to feel.
Though I'd a youngster's heavy eyes
    All sleep from them he drove;
It seemed to me the dead must rise
    When father shook the stove.

Now radiators thump and pound
    And every room is warm,
And modern men new ways have found
    To shield us from the storm.
The window panes are seldom glossed
    The way they used to be;
The pictures left by old Jack Frost
    Our children never see.
And now that he has gone to rest
    In God's great slumber grove,
I often think those days were best
    When father shook the stove.

AN EASY WORLD

It's an easy world to live in if you choose to
    make it so;
You never need to suffer, save the griefs that
    all must know;
If you'll stay upon the level and will do the
    best you can
You will never lack the friendship of a kindly
    fellow man.

Life's an easy road to travel if you'll only walk
    it straight;
There are many here to help you in your little
    bouts with fate;
When the clouds begin to gather and your hopes
    begin to fade,
If you've only toiled in honor you won't have
    to call for aid.

But if you've bartered friendship and the faith
    on which it rests
For a temporary winning; if you've cheated in
    the tests,
If with promises you've broken, you have chilled
    the hearts of men;
It is vain to look for friendship for it will not
    come again.

Oh, the world is full of kindness, thronged with
    men who want to be
Of some service to their neighbors and they'll
    run to you or me
When we're needing their assistance if we've
    lived upon the square,
But they'll spurn us in our trouble if we've
    always been unfair.

It's an easy world to live in; all you really need
    to do
Is the decent thing and proper and then friends
    will flock to you;
But let dishonor trail you and some stormy day
    you'll find
To your heart's supremest sorrow that you've
    made the world unkind.

THE OBLIGATION OF FRIENDSHIP

You ought to be fine for the sake of the folks
    Who think you are fine.
If others have faith in you doubly you're bound
    To stick to the line.
It's not only on you that dishonor descends:
You can't hurt yourself without hurting your
    friends.

You ought to be true for the sake of the folks
    Who believe you are true.
You never should stoop to a deed that your
    friends
        Think you wouldn't do.
If you're false to yourself, be the blemish but
    small,
You have injured your friends; you've been false
    to them all.

For friendship, my boy, is a bond between men
    That is founded on truth:
It believes in the best of the ones that it loves,
    Whether old man or youth;
And the stern rule it lays down for me and for
    you
Is to be what our friends think we are, through
    and through.

THE FINER THOUGHT

How fine it is at night to say:
" I have not wronged a soul to-day.
I have not by a word or deed,
In any breast sowed anger's seed,
Or caused a fellow being pain;
Nor is there on my crest a stain
That shame has left. In honor's way,
With head erect, I've lived this day."

When night slips down and day departs
And rest returns to weary hearts,
How fine it is to close the book
Of records for the day, and look
Once more along the traveled mile
And find that all has been worth while;
To say: " In honor I have toiled;
My plume is spotless and unsoiled."

Yet cold and stern a man may be
Retaining his integrity;
And he may pass from day to day
A spirit dead, in living clay,
Observing strictly morals, laws,
Yet serving but a selfish cause;
So it is not enough to say:
" I have not stooped to shame to-day! "

It is a finer, nobler thought
When day is done and night has brought
The contemplative hours and sweet,
And rest to weary hearts and feet,
If man can stand in truth and say:
"I have been useful here to-day.
Back there is one I chanced to see
With hope newborn because of me.

"This day in honor I have toiled;
My shining crest is still unsoiled,
But on the mile I leave behind
Is one who says that I was kind;
And someone hums a cheerful song
Because I chanced to come along."
Sweet rest at night that man shall own
Who has not lived his day alone.

A REAL MAN

Men are of two kinds, and he
Was of the kind I'd like to be.
Some preach their virtues, and a few
Express their lives by what they do.
That sort was he. No flowery phrase
Or glibly spoken words of praise
Won friends for him. He wasn't cheap
Or shallow, but his course ran deep,
And it was pure. You know the kind.
Not many in a life you find
Whose deeds outrun their words so far
That more than what they seem they are.

There are two kinds of lies as well:
The kind you live, the ones you tell.
Back through his years from age to youth
He never acted one untruth.
Out in the open light he fought
And didn't care what others thought
Nor what they said about his fight
If he believed that he was right.
The only deeds he ever hid
Were acts of kindness that he did.

What speech he had was plain and blunt.
His was an unattractive front.
Yet children loved him; babe and boy
Played with the strength he could employ,

Without one fear, and they are fleet
To sense injustice and deceit.
No back door gossip linked his name
With any shady tale of shame.
He did not have to compromise
With evil-doers, shrewd and wise,
And let them ply their vicious trade
Because of some past escapade.

Men are of two kinds, and he
Was of the kind I'd like to be.
No door at which he ever knocked
Against his manly form was locked.
If ever man on earth was free
And independent, it was he.
No broken pledge lost him respect,
He met all men with head erect,
And when he passed I think there went
A soul to yonder firmament
So white, so splendid and so fine
It came almost to God's design.

THE NEIGHBORLY MAN

Some are eager to be famous, some are striving
    to be great,
Some are toiling to be leaders of their nation
    or their state,
And in every man's ambition, if we only under-
    stood,
There is much that's fine and splendid; every
    hope is mostly good.
So I cling unto the notion that contented I
    will be
If the men upon life's pathway find a needed
    friend in me.

I rather like to putter 'round the walks and
    yards of life,
To spray at night the roses that are burned and
    browned with strife;
To eat a frugal dinner, but always to have a
    chair
For the unexpected stranger that my simple
    meal would share.
I don't care to be a traveler, I would rather be
    the one
Sitting calmly by the roadside helping weary
    travelers on.

I'd like to be a neighbor in the good old-fash-
ioned way,
Finding much to do for others, but not over
much to say.
I like to read the papers, but I do not yearn
to see
What the journal of the morning has been
moved to say of me;
In the silences and shadows I would live my
life and die
And depend for fond remembrance on some
grateful passers-by.

I guess I wasn't fashioned for the brilliant
things of earth,
Wasn't gifted much with talent or designed for
special worth,
But was just sent here to putter with life's little
odds and ends
And keep a simple corner where the stirring
highway bends,
And if folks should chance to linger, worn and
weary through the day,
To do some needed service and to cheer them
on their way.

ROSES

When God first viewed the rose He'd made
  He smiled, and thought it passing fair;
Upon the bloom His hands He laid,
  And gently blessed each petal there.
He summoned in His artists then
  And bade them paint, as ne'er before,
Each petal, so that earthly men
  Might love the rose for evermore.

With Heavenly brushes they began
  And one with red limned every leaf,
To signify the love of man;
  The first rose, white, betokened grief;
"My rose shall deck the bride," one said
  And so in pink he dipped his brush,
"And it shall smile beside the dead
  To typify the faded blush."

And then they came unto His throne
  And laid the roses at His feet,
The crimson bud, the bloom full blown,
  Filling the air with fragrance sweet.
"Well done, well done!" the Master spake;
  "Henceforth the rose shall bloom on earth:
One fairer blossom I will make,"
  And then a little babe had birth.

On earth a loving mother lay
  Within a rose-decked room and smiled,
But from the blossoms turned away
  To gently kiss her little child,
And then she murmured soft and low,
  " For beauty, here, a mother seeks.
None but the Master made, I know,
  The roses in a baby's cheeks."

THE JUNK BOX

My father often used to say:
" My boy don't throw a thing away:
You'll find a use for it some day."

So in a box he stored up things,
Bent nails, old washers, pipes and rings,
And bolts and nuts and rusty springs.

Despite each blemish and each flaw,
Some use for everything he saw;
With things material, this was law.

And often when he'd work to do,
He searched the junk box through and through
And found old stuff as good as new.

And I have often thought since then,
That father did the same with men;
He knew he'd need their help again.

It seems to me he understood
That men, as well as iron and wood,
May broken be and still be good.

Despite the vices he'd display
He never threw a man away,
But kept him for another day.

A human junk box is this earth
And into it we're tossed at birth,
To wait the day we'll be of worth.

Though bent and twisted, weak of will,
And full of flaws and lacking skill,
Some service each can render still.

THE BOY THAT WAS

When the hair about the temples starts to show
      the signs of gray,
And a fellow realizes that he's wandering far
      away
From the pleasures of his boyhood and his
      youth, and never more
Will know the joy of laughter as he did in days
      of yore,

Oh, it's then he starts to thinking of a stubby
     little lad
With a face as brown as berries and a soul
     supremely glad.

When a gray-haired dreamer wanders down the
     lanes of memory
And forgets the living present for the time of
     " used-to-be,"
He takes off his shoes and stockings, and he
     throws his coat away,
And he's free from all restrictions, save the rules
     of manly play.
He may be in richest garments, but bareheaded
     in the sun
He forgets his proud successes and the riches
     he has won.

Oh, there's not a man alive but that would give
     his all to be
The stubby little fellow that in dreamland he
     can see,
And the splendors that surround him and the
     joys about him spread
Only seem to rise to taunt him with the boyhood
     that has fled.
When the hair about the temples starts to show
     Time's silver stain,
Then the richest man that's living yearns to be
     a boy again.

Just Folks

We're queer folks here.
　　We'll talk about the weather,
　　The good times we have had together,
The good times near,
　　The roses buddin', an' the bees
　　Once more upon their nectar sprees;
　　The scarlet fever scare, an' who
　　Came mighty near not pullin' through,
　　An' who had light attacks, an' all
　　The things that int'rest, big or small;
But here you'll never hear of sinnin'
Or any scandal that's beginnin'.
We've got too many other labors
To scatter tales that harm our neighbors.

We're strange folks here.
　　We're tryin' to be cheerful,
　　An' keep this home from gettin' tearful.
We hold it dear;
　　Too dear for pettiness an' meanness,
　　An' nasty tales of men's uncleanness.
　　Here you shall come to joyous smilin',
　　Secure from hate an' harsh revilin';
　　Here, where the wood fire brightly blazes,
　　You'll hear from us our neighbor's praises.

Here, that they'll never grow to doubt us,
We keep our friends always about us;
An' here, though storms outside may pelter
Is refuge for our friends, an' shelter.

We've one rule here,
   An' that is to be pleasant.
   The folks we know are always present,
Or very near.
   An' though they dwell in many places,
   We think we're talkin' to their faces;
   An' that keeps us from only seein'
   The faults in any human bein',
   An' checks our tongues when they'd go trailin'
   Into the mire of mortal failin'.
Flaws aren't so big when folks are near you;
You don't talk mean when they can hear you.
An' so no scandal here is started,
Because from friends we're never parted.

As It Goes

In the corner she's left the mechanical toy,
   On the chair is her Teddy Bear fine;
The things that I thought she would really enjoy
   Don't seem to be quite in her line.

There's the flaxen-haired doll that is lovely to see
   And really expensively dressed,
Left alone, all uncared for, and strange though
      it be,
   She likes her rag dolly the best.

Oh, the money we spent and the plans that we
      laid
   And the wonderful things that we bought!
There are toys that are cunningly, skillfully
      made,
   But she seems not to give them a thought.
She was pleased when she woke and discovered
      them there,
   But never a one of us guessed
That it isn't the splendor that makes a gift
      rare—
   She likes her rag dolly the best.

There's the flaxen-haired doll, with the real
      human hair,
   There's the Teddy Bear left all alone,
There's the automobile at the foot of the stair,
   And there is her toy telephone;
We thought they were fine, but a little child's
      eyes
   Look deeper than ours to find charm,
And now she's in bed, and the rag dolly lies
   Snuggled close on her little white arm.

Hollyhocks

Old-fashioned flowers! I love them all:
The morning-glories on the wall,
The pansies in their patch of shade,
The violets, stolen from a glade,
The bleeding hearts and columbine,
Have long been garden friends of mine;
But memory every summer flocks
About a clump of hollyhocks.

The mother loved them years ago;
Beside the fence they used to grow,
And though the garden changed each year
And certain blooms would disappear
To give their places in the ground
To something new that mother found,
Some pretty bloom or rosebush rare—
The hollyhocks were always there.

It seems but yesterday to me
She led me down the yard to see
The first tall spires, with bloom aflame,
And taught me to pronounce their name.
And year by year I watched them grow,
The first flowers I had come to know.
And with the mother dear I'd yearn
To see the hollyhocks return.

The garden of my boyhood days
With hollyhocks was kept ablaze;
In all my recollections they
In friendly columns nod and sway;
And when to-day their blooms I see,
Always the mother smiles at me;
The mind's bright chambers, life unlocks
Each summer with the hollyhocks.

Sacrifice

When he has more than he can eat
To feed a stranger's not a feat.

When he has more than he can spend
It isn't hard to give or lend.

Who gives but what he'll never miss
Will never know what giving is.

He'll win few praises from his Lord
Who does but what he can afford.

The widow's mite to heaven went
Because real sacrifice it meant.

Reward

Don't want medals on my breast,
    Don't want all the glory,
I'm not worrying greatly lest
    The world won't hear my story.
A chance to dream beside a stream
    Where fish are biting free;
A day or two, 'neath skies of blue,
    Is joy enough for me.

I do not ask a hoard of gold,
    Nor treasures rich and rare;
I don't want all the joys to hold;
    I only want a share.
Just now and then, away from men
    And all their haunts of pride,
If I can steal, with rod and reel,
    I will be satisfied.

I'll gladly work my way through life;
    I would not always play;
I only ask to quit the strife
    For an occasional day.
If I can sneak from toil a week
    To chum with stream and tree,
I'll fish away and smiling say
    That life's been good to me.

See It Through

When you're up against a trouble,
　Meet it squarely, face to face;
Lift your chin and set your shoulders,
　Plant your feet and take a brace.
When it's vain to try to dodge it,
　Do the best that you can do;
You may fail, but you may conquer,
　See it through!

Black may be the clouds about you
　And your future may seem grim,
But don't let your nerve desert you;
　Keep yourself in fighting trim.
If the worst is bound to happen,
　Spite of all that you can do,
Running from it will not save you,
　See it through!

Even hope may seem but futile,
　When with troubles you're beset,
But remember you are facing
　Just what other men have met.
You may fail, but fall still fighting;
　Don't give up, whate'er you do;
Eyes front, head high to the finish.
　See it through!

To the Humble

If all the flowers were roses,
  If never daisies grew,
If no old-fashioned posies
  Drank in the morning dew,
Then man might have some reason
  To whimper and complain,
And speak these words of treason,
  That all our toil is vain.

If all the stars were Saturns
  That twinkle in the night,
Of equal size and patterns,
  And equally as bright,
Then men in humble places,
  With humble work to do,
With frowns upon their faces
  Might trudge their journey through.

But humble stars and posies
  Still do their best, although
They're planets not, nor roses,
  To cheer the world below.
And those old-fashioned daisies
  Delight the soul of man;
They're here, and this their praise is:
  They work the Master's plan.

Though humble be your labor,
　　And modest be your sphere,
Come, envy not your neighbor
　　Whose light shines brighter here.
Does God forget the daisies
　　Because the roses bloom?
Shall you not win His praises
　　By toiling at your loom?

Have you, the toiler humble,
　　Just reason to complain,
To shirk your task and grumble
　　And think that it is vain
Because you see a brother
　　With greater work to do?
No fame of his can smother
　　The merit that's in you.

When Nellie's on the Job

The bright spots in my life are when the servant
    quits the place,
Although that grim disturbance brings a frown
    to Nellie's face;
The week between the old girl's reign and entry
    of the new
Is one that's filled with happiness and comfort
    through and through.
The charm of living's back again—a charm that
    servants rob—
I like the home, I like the meals, when Nellie's
    on the job.

There's something in a servant's ways, however
    fine they be,
That has a cold and distant touch and frets the
    soul of me.
The old home never looks so well, as in that
    week or two
That we are servantless and Nell has all the
    work to do.
There is a sense of comfort then that makes my
    pulses throb
And home is as it ought to be when Nellie's on
    the job.

Think not that I'd deny her help or grudge the
    servant's pay;
When one departs we try to get another right
    away;
I merely state the simple fact that no such joys
    I've known
As in those few brief days at home when we've
    been left alone.
There is a gentleness that seems to soothe this
    selfish elf
And, Oh, I like to eat those meals that Nellie
    gets herself!

You cannot buy the gentle touch that mother
    gives the place;
No servant girl can do the work with just the
    proper grace.
And though you hired the queen of cooks to
    fashion your croquettes,
Her meals would not compare with those your
    loving comrade gets;
So, though the maid has quit again, and she is
    moved to sob,
The old home's at its finest now, for Nellie's
    on the job.

The Old, Old Story

I have no wish to rail at fate,
    And vow that I'm unfairly treated;
I do not give vent to my hate
    Because at times I am defeated.
Life has its ups and downs, I know,
    But tell me why should people say
Whenever after fish I go:
    "You should have been here yesterday"?

It is my luck always to strike
    A day when there is nothing doing,
When neither perch, nor bass, nor pike
    My baited hooks will come a-wooing.
Must I a day late always be?
    When not a nibble comes my way
Must someone always say to me:
    "We caught a bunch here yesterday"?

I am not prone to discontent,
    Nor over-zealous now to climb;
If victory is not yet meant
    For me I'll calmly bide my time.
But I should like just once to go
    Out fishing on some lake or bay
And not have someone mutter: "Oh,
    You should have been here yesterday."

The Pup

He tore the curtains yesterday,
    And scratched the paper on the wall;
Ma's rubbers, too, have gone astray—
    She says she left them in the hall;
He tugged the table cloth and broke
    A fancy saucer and a cup;
Though Bud and I think it a joke
    Ma scolds a lot about the pup.

The sofa pillows are a sight,
    The rugs are looking somewhat frayed,
And there is ruin, left and right,
    That little Boston bull has made.
He slept on Buddy's counterpane—
    Ma found him there when she woke up.
I think it needless to explain
    She scolds a lot about the pup.

And yet he comes and licks her hand
    And sometimes climbs into her lap
And there, Bud lets me understand,
    He very often takes his nap.
And Bud and I have learned to know
    She wouldn't give the rascal up:
She's really fond of him, although
    She scolds a lot about the pup.

Since Jessie Died

We understand a lot of things we never did
    before,
And it seems that to each other Ma and I are
    meaning more.
I don't know how to say it, but since little Jessie
    died
We have learned that to be happy we must travel
    side by side.
You can share your joys and pleasures, but you
    never come to know
The depth there is in loving, till you've got a
    common woe.

We're past the hurt of fretting—we can talk
    about it now:
She slipped away so gently and the fever left
    her brow
So softly that we didn't know we'd lost her, but,
    instead,
We thought her only sleeping as we watched
    beside her bed.
Then the doctor, I remember, raised his head, as
    if to say
What his eyes had told already, and Ma fainted
    dead away.

Up to then I thought that money was the thing
      I ought to get;
And I fancied, once I had it, I should never have
      to fret.
But I saw that I had wasted precious hours in
      seeking wealth;
I had made a tidy fortune, but I couldn't buy
      her health.
And I saw this truth much clearer than I'd ever
      seen before:
That the rich man and the poor man have to let
      death through the door.

We're not half so keen for money as one time
      we used to be;
I am thinking more of mother and she's think-
      ing more of me.
Now we spend more time together, and I know
      we're meaning more
To each other on life's journey, than we ever
      meant before.
It was hard to understand it! Oh, the dreary
      nights we've cried!
But we've found the depth of loving, since the
      day that Jessie died.

Hard Luck

Ain't no use as I can see
In sittin' underneath a tree
An' growlin' that your luck is bad,
An' that your life is extry sad;
Your life ain't sadder than your neighbor's
Nor any harder are your labors;
It rains on him the same as you,
An' he has work he hates to do;
An' he gits tired an' he gits cross,
An' he has trouble with the boss;
You take his whole life, through an' through,
Why, he's no better off than you.

If whinin' brushed the clouds away
I wouldn't have a word to say;
If it made good friends out o' foes
I'd whine a bit, too, I suppose;
But when I look around an' see
A lot o' men resemblin' me,
An' see 'em sad, an' see 'em gay
With work t' do most every day,
Some full o' fun, some bent with care,
Some havin' troubles hard to bear,
I reckon, as I count my woes,
They're 'bout what everybody knows.

The day I find a man who'll say
He's never known a rainy day,

Who'll raise his right hand up an' swear
In forty years he's had no care,
Has never had a single blow,
An' never known one touch o' woe,
Has never seen a loved one die,
Has never wept or heaved a sigh,
Has never had a plan go wrong,
But allus laughed his way along;
Then I'll sit down an' start to whine
That all the hard luck here is mine.

Vacation Time

Vacation time! How glad it seemed
When as a boy I sat and dreamed
Above my school books, of the fun
That I should claim when toil was done;
And, Oh, how oft my youthful eye
Went wandering with the patch of sky
That drifted by the window panes
O'er pleasant fields and dusty lanes,
Where I would race and romp and shout
The very moment school was out.
My artful little fingers then
Feigned labor with the ink and pen,
But heart and mind were far away,
Engaged in some glad bit of play.

The last two weeks dragged slowly by;
Time hadn't then learned how to fly.
It seemed the clock upon the wall
From hour to hour could only crawl,
And when the teacher called my name,
Unto my cheeks the crimson came,
For I could give no answer clear
To questions that I didn't hear.
"Wool gathering, were you?" oft she said
And smiled to see me blushing red.
Her voice had roused me from a dream
Where I was fishing in a stream,
And, if I now recall it right,
Just at the time I had a bite.

And now my youngsters dream of play
In just the very selfsame way;
And they complain that time is slow
And that the term will never go.
Their little minds with plans are filled
For joyous hours they soon will build,
And it is vain for me to say,
That have grown old and wise and gray,
That time is swift, and joy is brief;
They'll put no faith in such belief.
To youthful hearts that long for play
Time is a laggard on the way.
'Twas, Oh, so slow to me back then
Ere I had learned the ways of men!

The Little Hurts

Every night she runs to me
With a bandaged arm or a bandaged knee,
A stone-bruised heel or a swollen brow,
And in sorrowful tones she tells me how
She fell and "hurted herse'f to-day"
While she was having the "bestest play."

And I take her up in my arms and kiss
The new little wounds and whisper this:
"Oh, you must be careful, my little one,
You mustn't get hurt while your daddy's gone,
For every cut with its ache and smart
Leaves another bruise on your daddy's heart."

Every night I must stoop to see
The fresh little cuts on her arm or knee;
The little hurts that have marred her play,
And brought the tears on a happy day;
For the path of childhood is oft beset
With care and trouble and things that fret.

Oh, little girl, when you older grow,
Far greater hurts than these you'll know;
Greater bruises will bring your tears,
Around the bend of the lane of years,
But come to your daddy with them at night
And he'll do his best to make all things right.

The Lanes of Memory

Adown the lanes of memory bloom all the
flowers of yesteryear,
And looking back we smile to see life's bright
red roses reappear,
The little sprigs of mignonette that smiled upon
us as we passed,
The pansy and the violet, too sweet, we thought
those days, to last.

The gentle mother by the door caresses still her
lilac blooms,
And as we wander back once more we seem to
smell the old perfumes,
We seem to live again the joys that once were
ours so long ago
When we were little girls and boys, with all the
charms we used to know.

But living things grow old and fade; the dead
in memory remain,
In all their splendid youth arrayed, exempt from
suffering and pain;
The little babe God called away, so many, many
years ago,
Is still a little babe to-day, and I am glad that
this is so.

Time has not changed the joys we knew; the
    summer rains or winter snows
Have failed to harm the wondrous hue of any
    dew-kissed bygone rose;
In memory 'tis still as fair as when we plucked
    it for our own,
And we can see it blooming there, if anything,
    more lovely grown.

Adown the lanes of memory bloom all the joys
    of yesteryear,
And God has given you and me the power to
    make them reappear;
For we can settle back at night and live again
    the joys we knew
And taste once more the old delight of days
    when all our skies were blue.

The Day of Days

A year is filled with glad events:
    The best is Christmas day,
But every holiday presents
    Its special round of play,
And looking back on boyhood now
    And all the charms it knew,
One day, above the rest, somehow,
    Seems brightest in review.

That day was finest, I believe,
　　Though many grown-ups scoff,
When mother said that we could leave
　　Our shoes and stockings off.

Through all the pleasant days of spring
　　We begged to know once more
The joy of barefoot wandering
　　And quit the shoes we wore;
But always mother shook her head
　　And answered with a smile:
"It is too soon, too soon," she said.
　　"Wait just a little while."
Then came that glorious day at last
　　When mother let us know
That fear of taking cold was past
　　And we could barefoot go.

Though Christmas day meant much to me,
　　And eagerly I'd try
The first boy on the street to be
　　The Fourth day of July,
I think the summit of my joy
　　Was reached that happy day
Each year, when, as a barefoot boy,
　　I hastened out to play.
Could I return to childhood fair,
　　That day I think I'd choose
When mother said I needn't wear
　　My stockings and my shoes.

A Fine Sight

I reckon the finest sight of all
  That a man can see in this world of ours
Ain't the works of art on the gallery wall,
  Or the red an' white o' the fust spring flowers,
Or a hoard o' gold from the yellow mines;
  But the sight that'll make ye want t' yell
Is t' catch a glimpse o' the fust pink signs
  In yer baby's cheek, that she's gittin well.

When ye see the pink jes' a-creepin' back
  T' the pale, drawn cheek, an' ye note a smile,
Then th' cords o' yer heart that were tight, grow
      slack
  An' ye jump fer joy every little while,
An' ye tiptoe back to her little bed
  As though ye doubted yer eyes, or were
Afraid it was fever come back instead,
  An' ye found that th' pink still blossomed there.

Ye've watched fer that smile an' that bit o' bloom
  With a heavy heart fer weeks an' weeks;
An' a castle o' joy becomes that room
  When ye glimpse th' pink in yer baby's cheeks.
An' out o' yer breast flies a weight o' care,
  An' ye're lifted up by some magic spell,
An' yer heart jes' naturally beats a prayer
  O' joy to the Lord 'cause she's gittin' well.

Manhood's Greeting

I've felt some little thrills of pride, I've inwardly
    rejoiced
Along the pleasant lanes of life to hear my
    praises voiced;
No great distinction have I claimed, but in a
    humble way
Some satisfactions sweet have come to brighten
    many a day;
But of the joyous thrills of life the finest that
    could be
Was mine upon that day when first a stranger
    "mistered" me.

I had my first long trousers on, and wore a
    derby too,
But I was still a little boy to everyone I knew.
I dressed in manly fashion, and I tried to act
    the part,
But I felt that I was awkward and lacked the
    manly art.
And then that kindly stranger spoke my name
    and set me free;
I was sure I'd come to manhood on the day he
    "mistered" me.

I never shall forget the joy that suddenly was
    mine,
The sweetness of the thrill that seemed to dance
    along my spine,
The pride that swelled within me, as he shook
    my youthful hand
And treated me as big enough with grown up
    men to stand.
I felt my body straighten and a stiffening at each
    knee,
And was gloriously happy, just because he'd
    "mistered" me.

I cannot now recall his name, I only wish I
    could.
I've often wondered if that day he really under-
    stood
How much it meant unto a boy, still wearing
    boyhood's tan,
To find that others noticed that he'd grown to
    be a man.
Now I try to treat as equal every growing boy
    I see
In memory of that kindly man—the first to
    "mister" me.

Fishing Nooks

"Men will grow weary," said the Lord,
"Of working for their bed and board.
They'll weary of the money chase
And want to find a resting place
Where hum of wheel is never heard
And no one speaks an angry word,
And selfishness and greed and pride
And petty motives don't abide.
They'll need a place where they can go
To wash their souls as white as snow.
They will be better men and true
If they can play a day or two."

The Lord then made the brooks to flow
And fashioned rivers here below,
And many lakes; for water seems
Best suited for a mortal's dreams.
He placed about them willow trees
To catch the murmur of the breeze,
And sent the birds that sing the best
Among the foliage to nest.
He filled each pond and stream and lake
With fish for man to come and take;
Then stretched a velvet carpet deep
On which a weary soul could sleep.

It seemed to me the Good Lord knew
That man would want something to do

When worn and wearied with the stress
Of battling hard for world success.
When sick at heart of all the strife
And pettiness of daily life,
He knew he'd need, from time to time,
To cleanse himself of city grime,
And he would want some place to be
Where hate and greed he'd never see.
And so on lakes and streams and brooks
The Good Lord fashioned fishing nooks.

Show the Flag

Show the flag and let it wave
As a symbol of the brave;
Let it float upon the breeze
As a sign for each who sees
That beneath it, where it rides,
Loyalty to-day abides.

Show the flag and signify
That it wasn't born to die;
Let its colors speak for you
That you still are standing true,
True in sight of God and man
To the work that flag began.

Show the flag that all may see
That you serve humanity.
Let it whisper to the breeze
That comes singing through the trees
That whatever storms descend
You'll be faithful to the end.

Show the flag and let it fly,
Cheering every passer-by.
Men that may have stepped aside,
May have lost their old-time pride,
May behold it there, and then,
Consecrate themselves again.

Show the flag! The day is gone
When men blindly hurry on
Serving only gods of gold;
Now the spirit that was cold
Warms again to courage fine.
Show the flag and fall in line!

Constant Beauty

It's good to have the trees again, the singing of
the breeze again,
It's good to see the lilacs bloom as lovely as
of old.
It's good that we can feel again the touch of
beauties real again,

For hearts and minds, of sorrow now, have
all that they can hold.

The roses haven't changed a bit, nor have the
lilacs stranged a bit,
They bud and bloom the way they did before
the war began.
The world is upside down to-day, there's much
to make us frown to-day,
And gloom and sadness everywhere beset the
path of man.

But now the lilacs bloom again and give us their
perfume again,
And now the roses smile at us and nod along
the way;
And it is good to see again the blossoms on each
tree again,
And feel that nature hasn't changed the way
we have to-day.

Oh, we have changed from what we were; we're
not the carefree lot we were;
Our hearts are filled with sorrow now and
grave concern and pain,
But it is good to see once more, the blooming
lilac tree once more,
And find the constant roses here to comfort
us again.

Home

The road to laughter beckons me,
   The road to all that's best;
The home road where I nightly see
   The castle of my rest;
The path where all is fine and fair,
   And little children run,
For love and joy are waiting there
   As soon as day is done.

There is no rich reward of fame
   That can compare with this:
At home I wear an honest name,
   My lips are fit to kiss.
At home I'm always brave and strong,
   And with the setting sun
They find no trace of shame or wrong
   In anything I've done.

There shine the eyes that only see
   The good I've tried to do;
They think me what I'd like to be;
   They know that I am true.
And whether I have lost my fight
   Or whether I have won,
I find a faith that I've been right
   As soon as day is done.

The Old-Time Family

It makes me smile to hear 'em tell each other
    nowadays
The burdens they are bearing, with a child or
    two to raise.
Of course the cost of living has gone soaring
    to the sky
And our kids are wearing garments that my par-
    ents couldn't buy.
Now my father wasn't wealthy, but I never
    heard him squeal
Because eight of us were sitting at the table
    every meal.

People fancy they are martyrs if their children
    number three,
And four or five they reckon makes a large-
    sized family.
A dozen hungry youngsters at a table I have
    seen
And their daddy didn't grumble when they
    licked the platter clean.
Oh, I wonder how these mothers and these
    fathers up-to-date
Would like the job of buying little shoes for
    seven or eight.

We were eight around the table in those happy
    days back them,

Eight that cleaned our plates of pot-pie and then
    passed them up again;
Eight that needed shoes and stockings, eight to
    wash and put to bed,
And with mighty little money in the purse, as I
    have said,
But with all the care we brought them, and
    through all the days of stress,
I never heard my father or my mother wish for
    less.

The Job

The job will not make you, my boy;
    The job will not bring you to fame
Or riches or honor or joy
    Or add any weight to your name.
You may fail or succeed where you are,
    May honestly serve or may rob;
      From the start to the end
      Your success will depend
On just what you make of your job.

Don't look on the job as the thing
    That shall prove what you're able to do;
The job does no more than to bring
    A chance for promotion to you.

Men have shirked in high places and won
  Very justly the jeers of the mob;
    And you'll find it is true
    That it's all up to you
  To say what shall come from the job.

The job is an incident small;
  The thing that's important is man.
The job will not help you at all
  If you won't do the best that you can.
It is you that determines your fate,
  You stand with your hand on the knob
    Of fame's doorway to-day,
    And life asks you to say
  Just what you will make of your job.

Toys

I can pass up the lure of a jewel to wear
  With never the trace of a sigh,
The things on a shelf that I'd like for myself
  I never regret I can't buy.
I can go through the town passing store after
    store
  Showing things it would please me to own,
With never a trace of despair on my face,
  But I can't let a toy shop alone.

I can throttle the love of fine raiment to death
   And I don't know the craving for rum,
But I do know the joy that is born of a toy,
   And the pleasure that comes with a drum.
I can reckon the value of money at times,
   And govern my purse strings with sense,
But I fall for a toy for my girl or my boy
   And never regard the expense.

It's seldom I sigh for unlimited gold
   Or the power of a rich man to buy;
My courage is stout when the doing without
   Is only my duty, but I
Curse the shackles of thrift when I gaze at the
     toys
   That my kiddies are eager to own,
And I'd buy everything that they wish for, by
     Jing!
   If their mother would let me alone.

There isn't much fun spending coin on myself
   For neckties and up-to-date lids,
But there's pleasure tenfold, in the silver and gold
   I part with for things for the kids.
I can go through the town passing store after
     store
   Showing things it would please me to own,
But to thrift I am lost; I won't reckon the cost
   When I'm left in a toy shop alone.

The Stick-Together Families

The stick-together families are happier by far
Than the brothers and the sisters who take sepa-
rate highways are.
The gladdest people living are the wholesome
folks who make
A circle at the fireside that no power but death
can break.
And the finest of conventions ever held beneath
the sun
Are the little family gatherings when the busy
day is done.

There are rich folk, there are poor folk, who
imagine they are wise,
And they're very quick to shatter all the little
family ties.
Each goes searching after pleasure in his own
selected way,
Each with strangers likes to wander, and with
strangers likes to play.
But it's bitterness they harvest, and it's empty
joy they find,
For the children that are wisest are the stick-
together kind.

There are some who seem to fancy that for
  gladness they must roam,
That for smiles that are the brightest they must
  wander far from home.
That the strange friend is the true friend, and
  they travel far astray
And they waste their lives in striving for a joy
  that's far away,
But the gladdest sort of people, when the busy
  day is done,
Are the brothers and the sisters who together
  share their fun.

It's the stick-together family that wins the joys
  of earth,
That hears the sweetest music and that finds the
  finest mirth;
It's the old home roof that shelters all the charm
  that life can give;
There you find the gladdest play-ground, there
  the happiest spot to live.
And, O weary, wandering brother, if content-
  ment you would win,
Come you back unto the fireside and be comrade
  with your kin.

Childless

If certain folks that I know well
Should come to me their woes to tell
I'd read the sorrow in their faces
And I could analyze their cases.
I watch some couples day by day
Go madly on their selfish way
Forever seeking happiness
And always finding something less.
If she whose face is fair to see,
Yet lacks one charm that there should be,
Should open wide her heart to-day
I think I know what she would say.

She'd tell me that his love seems cold
And not the love she knew of old;
That for the home they've built to share
No longer does her husband care;
That he seems happier away
Than by her side, and every day
That passes leaves them more apart;
And then perhaps her tears would start
And in a softened voice she'd add:
"Sometimes I wonder, if we had
A baby now to love, if he
Would find so many faults in me?"

And if he came to tell his woe
Just what he'd say to me, I know:

"There's something dismal in the place
That always stares me in the face.
I love her. She is good and sweet
But still my joy is incomplete.
And then it seems to me that she
Can only see the faults in me.
I wonder sometimes if we had
A little girl or little lad,
If life with all its fret and fuss
Would then seem so monotonous?"

And what I'd say to them I know.
I'd bid them straightway forth to go
And find that child and take him in
And start the joy of life to win.
You foolish, hungry souls, I'd say,
You're living in a selfish way.
A baby's arms stretched out to you
Will give you something real to do.
And though God has not sent one down
To you, within this very town
Somewhere a little baby lies
That would bring gladness to your eyes.

You cannot live this life for gold
Or selfish joys. As you grow old
You'll find that comfort only springs
From living for the living things.
And home must be a barren place
That never knows a baby's face.

Take in a child that needs your care,
Give him your name and let him share
Your happiness and you will own
More joy than you have ever known,
And, what is more, you'll come to feel
That you are doing something real.

The Crucible of Life

Sunshine and shadow, blue sky and gray,
Laughter and tears as we tread on our way;
Hearts that are heavy, then hearts that are light,
Eyes that are misty and eyes that are bright;
Losses and gains in the heat of the strife,
Each in proportion to round out his life.

Into the crucible, stirred by the years,
Go all our hopes and misgivings and fears;
Glad days and sad days, our pleasures and pains,
Worries and comforts, our losses and gains.
Out of the crucible shall there not come
Joy undefiled when we pour off the scum?

Out of the sadness and anguish and woe,
Out of the travail and burdens we know,
Out of the shadow that darkens the way,
Out of the failure that tries us to-day,

Have you a doubt that contentment will come
When you've purified life and discarded the
    scum?

Tinctured with sorrow and flavored with sighs,
Moistened with tears that have flowed from your
    eyes;
Perfumed with sweetness of loves that have died,
Leavened with failures, with grief sanctified,
Sacred and sweet is the joy that must come
From the furnace of life when you've poured off
    the scum.

Unimportant Differences

If he is honest, kindly, true,
    And glad to work from day to day;
If when his bit of toil is through
    With children he will stoop to play;
If he does always what he can
    To serve another's time of need,
Then I shall hail him as a man
    And never ask him what's his creed.

If he respects a woman's name
    And guards her from all thoughtless jeers;
If he is glad to play life's game
    And not risk all to get the cheers;

If he disdains to win by bluff
  And scorns to gain by shady tricks,
I hold that he is good enough
  Regardless of his politics.

If he is glad his much to share
  With them who little here possess,
If he will stand by what is fair
  And not desert to claim success,
If he will leave a smile behind
  As he proceeds from place to place,
He has the proper frame of mind,
  And I won't stop to ask his race.

For when at last life's battle ends
  And all the troops are called on high
We shall discover many friends
  That thoughtlessly we journeyed by.
And we shall learn that God above
  Has judged His creatures by their deeds,
That millions there have won His love
  Who spoke in different tongues and creeds.

The Fishing Outfit

You may talk of stylish raiment,
  You may boast your broadcloth fine,
And the price you gave in payment

May be treble that of mine.
But there's one suit I'd not trade you
   Though it's shabby and it's thin,
For the garb your tailor made you:
     That's the tattered,
     Mud-bespattered
Suit that I go fishing in.

There's no king in silks and laces
   And with jewels on his breast,
With whom I would alter places.
   There's no man so richly dressed
Or so like a fashion panel
   That, his luxuries to win,
I would swap my shirt of flannel
     And the rusty,
     Frayed and dusty
Suit that I go fishing in.

'Tis an outfit meant for pleasure;
   It is freedom's raiment, too;
It's a garb that I shall treasure
   Till my time of life is through.
Though perhaps it looks the saddest
   Of all robes for mortal skin,
I am proudest and I'm gladdest
     In that easy,
     Old and greasy
Suit that I go fishing in.

Grown-Up

Last year he wanted building blocks,
  And picture books and toys,
A saddle horse that gayly rocks,
  And games for little boys.
But now he's big and all that stuff
  His whim no longer suits;
He tells us that he's old enough
  To ask for rubber boots.

Last year whatever Santa brought
  Delighted him to own;
He never gave his wants a thought
  Nor made his wishes known.
But now he says he wants a gun,
  The kind that really shoots,
And I'm confronted with a son
  Demanding rubber boots.

The baby that we used to know
  Has somehow slipped away,
And when or where he chanced to go
  Not one of us can say.
But here's a helter-skelter lad
  That to me nightly scoots
And boldly wishes that he had
  A pair of rubber boots.

I'll bet old Santa Claus will sigh
    When down our flue he comes,
And seeks the babe that used to lie
    And suck his tiny thumbs,
And finds within that little bed
    A grown up boy who hoots
At building blocks, and wants instead
    A pair of rubber boots.

Departed Friends

The dead friends live and always will;
Their presence hovers round us still.
It seems to me they come to share
Each joy or sorrow that we bear.
Among the living I can feel
The sweet departed spirits steal,
And whether it be weal or woe,
I walk with those I used to know.
I can recall them to my side
Whenever I am struggle-tried;
I've but to wish for them, and they
Come trooping gayly down the way,
And I can tell to them my grief
And from their presence find relief.
In sacred memories below
Still live the friends of long ago.

Laughter

Laughter sort o' settles breakfast better than
     digestive pills;
Found it, somehow in my travels, cure for every
     sort of ills;
When the hired help have riled me with their
     slipshod, careless ways,
An' I'm bilin' mad an' cussin' an' my temper's
     all ablaze,
If the calf gets me to laughin' while they're
     teachin' him to feed
Pretty soon I'm feelin' better, 'cause I've found
     the cure I need.

Like to start the day with laughter; when I've had
     a peaceful night,
An' can greet the sun all smilin', that day's goin'
     to be all right.
But there's nothing goes to suit me, when my
     system's full of bile;
Even horses quit their pullin' when the driver
     doesn't smile,
But they'll buckle to the traces when they hear a
     glad giddap,
Just as though they like to labor for a cheerful
     kind o' chap.

Laughter keeps me strong an' healthy.   You can
        bet I'm all run down,
Fit for doctor folks an' nurses when I cannot
        shake my frown.
Found in farmin' laughter's useful, good for
        sheep an' cows an' goats;
When I've laughed my way through summer,
        reap the biggest crop of oats.
Laughter's good for any business, leastwise so it
        seems to me—
Never knew a smilin' feller but was busy as could
        be.

Sometimes sit an' think about it, ponderin' on the
        ways of life,
Wonderin' why mortals gladly face the toil an'
        care an' strife,
Then I come to this conclusion—take it now for
        what it's worth—
It's the joy of laughter keeps us plodding on this
        stretch of earth.
Men the fun o' life are seeking—that's the reason
        for the calf
Spillin' mash upon his keeper—men are hungry
        for a laugh.

The Scoffer

If I had lived in Franklin's time I'm most afraid
that I,
Beholding him out in the rain, a kite about to fly,
And noticing upon its tail the barn door's rusty
key,
Would, with the scoffers on the street, have
chortled in my glee;
And with a sneer upon my lips I would have said
of Ben,
"His belfry must be full of bats. He's raving,
boys, again!"

I'm glad I didn't live on earth when Fulton had
his dream,
And told his neighbors marvelous tales of what
he'd do with steam,
For I'm not sure I'd not have been a member of
the throng
That couldn't see how paddle wheels could shove
a boat along.
At "Fulton's Folly" I'd have sneered, as thou-
sands did back then,
And called the Clermont's architect the craziest
of men.

Yet Franklin gave us wonders great and Fulton
      did the same,
And many "boobs" have left behind an everlast-
      ing fame.
And dead are all their scoffers now and all their
      sneers forgot
And scarce a nickel's worth of good was brought
      here by the lot.
I shudder when I stop to think, had I been living
      then,
I might have been a scoffer, too, and jeered at
      Bob and Ben.

I am afraid to-day to sneer at any fellow's dream.
Time was I thought men couldn't fly or sail be-
      neath the stream.
I never call a man a boob who toils throughout
      the night
On visions that I cannot see, because he may be
      right.
I always think of Franklin's trick, which brought
      the jeers of men,
And to myself I say, "Who knows but here's an-
      other Ben?"

The Pathway of the Living

The pathway of the living is our ever-present
care.
Let us do our best to smooth it and to make it
bright and fair;
Let us travel it with kindness, let's be careful as
we tread,
And give unto the living what we'd offer to the
dead.

The pathway of the living we can beautify and
grace;
We can line it deep with roses and make earth a
happier place.
But we've done all mortals can do, when our
prayers are softly said
For the souls of those that travel o'er the path-
way of the dead.

The pathway of the living all our strength and
courage needs,
There we ought to sprinkle favors, there we ought
to sow our deeds,
There our smiles should be the brightest, there
our kindest words be said,
For the angels have the keeping of the pathway
of the dead.

Lemon Pie

The world is full of gladness,
    There are joys of many kinds,
There's a cure for every sadness,
    That each troubled mortal finds.
And my little cares grow lighter
    And I cease to fret and sigh,
And my eyes with joy grow brighter
    When she makes a lemon pie.

When the bronze is on the filling
    That's one mass of shining gold,
And its molten joy is spilling
    On the plate, my heart grows bold.
And the kids and I in chorus
    Raise one glad exultant cry
And we cheer the treat before us—
    Which is mother's lemon pie.

Then the little troubles vanish,
    And the sorrows disappear,
Then we find the grit to banish
    All the cares that hovered near,
And we smack our lips in pleasure
    O'er a joy no coin can buy,
And we down the golden treasure
    Which is known as lemon pie.

The Flag on the Farm

We've raised a flagpole on the farm
   And flung Old Glory to the sky,
And it's another touch of charm
   That seems to cheer the passer-by,
But more than that, no matter where
   We're laboring in wood and field,
We turn and see it in the air,
   Our promise of a greater yield.
It whispers to us all day long,
From dawn to dusk: "Be true, be strong;
Who falters now with plow or hoe
Gives comfort to his country's foe."

It seems to me I've never tried
   To do so much about the place,
Nor been so slow to come inside,
   But since I've got the flag to face,
Each night when I come 'ome to rest
   I feel that I must look up there
And say: "Old Flag, I've done my best,
   To-day I've tried to do my share."
And sometimes, just to catch the breeze,
I stop my work, and o'er the trees
Old Glory fairly shouts my way:
"You're shirking far too much to-day!"

The help have caught the spirit, too;
   The hired man takes off his cap

Before the old red, white and blue,
  Then to the horses says: "giddap!"
And starting bravely to the field
  He tells the milkmaid by the door:
"We're going to make these acres yield
  More than they've ever done before."
She smiles to hear his gallant brag,
Then drops a curtsey to the flag.
And in her eyes there seems to shine
A patriotism that is fine.

We've raised a flagpole on the farm
  And flung Old Glory to the sky;
We're far removed from war's alarm,
  But courage here is running high.
We're doing things we never dreamed
  We'd ever find the time to do;
Deeds that impossible once seemed
  Each morning now we hurry through.
The flag now waves above our toil
And sheds its glory on the soil,
And boy and man looks up to it
As if to say: "I'll do my bit!"

Heroes

There are different kinds of heroes, there are
    some you hear about.
They get their pictures printed, and their names
    the newsboys shout;
There are heroes known to glory that were not
    afraid to die
In the service of their country and to keep the
    flag on high;
There are brave men in the trenches, there are
    brave men on the sea,
But the silent, quiet heroes also prove their
    bravery.

I am thinking of a hero that was never known
    to fame,
Just a manly little fellow with a very common
    name;
He was freckle-faced and ruddy, but his head
    was nobly shaped,
And he one day took the whipping that his com-
    rades all escaped.
And he never made a murmur, never whimpered
    in reply;
He would rather take the censure than to stand
    and tell a lie.

And I'm thinking of another that had courage
    that was fine,
And I've often wished in moments that such
    strength of will were mine.
He stood against his comrades, and he left them
    then and there
When they wanted him to join them in a deed
    that wasn't fair.
He stood alone, undaunted, with his little head
    erect;
He would rather take the jeering than to lose
    his self-respect.

And I know a lot of others that have grown
    to manhood now,
Who have yet to wear the laurel that adorns the
    victor's brow.
They have plodded on in honor through the dusty,
    dreary ways,
They have hungered for life's comforts and the
    joys of easy days,
But they've chosen to be toilers, and in this their
    splendor's told:
They would rather never have it than to do some
    things for gold.

The Mother's Question

When I was a boy, and it chanced to rain,
  Mother would always watch for me;
She used to stand by the window pane,
  Worried and troubled as she could be.
And this was the question I used to hear,
The very minute that I drew near;
The words she used, I can't forget:
"Tell me, my boy, if your feet are wet."

Worried about me was mother dear,
  As healthy a lad as ever strolled
Over a turnpike, far or near,
  'Fraid to death that I'd take a cold.
Always stood by the window pane,
Watching for me in the pouring rain;
And her words in my ears are ringing yet:
"Tell me, my boy, if your feet are wet."

Stockings warmed by the kitchen fire,
  And slippers ready for me to wear;
Seemed that mother would never tire,
  Giving her boy the best of care,
Thinking of him the long day through,
In the worried way that all mothers do;
Whenever it rained she'd start to fret,
Always fearing my feet were wet.

And now, whenever it rains, I see
    A vision of mother in days of yore,
Still waiting there to welcome me,
    As she used to do by the open door.
And always I think as I enter there
Of a mother's love and a mother's care;
Her words in my ears are ringing yet:
"Tell me, my boy, if your feet are wet."

The Blue Flannel Shirt

I am eager once more to feel easy,
I'm weary of thinking of dress;
I'm heartily sick of stiff collars,
And trousers the tailor must press.
I'm eagerly waiting the glad days—
When fashion will cease to assert
What I must put on every morning —
The days of the blue flannel shirt.

I want to get out in the country
And rest by the side of the lake;
To go a few days without shaving,
And give grim old custom the shake.
A week's growth of whiskers, I'm thinking,
At present my chin wouldn't hurt;

And I'm yearning to don those old trousers
And loaf in that blue flannel shirt.

You can brag all you like of your fashions,
The style of your cutaway coat;
You can boast of your tailor-made raiment,
And the collar that strangles your throat;
But give me the old pair of trousers
That seem to improve with the dirt,
And let me get back to the comfort
That's born of a blue flannel shirt.

Grandpa

My grandpa is the finest man
Excep' my pa.   My grandpa can
Make kites an' carts an' lots of things
You pull along the ground with strings,
And he knows all the names of birds,
And how they call 'thout using words,
And where they live and what they eat,
And how they build their nests so neat.
He's lots of fun!   Sometimes all day
He comes to visit me and play.
You see he's getting old, and so
To work he doesn't have to go,
And when it isn't raining, he
Drops in to have some fun with me.

He takes my hand and we go out
And everything we talk about.
He tells me how God makes the trees,
And why it hurts to pick up bees.
Sometimes he stops and shows to me
The place where fairies used to be;
And then he tells me stories, too,
And I am sorry when he's through.
When I am asking him for more
He says: "Why there's a candy store!
Let's us go there and see if they
Have got the kind we like to-day."
Then when we get back home my ma
Says: "You are spoiling Buddy, Pa."

My grandpa is my mother's pa,
I guess that's what all grandpas are.
And sometimes ma, all smiles, will say:
"You didn't always act that way.
When I was little, then you said
That children should be sent to bed
And not allowed to rule the place
And lead old folks a merry chase."
And grandpa laughs and says: "That's true,
That's what I used to say to you.
It is a father's place to show
The young the way that they should go,
But grandpas have a different task,
Which is to get them all they ask."

When I get big and old and gray
I'm going to spend my time in play;
I'm going to be a grandpa, too,
And do as all the grandpas do.
I'll buy my daughter's children things
Like horns and drums and tops with strings,
And tell them all about the trees
And frogs and fish and birds and bees
And fairies in the shady glen
And tales of giants, too, and when
They beg of me for just one more,
I'll take them to the candy store;
I'll buy them everything they see
The way my grandpa does for me

Pa Did It

The train of cars that Santa brought is out of
    kilter now;
While pa was showing how they went he broke
    the spring somehow.
They used to run around a track—at least they
    did when he
Would let me take them in my hands an' wind 'em
    with a key.

I could 'a' had some fun with 'em, if only they
      would go,
But, gee! I never had a chance, for pa enjoyed
      'em so.

The automobile that I got that ran around the
      floor
Was lots of fun when it was new, but it won't
      go no more.
Pa wound it up for Uncle Jim to show him how
      it went,
And when those two got through with it the
      runnin' gear was bent,
An' now it doesn't go at all. I mustn't grumble
      though,
'Cause while it was in shape to run my pa enjoyed
      it so.

I've got my blocks as good as new, my mitts are
      perfect yet;
Although the snow is on the ground I haven't got
      'em wet.
I've taken care of everything that Santa brought
      to me,
Except the toys that run about when wound up
      with a key.
But next year you can bet I won't make any such
      mistake;
I'm going to ask for toys an' things that my pa
      cannot break.

The Real Successes

You think that the failures are many,
   You think the successes are few,
But you judge by the rule of the penny,
   And not by the good that men do.
You judge men by standards of treasure
   That merely obtain upon earth,
When the brother you're snubbing may measure
   Full-length to God's standard of worth.

The failures are not in the ditches,
   The failures are not in the ranks,
They have missed the acquirement of riches,
   Their fortunes are not in the banks.
Their virtues are never paraded,
   Their worth is not always in view,
But they're fighting their battles unaided,
   And fighting them honestly, too.

There are failures to-day in high places
   The failures aren't all in the low;
There are rich men with scorn in their faces
   Whose homes are but castles of woe.
The homes that are happy are many,
   And numberless fathers are true;
And this is the standard, if any,
   By which we must judge what men do.

Wherever loved ones are awaiting
   The toiler to kiss and caress,
Though in Bradstreet's he hasn't a rating,
   He still is a splendid success.
If the dear ones who gather about him
   And know what he's striving to do
Have never a reason to doubt him,
   Is he less successful than you?

You think that the failures are many,
   You judge by men's profits in gold;
You judge by the rule of the penny—
   In this true success isn't told.
This falsely man's story is telling,
   For wealth often brings on distress,
But wherever love brightens a dwelling,
   There lives, rich or poor, a success.

The Sorry Hostess

She said she was sorry the weather was bad
The night that she asked us to dine;
And she really appeared inexpressibly sad
Because she had hoped 'twould be fine.
She was sorry to hear that my wife had a cold,
And she almost shed tears over that,
And how sorry she was, she most feelingly told,
That the steam wasn't on in the flat.

She was sorry she hadn't asked others to come,
She might just as well have had eight;
She said she was downcast and terribly glum
Because her dear husband was late.
She apologized then for the home she was in,
For the state of the rugs and the chairs,
For the children who made such a horrible din,
And then for the squeak in the stairs.

When the dinner began she apologized twice
For the olives, because they were small;
She was certain the celery, too, wasn't nice,
And the soup didn't suit her at all.
She was sorry she couldn't get whitefish instead
Of the trout that the fishmonger sent,
But she hoped that we'd manage somehow to be
        fed,
Though her dinner was not what she meant.

She spoke her regrets for the salad, and then
Explained she was really much hurt,
And begged both our pardons again and again
For serving a skimpy dessert.
She was sorry for this and sorry for that,
Though there really was nothing to blame.
But I thought to myself as I put on my hat,
Perhaps she is sorry we came.

Yesterday

I've trod the links with many a man,
    And played him club for club;
'Tis scarce a year since I began
    And I am still a dub.
But this I've noticed as we strayed
    Along the bunkered way,
No one with me has ever played
    As he did yesterday.

It makes no difference what the drive,
    Together as we walk,
Till we up to the ball arrive,
    I get the same old talk:
"To-day there's something wrong with me,
    Just what I cannot say.

Would you believe I got a three
   For this hole—yesterday?"

I see them top and slice a shot,
   And fail to follow through,
And with their brassies plough the lot,
   The very way I do.
To six and seven their figures run,
   And then they sadly say:
"I neither dubbed nor foozled one
   When I played—yesterday."

I have no yesterdays to count,
   No good work to recall;
Each morning sees hope proudly mount,
   Each evening sees it fall.
And in the locker room at night,
   When men discuss their play,
I hear them and I wish I might
   Have seen them—yesterday.

Oh, dear old yesterday! What store
   Of joys for men you hold!
I'm sure there is no day that's more
   Remembered or extolled.
I'm off my task myself a bit,
   My mind has run astray;
I think, perhaps, I should have writ
   These verses—yesterday.

The Beauty Places

Here she walked and romped about,
  And here beneath this apple tree
Where all the grass is trampled out
  The swing she loved so used to be.
This path is but a path to you,
Because my child you never knew.

'Twas here she used to stoop to smell
  The first bright daffodil of spring;
'Twas here she often tripped and fell
  And here she heard the robins sing.
You'd call this but a common place,
But you have never seen her face.

And it was here we used to meet.
  How beautiful a spot is this,
To which she gayly raced to greet
  Her daddy with his evening kiss!
You see here nothing grand or fine,
But, Oh, what memories are mine!

The people pass from day to day
  And never turn their heads to see
The many charms along the way
  That mean so very much to me.
For all things here are speaking of
The babe that once was mine to love.

The Little Old Man

The little old man with the curve in his back
And the eyes that are dim and the skin that is
       slack,
So slack that it wrinkles and rolls on his cheeks,
With a thin little voice that goes "crack!" when
       he speaks,
Never goes to the store but that right at his feet
Are all of the youngsters who live on the street.

And the little old man in the suit that was black,
And once might have perfectly fitted his back,
Has a boy's chubby fist in his own wrinkled hand,
And together they trudge off to Light-Hearted
       Land;
Some splendid excursions he gives every day
To the boys and the girls in his funny old way.

The little old man is as queer as can be;
He'd spend all his time with a child on his knee;
And the stories he tells I could never repeat,
But they're always of good boys and little girls
       sweet;
And the children come home at the end of the day
To tell what the little old man had to say.

Once the little old man didn't trudge to the store,
And the tap of his cane wasn't heard any more;
The children looked eagerly for him each day

And wondered why he didn't come out to play
Till some of them saw Doctor Brown ring his bell,
And they wept when they heard that he might
      not get well.

But after awhile he got out with his cane,
And called all the children around him again;
And I think as I see him go trudging along
In the center, once more, of his light-hearted
      throng,
That earth has no glory that's greater than this:
The little old man whom the children would miss.

The Little Velvet Suit

Last night I got to thinkin' of the pleasant long
      ago,
When I still had on knee breeches, an' I wore a
      flowing bow,
An' my Sunday suit was velvet. Ma an' Pa
      thought it was fine,
But I know I didn't like it—either velvet or
      design;
It was far too girlish for me, for I wanted some-
      thing rough
Like what other boys were wearing, but Ma
      wouldn't buy such stuff.

Ma answered all my protests in her sweet an'
      kindly way;
She said it didn't matter what I wore to run an'
      play,
But on Sundays when all people went to church
      an' wore their best,
Her boy must look as stylish an' as well kept as
      the rest.
So she dressed me up in velvet, an' she tied the
      flowing bow,
An' she straightened out my stockings, so that
      not a crease would show.

An' then I chuckled softly to myself while dream-
      ing there
An' I saw her standing o'er me combing out my
      tangled hair.
I could feel again the tugging, an' I heard the
      yell I gave
When she struck a snarl, an' softly I could hear
      her say: "Be brave.
'Twill be over in a minute, and a little man like
      you
Shouldn't whimper at a little bit of pain the way
      you do."

Oh, I wouldn't mind the tugging at my scalp lock,
      and I know
That I'd gladly wear to please her that old flow-
      ing girlish bow;

And I think I'd even try to don once more that
    velvet suit,
And blush the same old blushes, as the women
    called me cute,
Could the dear old mother only take me by the
    hand again,
And be as proud of me right now as she was
    always then.

The First Steps

Last night I held my arms to you
And you held yours to mine
And started out to march to me
As any soldier fine.
You lifted up your little feet
And laughingly advanced;
And I stood there and gazed upon
Your first wee steps, entranced.

You gooed and gurgled as you came
Without a sign of fear;
As though you knew, your journey o'er,
I'd greet you with a cheer.
And, what is more, you seemed to know,
Although you are so small,
That I was there, with eager arms,
To save you from a fall.

Three tiny steps you took, and then,
Disaster and dismay!
Your over-confidence had led
Your little feet astray.
You did not see what we could see
Nor fear what us alarms;
You stumbled, but ere you could fall
I caught you in my arms.

You little tyke, in days to come
You'll bravely walk alone,
And you may have to wander paths
Where dangers lurk unknown.
And, Oh, I pray that then, as now,
When accidents befall
You'll still remember that I'm near
To save you from a fall.

Signs

It's "be a good boy, Willie,"
    And it's "run away and play,
For Santa Slaus is coming
    With his reindeer and his sleigh."
It's "mind what mother tells you,"
    And it's "put away your toys,
For Santa Claus is coming
    To the good girls and the boys."

Ho, Santa Claus is coming, there is Christmas in
 the air,
And little girls and little boys are good now
 everywhere.

World-wide the little fellows
 Now are sweetly saying "please,"
And "thank you," and "excuse me,"
 And those little pleasantries
That good children are supposed to
 When there's company to hear;
And it's just as plain as can be
 That the Christmas time is near.
Ho, it's just as plain as can be that old Santa's
 on his way,
For there are no little children that are really bad
 to-day.

And when evening shadows lengthen,
 Every little curly head
Now is ready, aye, and willing
 To be tucked away in bed;
Not one begs to stay up longer,
 Not one even sheds a tear;
Ho, the goodness of the children
 Is a sign that Santa's near.
It's wonderful, the goodness of the little tots
 to-day,
When they know that good old Santa has begun
 to pack his sleigh.

The Family's Homely Man

There never was a family without its homely
    man,
With legs a little longer than the ordinary plan,
An' a shock of hair that brush an' comb can't ever
    straighten out,
An' hands that somehow never seem to know
    what they're about;
The one with freckled features and a nose that
    looks as though
It was fashioned by the youngsters from a chunk
    of mother's dough.
You know the man I'm thinking of, the homely
    one an' plain,
That fairly oozes kindness like a rosebush drip-
    ping rain.
His face is never much to see, but back of it there
    lies
A heap of love and tenderness and judgment,
    sound and wise.

And so I sing the homely man that's sittin' in his
    chair,
And pray that every family will always have him
    there.
For looks don't count for much on earth; it's
    hearts that wear the gold;
An' only that is ugly which is selfish, cruel, cold.

The family needs him, Oh, so much; more, may-
be, than they know;
Folks seldom guess a man's real worth until he
has to go,
But they will miss a heap of love an' tenderness
the day
God beckons to their homely man, an' he must go
away.

He's found in every family, it doesn't matter
where
They live or be they rich or poor, the homely man
is there.
You'll find him sitting quiet-like and sort of
drawn apart,
As though he felt he shouldn't be where folks
are fine an' smart.
He likes to hide himself away, a watcher of the
fun,
An' seldom takes a leading part when any game's
begun.
But when there's any task to do, like need for
extra chairs,
I've noticed it's the homely man that always
climbs the stairs.

And always it's the homely man that happens in
to mend
The little toys the youngsters break, for he's the
children's friend.

And he's the one that sits all night to watch beside
    the dead,
And sends the worn-out sorrowers and broken
    hearts to bed.
The family wouldn't be complete without him
    night or day,
To smooth the little troubles out and drive the
    cares away.

When Mother Cooked with Wood

I do not quarrel with the gas,
    Our modern range is fine,
The ancient stove was doomed to pass
    From Time's grim firing line,
Yet now and then there comes to me
    The thought of dinners good
And pies and cake that used to be
    When mother cooked with wood.

The axe has vanished from the yard,
    The chopping block is gone,
There is no pile of cordwood hard
    For boys to work upon;
There is no box that must be filled
    Each morning to the hood;
Time in its ruthlessness has willed
    The passing of the wood.

And yet those days were fragrant days
    And spicy days and rare;
The kitchen knew a cheerful blaze
    And friendliness was there.
And every appetite was keen
    For breakfasts that were good
When I had scarcely turned thirteen
    And mother cooked with wood.

I used to dread my daily chore,
    I used to think it tough
When mother at the kitchen door
    Said I'd not chopped enough.
And on her baking days, I know,
    I shirked whene'er I could
In that now happy long ago
    When mother cooked with wood.

I never thought I'd wish to see
    That pile of wood again;
Back then it only seemed to me
    A source of care and pain.
But now I'd gladly give my all
    To stand where once I stood,
If those rare days I could recall
    When mother cooked with wood.

Midnight in the Pantry

You can boast your round of pleasures, praise
    the sound of popping corks,
Where the orchestra is playing to the rattle of
    the forks;
And your after-opera dinner you may think
    superbly fine,
But that can't compare, I'm certain, to the joy
    that's always mine
When I reach my little dwelling—source of all
    sincere delight—
And I prowl around the pantry in the waning
    hours of night.

When my business, or my pleasure, has detained
    me until late,
And it's midnight, say, or after, when I reach my
    own estate,
Though I'm weary with my toiling I don't hustle
    up to bed,
For the inner man is hungry and he's anxious to
    be fed;
Then I feel a thrill of glory from my head down
    to my feet
As I prowl around the pantry after something
    good to eat.

Oft I hear a call above me: "Goodness gracious,
     come to bed!"
And I know that I've disturbed her by my over-
     eager tread,
But I've found a glass of jelly and some bread
     and butter, too,
And a bit of cold fried chicken and I answer:
     "When I'm through!"
Oh, there's no cafe that better serves my precious
     appetite
Than the pantry in our kitchen when I get home
     late at night.

You may boast your shining silver, and the linen
     and the flowers,
And the music and the laughter and the lights
     that hang in showers;
You may have your cafe table with its brilliant
     array,
But it doesn't charm yours truly when I'm on my
     homeward way;
For a greater joy awaits me, as I hunger for a
     bite—
Just the joy of pantry-prowling in the middle of
     the night.

The World Is Against Me

"The world is against me," he said with a sigh
"Somebody stops every scheme that I try.
The world has me down and it's keeping me there;
I don't get a chance. Oh, the world is unfair!
When a fellow is poor then he can't get a show;
The world is determined to keep him down low."

"What of Abe Lincoln?" I asked. "Would you
    say
That he was much richer than you are to-day?
He hadn't your chance of making his mark,
And his outlook was often exceedingly dark;
Yet he clung to his purpose with courage most
    grim
And he got to the top. Was the world against
    him?"

"What of Ben Franklin? I've oft heard it said
That many a time he went hungry to bed.
He started with nothing but courage to climb,
But patiently struggled and waited his time.
He dangled awhile from real poverty's limb,
Yet he got to the top. Was the world against him?

"I could name you a dozen, yes, hundreds, I guess,
Of poor boys who've patiently climbed to success;
All boys who were down and who struggled alone,

Who'd have thought themselves rich if your for-
      tune they'd known;
Yet they rose in the world you're so quick to
      condemn,
And I'm asking you now, was the world against
      them?"

Bribed

I know that what I did was wrong;
    I should have sent you far away.
You tempted me, and I'm not strong;
    I tried but couldn't answer nay.
I should have packed you off to bed;
    Instead I let you stay awhile,
And mother scolded when I said
    That you had bribed me with your smile.

And yesterday I gave to you
    Another piece of chocolate cake,
Some red-ripe watermelon, too,
    And that gave you the stomach ache.
And that was after I'd been told
    You'd had enough, you saucy miss;
You tempted me, you five-year-old,
    And bribed me with a hug and kiss.

And mother said I mustn't get
    You roller skates, yet here they are;
I haven't dared to tell her yet;
    Some time, she says, I'll go too far.
I gave my word I wouldn't buy
    These things, for accidents she fears;
Now I must tell, when questioned why,
    Just how you bribed me with your tears.

I've tried so hard to do the right,
    Yet I have broken every vow.
I let you do, most every night,
    The things your mother won't allow.
I know that I am doing wrong,
    Yet all my sense of honor flies,
The moment that you come along
    And bribe me with those wondrous eyes.

The Home Builders

The world is filled with bustle and with selfishness
    and greed,
It is filled with restless people that are dreaming
    of a deed.
You can read it in their faces; they are dreaming
    of the day
When they'll come to fame and fortune and put
    all their cares away.

And I think as I behold them, though it's **far**
  indeed they roam,
They will never find contentment save they seek
  for it at home.

I watch them as they hurry through the surging
  lines of men,
Spurred to speed by grim ambition, and I know
  they're dreaming then.
They are weary, sick and footsore, but their goal
  seems far away,
And it's little they've accomplished at the ending
  of the day.
It is rest they're vainly seeking, love and laugh-
  ter in the gloam,
But they'll never come to claim it, save they claim
  it here at home.

For the peace that is the sweetest isn't born of
  minted gold,
And the joy that lasts the longest and still lingers
  when we're old
Is no dim and distant pleasure—it is not to-mor-
  row's prize,
It is not the end of toiling, or the rainbow of our
  sighs.
It is every day within us—all the rest is hippo-
  drome—
And the soul that is the gladdest is the soul that
  builds a home.

They are fools who build for glory! They are
    fools who pin their hopes
On the come and go of battles or some vessel's
    slender ropes.
They shall sicken and shall wither and shall never
    peace attain
Who believe that real contentment only men vic-
    torious gain.
For the only happy toilers under earth's majestic
    dome
Are the ones who find their glories in the little
    spot called home.

My Books and I

My books and I are good old pals:
    My laughing books are gay,
Just suited for my merry moods
    When I am wont to play.
Bill Nye comes down to joke with me
    And, Oh, the joy he spreads.
Just like two fools we sit and laugh
    And shake our merry heads.

When I am in a thoughtful mood,
    With Stevenson I sit,
Who seems to know I've had enough
    Of Bill Nye and his wit.

And so, more thoughtful than I am,
   He talks of lofty things,
And thus an evening hour we spend
   Sedate and grave as kings.

And should my soul be torn with grief
   Upon my shelf I find
A little volume, torn and thumbled,
   For comfort just designed.
I take my little Bible down
   And read its pages o'er,
And when I part from it I find
   I'm stronger than before.

Success

I hold no dream of fortune vast,
   Nor seek undying fame.
I do not ask when life is past
   That many know my name.

I may not own the skill to rise
   To glory's topmost height,
Nor win a place among the wise,
   But I can keep the right.

And I can live my life on earth
   Contented to the end,
If but a few shall know my worth
   And proudly call me friend.

Questions

Would you sell your boy for a stack of gold?
Would you miss that hand that is yours to hold?
Would you take a fortune and never see
The man, in a few brief years, he'll be?
Suppose that his body were racked with pain,
How much would you pay for his health again?

Is there money enough in the world to-day
To buy your boy? Could a monarch pay
You silver and gold in so large a sum
That you'd have him blinded or stricken dumb?
How much would you take, if you had the choice,
Never to hear, in this world, his voice?

How much would you take in exchange for all
The joy that is wrapped in that youngster small?
Are there diamonds enough in the mines of earth
To equal your dreams of that youngster's worth?
Would you give up the hours that he's on your
            knee
The richest man in the world to be?

You may prate of gold, but your fortune lies,
And you know it well, in your boy's bright eyes.
And there's nothing that money can buy or do
That means so much as that boy to you.
Well, which does the most of your time employ,
The chase for gold—or that splendid boy?

Sausage

You may brag about your breakfast foods you
    eat at break of day,
Your crisp, delightful shavings and your stack of
    last year's hay,
Your toasted flakes of rye and corn that fairly
    swim in cream,
Or rave about a sawdust mash, an epicurean
    dream.
But none of these appeals to me, though all of
    them I've tried—
The breakfast that I liked the best was sausage
    mother fried.

Old country sausage was its name; the kind, of
    course, you know,
The little links that seemed to be almost as white
    as snow,
But turned unto a ruddy brown, while sizzling in
    the pan;
Oh, they were made both to appease and charm
    the inner man.
All these new-fangled dishes make me blush and
    turn aside,
When I think about the sausage that for break-
    fast mother fried.

When they roused me from my slumbers and I
    left to do the chores,

It wasn't long before I breathed a fragrance out
of doors
That seemed to grip my spirit, and to thrill my
body through,
For the spice of hunger tingled, and 'twas then I
plainly knew
That the gnawing at my stomach would be quickly
satisfied
By a plate of country sausage that my dear old
mother fried.

There upon the kitchen table, with its cloth of
turkey red,
Was a platter heaped with sausage and a plate of
home-made bread,
And a cup of coffee waiting—not a puny demi-
tasse
That can scarcely hold a mouthful, but a cup of
greater class;
And I fell to eating largely, for I could not be
denied—
Oh, I'm sure a king would relish the sausage
mother fried.

Times have changed and so have breakfasts; now
each morning when I see
A dish of shredded something or of flakes passed
up to me,
All my thoughts go back to boyhood, to the days
of long ago,

When the morning meal meant something more
    than vain and idle show.
And I hunger, Oh, I hunger, in a way I cannot
    hide,
For a plate of steaming sausage like the kind my
    mother fried.

Friends

Ain't it fine when things are going
    Topsy-turvy and askew
To discover someone showing
    Good old-fashioned faith in you?

Ain't it good when life seems dreary
    And your hopes about to end,
Just to feel the handclasp cheery
    Of a fine old loyal friend?

Gosh! one fellow to another
    Means a lot from day to day,
Seems we're living for each other
    In a friendly sort of way.

When a smile or cheerful greetin'
    Means so much to fellows sore,
Seems we ought to keep repeatin'
    Smiles an' praises more an' more.

A Boost for Modern Methods

In some respects the old days were perhaps ahead
    of these,
Before we got to wanting wealth and costly
    luxuries;
Perhaps the world was happier then, I'm not the
    one to say,
But when it's zero weather I am glad I live to-day.

Old-fashioned winters I recall—the winters of
    my youth—
I have no great desire for them to-day, I say in
    truth;
The frost upon the window panes was beautiful
    to see,
But the chill upon that bedroom floor was not a
    joy to me.

I do not now recall that it was fun in those days
    when
I woke to learn the water pipes were frozen tight
    "again."
To win once more the old-time joys, I don't
    believe I'd care
To have to sleep, for comfort's sake, dressed in
    my underwear.

Old-fashioned winters had their charms, a fact I
can't deny,
But after all I'm really glad that they have wan-
dered by;
We used to tumble out of bed, like firemen, I
declare,
And grab our clothes and hike down stairs and
finish dressing there.

Yes, brag about those days of old, boast of them
as you will,
I sing the modern methods that have robbed them
of their chill;
I sing the cheery steam pipe and the upstairs
snug and warm
And a spine that's free from shivers as I robe
my manly form.

The Summer Children

I like 'em in the winter when their cheeks are
    slightly pale,
I like 'em in the spring time when the March
    winds blow a gale;
But when summer suns have tanned 'em and
    they're racing to and fro,
I somehow think the children make the finest
    sort of show.

When they're brown as little berries and they're
    bare of foot and head,
And they're on the go each minute where the
    velvet lawns are spread,
Then their health is at its finest and they never
    stop to rest,
Oh, it's then I think the children look and are
    their very best.

We've got to know the winter and we've got to
    know the spring,
But for children, could I do it, unto summer I
    would cling;
For I'm happiest when I see 'em, as a wild and
    merry band
Of healthy, lusty youngsters that the summer
    sun has tanned.

October

Days are gettin' shorter an' the air a keener snap;
Apples now are droppin' into Mother Nature's
lap;
The mist at dusk is risin' over valley, marsh an'
fen
An' it's just as plain as sunshine, winter's comin'
on again.

The turkeys now are struttin' round the old farm-
house once more;
They are done with all their nestin', and their
hatchin' days are o'er;
Now the farmer's cuttin' fodder for the silo
towerin' high
An' he's frettin' an' complainin' 'cause the corn's
a bit too dry.

But the air is mighty peaceful an' the scene is
good to see,
An' there's somethin' in October that stirs deep
inside o' me;
An' I just can't help believin' in a God above us
when
Everything is ripe for harvest an' the frost is
back again.

On Quitting

How much grit do you think you've got?
Can you quit a thing that you like a lot?
You may talk of pluck; it's an easy word,
And where'er you go it is often heard;
But can you tell to a jot or guess
Just how much courage you now possess?

You may stand to trouble and keep your grin,
But have you tackled self-discipline?
Have you ever issued commands to you
To quit the things that you like to do,
And then, when tempted and sorely swayed,
Those rigid orders have you obeyed?

Don't boast of your grit till you've tried it out,
Nor prate to men of your courage stout,
For it's easy enough to retain a grin
In the face of a fight there's a chance to win,
But the sort of grit that is good to own
Is the stuff you need when you're all alone.

How much grit do you think you've got?
Can you turn from joys that you like a lot?
Have you ever tested yourself to know
How far with yourself your will can go?
If you want to know if you have grit,
Just pick out a joy that you like, and quit.

It's bully sport and it's open fight;
It will keep you busy both day and night;
For the toughest kind of a game you'll find
Is to make your body obey your mind.
And you never will know what is meant by grit
Unless there's something you've tried to quit.

The Price of Riches

Nobody stops at the rich man's door to pass the
time of day.
Nobody shouts a "hello!" to him in the good old-
fashioned way.
Nobody comes to his porch at night and sits in
that extra chair
And talks till it's time to go to bed. He's all by
himself up there.

Nobody just happens in to call on the long, cold
winter nights.
Nobody feels that he's welcome now, though the
house is ablaze with lights.
And never an unexpected guest will tap at his
massive door
And stay to tea as he used to do, for his neigh-
borly days are o'er.

It's a distant life that the rich man leads and many
    an hour is glum,
For never the neighbors call on him save when
    they are asked to come.
At heart he is just as he used to be and he longs
    for his friends of old,
But they never will venture unbidden there.
    They're afraid of his wall of gold.

For silver and gold in a large amount there's a
    price that all men must pay,
And who will dwell in a rich man's house must
    live in a lonely way.
For once you have builded a fortune vast you
    will sigh for the friends you knew
But never they'll tap at your door again in the
    way that they used to do.

The Other Fellow

Whose luck is better far than ours?
    The other fellow's.
Whose road seems always lined with flowers?
    The other fellow's.
Who is the man who seems to get
Most joy in life, with least regret,
Who always seems to win his bet?
    The other fellow.

Who fills the place we think we'd like?
  The other fellow.
Whom does good fortune always strike?
  The other fellow.
Whom do we envy, day by day?
Who has more time than we to play?
Who is it, when we mourn, seems gay?
  The other fellow.

Who seems to miss the thorns we find?
  The other fellow.
Who seems to leave us all behind?
  The other fellow.
Who never seems to feel the woe,
The anguish and the pain we know?
Who gets the best seats at the show?
  The other fellow.

And yet, my friend, who envies you?
  The other fellow.
Who thinks he gathers only rue?
  The other fellow.
Who sighs because he thinks that he
Would infinitely happier be,
If he could be like you or me?
  The other fellow.

The Open Fire

There in the flame of the open grate,
   All that is good in the past I see:
Red-lipped youth on the swinging gate,
    Bright-eyed youth with its minstrelsy;
      Girls and boys that I used to know,
      Back in the days of Long Ago,
Troop before in the smoke and flame,
   Chatter and sing, as the wild birds do.
Everyone I can call by name,
   For the fire builds all of my youth anew.

Outside, people go stamping by,
   Squeak of wheel on the evening air,
Stars and planets race through the sky,
    Here are darkness and silence rare;
      Only the flames in the open grate
      Crackle and flare as they burn up hate,
Malice and envy and greed for gold,
   Dancing, laughing my cares away;
I've forgotten that I am old,
   Once again I'm a boy at play.

There in the flame of the open grate
   Bright the pictures come and go;
Lovers swing on the garden gate,
    Lovers kiss 'neath the mistletoe.
      I've forgotten that I am old,
      I've forgotten my story's told;

Whistling boy down the lane I stroll,
   All untouched by the blows of fate,
Time turns back and I'm young of soul,
   Dreaming there by the open grate.

Improvement

The joy of life is living it, or so it seems to me;
In finding shackles on your wrists, then struggling
     till you're free;
In seeing wrongs and righting them, in dreaming
     splendid dreams,
Then toiling till the vision is as real as moving
     streams.
The happiest mortal on the earth is he who ends
     his day
By leaving better than he found to bloom along
     the way.

Were all things perfect here there would be
     naught for man to do;
If what is old were good enough we'd never need
     the new.
The only happy time of rest is that which follows
     strife
And sees some contribution made unto the joy of
     life.

And he who has oppression felt and conquered it
      is he
Who really knows the happiness and peace of
      being free.

The miseries of earth are here and with them all
      must cope.
Who seeks for joy, through hedges thick of care
      and pain must grope.
Through disappointment man must go to value
      pleasure's thrill;
To really know the joy of health a man must first
      be ill.
The wrongs are here for man to right, and happi-
      ness is had
By striving to supplant with good the evil and the
      bad.

The joy of life is living it and doing things of
      worth,
In making bright and fruitful all the barren spots
      of earth.
In facing odds and mastering them and rising
      from defeat,
And making true what once was false, and what
      was bitter, sweet.
For only he knows perfect joy whose little bit of
      soil
Is richer ground than what it was when he began
      to toil.

Send Her a Valentine

Send her a valentine to say
You love her in the same old way.
Just drop the long familiar ways
And live again the old-time days
When love was new and youth was bright
And all was laughter and delight,
And treat her as you would if she
Were still the girl that used to be.

Pretend that all the years have passed
Without one cold and wintry blast;
That you are coming still to woo
Your sweetheart as you used to do;
Forget that you have walked along
The paths of life where right and wrong
And joy and grief in battle are,
And play the heart without a scar.

Be what you were when youth was fine
And send to her a valentine;
Forget the burdens and the woe
That have been given you to know
And to the wife, so fond and true,
The pledges of the past renew.
'Twill cure her life of every ill
To find that you're her sweetheart still.

Bud

Who is it lives to the full every minute,
Gets all the joy and the fun that is in it?
Tough as they make 'em, and ready to race,
Fit for a battle and fit for a chase,
Heedless of buttons on blouses and pants,
Laughing at danger and taking a chance,
Gladdest, it seems, when he wallows in mud,
Who is the rascal?   I'll tell you, it's Bud!

Who is it wakes with a shout of delight,
And comes to our room with a smile that is
      bright?
Who is it springs into bed with a leap
And thinks it is queer that his dad wants to sleep?
Who answers his growling with laughter and tries
His patience by lifting the lids of his eyes?
Who jumps in the air and then lands with a thud
On his poor daddy's stomach?   I'll tell you, it's
      Bud!

Who is it thinks life is but laughter and play
And doesn't know care is a part of the day?
Who is reckless of stockings and heedless of
      shoes?
Who laughs at a tumble and grins at a bruise?
Who climbs over fences and clambers up trees,
And scrapes all the skin off his shins and his
      knees?

Who sometimes comes home all bespattered with
      blood
That was drawn by a fall?   It's that rascal called
      Bud.

Yet, who is it makes all our toiling worth while?
Who can cure every ache that we know, by his
      smile?
Who is prince to his mother and king to his dad
And makes us forget that we ever were sad?
Who is center of all that we dream of and plan,
Our baby to-day but to-morrow our man?
It's that tough little, rough little tyke in the mud,
That tousled-haired, fun-loving rascal called Bud!

The Front Seat

When I was but a little lad I always liked to ride,
No matter what the rig we had, right by the
      driver's side.
The front seat was the honor place in bob-sleigh,
      coach or hack,
And I maneuvered to avoid the cushions in the
      back.
We children used to scramble then to share the
      driver's seat,
And long the pout I wore when I was not allowed
      that treat.

Though times have changed and I am old I still
confess I race
With other grown-ups now and then to get my
favorite place.

The auto with its cushions fine and big and easy
springs
Has altered in our daily lives innumerable things,
But hearts of men are still the same as what they
used to be,
When surreys were the stylish rigs, or so they
seem to me,
For every grown-up girl to-day and every grown-
up boy
Still hungers for the seat in front and scrambles
for its joy,
And riding by the driver's side still holds the
charm it did
In those glad, youthful days gone by when I was
just a kid.

I hurry, as I used to do, to claim that favorite
place,
And when a tonneau seat is mine I wear a solemn
face.
I try to hide the pout I feel, and do my best to
smile,

But envy of the man in front gnaws at me all
the while.
I want to be where I can see the road that lies
ahead,
To watch the trees go flying by and see the
country spread
Before me as we spin along, for there I miss the
fear
That seems to grip the soul of me while riding
in the rear.

And I am not alone in this. To-day I drive a car
And three glad youngsters madly strive to share
the "seat with Pa."
And older folks that ride with us, I very plainly
see,
Maneuver in their artful ways to sit in front with
me;
Though all the cushions in the world were piled
up in the rear,
The child in all of us still longs to watch the
engineer.
And happier hearts we seem to own when we're
allowed to ride,
No matter what the car may be, close by the
driver's side.

There Are No Gods

There are no gods that bring to youth
   The rich rewards that stalwarts claim;
The god of fortune is in truth
   A vision and an empty name.
The toiler who through doubt and care
   Unto his goal and victory plods,
With no one need his glory share:
   He is himself his favoring gods.

There are no gods that will bestow
   Earth's joys and blessings on a man.
Each one must choose the path he'll go,
   Then win from it what joy he can.
And he that battles with the odds
   Shall know success, but he who waits
The favors of the mystic gods,
   Shall never come to glory's gates.

No man is greater than his will;
   No gods to him will lend a hand!
Upon his courage and his skill
   The record of his life must stand.
What honors shall befall to him,
   What he shall claim of fame or pelf,
Depend not on the favoring whim
   Of fortune's god, but on himself.

The Auto

An auto is a helpful thing;
I love the way the motor hums,
I love each cushion and each spring,
The way it goes, the way it comes;
It saves me many a dreary mile,
It brings me quickly to the smile
Of those at home, and every day
It adds unto my time for play.

It keeps me with my friends in touch;
No journey now appears too much
To make with meetings at the end:
It gives me time to be a friend.
It laughs at distance, and has power
To lengthen every fleeting hour.
It bears me into country new
That otherwise I'd never view.

It's swift and sturdy and it strives
To fill with happiness our lives;
When for the doctor we've a need
It brings him to our door with speed.
It saves us hours of anxious care
And heavy heartache and despair.
It has its faults, but still I sing:
The auto is a helpful thing.

The Handy Man

The handy man about the house
Is old and bent and gray;
Each morning in the yard he toils,
Where all the children play;
Some new task every day he finds,
Some task he loves to do,
The handy man about the house,
Whose work is never through.

The children stand to see him toil.
And watch him mend a chair;
They bring their broken toys to him;
He keeps them in repair.
No idle moment Grandpa spends,
But finds some work to do,
And hums a snatch of some old song,
That in his youth he knew.

He builds with wood most wondrous things:
A table for the den,
A music rack to please the girls,
A gun case for the men.
And 'midst his paints and tools he smiles,
And seems as young and gay
As any of the little ones
Who round him run in play.

I stopped to speak with him awhile;
"Oh, tell me, Grandpa, pray,"
I said, "why do you work so hard
Throughout the livelong day?
Your hair is gray, your back is bent,
With weight of years oppressed;
This is the evening of your life—
Why don't you sit and rest?"

"Ah, no," the old man answered me,
"Although I'm old and gray,
I like to work out here where I
Can watch the children play.
The old have tasks that they must do;
The greatest of my joys
Is working on this shaded porch,
And mending children's toys."

And as I wandered on, I thought,
Oh, shall I lonely be
When time has powdered white my hair,
And left his mark on me?
Will little children round me play,
Shall I have work to do?
Or shall I be, when age is mine,
Lonely and useless too?

The New Days

The old days, the old days, how oft the poets
  sing,
The days of hope at dewy morn, the days of
  early spring,
The days when every mead was fair, and every
  heart was true,
And every maiden wore a smile, and every sky
  was blue;
The days when dreams were golden and every
  night brought rest,
The old, old days of youth and love, the days
  they say were best;
But I—I sing the new days, the days that lie
  before,
The days of hope and fancy, the days that I
  adore.

The new days, the new days, the selfsame days
  they are;
The selfsame sunshine heralds them, the self-
  same evening star
Shines out to light them on their way unto the
  Bygone Land,
And with the selfsame arch of blue the world
  to-day is spanned.
The new days, the new days, when friends are
  just as true,

And maidens smile upon us all, the way they
used to do,
Dreams we know are golden dreams, hope springs
in every breast;
It cheers us in the dewy morn and soothes us
when we rest.

The new days, the new days, of them I want to
sing,
The new days with the fancies and the golden
dreams they bring;
The old days had their pleasures, but likewise
have the new
The gardens with their roses and the meadows
bright with dew;
We love to-day the selfsame way they loved in
days of old;
The world is bathed in beauty and it isn't growing
cold;
There's joy for us a-plenty, there are tasks for us
to do,
And life is worth the living, for the friends we
know are true.

The Call

Joy stands on the hilltops,
　Beckoning to me,
Urging me to journey
　Up where I can see
Blue skies ever smiling,
　Cool green fields below,
Hear the songs of children
　Still untouched by woe.

Joy stands on the hilltops,
　Urging me to stay,
Spite of toil and trouble,
　To life's rugged way,
Holding out a promise
　Of a life serene
When the steeps I've mastered
　Lying now between.

Joy stands on the hilltops,
　Smiling down at me,
Urging me to clamber
　Up where I can see
Over toil and trouble
　Far beyond despair,
And I answer smiling:
　Some day I'll be there.

Songs of Rejoicing

Songs of rejoicin',
    Of love and of cheer,
Are the songs that I'm yearnin' for
    Year after year.
The songs about children
    Who laugh in their glee
Are the songs worth the singin',
    The bright songs for me.

Songs of rejoicin',
    Of kisses and love,
Of faith in the Father,
    Who sends from above
The sunbeams to scatter
    The gloom and the fear;
These songs worth the singin',
    The songs of good cheer.

Songs of rejoicin',
    Oh, sing them again,
The brave songs of courage
    Appealing to men.
Of hope in the future
    Of heaven the goal;
The songs of rejoicin'
    That strengthen the soul.

Another Mouth to Feed

We've got another mouth to feed,
    From out our little store;
To satisfy another's need
    Is now my daily chore.
A growing family is ours,
    Beyond the slightest doubt;
It takes all my financial powers
    To keep them looking stout.
With us another makes his bow
    To breakfast, dine and sup;
Our little circle's larger now,
    For Buddy's got a pup.

If I am frayed about the heels
    And both my elbows shine
And if my overcoat reveals
    The poverty that's mine,
'Tis not because I squander gold
    In folly's reckless way;
The cost of foodstuffs, be it told,
    Takes all my weekly pay.
'Tis putting food on empty plates
    That eats my wages up;
And now another mouth awaits,
    For Buddy's got a pup.

And yet I gladly stand the strain,
    And count the task worth while,

Nor will I dismally complain
    While Buddy wears a smile.
What's one mouth more at any board
    Though costly be the fare?
The poorest of us can afford
    His frugal meal to share.
And so bring on the extra plate,
    He will not need a cup,
And gladly will I pay the freight
    Now Buddy's got a pup.

The Little Church

The little church of Long Ago, where as a boy
    I sat
With mother in the family pew, and fumbled
    with my hat—
How I would like to see it now the way I saw
    it then,
The straight-backed pews, the pulpit high, the
    women and the men
Dressed stiffly in their Sunday clothes and sol-
    emnly devout,
Who closed their eyes when prayers were said
    and never looked about—
That little church of Long Ago, it wasn't grand
    to see,
But even as a little boy it meant a lot to me.

The choir loft where father sang comes back to
    me again;
I hear his tenor voice once more the way I
    heard it when
The deacons used to pass the plate, and once
    again I see
The people fumbling for their coins, as glad as
    they could be
To drop their quarters on the plate, and I'm a
    boy once more
With my two pennies in my fist that mother gave
    before
We left the house, and once again I'm reaching
    out to try
To drop them on the plate before the deacon
    passes by.

It seems to me I'm sitting in that high-backed
    pew, the while
The minister is preaching in that good old-
    fashioned style;
And though I couldn't understand it all some-
    how I know
The Bible was the text book in that church of
    Long Ago;
He didn't preach on politics, but used the word
    of God,
And even now I seem to see the people gravely
    nod,

As though agreeing thoroughly with all he had
     to say,
And then I see them thanking him before they
     go away.

The little church of Long Ago was not a struc-
     ture huge,
It had no hired singers or no other subterfuge
To get the people to attend, 'twas just a simple
     place
Where every Sunday we were told about God's
     saving grace;
No men of wealth were gathered there to help
     it with a gift;
The only worldly thing it had—a mortgage hard
     to lift.
And somehow, dreaming here to-day, I wish
     that I could know
The joy of once more sitting in that church of
     Long Ago.

Sue's Got a Baby

Sue's got a baby now, an' she
Is like her mother used to be;
Her face seems prettier, an' her ways
More settled-like. In these few days
She's changed completely, an' her smile
Has taken on the mother-style.
Her voice is sweeter, an' her words
Are clear as is the song of birds.
She still is Sue, but not the same—
She's different since the baby came.

There is a calm upon her face
That marks the change that's taken place;
It seems as though her eyes now see
The wonder things that are to be,
An' that her gentle hands now own
A gentleness before unknown.
Her laughter has a clearer ring
Than all the bubbling of a spring,
An' in her cheeks love's tender flame
Glows brighter since the baby came.

I look at her an' I can see
Her mother as she used to be.
How sweet she was, an' yet how much
She sweetened by the magic touch

That made her mother! In her face
It seemed the angels left a trace
Of Heavenly beauty to remain
Where once had been the lines of pain
An' with the baby in her arms
Enriched her with a thousand charms.

Sue's got a baby now an' she
Is prettier than she used to be.
A wondrous change has taken place,
A softer beauty marks her face
An' in the warmth of her caress
There seems the touch of holiness,
An' all the charms her mother knew
Have blossomed once again in Sue.
I sit an' watch her an' I claim
My lost joys since her baby came.

The Lure That Failed

I know a wonderful land, I said,
    Where the skies are always blue,
Where on chocolate drops are the children fed,
    And cocoanut cookies, too;
Where puppy dogs romp at the children's feet,
    And the liveliest kittens play,
And little tin soldiers guard the street
    To frighten the bears away.

This land is reached by a wonderful ship
    That sails on a golden tide;
But never a grown-up makes the trip—
    It is only a children's ride.
And never a cross-patch journeys there,
    And never a pouting face,
For it is the Land of Smiling, where
    A frown is a big disgrace.

Oh, you board the ship when the sun goes down,
    And over a gentle sea
You slip away from the noisy town
    To the land of the chocolate tree.
And there, till the sun comes over the hill,
    You frolic and romp and play,
And of candy and cake you eat your fill,
    With no one to tell you "Nay!"

So come! It is time for the ship to go
   To this wonderful land so fair,
And gently the summer breezes blow
   To carry you safely there.
So come! Set sail on this golden sea,
   To the land that is free from dread!
"I know what you mean," she said to me,
   "An' I don't wanna go to bed."

The Old-Fashioned Thanksgiving

It may be I am getting old and like too much to
    dwell
Upon the days of bygone years, the days I loved
    so well;
But thinking of them now I wish somehow that
    I could know
A simple old Thanksgiving Day, like those of
    long ago,
When all the family gathered round a table richly
    spread,
With little Jamie at the foot and grandpa at the
    head,
The youngest of us all to greet the oldest with a
    smile,
With mother running in and out and laughing all
    the while.

It may be I'm old-fashioned, but it seems to me
    to-day
We're too much bent on having fun to take the
    time to pray;
Each little family grows up with fashions of its
    own;
It lives within a world itself and wants to be
    alone.
It has its special pleasures, its circle, too, of
    friends;
There are no get-together days; each one his jour-
    ney wends,
Pursuing what he likes the best in his particular
    way,
Letting the others do the same upon Thanksgiving
    Day.

I like the olden way the best, when relatives were
    glad
To meet the way they used to do when I was but
    a lad;
The old home was a rendezvous for all our kith
    and kin,
And whether living far or near they all came
    trooping in
With shouts of "Hello, daddy!" as they fairly
    stormed the place

And made a rush for mother, who would stop to
        wipe her face
Upon her gingham apron before she kissed them
        all,
Hugging them proudly to her breast, the grown-
        ups and the small.

Then laughter rang throughout the home, and,
        Oh, the jokes they told;
From Boston, Frank brought new ones, but
        father sprang the old;
All afternoon we chatted, telling what we hoped
        to do,
The struggles we were making and the hardships
        we'd gone through;
We gathered round the fireside. How fast the
        hours would fly—
It seemed before we'd settled down 'twas time to
        say good-bye.
Those were the glad Thanksgivings, the old-time
        families knew
When relatives could still be friends and every
        heart was true.

The Old-Fashioned Pair

'Tis a little old house with a squeak in the stairs,
And a porch that seems made for just two easy
    chairs;
In the yard is a group of geraniums red,
And a glorious old-fashioned peony bed.
Petunias and pansies and larkspurs are there
Proclaiming their love for the old-fashioned pair.

Oh, it's hard now to picture the peace of the
    place!
Never lovelier smile lit a fair woman's face
Than the smile of the little old lady who sits
On the porch through the bright days of summer
    and knits.
And a courtlier manner no prince ever had
Than the little old man that she speaks of as
    "dad."

In that little old house there is nothing of hate;
There are old-fashioned things by an old-fash-
    ioned grate;
On the walls there are pictures of fine looking
    men
And beautiful ladies to look at, and then
Time has placed on the mantel to comfort them
    there
The pictures of grandchildren, radiantly fair

Every part of the house seems to whisper of joy,
Save the trinkets that speak of a lost little boy.
Yet Time has long since soothed the hurt and
     the pain,
And his glorious memories only remain:
The laughter of children the old walls have
     known,
And the joy of it stays, though the babies have
     flown.

I am fond of that house and that old-fashioned
     pair
And the glorious calm that is hovering there.
The riches of life are not silver and gold
But fine sons and daughters when we are grown
     old,
And I pray when the years shall have silvered
     our hair
We shall know the delights of that old-fashioned
     pair.

At Pelletier's

We've been out to Pelletier's
Brushing off the stain of years,
Quitting all the moods of men
And been boys and girls again.
We have romped through orchards blazing,
Petted ponies gently grazing,
Hidden in the hayloft's spaces,
And the queerest sort of places
That are lost (and it's a pity!)
To the youngsters in the city.
And the hired men have let us
Drive their teams, and stopped to get us
Apples from the trees, and lingered
While a cow's cool nose we fingered;
And they told us all about her
And her grandpa who was stouter.

We've been out to Pelletier's
Watching horses raise their ears,
And their joyous whinnies hearing
When the man with oats was nearing.
We've been climbing trees an' fences
Never minding consequences.
And we helped the man to curry
The fat ponies' sides so furry.
And we saw a squirrel taking
Walnuts to the nest he's making,

Storing them for winter, when he
Can't get out to hunt for any.
And we watched the turkeys, growing
Big and fat and never knowing
That the reason they were living
Is to die for our Thanksgiving.

We've been out to Pelletier's,
Brushing off the stain of years.
We were kids set free from shamming
And the city's awful cramming,
And the clamor and the bustle
And the fearful rush and hustle—
Out of doors with room to race in
And broad acres soft to chase in.
We just stretched our souls and let them
Drop the petty cares that fret them,
Left our narrow thoughts behind us,
Loosed the selfish traits that bind us
And were wholesomer and plainer
Simpler, kinder folks and saner,
And at night said: "It's a pity
Mortals ever built a city."

At Christmas

A man is at his finest towards the finish of the
       year;
He is almost what he should be when the Christ-
       mas season's here;
Then he's thinking more of others than he's
       thought the months before,
And the laughter of his children is a joy worth
       toiling for.
He is less a selfish creature than at any other
       time;
When the Christmas spirit rules him he comes
       close to the sublime.

When it's Christmas man is bigger and is better
       in his part;
He is keener for the service that is prompted by
       the heart.
All the petty thoughts and narrow seem to vanish
       for awhile
And the true reward he's seeking is the glory of
       a smile.
Then for others he is toiling and somehow it
       seems to me
That at Christmas he is almost what God wanted
       him to be.

If I had to paint a picture of a man I think I'd
    wait
Till he'd fought his selfish battles and had put
    aside his hate.
I'd not catch him at his labors when his thoughts
    are all of pelf,
On the long days and the dreary when he's striv-
    ing for himself.
I'd not take him when he's sneering, when he's
    scornful or depressed,
But I'd look for him at Christmas when he's
    shining at his best.

Man is ever in a struggle and he's oft misunder-
    stood;
There are days the worst that's in him is the
    master of the good,
But at Christmas kindness rules him and he puts
    himself aside
And his petty hates are vanquished and his heart
    is opened wide.
Oh, I don't know how to say it, but somehow it
    seems to me
That at Christmas man is almost what God sent
    him here to be.

Who Is Your Boss?

"I work for someone else," he said;
"I have no chance to get ahead.
At night I leave the job behind;
At morn I face the same old grind.
And everything I do by day
Just brings to me the same old pay.
While I am here I cannot see
The semblance of a chance for me."

I asked another how he viewed
The occupation he pursued.
"It's dull and dreary toil," said he,
"And brings but small reward to me.
My boss gets all the profits fine
That I believe are rightly mine.
My life's monotonously grim
Because I'm forced to work for him."

I stopped a third young man to ask
His attitude towards his task.
A cheerful smile lit up his face;
"I shan't be always in this place,"
He said, "because some distant day
A better job will come my way."
"Your boss?" I asked, and answered he:
"I'm going to make him notice me.

"He pays me wages and in turn
That money I am here to earn,
But I don't work for him alone;
Allegiance to myself I own.
I do not do my best because
It gets me favors or applause—
I work for him, but I can see
That actually I work for me.

"It looks like business good to me
The best clerk on the staff to be.
If customers approve my style
And like my manner and my smile
I help the firm to get the pelf,
But what is more I help myself.
From one big thought I'm never free:
That every day I work for me."

Oh, youth, thought I, you're bound to climb
The ladder of success in time.
Too many self-impose the cross
Of daily working for a boss,
Forgetting that in failing him
It is their own stars that they dim.
And when real service they refuse
They are the ones who really lose.

Living

If through the years we're not to do
  Much finer deeds than we have done;
If we must merely wander through
  Time's garden, idling in the sun;
If there is nothing big ahead,
Why do we fear to join the dead?

Unless to-morrow means that we
  Shall do some needed service here;
That tasks are waiting you and me
  That will be lost, save we appear;
Then why this dreadful thought of sorrow
That we may never see to-morrow?

If all our finest deeds are done,
  And all our splendor's in the past;
If there's no battle to be won,
  What matter if to-day's our last?
Is life so sweet that we would live
Though nothing back to life we give?

It is not greatness to have clung
  To life through eighty fruitless years;
The man who dies in action, young,
  Deserves our praises and our cheers,
Who ventures all for one great deed
And gives his life to serve life's need.

On Being Broke

Don't mind being broke at all,
    When I can say that what I had
Was spent for toys for kiddies small
    And that the spending made 'em glad.
I don't regret the money gone,
    If happiness it left behind.
An empty purse I'll look upon
    Contented, if its record's kind.
There's no disgrace in being broke,
    Unless it's due to flying high;
Though poverty is not a joke,
    The only thing that counts is "why?"

The dollars come to me and go;
    To-day I've eight or ten to spend;
To-morrow I'll be sailing low,
    And have to lean upon a friend.
But if that little bunch of mine
    Is richer by some toy or frill,
I'll face the world and never whine
    Because I lack a dollar bill.
I'm satisfied, if I can see
    One smile that hadn't bloomed before.
The only thing that counts with me
    Is what I've spent my money for.

I might regret my sorry plight,
    If selfishness brought it about;

If for the fun I had last night,
　Some joy they'd have to go without.
But if I've swapped my bit of gold,
　For laughter and a happier pack
Of youngsters in my little fold,
　I'll never wish those dollars back.
If I have traded coin for things
　They needed and have left them glad,
Then being broke no sorrow brings—
　I've done my best with what I had.

The Broken Drum

There is sorrow in the household;
There's a grief too hard to bear;
There's a little cheek that's tear-stained;
There's a sobbing baby there.
And try how we will to comfort,
Still the tiny teardrops come;
For, to solve a vexing problem,
Curly Locks has wrecked his drum.

It had puzzled him and worried,
How the drum created sound;
For he couldn't understand it;
It was not enough to pound
With his tiny hands and drumsticks,
And at last the day has come,

When another hope is shattered;
Now in ruins lies his drum.

With his metal bank he broke it,
Tore the tightened skin aside,
Gazed on vacant space bewildered,
Then he broke right down and cried.
For the broken bubble shocked him
And the baby tears must come;
Now a joy has gone forever:
Curly Locks has wrecked his drum.

While his mother tries to soothe him,
I am sitting here alone;
In the life that lies behind me,
Many shocks like that I've known.
And the boy who's upstairs weeping,
In the years that are to come
Will learn that many pleasures
Are as empty as his drum.

Mother's Excuses

Mother for me made excuses
When I was a little tad;
Found some reason for my conduct
When it had been very bad.

Blamed it on a recent illness
Or my nervousness and told
Father to be easy with me
Every time he had to scold.

And I knew, as well as any
Roguish, healthy lad of ten,
Mother really wasn't telling
Truthful things to father then.
I knew I deserved the whipping,
Knew that I'd been very bad,
Knew that mother knew it also
When she intervened with dad.

I knew that my recent illness
Hadn't anything to do
With the mischief I'd been up to,
And I knew that mother knew.
But remembering my fever
And my nervous temperament,
Father put away the shingle
And postponed the sad event.

Now his mother, when I threaten
Punishment for this and that,
Calls to mind the dreary night hours
When beside his bed we sat.
Comes and tells me that he's nervous,
That's the reason he was bad,

And the boy and doting mother
Put it over on the dad.

Some day when he's grown as I am,
With a boy on mischief bent,
He will hear the timeworn story
Of the nervous temperament.
And remembering the shingle
That aside I always threw,
All I hope is that he'll let them
Put it over on him, too.

As It Is

I might wish the world were better,
  I might sit around and sigh
For a water that is wetter
  And a bluer sort of sky.
There are times I think the weather
  Could be much improved upon,
But when taken altogether
  It's a good old world we're on.
I might tell how I would make it,
  But when I have had my say
It is still my job to take it
  As it is, from day to day.

I might wish that men were kinder,
   And less eager after gold;
I might wish that they were blinder
   To the faults they now behold.
And I'd try to make them gentle,
   And more tolerant in strife
And a bit more sentimental
   O'er the finer things of life.
But I am not here to make them,
   Or to work in human clay;
It is just my work to take them
   As they are from day to day.

Here's a world that suffers sorrow,
   Here are bitterness and pain,
And the joy we plan to-morrow
   May be ruined by the rain.
Here are hate and greed and badness,
   Here are love and friendship, too,
But the most of it is gladness
   When at last we've run it through.
Could we only understand it
   As we shall some distant day,
We should see that He who planned it
   Knew our needs along the way.

A Boy's Tribute

Prettiest girl I've ever seen
    Is Ma.
Lovelier than any queen
    Is Ma.
Girls with curls go walking by,
Dainty, graceful, bold an' shy,
But the one that takes my eye
    Is Ma.

Every girl made into one
    Is Ma.
Sweetest girl to look upon
    Is Ma.
Seen 'em short and seen 'em tall,
Seen 'em big and seen 'em small,
But the finest one of all
    Is Ma.

Best of all the girls on earth
    Is Ma.
One that all the rest is worth
    Is Ma.
Some have beauty, some have grace,
Some look nice in silk and lace,
But the one that takes first place
    Is Ma.

Sweetest singer in the land
  Is Ma.
She that has the softest hand
  Is Ma.
Tenderest, gentlest nurse is she,
Full of fun as she can be,
An' the only girl for me
  Is Ma.

Bet if there's an angel here
  It's Ma.
If God has a sweetheart dear
  It's Ma.
Take the girls that artists draw,
An' all the girls I ever saw,
The only one without a flaw
  Is Ma.

America

God has been good to men. He gave
His Only Son their souls to save,
And then he made a second gift,
Which from their dreary lives should lift
The tyrant's yoke and set them free
From all who'd throttle liberty.
He gave America to men —
Fashioned this land we love, and then
Deep in her forests sowed the seed
Which was to serve man's earthly need.

When wisps of smoke first upwards curled
From pilgrim fires, upon the world
Unnoticed and unseen, began
God's second work of grace for man.
Here where the savage roamed and fought,
God sowed the seed of nobler thought;
Here to the land we love to claim,
The pioneers of freedom came;
Here has been cradled all that's best
In every human mind and breast.

For full four hundred years and more
Our land has stretched her welcoming shore
To weary feet from soils afar;
Soul-shackled serfs of king and czar
Have journeyed here and toiled and sung

And talked of freedom to their young,
And God above has smiled to see
This precious work of liberty,
And watched this second gift He gave
The dreary lives of men to save.

And now, when liberty's at bay,
And blood-stained tyrants force the fray,
Worn warriors, battling for the right,
Crushed by oppression's cruel might,
Hear in the dark through which they grope
America's glad cry of hope:
Man's liberty is not to die!
America is standing by!
World-wide shall human lives be free:
America has crossed the sea!

America! the land we love!
God's second gift from Heaven above,
Builded and fashioned out of truth,
Sinewed by Him with splendid youth
For that glad day when shall be furled
All tyrant flags throughout the world.
For this our banner holds the sky:
That liberty shall never die.
For this, America began:
To make a brotherhood of man.

Kelly Ingram

His name was Kelly Ingram; he was Alabama's
    son,
And he whistled " Yankee Doodle," as he stood
    beside his gun;
There was laughter in his make-up, there was
    manhood in his face,
And he knew the best traditions and the courage
    of his race;
Now there's not a heart among us but should
    swell with loyal pride
When he thinks of Kelly Ingram and the splendid
    way he died.

On the swift Destroyer Cassin he was merely
    gunner's mate,
But up there to-day, I fancy, he is standing with
    the great.
On that grim day last October his position on
    the craft
Was that portion of the vessel which the sailors
    christen aft;
There were deep sea bombs beside him to be
    dropped upon the Hun
Who makes women folks his victims and then
    gloats o'er what he's done.

From the lookout came a warning; came the
    cry all sailors fear,

A torpedo was approaching, and the vessel's
    doom was near;
Ingram saw the streak of danger, but he saw a
    little more,
A greater menace faced them than that missile
    had in store;
If those deep sea bombs beside him were not
    thrown beneath the wave,
Every man aboard the Cassin soon would find a
    watery grave.

It was death for him to linger, but he figured
    if he ran
And quit his post of duty, 'twould be death for
    every man;
So he stood at his position, threw those depth
    bombs overboard,
And when that torpedo struck them, he went
    forth to meet his Lord.
Oh, I don't know how to say it, but these whole
    United States
Should remember Kelly Ingram — he who died
    to save his mates.

Runner McGee

(Who had "Return if Possible" Orders.)

"You've heard a good deal of the telephone
      wires," he said as we sat at our ease,
And talked of the struggle that's taking men's
      lives in these terrible days o'er the seas,
"But I've been through the thick of the thing
      and I know when a battle's begun,
It isn't the phone you depend on for help. It's
      the legs of a boy who can run.

"It isn't because of the phone that I'm here.
      To-day you are talking to me
Because of the grit and the pluck of a boy. His
      title was Runner McGee.
We were up to our dead line an' fighting alone;
      some plan had miscarried, I guess,
And the help we were promised had failed to
      arrive. We were showing all signs of
      distress.

"Our curtain of fire was ahead of us still, an'
      theirs was behind us an' thick,
An' there wasn't a thing we could do for our-
      selves—the few of us left had to stick.
You haven't much chance to get central an' talk
      on the phone to the music of guns;
Gettin' word to the chief is a matter right then
      that is up to the fellow who runs.

" I'd sent four of 'em back with the R. I. P.
     sign, which means to return if you can,
But none of 'em got through the curtain of fire;
     my hurry call died with the man.
Then Runner McGee said he'd try to get through.
     I hated to order the kid
On his mission of death; thought he'd never get
     by, but somehow or other he did.

" Yes, he's dead. Died an hour after bringing
     us word that the chief was aware of our
     plight,
An' for us to hang on to the ditch that we held;
     the reserves would relieve us at night.
Then we stuck to our trench an' we stuck to our
     guns; you know how you'll fight when
     you know
That new strength is coming to fill up the gaps.
     There's heart in the force of your blow.

" It wasn't till later I got all the facts. They
     wanted McGee to remain.
They begged him to stay. He had cheated death
     once an' was foolish to try it again.
' R. I. P. are my orders,' he answered them all,
     ' an' back to the boys I must go;
Four of us died comin' out with the news. It
     will help them to know that you know.' "

Spring in the Trenches

It's coming time for planting in that little patch
      of ground,
Where the lad and I made merry as he followed
      me around;
The sun is getting higher, and the skies above
      are blue,
And I'm hungry for the garden, and I wish the
      war were through.

    But it's tramp, tramp, tramp,
      And it's never look behind,
    And when you see a stranger's kids,
      Pretend that you are blind.

The spring is coming back again, the birds begin
      to mate;
The skies are full of kindness, but the world is
      full of hate.
And it's I that should be bending now in peace
      above the soil,
With laughing eyes and little hands about to bless
      the toil.

    But it's fight, fight, fight,
      And it's charge at double-quick;
    A soldier thinking thoughts of home
      Is one more soldier sick.

Last year I brought the bulbs to bloom and saw
    the roses bud;
This year I'm ankle deep in mire, and most of
    it is blood.
Last year the mother in the door was glad as
    she could be;
To-day her heart is full of pain, and mine is
    hurting me.

    But it's shoot, shoot, shoot,
      And when the bullets hiss,
    Don't let the tears fill up your eyes,
      For weeping soldiers miss.

Oh, who will tend the roses now and who will
    sow the seeds?
And who will do the heavy work the little gar-
    den needs?
And who will tell the lad of mine the things he
    wants to know,
And take his hand and lead him round the paths
    we used to go?

    For it's charge, charge, charge,
      And it's face the foe once more;
    Forget the things you love the most
      And keep your mind on war.

The Struggle

Life is a struggle for peace,
  A longing for rest,
A hope for the battles to cease,
  A dream for the best;
And he is not living who stays
  Contented with things,
Unconcerned with the work of the days
  And all that it brings.

He is dead who sees nothing to change,
  No wrong to make right;
Who travels no new way or strange
  In search of the light;
Who never sets out for a goal
  That he sees from afar
But contents his indifferent soul
  With things as they are.

Life isn't rest — it is toil;
  It is building a dream;
It is tilling a parcel of soil
  Or bridging a stream;
It's pursuing the light of a star
  That but dimly we see,
And in wresting from things as they are
  The joy that should be.

The Undaunted

He tried to travel No Man's Land, that's guarded
    well with guns,
He tried to race the road of death, where never
    a coward runs.
Now he's asking of his doctor, and he's panting
    hard for breath,
How soon he will be ready for another bout with
    death.

You'd think if you had wakened in a shell hole's
    slime and mud
That was partly dirty water, but was mostly
    human blood,
And you had to lie and suffer till the bullets
    ceased to hum
And the night time dropped its cover, so the
    stretcher boys could come —

You'd think if you had suffered from a fever
    and its thirst,
And could hear the "rapids" spitting and the
    high explosives burst,
And had lived to tell that story — you could face
    your fellow men
In the little peaceful village, though you never
    fought again.

You'd think that once you'd fallen in the shrap-
    nel's deadly rain,
Once you'd shed your blood for honor, you had
    borne your share of pain;
Once you'd traveled No Man's country, you'd be
    satisfied to quit
And be invalided homeward, and could say you'd
    done your bit.

But he's lying, patched and bandaged, **very white**
    and very weak,
And he's trying to be cheerful, though it's agony
    to speak;
He is pleading with the doctor, though he's
    panting hard for breath,
To return him to the trenches for another bout
    with death.

The Chaplain

He was just a small church parson when the
     war broke out, and he
Looked and dressed and acted like all parsons
     that we see.
He wore the cleric's broadcloth and he hooked
     his vest behind,
But he had a man's religion and he had a strong
     man's mind,
And he heard the call to duty, and he quit his
     church and went,
And he bravely tramped right with 'em every-
     where the boys were sent.

He put aside his broadcloth and he put the
     khaki on;
Said he'd come to be a soldier and was going
     to live like one.
Then he refereed the prize fights that the boys
     pulled off at night,
And if no one else was handy he'd put on the
     gloves and fight.
He wasn't there a fortnight ere he saw the sol-
     diers' needs,
And he said: "I'm done with preaching; this
     is now the time for deeds."

He learned the sound of shrapnel, he could tell
     the size of shell

From the shriek it make above him, and he knew
    just where it fell.
In the front line trench he labored, and he knew
    the feel of mud,
And he didn't run from danger and he wasn't
    scared of blood.
He wrote letters for the wounded, and he cheered
    them with his jokes,
And he never made a visit without passing round
    the smokes.

Then one day a bullet got him, as he knelt be-
    side a lad
Who was " going west " right speedy, and they
    both seemed mighty glad,
'Cause he held the boy's hand tighter, and he
    smiled and whispered low,
" Now you needn't fear the journey; over there
    with you I'll go."
And they both passed out together, arm in arm
    I think they went.
He had kept his vow to follow everywhere the
    boys were sent.

Thanksgiving

For strength to face the battle's might,
For men that dare to die for right,
　For hearts above the lure of gold
　　And fortune's soft and pleasant way,
　For courage of our days of old,
　　Great God of All, we kneel and pray.

We thank Thee for our splendid youth.
Who fight for liberty and truth,
　Within whose breasts there glows anew
　　The glory of the altar fires
　Which our heroic fathers knew —
　　God make them worthy of their sires!

We thank Thee for our mothers fair
Who through the sorrows they must bear
　Still smile, and give their hearts to woe,
　　Yet bravely heed the day's command —
　That mothers, yet to be, may know
　　A free and glorious motherland.

Oh, God, we thank Thee for the skies
Where our flag now in glory flies!
　We thank Thee that no love of gain
　　Is leading us, but that we fight
　To keep our banner free from stain
　　And that we die for what is right.

Oh, God, we thank Thee that we may
Lift up our eyes to Thee to-day;
  We thank Thee we can face this test
    With honor and a spotless name,
And that we serve a world distressed
  Unselfishly and free from shame.

A Patriotic Wish

I'd like to be the sort of man the flag could boast
      about;
I'd like to be the sort of man it cannot live with-
      out;
I'd like to be the type of man
That really is American:
The head-erect and shoulders-square,
Clean-minded fellow, just and fair,
That all men picture when they see
The glorious banner of the free.

I'd like to be the sort of man the flag now typifies,
The kind of man we really want the flag to
      symbolize;
The loyal brother to a trust,
The big, unselfish soul and just,
The friend of every man oppressed,
The strong support of all that's best —

The sturdy chap the banner's meant,
Where'er it flies, to represent.

I'd like to be the sort of man the flag's supposed
    to mean,
The man that all in fancy see, wherever it is
    seen;
The chap that's ready for a fight
Whenever there's a wrong to right,
The friend in every time of need,
The doer of the daring deed,
The clean and generous handed man
That is a real American.

A Patriot

It's funny when a feller wants to do his little bit,
And wants to wear a uniform and lug a soldier's
    kit,
And ain't afraid of submarines nor mines that
    fill the sea,
They will not let him go along to fight for liberty.
They make him stay at home and be his mother's
    darling pet,
But you can bet there'll come a time when they
    will want me yet.

I want to serve the Stars and Stripes, I want to
    go and fight,
I want to lick the Kaiser good, and do the job
    up right.
I know the way to use a gun and I can dig a
    trench
And I would like to go and help the English and
    the French.
But no, they say, you cannot march away to
    stirring drums;
Be mother's angel boy at home; stay there and
    twirl your thumbs.

I've read about the daring boys that fight up in
    the sky;
It seems to me that that must be a splendid way
    to die.
I'd like to drive an aeroplane and prove my cour-
    age grim
And get above a German there and drop a bomb
    on him,
But they won't let me go along to help the latest
    drive;
They say my mother needs me here because I'm
    only five.

Memorial Day

The finest tribute we can pay
Unto our hero dead to-day,
Is not a rose wreath, white and red,
In memory of the blood they shed;
It is to stand beside each mound,
Each couch of consecrated ground,
And pledge ourselves as warriors true
Unto the work they died to do.

Into God's valleys where they lie
At rest, beneath the open sky,
Triumphant now, o'er every foe,
As living tributes let us go.
No wreath of rose or immortelles
Or spoken word or tolling bells
Will do to-day, unless we give
Our pledge that liberty shall live.

Our hearts must be the roses red
We place above our hero dead;
To-day beside their graves we must
Renew allegiance to their trust;
Must bare our heads and humbly say
We hold the Flag as dear as they,
And stand, as once they stood, to die
To keep the Stars and Stripes on high.

The finest tribute we can pay
Unto our hero dead to-day
Is not of speech or roses red,
But living, throbbing hearts instead
That shall renew the pledge they sealed
With death upon the battlefield:
That freedom's flag shall bear no stain
And free men wear no tyrant's chain.

The Soldier on Crutches

He came down the stairs on the laughter-filled
    grill
Where patriots were eating and drinking their
    fill,
The tap of his crutch on the marble of white
Caught my ear as I sat all alone there that night.
I turned — and a soldier my eyes fell upon,
He had fought for his country, and one leg was
    gone!

As he entered a silence fell over the place;
Every eye in the room was turned up to his face.
His head was up high and his eyes seemed aflame
With a wonderful light, and he laughed as he
    came.
He was young — not yet thirty — yet never he
    made
One sign of regret for the price he had paid.

One moment before this young soldier came in
I had caught bits of speech in the clatter and din
From the fine men about me in life's dress parade
Who were boasting the cash sacrifices they'd
      made;
And I'd thought of my own paltry service with
      pride,
When I turned and that hero of battle I spied.

I shall never forget the hot flushes of shame
That rushed to my cheeks as that young fellow
      came.
He was cheerful and smiling and clear-eyed and
      fine
And out of his face golden light seemed to shine.
And I thought as he passed me on crutches:
      " How small
Are the gifts that I make if I don't give my all."

Some day in the future in many a place
More soldiers just like him we'll all have to face.
We must sit with them, talk with them, laugh
      with them, too,
With the signs of their service forever in view
And this was my thought as I looked at him
      then —
Oh, God! make me worthy to stand with such
      men.

Easy Service

When an empty sleeve or a sightless eye
   Or a legless form I see,
I breathe my thanks to my God on High
   For His watchful care o'er me.
And I say to myself, as the cripple goes
   Half stumbling on his way:
I may brag and boast, but that brother knows
   Why the old flag floats to-day.

I think as I sit in my cozy den
   Puffing one of my many pipes
That I've served with all of my fellow men
   The glorious Stars and Stripes.
Then I see a troop in the faded blue
   And a few in the dusty gray,
And I have to laugh at the deeds I do
   For the flag that floats to-day.

I see men tangled in pointed wire,
   The sport of the blazing sun,
Mangled and maimed by a leaden fire
   As the tides of battle run,
And I fancy I hear their piteous calls
   For merciful death, and then
The cannons cease and the darkness falls,
   And those fluttering things are men.

Out there in the night they beg for death,
   Yet the Reaper spurns their cries,
And it seems his jest to leave them breath
   For their pitiful pleas and sighs.
And I am here in my cozy room
   In touch with the joys of life,
I am miles away from the fields of doom
   And the gory scenes of strife.

I never have vainly called for aid,
   Nor suffered real pangs of thirst,
I have marched with life in its best parade
   And never have seen its worst.
In the flowers of ease I have ever basked,
   And I think as the Flag I see
How much of service from some it's asked,
   How little of toil from me.

Spoiling Them

" You're spoiling them!" the mother cries
When I give way to weepy eyes
And let them do the things they wish,
Like cleaning up the jelly dish,
Or finishing the chocolate cake,
Or maybe let the rascal take
My piece of huckleberry pie,
Because he wants it more than I.

" You're spoiling them!" the mother tells,
When I am heedless to their yells,
And let them race and romp about
And do not put their joy to rout.
I know I should be firm, and yet
I tried it once to my regret;
I will remember till I'm old
The day I started in to scold.

I stamped my foot and shouted: " Stop!"
And Bud just let his drum sticks drop,
And looked at me, and turned away;
That night there was no further play.
The girls were solemn-like and still,
Just as girls are when they are ill,
And when unto his cot I crept,
I found him sobbing as he slept.

That was my first attempt and last
To play the scold. I'm glad it passed
So quickly and has left no trace
Of memory on each little face;
But now when mother whispers low:
"You're spoiling them," I answer, "No!
But it is plain, as plain can be,
Those little tykes are spoiling me."

An Old-Fashioned Welcome

There's nothing cheers a fellow up just like a
    hearty greeting,
A handclasp and an honest smile that flash the
    joy of meeting;
And when at friendly doors you ring, somehow
    it seems to free you
From all life's doubts to hear them say: "Come
    in! We're glad to see you!"

At first the portal slips ajar in answer to your
    ringing,
And then your eyes meet friendly eyes, and wide
    the door goes flinging;
And something seems to stir the soul, however
    troubled be you,
If but the cheery host exclaims: "Come in!
    We're glad to see you!"

The Mother Watch

She never closed her eyes in sleep till we were
    all in bed;
On party nights till we came home she often sat
    and read,
We little thought about it then, when we were
    young and gay,
How much the mother worried when we children
    were away.
We only knew she never slept when we were out
    at night,
And that she waited just to know that we'd come
    home all right.

Why, sometimes when we'd stayed away till one
    or two or three,
It seemed to us that mother heard the turning
    of the key;
For always when we stepped inside she'd call
    and we'd reply,
But we were all too young back then to under-
    stand just why.
Until the last one had returned she always kept
    a light,
For mother couldn't sleep until she'd kissed us
    all good night.

She had to know that we were safe before she
went to rest;
She seemed to fear the world might harm the
ones she loved the best.
And once she said: "When you are grown to
women and to men,
Perhaps I'll sleep the whole night through; I may
be different then."
And so it seemed that night and day we knew a
mother's care —
That always when we got back home we'd find
her waiting there.

Then came the night that we were called to gather
round her bed:
"The children all are with you now," the kindly
doctor said.
And in her eyes there gleamed again the old-time
tender light
That told she had been waiting just to know we
were all right.
She smiled the old-familiar smile, and prayed to
God to keep
Us safe from harm throughout the years, and
then she went to sleep.

Faces

I look into the faces of the people passing by,
  The glad ones and the sad ones, and the lined
    with misery,
And I wonder why the sorrow or the twinkle in
    the eye;
  But the pale and weary faces are the ones that
    trouble me.

I saw a face this morning, and time was when it
    was fair;
  Youth had brushed it bright with color in the
    distant long ago,
And the goddess of the lovely once had kept a
    temple there,
  But the cheeks were pale with grieving and
    the eyes were dull with woe.

Who has done this thing I wondered; what has
    wrought the ruin here?
  Why these sunken cheeks and pallid where the
    roses once were pink?
Why has beauty fled her palace; did some vandal
    hand appear?
  Did her lover prove unfaithful or her husband
    take to drink?

Once the golden voice of promise whispered
    sweetly in her ears;
  She was born to be a garden where the smiles
    of love might lurk;
Now the eyes that shone like jewels are but gate-
    ways for her tears,
  And she takes her place among us, toilers early
    bound for work.

Is it fate that writes so sadly, or the cruelty of
    man?
  What foul deed has marred the parchment of
    a life so fair as this?
Who has wrecked this lovely temple and de-
    stroyed the Maker's plan,
  Raining blows on cheeks of beauty God had
    fashioned just to kiss?

Oh, the pale and weary faces of the people that
    I see
  Are the ones that seem to haunt me, and I
    pray to God above
That such cruel desolation shall not ever come
    to be
  Stamped forever in the future on the faces
    that I love.

The Lost Purse

I remember the excitement and the terrible alarm
That worried everybody when William broke
    his arm;
An' how frantic Pa and Ma got only jes' the
    other day
When they couldn't find the baby coz he'd up
    an' walked away;
But I'm sure there's no excitement that our house
    has ever shook
Like the times Ma can't remember where she's
    put her pocketbook.

When the laundry man is standin' at the door an'
    wants his pay
Ma hurries in to get it, an' the fun starts right
    away.
She hustles to the sideboard, coz she knows
    exactly where
She can put her hand right on it, but alas! it isn't
    there.
She tries the parlor table an' she goes upstairs
    to look,
An' once more she can't remember where she put
    her pocketbook.

She tells us that she had it just a half an hour
    ago,

An' now she cannot find it though she's hunted
    high and low;
She's searched the kitchen cupboard an' the
    bureau drawers upstairs,
An' it's not behind the sofa nor beneath the par-
    lor chairs.
She makes us kids get busy searching every little
    nook,
An' this time says she's certain that she's lost
    her pocketbook.

She calls Pa at the office an' he laughs I guess,
    for then
She always mumbles something 'bout the heart-
    lessness of men.
She calls to mind a peddler who came to the
    kitchen door,
An' she's certain from his whiskers an' the
    shabby clothes he wore
An' his dirty shirt an' collar that he must have
    been a crook,
An' she's positive that feller came and got her
    pocketbook.

But at last she allus finds it in some queer an'
    funny spot,
Where she'd put it in a hurry, an' had somehow
    clean forgot;

An' she heaves a sigh of gladness, an' she says,
    " Well, I declare,
I would take an oath this minute that I never put
    it there."
An' we're peaceable an' quiet till next time Ma
    goes to look
An' finds she can't remember where she put her
    pocketbook.

The Doctor

I don't see why Pa likes him so,
    And seems so glad to have him come;
He jabs my ribs and wants to know
    If here and there it's hurting some.
He holds my wrist, coz there are things
    In there, which always jump and jerk,
Then, with a telephone he brings,
    He listens to my breather work.

He taps my back and pinches me,
    Then hangs a mirror on his head
And looks into my throat to see
    What makes it hurt and if it's red.
Then on his knee he starts to write
    And says to mother, with a smile:
" This ought to fix him up all right,
    We'll cure him in a little while."

I don't see why Pa likes him so.
　　Whenever I don't want to play
He says: " The boy is sick, I know!
　　Let's get the doctor right away."
And when he comes, he shakes his hand,
　　And hustles him upstairs to me,
And seems contented just to stand
　　Inside the room where he can see.

Then Pa says every time he goes:
　　" That's money I am glad to pay;
It's worth it, when a fellow knows
　　His pal will soon be up to play."
But maybe if my Pa were me,
　　And had to take his pills and all,
He wouldn't be so glad to see
　　The doctor come to make a call.

Compensation

I'd like to think when life is done
   That I had filled a needed post,
That here and there I'd paid my fare
   With more than idle talk and boast;
That I had taken gifts divine,
The breath of life and manhood fine,
And tried to use them now and then
In service for my fellow men.

I'd hate to think when life is through
   That I had lived my round of years
A useless kind, that leaves behind
   No record in this vale of tears;
That I had wasted all my days
By treading only selfish ways,
And that this world would be the same
If it had never known my name.

I'd like to think that here and there,
   When I am gone, there shall remain
A happier spot that might have not
   Existed had I toiled for gain;
That some one's cheery voice and smile
Shall prove that I had been worth while;
That I had paid with something fine
My debt to God for life divine.

It Couldn't Be Done

Somebody said that it couldn't be done,
  But he with a chuckle replied
That " maybe it couldn't," but he would be one
  Who wouldn't say so till he'd tried.
So he buckled right in with the trace of a grin
  On his face. If he worried he hid it.
He started to sing as he tackled the thing
  That couldn't be done, and he did it.

Somebody scoffed: "Oh, you'll never do that;
  At least no one ever has done it";
But he took off his coat and he took off his hat,
  And the first thing we knew he'd begun it.
With a lift of his chin and a bit of a grin,
  Without any doubting or quiddit,
He started to sing as he tackled the thing
  That couldn't be done, and he did it.

There are thousands to tell you it cannot be done,
  There are thousands to prophesy failure;
There are thousands to point out to you one by
      one,
  The dangers that wait to assail you.
But just buckle in with a bit of a grin,
  Just take off your coat and go to it;
Just start in to sing as you tackle the thing
  That " cannot be done," and you'll do it.

Service

You never hear the robins brag about the sweet-
ness of their song,
Nor do they stop their music gay whene'er a
poor man comes along.
God taught them how to sing an' when they'd
learned the art He sent them here
To use their talents day by day the dreary lives
o' men to cheer.
An' rich or poor an' sad or gay, the ugly an'
the fair to see,
Can stop most any time in June an' hear the
robins' melody.

I stand an' watch them in the sun, usin' their
gifts from day to day,
Swellin' their little throats with song, regardless
of man's praise or pay;
Jes' bein' robins, nothing else, nor claiming great-
ness for their deeds,
But jes' content to gratify one of the big world's
many needs,
Singin' a lesson to us all to be ourselves and
scatter cheer
By usin' every day the gifts God gave us when
He sent us here.

Why should we keep our talents hid, or think
    we favor men because
We use the gifts that God has given? The
    robins never ask applause,
Nor count themselves remarkable, nor strut in a
    superior way,
Because their music sweeter is than that God
    gave unto the jay.
Only a man conceited grows as he makes use of
    talents fine,
Forgetting that he merely does the working of
    the Will Divine.

Lord, as the robins, let me serve! Teach me to
    do the best I can
To make this world a better place, an' happier
    for my fellow man.
If gift o' mine can cheer his soul an' hearten him
    along his way
Let me not keep that talent hid; I would make
    use of it to-day.
An' since the robins ask no praise, or pay for all
    their songs o' cheer,
Let me in humbleness rejoice to do my bit o'
    service here.

At the Peace Table

Who shall sit at the table, then, when the terms
    of peace are made —
The wisest men of the troubled lands in their
    silver and gold brocade?
Yes, they shall gather in solemn state to speak
    for each living race,
But who shall speak for the unseen dead that shall
    come to the council place?

Though you see them not and you hear them not,
    they shall sit at the table, too;
They shall throng the room where the peace is
    made and know what it is you do;
The innocent dead from the sea shall rise to stand
    at the wise man's side,
And over his shoulder a boy shall look — a boy
    that was crucified.

You may guard the doors of that council hall with
    barriers strong and stout,
But the dead unbidden shall enter there, and never
    you'll shut them out.
And the man that died in the open boat, and the
    babes that suffered worse,
Shall sit at the table when peace is made by the
    side of a martyred nurse.

You may see them not, but they'll all be there;
    when they speak you may fail to hear;
You may think that you're making your pacts
    alone, but their spirits will hover near;
And whatever the terms of the peace you make
    with the tyrant whose hands are red,
You must please not only the living here, but must
    satisfy your dead.

Mrs. Malone and the Censor

When Mrs. Malone got a letter from Pat
She started to read it aloud in her flat.
"Dear Mary," it started, "I can't tell you much,
I'm somewhere in France, and I'm fightin' the
    Dutch;
I'm chokin' wid news thot I'd like to relate,
But it's little a soldier's permitted t' state.
Do ye mind Red McPhee — well, he fell in a
    ditch
An' busted an arrm, but I can't tell ye which.

"An' Paddy O'Hara was caught in a flame
An' rescued by — Faith, I can't tell ye his name.
Last night I woke up wid a terrible pain;
I thought for awhile it would drive me insane.
Oh, the suff'rin, I had was most dreadful t' bear!

I'm sorry, my dear, but I can't tell ye where.
The doctor he gave me a pill, but I find
It's conthrary to rules t' disclose here the kind.

" I've been t' the dintist an' had a tooth out.
I'm sorry t' leave you so shrouded in doubt
But the best I can say is that one tooth is gone,
The censor won't let me inform ye which one.
I met a young fellow who knows ye right well,
An' ye know him, too, but his name I can't tell.
He's Irish, red-headed, an' there with th' blarney,
His folks once knew your folks back home in
        Killarney."

" By gorry," said Mrs. Malone in her flat,
" It's hard t' make sinse out av writin' like that,
But I'll give him as good as he sends, that I will."
So she went right to work with her ink well an'
        quill,
An' she wrote, " I suppose ye're dead eager fer
        news —
You know when ye left we were buyin' the shoes;
Well, the baby has come, an' we're both doin'
        well;
It's a ——. Oh, but that's somethin' they won't
        let me tell."

First Name Friends

Though some may yearn for titles great, and
  seek the frills of fame,
I do not care to have an extra handle to my name.
I am not hungry for the pomp of life's high
  dignities,
I do not sigh to sit among the honored LL. D.'s.
I shall be satisfied if I can be unto the end,
To those I know and live with here, a simple,
  first-name friend.

There's nothing like the comradeship which
  warms the lives of those
Who make the glorious circle of the Jacks and
  Bills and Joes.
With all his majesty and power, Old Caesar never
  knew
The joy of first-name fellowship, as all the
  Eddies do.
Let them who will be "mistered" here and raised
  above the rest;
I hold a first-name greeting is by far the very
  best.

Acquaintance calls for dignity. You never really
  know
The man on whom the terms of pomp you feel
  you must bestow.

Professor William Joseph Wise may be your
　　　friend, but still
You are not certain of the fact till you can call
　　　him Bill.
But hearts grow warm and lips grow kind, and
　　　all the shamming ends,
When you are in the company of good old first-
　　　name friends.

The happiest men on earth are not the men of
　　　highest rank;
That joy belongs to George, and Jim, to Henry
　　　and to Frank;
With them the prejudice of race and creed and
　　　wealth depart,
And men are one in fellowship and always light
　　　of heart.
So I would live and laugh and love until my sun
　　　descends,
And share the joyous comradeship of honest
　　　first-name friends.

The Furnace Door

My father is a peaceful man;
He tries in every way he can
To live a life of gentleness
And patience all the while.
He says that needless fretting's vain,
That it's absurd to be profane,
That nearly every wrong can be
Adjusted with a smile.
Yet try no matter how he will,
There's one thing that annoys him still,
One thing that robs him of his calm
And leaves him very sore;
He cannot keep his self-control
When with a shovel full of coal
He misses where it's headed for,
And hits the furnace door.

He measures with a careful eye
The space for which he's soon to try,
Then grabs his trusty shovel up
And loads it in the bin,
Then turns and with a healthy lunge,
That's two parts swing and two parts plunge,
He lets go at the furnace fire,
Convinced it will go in!
And then we hear a sudden smack,
The cellar air turns blue and black;

Above the rattle of the coal
We hear his awful roar.
From dreadful language upward hissed
We know that father's aim has missed,
And that his shovel full of coal
Went up against the door.

The minister was here one day
For supper, and Pa went away
To fix the furnace fire, and soon
We heard that awful roar.
And through the furnace pipes there came
Hot words that made Ma blush for shame.
" It strikes me," said the minister,
" He hit the furnace door."
Ma turned away and hung her head;
" I'm so ashamed," was all she said.
And then the minister replied:
" Don't worry. I admit
That when I hit the furnace door,
And spill the coal upon the floor,
I quite forget the cloth I wear
And — er — swear a little bit."

Out Fishin'

A feller isn't thinkin' mean,
    Out fishin';
His thoughts are mostly good an' clean,
    Out fishin'.
He doesn't knock his fellow men,
Or harbor any grudges then;
A feller's at his finest when
    Out fishin'.

The rich are comrades to the poor,
    Out fishin';
All brothers of a common lure,
    Out fishin'.
The urchin with the pin an' string
Can chum with millionaire an' king;
Vain pride is a forgotten thing,
    Out fishin'.

A feller gits a chance to dream,
    Out fishin';
He learns the beauties of a stream,
    Out fishin';
An' he can wash his soul in air
That isn't foul with selfish care,
An' relish plain and simple fare,
    Out fishin'.

A feller has no time fer hate,
    Out fishin';
He isn't eager to be great,
    Out fishin'.
He isn't thinkin' thoughts of pelf,
Or goods stacked high upon a shelf,
But he is always just himself,
    Out fishin'.

A feller's glad to be a friend,
    Out fishin';
A helpin' hand he'll always lend,
    Out fishin'.
The brotherhood of rod an' line
An' sky and stream is always fine;
Men come real close to God's design,
    Out fishin'.

A feller isn't plotting schemes,
    Out fishin';
He's only busy with his dreams,
    Out fishin'.
His livery is a coat of tan,
His creed — to do the best he can;
A feller's always mostly man,
    Out fishin'.

Selling the Old Home

The little house has grown too small, or rather
    we have grown
Too big to dwell within the walls where all our
    joys were known.
And so, obedient to the wish of her we love so
    well,
I have agreed for sordid gold the little home to
    sell.
Now strangers come to see the place, and secretly
    I sigh,
And deep within my breast I hope that they'll
    refuse to buy.

"This bedroom's small," one woman said; up
    went her nose in scorn!
To me that is the splendid room where little
    Bud was born.
"The walls are sadly finger-marked," another
    stranger said.
A lump came rising in my throat; I felt my
    cheeks grow red.
"Yes, yes," I answered, "so they are.   The
    fingermarks are free
But I'd not leave them here if I could take them
    all with me."

" The stairway shows the signs of wear." I
answered her in heat,
" That's but the glorious sign to me of happy
little feet.
Most anyone can have a flight of shiny stairs
and new
But those are steps where joy has raced, and love
and laughter, too."
" This paper's ruined! Here are scrawled some
pencil marks, I note."
I'd treasured them for years. They were the
first he ever wrote.

Oh I suppose we'll sell the place; it's right that
we should go;
The children must have larger rooms in which
to live and grow.
But all my joys were cradled here; 'tis here I've
lived my best,
'Tis here, whatever else shall come, we've been
our happiest;
And though into a stranger's hands this home I
shall resign,
And take his gold in pay for it, I still shall call
it mine.

Tied Down

"They tie you down," a woman said,
Whose cheeks should have been flaming red
With shame to speak of children so.
"When babies come you cannot go
In search of pleasure with your friends,
And all your happy wandering ends.
The things you like you cannot do,
For babies make a slave of you."

I looked at her and said: "'Tis true
That children make a slave of you,
And tie you down with many a knot,
But have you never thought to what
It is of happiness and pride
That little babies have you tied?
Do you not miss the greater joys
That come with little girls and boys?

"They tie you down to laughter rare,
To hours of smiles and hours of care,
To nights of watching and to fears;
Sometimes they tie you down to tears
And then repay you with a smile,
And make your trouble all worth while.
They tie you fast to chubby feet,
And cheeks of pink and kisses sweet.

" They fasten you with cords of love
To God divine, who reigns above.
They tie you, whereso'er you roam,
Unto the little place called home;
And over sea or railroad track
They tug at you to bring you back.
The happiest people in the town
Are those the babies have tied down.

" Oh, go your selfish way and free,
But hampered I would rather be,
Yes rather than a kingly crown
I would be, what you term, tied down;
Tied down to dancing eyes and charms,
Held fast by chubby, dimpled arms,
The fettered slave of girl and boy,
And win from them earth's finest joy."

A Choice

Sure, they get stubborn at times; they worry and
    fret us a lot,
But I'd rather be crossed by a glad little boy and
    frequently worried than not.
There are hours when they get on my nerves
    and set my poor brain all awhirl,
But I'd rather be troubled that way than to be
    the man who has no little girl.

There are times they're a nuisance, that's true,
    with all of their racket and noise,
But I'd rather my personal pleasures be lost than
    to give up my girls and my boys.
Not always they're perfectly good; there are
    times when they're wilfully bad,
But I'd rather be worried by youngsters of mine
    than lonely and childless and sad.

So I try to be patient and calm whenever they're
    having their fling;
For the sum of their laughter and love is more
    than the worry they bring.
And each night when sweet peace settles down
    and I see them asleep in their cot,
I chuckle and say: "They upset me to-day, but
    I'd rather be that way than not."

Back Home

Glad to get back home again,
Where abide the friendly men;
Glad to see the same old scenes
And the little house that means
All the joys the soul has treasured —
Glad to be where smiles aren't measured,
Where I've blended with the gladness
All the heart has known of sadness,
Where some long-familiar steeple
Marks my town of friendly people.

Though it's fun to go a-straying
Where the bands are nightly playing
And the throngs of men and women
Drain the cup of pleasure brimmin',
I am glad when it is over
That I've ceased to play the Rover.
And when once the train starts chugging
Towards the children I'd be hugging,
All my thoughts and dreams are set there;
Fast enough I cannot get there.

Guess I wasn't meant for bright lights,
For the blaze of red and white lights,
For the throngs that seems to smother
In their selfishness, each other;
For whenever I've been down there,

Tramped the noisy, blatant town there,
Always in a week I've started
Yearning, hungering, heavy-hearted,
For the home town and its spaces
Lit by fine and friendly faces.

Like to be where men about me
Do not look on me to doubt me;
Where I know the men and women,
Know why tears some eyes are dimmin',
Know the good folks an' the bad folks
An' the glad folks an' the sad folks;
Where we live with one another,
Meanin' something to each other.
An' I'm glad to see the steeple,
Where the crowds aren't merely people.

Aunty

I'm sorry for a feller if he hasn't any aunt,
To let him eat and do the things his mother says
    he can't.
An aunt to come a visitin' or one to go and see
Is just about the finest kind of lady there could be.
Of course she's not your mother, an' she hasn't
    got her ways,
But a part that's most important in a feller's life
    she plays.

She is kind an' she is gentle, an' sometimes she's
    full of fun,
An' she's very sympathetic when some dreadful
    thing you've done.
An' she likes to buy you candy, an' she's always
    gettin' toys
That you wish your Pa would get you, for she
    hasn't any boys.
But sometimes she's over-loving, an' your cheeks
    turn red with shame
When she smothers you with kisses, but you like
    her just the same.

One time my father took me to my aunty's, an'
    he said:
" You will stay here till I get you, an' be sure you
    go to bed

"When your aunty says it's time to, an' be good
    an' mind her, too,
An' when you come home we'll try to have a big
    surprise for you."
I did as I was told to, an' when Pa came back
    for me
He said there was a baby at the house for me
    to see.

I've been visitin' at aunty's for a week or two,
    an' Pa
Has written that he's comin' soon to take me
    home to Ma.
He says they're gettin' lonely, an' I'm kind o'
    lonely, too,
Coz an aunt is not exactly what your mother is
    to you.
I am hungry now to see her, but I'm wondering
    to-day
If Pa's bought another baby in the time I've been
    away.

Toys and Life

You can learn a lot from boys
By the way they use their toys;
Some are selfish in their care,
Never very glad to share
Playthings with another boy;
Seem to want to hoard their joy.
And they hide away the drum
For the days that never come;
Hide the train of cars and skates,
Keeping them from all their mates,
And run all their boyhood through
With their toys as good as new.

Others gladly give and lend,
Heedless that the tin may bend,
Caring not that drum-heads break,
Minding not that playmates take
To themselves the joy that lies
In the little birthday prize.
And in homes that house such boys
Always there are broken toys,
Symbolizing moments glad
That the youthful lives have had.
There you'll never find a shelf
Dedicated unto self.

Toys are made for children's fun,

Very frail and quickly done,
And who keeps them long to view,
Bright of paint and good as new,
Robs himself and other boys
Of their swiftly passing joys.
So he looked upon a toy
When our soldier was a boy;
And somehow to-day we're glad
That the tokens of our lad
And the trinkets that we keep
Are a broken, battered heap.

Life itself is but a toy
Filled with duty and with joy;
Not too closely should we guard
Our brief time from being scarred;
Never high on musty shelves
Should we hoard it for ourselves.
It is something we should share
In another's hour of care —
Something we should gladly give
That another here may live;
We should never live it through
Keeping it as good as new.

Faith

It is faith that bridges the land of breath
   To the realms of the souls departed,
That comforts the living in days of death,
   And strengthens the heavy-hearted.
It is faith in his dreams that keeps a man
   Face front to the odds about him,
And he shall conquer who thinks he can,
   In spite of the throngs who doubt him.

Each must stand in the court of life
   And pass through the hours of trial;
He shall tested be by the rules of strife,
   And tried for his self-denial.
Time shall bruise his soul with the loss of friends,
   And frighten him with disaster,
But he shall find when the anguish ends
   That of all things faith is master.

So keep your faith in the God above,
   And faith in the righteous truth,
It shall bring you back to the absent love,
   And the joys of a vanished youth.
You shall smile once more when your tears are
     dried,
   Meet trouble and swiftly rout it,
For faith is the strength of the soul inside,
   And lost is the man without it.

The Burden Bearer

Oh, my shoulders grow aweary of the burdens
    I am bearin',
An' I grumble when I'm footsore at the rough
    road I am farin',
But I strap my knapsack tighter till I feel the
    leather bind me,
An' I'm glad to bear the burdens for the ones
    who come behind me.
It's for them that I am ploddin', for the chil-
    dren comin' after;
I would strew their path with roses and would
    fill their days with laughter.

Oh, there's selfishness within me, there are times
    it gets to talkin',
Times I hear it whisper to me, "It's a dusty
    road you're walkin';
Why not rest your feet a little; why not pause an'
    take your leisure?
Don't you hunger in your strivin' for the merry
    whirl of pleasure?"
Then I turn an' see them smilin' an' I grip my
    burdens tighter,
For the joy that I am seekin' is to see their eyes
    grow brighter.

Oh, I've sipped the cup of sorrow an' I've felt
    the gad of trouble,
An' I know the hurt of trudgin' through a field
    o'errun with stubble;
But a rougher road to travel had my father good
    before me,
An' I'm owin' all my gladness to the tasks he
    shouldered for me.
Oh, I didn't understand it, when a lad I played
    about him,
But he labored for my safety in the days I'd
    be without him.

Oh, my kindly father never gave himself a year
    of leisure —
Never lived one selfish moment, never turned
    aside for pleasure —
Though he must have grown aweary of the bur-
    dens he was bearin';
He was tryin' hard to better every road I'd
    soon be farin'.
Now I turn an' see them smilin' an' I hear their
    merry laughter,
An' I'm glad to bear the burdens for the ones
    that follow after.

"It's a Boy"

The doctor leads a busy life, he wages war with
      death;
Long hours he spends to help the one who's fight-
      ing hard for breath;
He cannot call his time his own, nor share in
      others' fun,
His duties claim him through the night when
      others' work is done.
And yet the doctor seems to be God's messenger
      of joy,
Appointed to announce this news of gladness:
      " It's a boy! "

In many ways unpleasant is the doctor's round
      of cares,
I should not like to have to bear the burdens
      that he bears;
His eyes must look on horrors grim, unmoved
      he must remain,
Emotion he must master if he hopes to conquer
      pain;
Yet to his lot this duty falls, his voice he must
      employ
To speak to man the happiest phrase that's
      sounded: "It's a boy! "

I wish 'twere given me to speak a message half
      so glad

As that the doctor brings unto the fear-distracted
    dad.
I wish that simple words of mine could change
    the skies to blue,
And lift the care from troubled hearts, as those
    he utters do.
I wish that I could banish all the thoughts that
    man annoy,
And cheer him as the doctor does, who whispers:
    "It's a boy."

Whoever through the hours of night has stood
    outside her door,
And wondered if she'd smile again; whoe'er has
    paced the floor,
And lived those years of fearful thoughts, and
    then been swept from woe
Up to the topmost height of bliss that's given
    man to know,
Will tell you there's no phrase so sweet, so
    charged with human joy
As that the doctor brings from God — that mes-
    sage: "It's a boy!"

There Will Always Be Something to Do

There will always be something to do, my boy;
  There will always be wrongs to right;
There will always be need for a manly breed
  And men unafraid to fight.
There will always be honor to guard, my boy;
  There will always be hills to climb,
And tasks to do, and battles new
  From now to the end of time.

There will always be dangers to face, my boy;
  There will always be goals to take;
Men shall be tried, when the roads divide,
  And proved by the choice they make.
There will always be burdens to bear, my boy;
  There will always be need to pray;
There will always be tears through the future
      years,
  As loved ones are borne away.

There will always be God to serve, my boy,
  And always the Flag above;
They shall call to you until life is through
  For courage and strength and love.
So these are things that I dream, my boy,
  And have dreamed since your life began:
That whatever befalls, when the old world calls,
  It shall find you a sturdy man.

Becoming a Dad

Old women say that men don't know
The pain through which all mothers go,
And maybe that is true, and yet
I vow I never shall forget
The night he came. I suffered, too,
Those bleak and dreary long hours through:
I paced the floor and mopped my brow
And waited for his glad wee-ow!
I went upstairs and then came down,
Because I saw the doctor frown
And knew beyond the slightest doubt
He wished to goodness I'd clear out.

I walked into the yard for air
And back again to hear her there,
And met the nurse, as calm as though
My world was not in deepest woe,
And when I questioned, seeking speech
Of consolation that would reach
Into my soul and strengthen me
For dreary hours that were to be:
" Progressing nicely! " that was all
She said and tip-toed down the hall;
" Progressing nicely! " nothing more,
And left me there to pace the floor.

And once the nurse came out in haste
For something that had been misplaced,

And I that had been growing bold
Then felt my blood grow icy cold;
And fear's stern chill swept over me.
I stood and watched and tried to see
Just what it was she came to get.
I haven't learned that secret yet.
I half-believe that nurse in white
Was adding fuel to my fright
And taking an unholy glee,
From time to time, in torturing me.

Then silence! To her room I crept
And was informed the doctor slept!
The doctor slept! Oh, vicious thought,
While she at death's door bravely fought
And suffered untold anguish deep,
The doctor lulled himself to sleep.
I looked and saw him stretched out flat
And could have killed the man for that.
Then morning broke, and oh, the joy;
With dawn there came to us our boy,
And in a glorious little while
I went in there and saw her smile!

I must have looked a human wreck,
My collar wilted at the neck,
My hair awry, my features drawn
With all the suffering I had borne.
She looked at me and softly said,

"If I were you, I'd go to bed."
Her's was the bitterer part, I know;
She traveled through the vale of woe,
But now when women folks recall
The pain and anguish of it all
I answer them in manner sad:
"It's no cinch to become a dad."

The Test

You can brag about the famous men you know;
    You may boast about the great men you have
        met,
Parsons, eloquent and wise; stars in histrionic
        skies;
    Millionaires and navy admirals, and yet
Fame and power and wealth and glory vanish
        fast;
    They are lusters that were never made to
        stick,
And the friends worth-while and true, are the
        happy smiling few
    Who come to call upon you when you're sick.

You may think it very fine to know the great;
    You may glory in some leader's words of
        praise;
You may tell with eyes aglow of the public men
        you know,

But the true friends seldom travel glory's
    ways,
And the day you're lying ill, lonely, pale and
    keeping still,
  With a fevered pulse, that's beating double
    quick,
Then it is you must depend on the old-familiar
    friend
  To come to call upon you when you're sick.

It is pleasing to receive a great man's nod,
  And it's good to know the big men of the land,
But the test of friendship true, isn't merely:
    " Howdy-do? "
  And a willingness to shake you by the hand.
If you want to know the friends who love you
    best,
  And the faithful from the doubtful you would
    pick,
It is not a mighty task; of yourself you've but
    to ask:
  " Does he come to call upon me when I'm
    sick? "

The Tramp

Eagerly he took my dime,
   Then shuffled on his way,
Thick with sin and filth and grime,
   But I wondered all that day
   How the man had gone astray.

Not to him the dime I gave;
   Not unto the man of woe,
Not to him who should be brave,
   Not to him who'd sunk so low,
   But the boy of long ago.

Passed his years of sin and shame
   Through the filth that all could see,
Out of what he is there came
   One more pitiful to me:
   Came the boy that used to be.

Smiling, full of promise glad,
   Stood a baby, like my own;
I beheld a glorious lad,
   Someone once had loved and known
   Out of which this wreck had grown!

Where, thought I, must lie the blame?
  Who has failed in such a way?
As all children come he came,
  There's a soul within his clay;
  Who has led his feet astray?

As he shuffled down the hall
  With the coin I'd never miss,
What, thought I, were fame and all
  Man may gain of earthly bliss,
  If my child should come to this!

The Lonely Garden

I wonder what the trees will say,
The trees that used to share his play,
An' knew him as the little lad
Who used to wander with his dad.
They've watched him grow from year to year
Since first the good Lord sent him here.
This shag-bark hick'ry, many a time,
The little fellow tried t' climb,
An' never a spring has come but he
Has called upon his favorite tree.
I wonder what they all will say
When they are told he's marched away.

I wonder what the birds will say,
The swallow an' the chatterin' jay,
The robin, an' the kill-deer, too.
For every one o' them, he knew,
An' every one o' them knew him,
An' hoppin' there from limb t' limb,
Waited each spring t' tell him all
They'd done an' seen since 'way last fall.
He was the first to greet 'em here
As they returned from year t' year;
An' now I wonder what they'll say
When they are told he's marched away.

I wonder how the roses there
Will get along without his care,
An' how the lilac bush will face
The loneliness about th' place;
For ev'ry spring an' summer, he
Has been the chum o' plant an' tree,
An' every livin' thing has known
A comradeship that's finer grown,
By havin' him from year t' year.
Now very soon they'll all be here,
An' I am wonderin' what they'll say
When they find out he's marched away.

Tinkerin' at Home

Some folks there be who seem to need excitement
    fast and furious,
An' reckon all the joys that have no thrill in 'em
    are spurious.
Some think that pleasure's only found down
    where the lights are shining,
An' where an orchestra's at work the while the
    folks are dining.
Still others seek it at their play, while some there
    are who roam,
But I am happiest when I am tinkerin' 'round the
    home.

I like to wear my oldest clothes, an' fuss around
    the yard,
An' dig a flower bed now an' then, and pensively
    regard
The mornin' glories climbin' all along the wooden
    fence,
An' do the little odds an' ends that aren't of
    consequence.
I like to trim the hedges, an' touch up the paint
    a bit,
An' sort of take a homely pride in keepin' all
    things fit.
An' I don't envy rich folks who are sailin' o'er
    the foam

When I can spend a day or two in tinkerin'
    'round the home.

If I were fixed with money, as some other people
    are,
I'd take things mighty easy; I'd not travel very
    far.
I'd jes' wear my oldest trousers an' my flannel
    shirt, an' stay
An' guard my vine an' fig tree in an old man's
    tender way.
I'd bathe my soul in sunshine every mornin',
    and I'd bend
My back to pick the roses; Oh, I'd be a watchful
    friend
To everything around the place, an' in the twi-
    light gloam
I'd thank the Lord for lettin' me jes' tinker
    'round the home.

But since I've got to hustle in the turmoil of the
    town,
An' don't expect I'll ever be allowed to settle
    down
An' live among the roses an' the tulips an' the
    phlox,
Or spend my time in carin' for the noddin' holly-
    hocks,

I've come to the conclusion that perhaps in
      Heaven I may
Get a chance to know the pleasures that I'm
      yearnin' for to-day;
An' I'm goin' to ask the good Lord, when I've
      climbed the golden stair,
If he'll kindly let me tinker 'round the home we've
      got up there.

When An Old Man Gets to Thinking

When an old man gets to thinking of the years
      he's traveled through,
He hears again the laughter of the little ones he
      knew.
He isn't counting money, and he isn't planning
      schemes;
He's at home with friendly people in the shadow
      of his dreams.

When he's lived through all life's trials and his
      sun is in the west,
When he's tasted all life's pleasures and he knows
      which ones were best,
Then his mind is stored with riches, not of silver
      and of gold,
But of happy smiling faces and the joys he
      couldn't hold.

Could we see what he is seeing as he's dreaming
    in his chair,
We should find no scene of struggle in the dis-
    tance over there.
As he counts his memory treasures, we should see
    some shady lane
Where's he walking with his sweetheart, young,
    and arm in arm again.

We should meet with friendly people, simple,
    tender folk and kind,
That had once been glad to love him. In his
    dreaming we should find
All the many little beauties that enrich the lives
    of men
That the eyes of youth scarce notice and the
    poets seldom pen.

Age will tell you that the memory is the treasure-
    house of man.
Gold and fleeting fame may vanish, but life's
    riches never can;
For the little home of laughter and the voice of
    every friend
And the joys of real contentment linger with us
    to the end.

The Evening Prayer

Little girlie, kneeling there,
Speaking low your evening prayer,
In your cunning little nightie
With your pink toes peeping through,
With your eyes closed and your hands
Tightly clasped, while daddy stands
In the doorway, just to hear the
"God bless papa," lisped by you,
You don't know just what I feel,
As I watch you nightly kneel
By your trundle bed and whisper
Soft and low your little prayer!
But in all I do or plan,
I'm a bigger, better man
Every time I hear you asking
God to make my journey fair.

Little girlie, kneeling there,
Lisping low your evening prayer,
Asking God above to bless me
At the closing of each day,
Oft the tears come to my eyes,
And I feel a big lump rise
In my throat, that I can't swallow,
And I sometimes turn away.
In the morning, when I wake,
And my post of duty take,

I go forth with new-born courage
To accomplish what is fair;
And, throughout the live-long day,
I am striving every way
To come back to you each evening
And be worthy of your prayer.

Thoughts of a Father

We've never seen the Father here, but we have
    known the Son,
The finest type of manhood since the world was
    first begun.
And, summing up the works of God, I write with
    reverent pen,
The greatest is the Son He sent to cheer the lives
    of men.

Through Him we learned the ways of God and
    found the Father's love;
The Son it was who won us back to Him who
    reigns above.
The Lord did not come down himself to prove
    to men His worth,
He sought our worship through the Child He
    placed upon the earth.

How can I best express my life? Wherein does
 greatness lie?
How can I long remembrance win, since I am
 born to die?
Both fame and gold are selfish things; their
 charms may quickly flee,
But I'm the father of a boy who came to speak
 for me.

In him lies all I hope to be; his splendor shall be
 mine;
I shall have done man's greatest work if only
 he is fine.
If some day he shall help the world long after
 I am dead,
In all that men shall say of him my praises shall
 be said.

It matters not what I may win of fleeting gold
 or fame,
My hope of joy depends alone on what my boy
 shall claim.
My story must be told through him, for him I
 work and plan,
Man's greatest duty is to be the father of a man.

Pleasing Dad

When I was but a little lad, not more than two or
    three,
I noticed in a general way my dad was proud of
    me.
He liked the little ways I had, the simple things
    I said;
Sometimes he gave me words of praise, sometimes
    he stroked my head;
And when I'd done a thing worth while, the
    thought that made me glad
Was always that I'd done my best, and that
    would please my dad.

I can look back to-day and see how proud he
    used to be
When I'd come home from school and say they'd
    recommended me.
I didn't understand it then, for school boys never
    do,
But in a vague and general way it seems to me
    I knew
That father took great pride in me, and wanted
    me to shine,
And that it meant a lot to him when I'd done
    something fine.

Then one day out of school I went, amid the
    great world's hum,

An office boy, and father watched each night to
    see me come.
And I recall how proud he was of me that
    wondrous day
When I could tell him that, unasked, the firm had
    raised my pay.
I still can feel that hug he gave, I understand the
    joy
It meant to him to learn that men were trusting
    in his boy.

I wonder will it please my dad? How oft the
    thought occurs
When I am stumbling on the paths, beset with
    briars and burrs!
He isn't here to see me now, alone my race I
    run,
And yet some day I'll go to him and tell him all
    I've done.
And oh I pray that when we meet beyond life's
    stormy sea
That he may claim the old-time joy of being
    proud of me.

The Change-Worker

A feller don't start in to think of himself, an'
    the part that he's playin' down here,
When there's nobody lookin' to him fer support,
    an' he don't give a thought to next year.
His faults don't seem big an' his habits no worse
    than a whole lot of others he knows,
An' he don't seem to care what his neighbors may
    say, as heedlessly forward he goes.
He don't stop to think if it's wrong or it's right;
    with his speech he is careless or glib,
Till the minute the nurse lets him into the room
    to see what's asleep in the crib.

An' then as he looks at that bundle o' red, an' the
    wee little fingers an' toes,
An' he knows it's his flesh an' his blood that is
    there, an' will be just like him when it
    grows,
It comes in a flash to a feller right then, there is
    more here than pleasure or pelf,
An' the sort of a man his baby will be is the sort
    of a man he's himself.
Then he kisses the mother an' kisses the child, an'
    goes out determined that he
Will endeavor to be just the sort of a man that
    he's wantin' his baby to be.

A feller don't think that it matters so much what
      he does till a baby arrives;
He sows his wild oats an' he has his gay fling an'
      headlong in pleasure he dives;
An' a drink more or less doesn't matter much
      then, for life is a comedy gay,
But the moment a crib is put in the home, an' a
      baby has come there to stay,
He thinks of the things he has done in the past,
      an' it strikes him as hard as a blow,
That the path he has trod in the past is a path
      that he don't want his baby to go.

I ain't much to preach, an' I can't just express
      in the way that your clever men can
The thoughts that I think, but it seems to me now
      that when God wants to rescue a man
From himself an' the follies that harmless ap-
      pear, but which, under the surface, are
      grim,
He summons the angel of infancy sweet, an' sends
      down a baby to him.
For in that way He opens his eyes to himself, and
      He gives him the vision to see
That his duty's to be just the sort of a man that
      he's wantin' his baby to be.

The Simple Things

I would not be too wise — so very wise
    That I must sneer at simple songs and creeds,
And let the glare of wisdom blind my eyes
    To humble people and their humble needs.

I would not care to climb so high that I
    Could never hear the children at their play,
Could only see the people passing by,
    And never hear the cheering words they say.

I would not know too much — too much to smile
    At trivial errors of the heart and hand,
Nor be too proud to play the friend the while,
    Nor cease to help and know and understand.

I would not care to sit upon a throne,
    Or build my house upon a mountain-top,
Where I must dwell in glory all alone
    And never friend come in or poor man stop.

God grant that I may live upon this earth
    And face the tasks which every morning
      brings
And never lose the glory and the worth
    Of humble service and the simple things.

What We Need

We were settin' there an' smokin' of our pipes,
　　discussin' things,
Like licker, votes for wimmin, an' the totterin'
　　thrones o' kings,
When he ups an' strokes his whiskers with his
　　hand an' says t'me:
"Changin' laws an' legislatures ain't, as fur as
　　I can see,
Goin' to make this world much better, unless
　　somehow we can
Find a way to make a better an' a finer sort
　　o' man.

"The trouble ain't with statutes or with systems
　　— not at all;
It's with humans jest like we air an' their petty
　　ways an' small.
We could stop our writin' law-books an' our
　　regulatin' rules
If a better sort of manhood was the product of
　　our schools.
For the things that we air needin' ain't no writin'
　　from a pen
Or bigger guns to shoot with, but a bigger type
　　of men.

" I reckon all these problems air jest ornery like
  the weeds.
They grow in soil that oughta nourish only
  decent deeds,
An' they waste our time an' fret us when, if we
  were thinkin' straight
An' livin' right, they wouldn't be so terrible
  an' great.
A good horse needs no snaffle, an' a good man,
  I opine,
Doesn't need a law to check him or to force him
  into line.

" If we ever start in teachin' to our children,
  year by year,
How to live with one another, there'll be less o'
  trouble here.
If we'd teach 'em how to neighbor an' to walk
  in honor's ways,
We could settle every problem which the mind
  o' man can raise.
What we're needin' isn't systems or some regu-
  latin' plan,
But a bigger an' a finer an' a truer type o' man."

Looking Back

I might have been rich if I'd wanted the gold
    instead of the friendships I've made.
I might have had fame if I'd sought for renown
    in the hours when I purposely played.
Now I'm standing to-day on the far edge of
    life, and I'm just looking backward to see
What I've done with the years and the days that
    were mine, and all that has happened to me.

I haven't built much of a fortune to leave to
    those who shall carry my name,
And nothing I've done shall entitle me now to
    a place on the tablets of fame.
But I've loved the great sky and its spaces of
    blue; I've lived with the birds and the trees;
I've turned from the splendor of silver and gold
    to share in such pleasures as these.

I've given my time to the children who came;
    together we've romped and we've played,
And I wouldn't exchange the glad hours spent
    with them for the money that I might have
    made.
I chose to be known and be loved by the few,
    and was deaf to the plaudits of men;

And I'd make the same choice should the chance
    come to me to live my life over again.

I've lived with my friends and I've shared in
    their joys, known sorrow with all of its
    tears;
I have harvested much from my acres of life,
    though some say I've squandered my years.
For much that is fine has been mine to enjoy,
    and I think I have lived to my best,
And I have no regret, as I'm nearing the end,
    for the gold that I might have possessed.

God Made This Day for Me

Jes' the sort o' weather and jes' the sort of sky
Which seem to suit my fancy, with the white
    clouds driftin' by
On a sea o' smooth blue water. Oh, I ain't an
    egotist,
With an " I " in all my thinkin', but I'm willin'
    to insist
That the Lord who made us humans an' the
    birds in every tree
Knows my special sort o' weather an' he made
    this day fer me.

This is jes' my style o' weather — sunshine
    floodin' all the place,

An' the breezes from the eastward blowin'
  gently on my face;
An' the woods chock full o' singin' till you'd
  think birds never had
A single care to fret 'em or a grief to make
  'em sad.
Oh, I settle down contented in the shadow of
  a tree,
An' tell myself right proudly that the day was
  made fer me.

It's my day, my sky an' sunshine, an' the temper
  o' the breeze —
Here's the weather I would fashion could I run
  things as I please:
Beauty dancin' all around me, music ringin'
  everywhere,
Like a weddin' celebration — why, I've plumb
  fergot my care
An' the tasks I should be doin' fer the rainy
  days to be,
While I'm huggin' the delusion that God made
  this day fer me.

The Grate Fire

I'm sorry for a fellow if he cannot look and see
In a grate fire's friendly flaming all the joys
    which used to be.
If in quiet contemplation of a cheerful ruddy
    blaze
He sees nothing there recalling all his happy
    yesterdays,
Then his mind is dead to fancy and his life is
    bleak and bare,
And he's doomed to walk the highways that are
    always thick with care.

When the logs are dry as tinder and they crackle
    with the heat,
And the sparks, like merry children, come
    a-dancing round my feet,
In the cold, long nights of autumn I can sit
    before the blaze
And watch a panorama born of all my yester-
    days.
I can leave the present burdens and the mo-
    ment's bit of woe,
And claim once more the gladness of the bygone
    long-ago.

No loved ones ever vanish from the grate fire's
    merry throng;
No hands in death are folded and no lips are
    stilled to song.
All the friends who were are living — like the
    sparks that fly about
They come romping out to greet me with the
    same old merry shout,
Till it seems to me I'm playing once again on
    boyhood's stage,
Where there's no such thing as sorrow and
    there's no such thing as age.

I can be the care-free schoolboy! I can play the
    lover, too!
I can walk through Maytime orchards with the
    old sweetheart I knew,
I can dream the glad dreams over, greet the old
    familiar friends
In a land where there's no parting and the
    laughter never ends.
All the gladness life has given from a grate fire
    I reclaim,
And I'm sorry for the fellow who sees nothing
    there but flame.

The Homely Man

Looks as though a cyclone hit him —
Can't buy clothes that seem to fit him;
An' his cheeks are rough like leather,
Made for standin' any weather.
Outwards he was fashioned plainly,
Loose o' joint an' blamed ungainly,
But I'd give a lot if I'd
Been built half as fine inside.

Best thing I can tell you of him
Is the way the children love him.
Now an' then I get to thinkin'
He's much like old Abe Lincoln;
Homely like a gargoyle graven —
Worse'n that when he's unshaven;
But I'd take his ugly phiz
Jes' to have a heart like his.

I ain't over-sentimental,
But old Blake is so blamed gentle
An' so thoughtful-like of others
He reminds us of our mothers.
Rough roads he is always smoothin',
An' his way is, Oh, so soothin',
That he takes away the sting
When your heart is sorrowing.

Children gather round about him
Like they can't get on without him.
An' the old depend upon him,
Pilin' all their burdens on him,
Like as though the thing that grieves 'em
Has been lifted when he leaves 'em.
Homely? That can't be denied,
But he's glorious inside.

The Joys We Miss

There never comes a lonely day but that we
    miss the laughing ways
Of those who used to walk with us through all
    our happy yesterdays.
We seldom miss the earthly great — the famous
    men that life has known —
But, as the years go racing by, we miss the
    friends we used to own.

The chair wherein he used to sit recalls the
    kindly father true,
For, Oh, so filled with fun he was, and, Oh,
    so very much he knew!
And as we face the problems grave with which
    the years of life are filled,
We miss the hand which guided us and miss
    the voice forever stilled.

We little guessed how much he did to smooth
    our pathway day by day,
How much of joy he brought to us, how much
    of care he brushed away;
But now that we must tread alone the thorough-
    fare of life, we find
How many burdens we were spared by him who
    was so brave and kind.

Death robs the living, not the dead — they
    sweetly sleep whose tasks are done;
But we are weaker than before who still must
    live and labor on.
For when come care and grief to us, and heavy
    burdens bring us woe,
We miss the smiling, helpful friends on whom
    we leaned long years ago.

We miss the happy, tender ways of those who
    brought us mirth and cheer;
We never gather round the hearth but that we
    wish our friends were near;
For peace is born of simple things — a kindly
    word, a goodnight kiss,
The prattle of a babe, and love — these are the
    vanished joys we miss.

The Better Job

If I were running a factory
I'd stick up a sign for all to see;
I'd print it large and I'd nail it high
On every wall that the men walked by;
And I'd have it carry this sentence clear:
" The 'better job' that you want is here! "

It's the common trait of the human race
To pack up and roam from place to place;
Men have done it for ages and do it now;
Seeking to better themselves somehow
They quit their posts and their tools they drop
For a better job in another shop.

It may be I'm wrong, but I hold to this —
That something surely must be amiss
When a man worth while must move away
For the better job with the better pay;
And something is false in our own renown
When men can think of a better town.

So if I were running a factory
I'd stick up this sign for all to see,
Which never an eye in the place could miss:
" There isn't a better town than this!
You need not go wandering, far or near —
The 'better job' that you want is here! "

My Religion

My religion's lovin' God, who made us, one
    and all,
Who marks, no matter where it be, the humble
    sparrow's fall;
An' my religion's servin' Him the very best I can
By not despisin' anything He made, especially
    man!
It's lovin' sky an' earth an' sun an' birds an'
    flowers an' trees,
But lovin' human beings more than any one
    of these.

I ain't no hand at preachin' an' I can't expound
    the creeds;
I fancy every fellow's faith must satisfy his
    needs
Or he would hunt for something else. An' I
    can't tell the why
An' wherefore of the doctrines deep — and
    what's more I don't try.
I reckon when this life is done and we can know
    His plan,
God won't be hard on anyone who's tried to be
    a man.

My religion doesn't hinge on some one rite or
    word;
I hold that any honest prayer a mortal makes
    is heard;
To love a church is well enough, but some get
    cold with pride
An' quite forget their fellowmen for whom the
    Saviour died;
I fancy he best worships God, when all is said
    an' done,
Who tries to be, from day to day, a friend to
    everyone.

If God can mark the sparrow's fall, I don't
    believe He'll fail
To notice us an' how we act when doubts an'
    fears assail;
I think He'll hold what's in our hearts above
    what's in our creeds,
An' judge all our religion here by our recorded
    deeds;
An' since man is God's greatest work since life
    on earth began,
He'll get to Heaven, I believe, who helps his
    fellowman.

What *I* Call Living

The miser thinks he's living when he's hoarding
    up his gold;
The soldier calls it living when he's doing
    something bold;
The sailor thinks it living to be tossed upon
    the sea,
And upon this vital subject no two of us agree.
But I hold to the opinion, as I walk my way
    along,
That living's made of laughter and good-fellow-
    ship and song.

I wouldn't call it living always to be seeking
    gold,
To bank all the present gladness for the days
    when I'll be old.
I wouldn't call it living to spend all my strength
    for fame,
And forego the many pleasures which to-day are
    mine to claim.
I wouldn't for the splendor of the world set out
    to roam,
And forsake my laughing children and the
    peace I know at home.

Oh, the thing that I call living isn't gold or
    fame at all!

It's good-fellowship and sunshine, and it's roses
    by the wall;
It's evenings glad with music and a hearth fire
    that's ablaze,
And the joys which come to mortals in a
    thousand different ways.
It is laughter and contentment and the struggle
    for a goal;
It is everything that's needful in the shaping
    of a soul.

If This Were All

If this were all of life we'll know,
    If this brief space of breath
Were all there is to human toil,
    If death were really death,
And never should the soul arise
    A finer world to see,
How foolish would our struggles seem,
    How grim the earth would be!

If living were the whole of life,
    To end in seventy years,
How pitiful its joys would seem!
    How idle all its tears!
There'd be no faith to keep us true,
    No hope to keep us strong,
And only fools would cherish dreams —
    No smile would last for long.

How purposeless the strife would be
  If there were nothing more,
If there were not a plan to serve,
  An end to struggle for!
No reason for a mortal's birth
  Except to have him die —
How silly all the goals would seem
  For which men bravely try.

There must be something after death;
  Behind the toil of man
There must exist a God divine
  Who's working out a plan;
And this brief journey that we know
  As life must really be
The gateway to a finer world
  That some day we shall see.

When the Minister Calls

My Paw says that it used to be,
Whenever the minister came for tea,
'At they sat up straight in their chairs at night
An' put all their common things out o' sight,
An' nobody cracked a joke or grinned,
But they talked o' the way that people sinned,
An' the burnin' fires that would cook you sure
When you came to die, if you wasn't pure —
Such a gloomy affair it used to be
Whenever the minister came for tea.

But now when the minister comes to call
I get him out for a game of ball,
And you'd never know if you'd see him bat,
Without any coat or vest or hat,
That he is a minister, no, siree!
He looks like a regular man to me.
An' he knows just how to go down to the dirt
For the grounders hot without gettin' hurt —
An' when they call us, both him an' me
Have to git washed up again for tea.

Our minister says if you'll just play fair
You'll be fit for heaven or anywhere;
An' fun's all right if your hands are clean
An' you never cheat an' you don't get mean.
He says that he never has understood

Why a feller can't play an' still be good.
An' my Paw says that he's just the kind
Of a minister that he likes to find —
So I'm always tickled as I can be
Whenever our minister comes for tea.

The Age of Ink

Swiftly the changes come. Each day
Sees some lost beauty blown away
And some new touch of lovely grace
Come into life to take its place.
The little babe that once we had
One morning woke a roguish lad;
The babe that we had put to bed
Out of our arms and lives had fled.

Frocks vanished from our castle then,
Ne'er to be worn or seen again,
And in his knickerbocker pride
He boasted pockets at each side
And stored them deep with various things—
Stones, tops and jacks and colored strings;
Then for a time we claimed the joy
Of calling him our little boy.

Brief was the reign of such a spell.
One morning sounded out a bell;

With tears I saw her brown eyes swim
And knew that it was calling him.
Time, the harsh master of us all,
Was bidding him to heed his call;
This shadow fell across life's pool—
Our boy was on his way to school.

Our little boy! And still we dreamed,
For such a little boy he seemed!
And yesterday, with eyes aglow
Like one who has just come to know
Some great and unexpected bliss,
He bounded in, announcing this:
"Oh, Dad! Oh, Ma! Say, what d'you think?
This year we're going to write with ink!"

Here was a change I'd not foreseen,
Another step from what had been.
I paused a little while to think
About this older age of ink—
What follows this great step, thought I,
What next shall come as the time goes by?
And something said: "His pathway leads
Unto the day he'll write with deeds."

No Use Sighin'

No use frettin' when the rain comes down,
No use grievin' when the gray clouds frown,
No use sighin' when the wind blows strong,
No use wailin' when the world's all wrong;
Only thing that a man can do
Is work an' wait till the sky gets blue.

No use mopin' when you lose the game,
No use sobbin' if you're free from shame,
No use cryin' when the harm is done,
Just keep on tryin' an' workin' on;
Only thing for a man to do,
Is take the loss an' begin anew.

No use weepin' when the milk is spilled,
No use growlin' when your hopes are killed,
No use kickin' when the lightnin' strikes
Or the floods come along an' wreck your dykes;
Only thing for a man right then
Is to grit his teeth an' start again.

For it's how life is an' the way things are
That you've got to face if you travel far;
An' the storms will come an' the failures, too,
An' plans go wrong spite of all you do;
An' the only thing that will help you win,
Is the grit of a man and a stern set chin.

Father To Son

The times have proved my judgment bad.
  I've followed foolish hopes in vain,
And as you look upon your dad
  You see him commonplace and plain.
No brilliant wisdom I enjoy;
  The jests I tell have grown to bore you,
But just remember this, my boy:
  'Twas I who chose your mother for you!

Against the blunders I have made
  And all the things I've failed to do,
The weaknesses which I've displayed,
  This fact remains forever true;
This to my credit still must stay
  And don't forget it, I implore you;
Whatever else you think or say:
  'Twas I who chose your mother for you!

Chuckle at times behind my back
  About the ties and hats I wear.
Sound judgment I am known to lack.
  Smile at the ancient views I air.
Say if you will I'm often wrong,
  But with my faults strewn out before you,
Remember this your whole life long:
  'Twas I who chose your mother for you!

Your life from babyhood to now
  Has known the sweetness of her care;
Her tender hand has soothed your brow;
  Her love gone with you everywhere.

Through every day and every night
  You've had an angel to adore you.
So bear in mind I once was right:
  'Twas I who chose your mother for you!

Nothing to Laugh At

'Taint nothin' to laugh at as I can see!
If you'd been stung by a bumble bee,
An' your nose wuz swelled an' it smarted, too,
You wouldn't want people to laugh at you.
If you had a lump that wuz full of fire,
Like you'd been touched by a red hot wire,
An' your nose spread out like a load of hay,
You wouldn't want strangers who come your
        way
To ask you to let 'em see the place
An' laugh at you right before your face.

What's funny about it, I'd like to know?
It isn't a joke to be hurted so!
An' how wuz I ever on earth to tell
'At the pretty flower which I stooped to smell
In our backyard wuz the very one

Which a bee wuz busily working on?
An' jus' as I got my nose down there,
He lifted his foot an' kicked for fair,
An' he planted his stinger right into me,
But it's nothin' to laugh at as I can see.

I let out a yell an' my Maw came out
To see what the trouble wuz all about.
She says from my shriek she wuz sure 'at I
Had been struck by a motor car passin' by;
But when she found what the matter wuz
She laughed just like ever'body does
An' she made me stand while she poked about
To pull his turrible stinger out.
An' my Pa laughed, too, when he looked at me,
But it's nothin' to laugh at, as I can see.

My Maw put witch hazel on the spot
To take down the swellin' but it has not.
It seems to git bigger as time goes by
An' I can't see good out o' this one eye;
An' it hurts clean down to my very toes
Whenever I've got to blow my nose.
An' all I can say is when this gits well
There ain't any flowers I'll stoop to smell.
I'm through disturbin' a bumble bee,
But it's nothin' to laugh at, as I can see.

Boy O' Mine

Boy o' mine, boy o' mine, this is my prayer for
you,
This is my dream and my thought and my care
for you:
Strong be the spirit which dwells in the breast
of you,
Never may folly or shame get the best of you;
You shall be tempted in fancied security,
But make no choice that is stained with im-
purity.

Boy o' mine, boy o' mine, time shall command
of you
Thought from the brain of you, work from the
hand of you;
Voices of pleasure shall whisper and call to you,
Luring you far from the hard tasks that fall
to you;
Then as you're meeting life's bitterest test of
men,
God grant you strength to be true as the best
of men.

Boy o' mine, boy o' mine, singing your way
　　along,
Cling to your laughter and cheerfully play
　　along;
Kind to your neighbor be, offer your hand to
　　him,
You shall grow great as your heart shall ex-
　　pand to him;
But when for victory sweet you are fighting
　　there,
Know that your record of life you are writing
　　there.

Boy o' mine, boy o' mine, this is my prayer for
　　you;
Never may shame pen one line of despair for
　　you;
Never may conquest or glory mean all to you;
Cling to your honor whatever shall fall to you;
Rather than victory, rather than fame to you,
Choose to be true and let nothing bring shame
　　to you.

A Feller's Hat

It's funny 'bout a feller's hat—
He can't remember where it's at,
Or where he took it off, or when,
The time he's wantin' it again.
He knows just where he leaves his shoes;
His sweater he won't often lose;
An' he can find his rubbers, but
He can't tell where his hat is put.

A feller's hat gets anywhere.
Sometimes he'll find it in a chair,
Or on the sideboard, or maybe
It's in the kitchen, just where he
Gave it a toss beside the sink
When he came in to get a drink,
An' then forgot—but anyhow
He never knows where it is now.

A feller's hat is never where
He thinks it is when he goes there;
It's never any use to look
For it upon a closet hook,
'Cause it is always in some place
It shouldn't be, to his disgrace,
An' he will find it, like as not,
Behind some radiator hot.

A feller's hat can get away
From him 'most any time of day,
So he can't ever find it when
He wants it to go out again;
It hides in corners dark an' grim
An' seems to want to bother him;
It disappears from sight somehow—
I wish I knew where mine is now.

The Scrubwoman

The woman who scrubs the floors appears
As old as one hundred and forty years.
Yet though aching and weary her bones must be,
When I say "good evening," she smiles at me.
There's a band of gold on her finger red.
The man who placed it there must be dead,

And I wonder what sorrowful, sordid tale
Has had its end in that mop and pail.
Youth and beauty are hers no more,
The close of her hope is a marble floor.
As she wrings out her mop this thought occurs:
So life has wrung dry every dream of hers.

She Mothered Five

She mothered five!
Night after night she watched a little bed,
Night after night she cooled a fevered head,
Day after day she guarded little feet,
Taught little minds the dangers of the street,
Taught little lips to utter simple prayers,
Whispered of strength that some day would be
    theirs,
And trained them all to use it as they should.
She gave her babies to the nation's good.

She mothered five!
She gave her beauty—from her cheeks let fade
Their rose-blush beauty—to her mother trade.
She saw the wrinkles furrowing her brow,
Yet smiling said: "My boy grows stronger
    now."
When pleasures called she turned away and
    said:
"I dare not leave my babies to be fed
By strangers' hands; besides they are too small;
I must be near to hear them when they call."

She mothered five!
Night after night they sat about her knee
And heard her tell of what some day would be.

From her they learned that in the world outside
Are cruelty and vice and selfishness and pride;
From her they learned the wrongs they ought
    to shun,
What things to love, what work must still be
    done.
She led them through the labyrinth of youth
And brought five men and women up to truth.

She mothered five!
Her name may be unknown save to the few;
Of her the outside world but little knew;
But somewhere five are treading virtue's ways,
Serving the world and brightening its days;
Somewhere are five, who, tempted, stand up-
    right,
Who cling to honor, keep her memory bright;
Somewhere this mother toils and is alive
No more as one, but in the breasts of five.

Little Girls Are Best

Little girls are mighty nice,
    Take 'em any way they come;
They are always worth their price;
    Life without 'em would be glum;
Run earth's lists of treasures through,
    Pile 'em high until they fall,
Gold an' costly jewels, too—
    Little girls are best of all.

Nothing equals 'em on earth!
   I'm an old man an' I know
Any little girl is worth
   More than all the gold below;
Eyes o' blue or brown or gray,
   Raven hair or golden curls,
There's no joy on earth to-day
   Quite so fine as little girls.

Pudgy nose or freckled face,
   Fairy-like or plain to see,
God has surely blessed the place
   Where a little girl may be;
They're the jewels of His crown
   Dropped to earth from heaven above,
Like wee angel souls sent down
   To remind us of His love.

God has made some lovely things—
   Roses red an' skies o' blue,
Trees an' babbling silver springs,
   Gardens glistening with dew—
But take every gift to man,
   Big an' little, great an' small,
Judge it on its merits, an'
   Little girls are best of all!

The Christmas Gift for Mother

In the Christmas times of the long ago,
There was one event we used to know
   That was better than any other;
It wasn't the toys that we hoped to get,
But the talks we had — and I hear them yet —
   Of the gift we'd buy for Mother.

If ever love fashioned a Christmas gift,
Or saved its money and practiced thrift,
   'Twas done in those days, my brother —
Those golden times of Long Gone By,
Of our happiest years, when you and I
   Talked over the gift for Mother.

We hadn't gone forth on our different ways
Nor coined our lives into yesterdays
   In the fires that smelt and smother,
And we whispered and planned in our youthful
    glee
Of that marvelous " something" which was to be
   The gift of our hearts to Mother.

It had to be all that our purse could give,
Something she'd treasure while she could live.
   And better than any other.
We gave it the best of our love and thought,
And, Oh, the joy when at last we'd bought
   That marvelous gift for Mother!

Now I think as we go on our different ways,
Of the joy of those vanished yesterdays.
  How good it would be, my brother,
If this Christmas-time we could only know
That same sweet thrill of the Long Ago
  When we shared in the gift for Mother.

Bedtime

It's bedtime, and we lock the door,
Put out the lights — the day is o'er;
All that can come of good or ill,
The record of this day to fill,
Is written down; the worries cease,
And old and young may rest in peace.

We knew not when we started out
What dangers hedged us all about,
What little pleasures we should gain,
What should be ours to bear of pain.
But now the fires are burning low,
And this day's history we know.

No harm has come. The laughter here
Has been unbroken by a tear;
We've met no hurt too great to bear
We have not had to bow to care;
The children all are safe in bed,
There's nothing now for us to dread.

When bedtime comes and we can say
That we have safely lived the day,
How sweet the calm that settles down
And shuts away the noisy town!
There is no danger now to fear
Until to-morrow shall appear.

When the long bedtime comes, and I
In sleep eternal come to lie —
When life has nothing more in store,
And silently I close the door,
God grant my weary soul may claim
Security from hurt and shame.

The Willing Horse

I'd rather be the willing horse that people ride
    to death
  Than be the proud and haughty steed that
    children dare not touch;
I'd rather haul a merry pack and finish out of
    breath
  Than never leave the barn to toil because I'm
    worth too much.
So boast your noble pedigrees
And talk of manners, if you please —
The weary horse enjoys his ease
  When all his work is done;
The willing horse, day in and out,
Can hear the merry children shout
And every time they are about
  He shares in all their fun.

I want no guards beside my door to pick and
    choose my friends for me;
  I would not be shut off from men as is the
    fancy steed;
I do not care when I go by that no one turns
    his eyes to see
  The dashing manner of my gait which marks
    my noble breed;

I am content to trudge the road
And willingly to draw my load —
Sometimes to know the spur and goad
  When I begin to lag;
I'd rather feel the collar jerk
And tug at me, the while I work,
Than all the tasks of life to shirk
  As does the stylish nag.

So let me be the willing horse that now and
    then is overtasked,
  Let me be one the children love and freely
    dare to ride —
I'd rather be the gentle steed of which too much
    is sometimes asked
  Than be the one that never knows the young-
    sters at his side.
So drive me wheresoe'er you will,
On level road or up the hill,
Pile on my back the burdens still
  And run me out of breath —
In love and friendship, day by day,
And kindly words I'll take my pay;
A willing horse; that is the way
  I choose to meet my death.

What Makes an Artist

We got to talking art one day, discussing in a
    general way
  How some can match with brush and paint
    the glory of a tree,
And some in stone can catch the things of which
    the dreamy poet sings,
  While others seem to have no way to tell the
    joys they see.

Old Blake had sat in silence there and let each
    one of us declare
  Our notions of what's known as art, until
    he'd heard us through;
And then said he: " It seems to me that any
    man, whoe'er he be,
  Becomes an artist by the good he daily tries
    to do.

" He need not write the books men read to be
    an artist. No, indeed!
  He need not work with paint and brush to
    show his love of art;
Who does a kindly deed to-day and helps
    another on his way,
  Has painted beauty on a face and played the
    poet's part.

" Though some of us cannot express our inmost
    thoughts of loveliness,
  We prove we love the beautiful by how we
    act and live;
The poet singing of a tree no greater poet is
    than he
  Who finds it in his heart some care unto a
    tree to give.

" Though he who works in marble stone the
    name of artist here may own,
  No less an artist is the man who guards his
    children well;
'Tis art to love the fine and true; by what we
    are and what we do
  How much we love life's nobler things to all
    the world we tell."

She Powders Her Nose

A woman is queer, there's no doubt about that.
She hates to be thin and she hates to be fat;
One minute it's laughter, the next it's a cry —
You can't understand her, however you try;
But there's one thing about her which everyone
    knows —
A woman's not dressed till she powders her nose.

You never can tell what a woman will say;
She's a law to herself every hour of the day.
It keeps a man guessing to know what to do,
And mostly he's wrong when his guessing is
    through;
But this you can bet on, wherever she goes
She'll find some occasion to powder her nose.

I've studied the sex for a number of years;
I've watched her in laughter and seen her in
    tears;
On her ways and her whims I have pondered
    a lot,
To find what will please her and just what will
    not;
But all that I've learned from the start to the
    close
Is that sooner or later she'll powder her nose.

At church or a ball game, a dance or a show,
There's one thing about her I know that I
    know —
At weddings or funerals, dinners of taste,
You can bet that her hand will dive into her
    waist,
And every few minutes she'll strike up a pose,
And the whole world must wait till she powders
    her nose.

The Chip on Your Shoulder

You'll learn when you're older that chip on
    your shoulder
  Which you dare other boys to upset,
And stand up and fight for and struggle and
    smite for,
  Has caused you much shame and regret.
When Time, life's adviser, has made you much
    wiser,
  You won't be so quick with the blow;
You won't be so willing to fight for a shilling,
  And change a good friend to a foe.

You won't be a sticker for trifles, and bicker
  And quarrel for nothing at all;
You'll grow to be kinder, more thoughtful and
    blinder
  To faults which are petty and small.
You won't take the trouble your two fists to
    double
  When someone your pride may offend;
When with rage now you bristle you'll smile
    or you'll whistle,
  And keep the good will of a friend.

You'll learn when you're older that chip on your
    shoulder
  Which proudly you battle to guard,

Has frequently shamed you and often defamed
    you
  And left you a record that's marred!
When you've grown calm and steady, you won't
    be so ready
  To fight for a difference that's small,
For you'll know, when you're older that chip
    on your shoulder
  Is only a chip after all.

All for the Best

Things mostly happen for the best.
However hard it seems to-day,
When some fond plan has gone astray
Or what you've wished for most is lost
An' you sit countin' up the cost
With eyes half-blind by tears o' grief
While doubt is chokin' out belief,
You'll find when all is understood
That what seemed bad was really good.

Life can't be counted in a day.
The present rain that will not stop
Next autumn means a bumper crop.
We wonder why some things must be —
Care's purpose we can seldom see —

An' yet long afterwards we turn
To view the past, an' then we learn
That what once filled our minds with doubt
Was good for us as it worked out.

I've never known an hour of care
But that I've later come to see
That it has brought some joy to me.
Even the sorrows I have borne,
Leavin' me lonely an' forlorn
An' hurt an' bruised an' sick at heart,
In life's great plan have had a part.
An' though I could not understand
Why I should bow to Death's command,
As time went on I came to know
That it was really better so.

Things mostly happen for the best.
So narrow is our vision here
That we are blinded by a tear
An' stunned by every hurt an' blow
Which comes to-day to strike us low.
An' yet some day we turn an' find
That what seemed cruel once was kind.
Most things, I hold, are wisely planned
If we could only understand.

Committee Meetings

For this and that and various things
   It seems that men must get together,
To purchase cups or diamond rings
   Or to discuss the price of leather.
From nine to ten, or two to three,
   Or any hour that's fast and fleeting,
There is a constant call for me
   To go to some committee meeting.

The church has serious work to do,
   The lodge and club has need of workers,
They ask for just an hour or two —
   Surely I will not join the shirkers?
Though I have duties of my own
   I should not drop before completing,
There comes the call by telephone
   To go to some committee meeting.

No longer may I eat my lunch
   In quietude and contemplation;
I must foregather with the bunch
   To raise a fund to save the nation.
And I must talk of plans and schemes
   The while a scanty bite I'm eating,
Until I vow to-day it seems
   My life is one committee meeting.

When over me the night shall fall,
 And my poor soul goes upwards winging
Unto that heavenly realm, where all
 Is bright with joy and gay with singing,
I hope to hear St. Peter say —
 And I shall thank him for the greeting:
" Come in and rest from day to day;
 Here there is no committee meeting!"

Pa and the Monthly Bills

When Ma gets out the monthly bills and sets
  them all in front of Dad,
She makes us children run away because she
  knows he may get mad;
An' then she smiles a bit and says: " I hope
  you will not fuss and fret —
There's nothing here except the things I abso-
  lutely had to get!"
An' Pa he looks 'em over first. " The things you
  had to have!" says he;
" I s'pose that we'd have died without that
  twenty dollar longeree."

Then he starts in to write the checks for laun-
  dry an' for light an' gas,
An' never says a word 'bout them — because
  they're small he lets 'em pass.

But when he starts to grunt an' groan, an'
    stops the while his pipe he fills,
We know that he is gettin' down to where Ma's
    hid the bigger bills.
"Just what we had to have," says he, "an' I'm
    supposed to pay the tolls;
Nine dollars an' a half for — say, what the
    deuce are camisoles?

"If you should break a leg," says Pa, "an
    couldn't get down town to shop,
I'll bet the dry goods men would see their busi-
    ness take an awful drop,
An' if they missed you for a week, they'd have
    to fire a dozen clerks!
Say, couldn't we have got along without this
    bunch of Billie Burkes?"
But Ma just sits an' grins at him, an' never has
    a word to say,
Because she says Pa likes to fuss about the
    bills he has to pay.

Bob White

Out near the links where I go to play
My favorite game from day to day,
There's a friend of mine that I've never met
Walked with or broken bread with, yet
I've talked to him oft and he's talked to me
Whenever I've been where he's chanced to be;
He's a cheery old chap who keeps out of sight,
A gay little fellow whose name is Bob White.

Bob White! Bob White! I can hear him call
As I follow the trail to my little ball —
Bob White! Bob White! with a note of cheer
That was just designed for a mortal ear.
Then I drift far off from the world of men
And I send an answer right back to him then;
An' we whistle away to each other there,
Glad of the life which is ours to share.

Bob White! Bob White! May you live to be
The head of a numerous family!
May you boldly call to your friends out here,
With never an enemy's gun to fear.
I'm a better man as I pass along,
For your cheery call and your bit of song.
May your food be plenty and skies be bright
To the end of your days, good friend Bob
    White!

Sittin' on the Porch

Sittin' on the porch at night when all the tasks
    are done,
Just restin' there an' talkin', with my easy slip-
    pers on,
An' my shirt band thrown wide open an' my feet
    upon the rail,
Oh, it's then I'm at my richest, with a wealth
    that cannot fail;
For the scent of early roses seems to flood the
    evening air,
An' a throne of downright gladness is my
    wicker rocking chair.

The dog asleep beside me, an' the children
    rompin' 'round
With their shrieks of merry laughter, Oh, there
    is no gladder sound
To the ears o' weary mortals, spite of all the
    scoffers say,
Or a grander bit of music than the children at
    their play!
An' I tell myself times over, when I'm sittin'
    there at night,
That the world in which I'm livin' is a place o'
    real delight.

Then the moon begins its climbin' an' the stars
    shine overhead,
An' the mother calls the children an' she takes
    'em up to bed,
An' I smoke my pipe in silence an' I think o'
    many things,
An' balance up my riches with the lonesomeness
    o' kings,
An' I come to this conclusion, an' I'll wager that
    I'm right —
That I'm happier than they are, sittin' on my
    porch at night.

With Dog and Gun

Out in the woods with a dog an' gun
Is my idee of a real day's fun.
'Tain't the birds that I'm out to kill
That furnish me with the finest thrill,
'Cause I never worry or fret a lot,
Or curse my luck if I miss a shot.
There's many a time, an' I don't know why,
That I shoot too low or I aim too high,
An' all I can see is the distant whirr
Of a bird that's gittin' back home to her —
Yep, gittin' back home at the end o' day,
An' I'm just as glad that he got away.

There's a whole lot more in the woods o' fall
Than the birds you bag — if you think at all.
There's colors o' gold an' red an' brown
As never were known in the busy town;
There's room to breathe in the purest air
An' something worth looking at everywhere;
There's the dog who's leadin' you on an' on
To a patch o' cover where birds have gone,
An' standin' there, without move or change,
Till you give the sign that you've got the range.
That's thrill enough for my blood, I say,
So why should I care if they get away?

Fact is, there are times that I'd ruther miss
Than to bring 'em down, 'cause I feel like this:
There's a heap more joy in a living thing
Than a breast crushed in or a broken wing,
An' I can't feel right, an' I never will,
When I look at a bird that I've dared to kill.
Oh, I'm jus' plumb happy to tramp about
An' follow my dog as he hunts 'em out,
Jus' watchin' him point in his silent way
Where the Bob Whites are an' the partridge
        stay;
For the joy o' the great outdoors I've had,
So why should I care if my aim is bad?

Lonely

They're all away
  And the house is still,
And the dust lies thick
  On the window sill,
And the stairway creaks
  In a solemn tone
This taunting phrase:
  "You are all alone."

They've gone away
  And the rooms are bare;
I miss his cap
  From a parlor chair,
And I miss the toys
  In the lonely hall,
But most of any
  I miss his call.

I miss the shouts
  And the laughter gay
Which greeted me
  At the close of day,
And there isn't a thing
  In the house we own
But sobbingly says:
  "You are all alone."

It's only a house
  That is mine to know,
An empty house
  That is cold with woe;
Like a prison grim
  With its bars of black,
And it won't be home
  Till they all come back.

The Cookie Jar

You can rig up a house with all manner of
    things,
The prayer rugs of sultans and princes and
    kings;
You can hang on its walls the old tapestries rare
Which some dead Egyptian once treasured with
    care;
But though costly and gorgeous its furnishings
    are,
It must have, to be homelike, an old cookie jar.

There are just a few things that a home must
    possess,
Besides all your money and all your success —
A few good old books which some loved one
    has read,
Some trinkets of those whose sweet spirits have
    fled,

And then in the pantry, not shoved back too far
For the hungry to get to, that old cookie jar.

Let the house be a mansion, I care not at all!
Let the finest of pictures be hung on each wall,
Let the carpets be made of the richest velour,
And the chairs only those which great wealth
    can procure,
I'd still want to keep for the joy of my flock
That homey, old-fashioned, well-filled cookie
    crock.

Like the love of the Mother it shines through our
    years;
It has soothed all our hurts and has dried away
    tears;
It has paid us for toiling; in sorrow or joy,
It has always shown kindness to each girl and
    boy;
And I'm sorry for people, whoever they are,
Who live in a house where there's no cookie jar.

Little Wrangles

Lord, we've had our little wrangles, an' we've
    had our little bouts;
There's many a time, I reckon, that we have
    been on the outs;
My tongue's a trifle hasty an' my temper's apt
    to fly,
An' Mother, let me tell you, has a sting in her
    reply,
But I couldn't live without her, an' it's plain
    as plain can be
That in fair or sunny weather Mother needs a
    man like me.

I've banged the door an' muttered angry words
    beneath my breath,
For at times when she was scoldin' Mother's
    plagued me most to death,
But we've always laughed it over, when we'd
    both cooled down a bit,
An' we never had a difference but a smile would
    settle it.
An' if such a thing could happen, we could
    share life's joys an' tears
An' live right on together for another thousand
    years.

Some men give up too easy in the game o
    married life;
They haven't got the courage to be worthy of
    a wife;
An' I've seen a lot o' women that have made
    their lives a mess,
'Cause they couldn't bear the burdens that are
    mixed with happiness.
So long as folks are human they'll have many
    faults that jar,
An' the way to live with people is to take them
    as they are.

We've been forty years together, good an' bad,
    an' rain an' shine;
I've forgotten Mother's faults now an' she
    never mentions mine.
In the days when sorrow struck us an' we shared
    a common woe
We just leaned upon each other, an' our weak-
    ness didn't show.
An' I learned how much I need her an' how
    tender she can be
An' through it, maybe, Mother saw the better
    side o' me.

I Ain't Dead Yet

Time was I used to worry and I'd sit around
    an' sigh,
And think with every ache I got that I was
    goin' to die,
I'd see disaster comin' from a dozen different
    ways
An' prophesy calamity an' dark and dreary days.
But I've come to this conclusion, that it's fool-
    ishness to fret;
I've had my share o' sickness, but I
                Ain't
                    Dead
                        Yet!

Wet springs have come to grieve me an' I've
    grumbled at the showers,
But I can't recall a June-time that forgot to
    bring the flowers.
I've had my business troubles, and looked fail-
    ure in the face,
But the crashes I expected seemed to pass right
    by the place.
So I'm takin' life more calmly, pleased with
    everything I get,
An' not over-hurt by losses, 'cause I
                Ain't
                    Dead
                        Yet!

I've feared a thousand failures an' a thousand
    deaths I've died,
I've had this world in ruins by the gloom I've
    prophesied.
But the sun shines out this mornin' an' the skies
    above are blue,
An' with all my griefs an' trouble, I have some-
    how lived 'em through.
There may be cares before me, much like those
    that I have met;
Death will come some day an' take me, but I

                Ain't

                    Dead

                        Yet!

The Cure for Weariness

Seemed like I couldn't stand it any more,
    The factory whistles blowin' day by day,
An' men an' children hurryin' by the door,
    An' street cars clangin' on their busy way.
The faces of the people seemed to be
    Washed pale by tears o' grief an' strife an'
        care,
Till everywhere I turned to I could see
    The same old gloomy pictures of despair.

The windows of the shops all looked the same,
  Decked out with stuff their owners wished
    to sell;
When visitors across our doorway came
  I could recite the tales they'd have to tell.
All things had lost their old-time power to
    please;
  Dog-tired I was an' irritable, too,
An' so I traded chimney tops for trees,
  An' shingled roof for open skies of blue.

I dropped my tools an' took my rod an' line
  An' tackle box an' left the busy town;
I found a favorite restin' spot of mine
  Where no one seeks for fortune or renown.
I whistled to the birds that flew about,
  An' built a lot of castles in my dreams;
I washed away the stains of care an' doubt
  An' thanked the Lord for woods an' running
    streams.

I've cooked my meals before an open fire,
  I've had the joy of green smoke in my face,
I've followed for a time my heart's desire
  An' now the path of duty I retrace.
I've had my little fishin' trip, an' go
  Once more contented to the haunts of men;
I'm ready now to hear the whistles blow
  An' see the roofs an' chimney tops again.

To an Old Friend

When we have lived our little lives and wandered
    all their byways through,
When we've seen all that we shall see and finished
    all that we must do,
When we shall take one backward look off yonder
    where our journey ends,
I pray that you shall be as glad as I shall be that
    we were friends.

Time was we started out to find the treasures and
    the joys of life;
We sought them in the land of gold through
    many days of bitter strife.
When we were young we yearned for fame; in
    search of joy we went afar,
Only to learn how very cold and distant all the
    strangers are.

When we have met all we shall meet and know
    what destiny has planned,
I shall rejoice in that last hour that I have known
    your friendly hand;
I shall go singing down the way off yonder as
    my sun descends
As one who's had a happy life, made glorious by
    the best of friends.

The Things You Can't Forget

They ain't much, seen from day to day—
The big elm tree across the way,
The church spire, an' the meetin' place
Lit up by many a friendly face.
You pass 'em by a dozen times
An' never think o' them in rhymes,
Or fit for poet's singin'.   Yet
They're all the things you can't forget;
An' they're the things you'll miss some day
If ever you should go away.

The people here ain't much to see—
Jes' common folks like you an' me,
Doin' the ordinary tasks
Which life of everybody asks:
Old Dr. Green, still farin' 'round
To where his patients can be found,
An' Parson Hill, serene o' face,
Carryin' God's message every place,
An' Jim, who keeps the grocery store—
Yet they are folks you'd hunger for.

They seem so plain when close to view—
Bill Barker, an' his brother too,
The Jacksons, men of higher rank
Because they chance to run the bank,
Yet friends to every one round here,

Quiet an' kindly an' sincere,
Not much to sing about or praise,
Livin' their lives in modest ways—
Yet in your memory they'd stay
If ever you should go away.

These are things an' these the men
Some day you'll long to see again.
Now it's so near you scarcely see
The beauty o' that big elm tree,
But some day later on you will
An' wonder if it's standin' still,
An' if the birds return to sing
An' make their nests there every spring.
Mebbe you scorn them now, but they
Will bring you back again some day.

The Making of Friends

If nobody smiled and nobody cheered and nobody
    helped us along,
If each every minute looked after himself and
    good things all went to the strong,
If nobody cared just a little for you, and nobody
    thought about me,
And we stood all alone to the battle of life, what
    a dreary old world it would be!

If there were no such a thing as a flag in the sky
    as a symbol of comradeship here,
If we lived as the animals live in the woods, with
    nothing held sacred or dear,
And selfishness ruled us from birth to the end,
    and never a neighbor had we,
And never we gave to another in need, what a
    dreary old world it would be!

Oh, if we were rich as the richest on earth and
    strong as the strongest that lives,
Yet never we knew the delight and the charm of
    the smile which the other man gives,
If kindness were never a part of ourselves,
    though we owned all the land we could see,
And friendship meant nothing at all to us here,
    what a dreary old world it would be!

Life is sweet just because of the friends we have
    made and the things which in common we
    share;
We want to live on not because of ourselves, but
    because of the people who care;
It's giving and doing for somebody else—on that
    all life's splendor depends,
And the joy of this world, when you've summed
    it all up, is found in the making of friends.

The Deeds of Anger

I used to lose my temper an' git mad an' tear
 around
An' raise my voice so wimmin folks would
 tremble at the sound;
I'd do things I was ashamed of when the fit of
 rage had passed,
An' wish I hadn't done 'em, an' regret 'em to
 the last;
But I've learned from sad experience how useless
 is regret,
For the mean things done in anger are the things
 you can't forget.

'Tain't no use to kiss the youngster once your
 hand has made him cry;
You'll recall the time you struck him till the
 very day you die;
He'll forget it an' forgive you an' to-morrow
 seem the same,
But you'll keep the hateful picture of your sor-
 row an' your shame,
An' it's bound to rise to taunt you, though you
 long have squared the debt,
For the things you've done in meanness are the
 things you can't forget.

Lord, I sometimes sit an' shudder when some
    scene comes back to me,
Which shows me big an' brutal in some act o'
    tyranny,
When some triflin' thing upset me an' I let my
    temper fly,
An' was sorry for it after—but it's vain to sit an'
    sigh.
So I'd be a whole sight happier now my sun
    begins to set,
If it wasn't for the meanness which I've done
    an' can't forget.

Now I think I've learned my lesson an' I'm
    treadin' gentler ways,
An' I try to build my mornings into happy yes-
    terdays;
I don't let my temper spoil 'em in the way I used
    to do
An' let some splash of anger smear the record
    when it's through;
I want my memories pleasant, free from shame
    or vain regret,
Without any deeds of anger which I never can
    forget.

Brothers All

Under the toiler's grimy shirt,
Under the sweat and the grease and dirt,
Under the rough outside you view,
Is a man who thinks and feels as you.

Go talk with him,
Go walk with him,
Sit down with him by a running stream,
Away from the things that are hissing steam,
Away from his bench,
His hammer and wrench,
And the grind of need
And the sordid deed,
And this you'll find
As he bares his mind:
In the things which count when this life is
    through
He's as tender and big and as good as you.

Be fair with him,
And share with him
An hour of time in a restful place,
Brother to brother and face to face,
And he'll whisper low
Of the long ago,
Of a loved one dead
And the tears he shed;
And you'll come to see
That in suffering he,
With you, is hurt by the self-same rod
And turns for help to the self-same God.

You hope as he,
You dream of splendors, and so does he,
His children must be as you'd have yours be;
He shares your love
For the Flag above,
He laughs and sings
For the self-same things;
When he's understood
He is mostly good,
Thoughtful of others and kind and true,
Brave, devoted—and much like you.

Under the toiler's grimy shirt,
Under the sweat and the grease and dirt,
Under the rough outside you view,
Is a man who thinks and feels as you.

Life's Single Standard

There are a thousand ways to cheat and a
    thousand ways to sin;
There are ways uncounted to lose the game, but
    there's only one way to win;
And whether you live by the sweat of your brow
    or in luxury's garb you're dressed,
You shall stand at last, when your race is run,
    to be judged by the single test.

Some men lie by the things they make; some
    lie in the deeds they do;
And some play false for a woman's love, and
    some for a cheer or two;
Some rise to fame by the force of skill, grow
    great by the might of power,
Then wreck the temple they toiled to build,
    in a single, shameful hour.

The follies outnumber the virtues good; sin
    lures in a thousand ways;
But slow is the growth of man's character and
    patience must mark his days;
For only those victories shall count, when the
    work of life is done,
Which bear the stamp of an honest man, and
    by courage and faith were won.

There are a thousand ways to fail, but only one
    way to win!
Sham cannot cover the wrong you do nor wash
    out a single sin,
And never shall victory come to you, whatever
    of skill you do,
Save you've done your best in the work of life
    and unto your best were true.

Learn to Smile

The good Lord understood us when He taught
    us how to smile;
He knew we couldn't stand it to be solemn all
    the while;
He knew He'd have to shape us so that when
    our hearts were gay,
We could let our neighbors know it in a quick
    and easy way.

So He touched the lips of Adam and He touched
    the lips of Eve,
And He said: "Let these be solemn when your
    sorrows make you grieve,

But when all is well in Eden and your life seems
    worth the while,
Let your faces wear the glory and the sunshine
    of a smile.

"Teach the symbol to your children, pass it
    down through all the years.
Though they know their share of sadness and
    shall weep their share of tears,
Through the ages men and women shall prove
    their faith in Me
By the smile upon their faces when their hearts
    are trouble-free."

The good Lord understood us when He sent us
    down to earth,
He knew our need for laughter and for happy
    signs of mirth;
He knew we couldn't stand it to be solemn all
    the while,
But must share our joy with others — so He
    taught us how to smile.

The True Man

This is the sort of a man was he:
True when it hurt him a lot to be;
Tight in a corner an' knowin' a lie
Would have helped him out, but he wouldn't
    buy
His freedom there in so cheap a way —
He told the truth though he had to pay.

Honest! Not in the easy sense,
When he needn't worry about expense —
We'll all play square when it doesn't count
And the sum at stake's not a large amount —
But he was square when the times were bad,
An' keepin' his word took all he had.

Honor is something we all profess,
But most of us cheat — some more, some less —
An' the real test isn't the way we do
When there isn't a pinch in either shoe;
It's whether we're true to our best or not
When the right thing's certain to hurt a lot.

That is the sort of a man was he:
Straight when it hurt him a lot to be;
Times when a lie would have paid him well,
No matter the cost, the truth he'd tell;
An' he'd rather go down to a drab defeat
Than save himself if he had to cheat.

Boy or Girl?

Some folks pray for a boy, and some
For a golden-haired little girl to come.
  Some claim to think there is more of joy
  Wrapped up in the smile of a little boy,
  While others pretend that the silky curls
  And plump, pink cheeks of the little girls
  Bring more of bliss to the old home place
  Than a small boy's queer little freckled face.

Now which is better, I couldn't say
If the Lord should ask me to choose to-day;
  If He should put in a call for me
  And say: "Now what shall your order be,
  A boy or girl? I have both in store —
  Which of the two are you waiting for?"
  I'd say with one of my broadest grins:
  "Send either one, if it can't be twins."

I've heard it said, to some people's shame,
They cried with grief when a small boy came,
  For they wanted a girl. And some folks I
      know
  Who wanted a boy, just took on so
  When a girl was sent. But it seems to me
  That mothers and fathers should happy be
  To think, when the Stork has come and gone,
  That the Lord would trust them with either
      one.

Boy or girl? There can be no choice;
There's something lovely in either voice.
     And all that I ask of the Lord to do
     Is to see that the mother comes safely through
     And guard the baby and have it well,
     With a perfect form and a healthy yell,
     And a pair of eyes and a shock of hair.
     Then, boy or girl — and its dad won't care.

They're Waiting Over There

     They're waiting for us over there;
     The young, the beautiful and fair
     Who left us, oh, so long ago,
     Lonely and hurt on earth below,
     Are waiting bravely, never fear,
     Until our faces shall appear.

     Then, when our journey here is done,
     And we set out to follow on
     Through the great, heavy mantled door
     Which leads to rest forevermore,
     They will be there to laugh away
     The loneliness we feel to-day.

     They'll welcome us with wondrous grace,
     And show us all about the place;
     They'll take us gently by the hand

And guide us through that radiant land;
They'll tell us all they've learned and seen
Through the long absence that has been.

We'll meet the friends who have been kind
To them the while we stayed behind —
Angels who long have dwelt above,
Who welcomed them with arms of love,
And sheltered them the long years through,
Just as we'd prayed for them to do.

Though now you mourn, who stay behind,
How sad 'twould be to leave, and find
Upon that distant other shore
No loved one who had gone before —
The gates of Heaven to enter through
With no one there to welcome you.

As now, when some long journey ends
And we're received by smiling friends
Who've watched and waited for our train,
So shall they welcome us again;
The young, the beautiful and fair
Will all be waiting for us there.

Visitors

We've had a lot of visitors, it seems, for weeks
    an' weeks,
And Pa is gettin' all run down. Ma says that
    when he speaks
He isn't civil any more. He mopes around the
    place
And always seems to wear a look of sadness
    on his face.
And yesterday he said to Ma when she began
    to fuss:
" I wonder when they're going to quit an' leave
    the home to us.

" It's nice to have your people come, but some
    of them should go;
Instead of that they're sticking here like bull dogs
    at a show.
' The more the merrier,' they shout, as other
    ones drop in.
I'm getting so I cannot stand to see your cousins
    grin
And, what is more, I'm getting tired of driving
    folks about
And mighty tired of visitors who must be taken
    out.

"Night after night when I've come home I've
      hauled them near and far,
You'd think I was the driver of a town sight-
      seeing car.
I've hauled them up to factories and monuments
      and parks,
Museums and aquariums; I've shown 'em seals
      and sharks
And bears and wolves and elephants; and now
      I want to quit.
I know they'd do the same for me, but I am sick
      of it.

"I wouldn't say a word at all about your folks,
      I know
They're just as nice as they can be, but still
      I wish they'd go.
I'm tired of all the buzz and talk, the tales of
      those who've died;
I'm tired of seeing all our chairs forever occu-
      pied."
"And I am tired myself," said Ma, "as tired as
      I can be,
You're only on the job at night, but it's all day
      long for me."

When Father Broke His Arm

Pa never gets a story straight.
He's always mixed about the date,
Or where it was, or what occurred,
Or who related what he heard;
And every time he starts to tell
Some little story he knows well,
Ma says: " No, Pa, as I recall,
That isn't how it was at all."

" Remember when I broke my arm,"
Says Pa, " when we were on the farm
And I went out that slippery morn
A few days after Bud was born,
To get some wood " — and Ma says then:
" Oh, Pa, don't tell that tale again!
And anyhow, I know right well
Bud wasn't born the day you fell."

" 'Twas months before he came," says Ma.
" 'Twas after he was born," says Pa;
" I rather think I ought to know
Just when it was I suffered so."
" Maybe you ought," says Ma, " but still,
I saw you tumble down the hill,
And it was March with snow drifts high —
Bud wasn't born till next July."

"I'd walk him round the floor," says Pa.
"You're all mixed up again," says Ma.
"We'll ask Aunt Lizzie, she was there,
She'd come to help." Says Ma: "I swear
You're just as crazy as a loon,
Aunt Lizzie didn't come till June.
To argue on is most absurd,
Bud wasn't born when that occurred."

I wish I knew just what is what
Or whether I was born or not,
But I'll just have to sit and wait
Until Pa gets his story straight;
And I have never heard at all
Just how it was he chanced to fall,
For Pa and Ma can't yet agree
Which one came first — the fall or me.

The Spirit of the Home

Dishes to wash and clothes to mend,
  And always another meal to plan,
Never the tasks of a mother end
  And oh, so early her day began!
Floors to sweep and the pies to bake,
And chairs to dust and the beds to make.

Oh, the home is fair when you come at night
  And the meal is good and the children gay,

And the kettle sings in its glad delight
   And the mother smiles in her gentle way;
So great her love that you seldom see
Or catch a hint of the drudgery.

Home, you say, when the day is done,
   Home to comfort and peace and rest;
Home, where the children romp and run—
   There is the place that you love the best!
Yet what would the home be like if you
Had all of its endless tasks to do?

Would it be home if she were not there,
   Brave and gentle and fond and true?
Could you so fragrant a meal prepare?
   Could you the numberless duties do?
What were the home that you love so much,
Lacking her presence and gracious touch?

She is the spirit of all that's fair;
   She is the home that you think you build;
She is the beauty you dream of there;
   She is the laughter with which it's filled—
She, with her love and her gentle smile,
Is all that maketh the home worth while.

If I Were Sending My Boy Afar

If I were sending my boy afar
To live and labor where strangers are,
I should hold him close till the time to go,
Telling him things which he ought to know;
I should whisper counsel and caution wise,
Hinting of dangers which might arise,
And tell him the things I have learned from life.
Of its bitter pain and its cruel strife
And the sore temptations which men beset,
And then add this: "Boy, don't forget
When your strength gives out and your hope
      grows dim,
Your father will help if you'll come to him."

If I were sending a boy away,
I should hold him close on the parting day
And give him my trust. Through thick and thin
I should tell him I counted on him to win,
To keep his word at whatever cost,
To play the man though his fight be lost.
But beyond all that I should whisper low:
"If trouble comes, let your father know;
Come to him, son, as you used to do
When you were little — he'll see you through.
I am trusting you in a distant land.
You trust your father to understand.

" Trust me wherever you chance to be,
Know there is nothing to hide from me,
Tell me it all — your tale of woe,
The sting of failure that hurts you so.
Never, whatever your plight may be,
Think it something to hide from me;
Come to me first in your hour of need,
Come though you know that my heart will bleed!
Boy, when the shadows of trouble fall,
Come to your father first of all."

The White Oak

The white oak keeps its leaves till spring when
    other trees are bare,
And who will take the time to look, will find the
    young bud there;
The young bud nestled snug and warm against
    the winter's cold;
The young bud being sheltered by the knowledge
    of the old.

And when the spring shall come again — and
    gentle turns the day,
The youthful bud will swell with strength and
    thrust the old away;
The youthful bud will seek the breeze and hunger
    for the sun,
And down to earth will fall the old with all its
    duty done.

Then, heedless of the parent leaf, the youthful
    bud will grow
And watch the robins build their nests and watch
    the robins go.
Then something strange will come to it when
    that young leaf grows old,
It, too, will want to shield its babe against the
    winter's cold.

It, too, will cling unto the tree through many a
    dreary day
Until the spring-time comes again and it is thrust
    away;
Then it will flutter down to earth with all its
    duty done,
And leave behind its happy child to drink the
    morning sun.

How like man's life from birth to close! How
    like the white oak tree
Which keeps a shelter for its young against the
    storms, are we!
We guard our children through the night and
    watch them through the day,
And when at last our work is done, like leaves,
    we fall away.

Dirty Hands

I have to wash myself at night before I go to bed,
An' wash again when I get up, and wash before
    I'm fed,
An' Ma inspects my neck an' ears an' Pa my
    hands an' shirt —
They seem to wonder why it is that I'm so fond
    of dirt.
But Bill — my chum — an' I agree that we have
    never seen
A feller doing anything whose hands were white
    an' clean.

Bill's mother scolds the same as mine an' calls
    him in from play
To make him wash his face an' hands a dozen
    times a day.
Dirt seems to worry mothers so. But when the
    plumber comes
To fix the pipes, it's plain to see he never scrubs
    his thumbs;
His clothes are always thick with grease, his face
    is smeared with dirt,
An' he is not ashamed to show the smudges on
    his shirt.

The motorman who runs the car has hands much
    worse than mine,
An' I have noticed when we ride there's dirt in
    every line.
The carpenter who works around our house can
    mend a chair
Or put up shelves or fix the floor, an' mother
    doesn't care
That he's not in his Sunday best; she never
    interferes
An' makes him stop his work to go upstairs to
    wash his ears.

The fellers really doing things, as far as I can see,
Have hands and necks and ears that are as dirty
    as can be.
The man who fixes father's car when he can't
    make it go,
Most always has a smudgy face — his hands
    aren't white as snow.
But I must wash an' wash an' wash while every-
    body knows
The most important men in town have dirty
    hands and clo'es.

Bread and Butter

I've eaten chicken a la king
   And many a fancy dish,
I think I've tasted everything
   The heart of man can wish;
But nightly when we dine alone,
   My grateful praise I utter
Unto that good old stand-by, known
   As mother's bread and butter.

Some think it very common fare
   And may be they are right,
But I can take that wholesome pair
   At morning, noon and night;
And there's a happy thrill I feel
   That sets my heart a-flutter
As I sit down to make a meal
   Of mother's bread and butter.

Though poets sing their favorite foods
   In lilting lines and sweet,
And each unto his different moods
   Tells what he likes to eat,
I still remain the little boy
   Who gleefully would mutter
A youngster's gratitude and joy
   For mother's bread and butter.

So now, for all the joy I've had
  From such a wholesome pair
Since first I was a little lad
  In hunger's deep despair,
I hold the finest food of all —
  Though epicures may sputter
And sneer me from the banquet hall —
  Is mother's bread and butter.

The Little Clothes Line

The little clothes line by the kitchen door!
  My mother stretched it once when I was young,
And there the garments which the baby wore,
  Each morning, very carefully, she hung.

Square bits of flannel fluttered in the breeze,
  White stockings very delicate and small,
Long flowing dresses and the glad bootees,
  A little blanket and a knitted shawl.

Then came the day when mother took it down,
  And we forgot what symbols fluttered there;
We'd grown to breast the current of the town,
  To fight for conquest and to stand to care.

Ten years ago she smiled and said to me:
  "I want a little clothes line by the door."
And there she hung, for all the world to see,
  The various bits of raiment which he wore.

Even the ragman on his alley round
　　Knew, by the symbols fluttering on that line,
That there a little baby would be found,
　　And day by day he saw that glorious sign.

Then boyhood came and called our babe away,
　　Muscled him strong and turned his cheeks to
　　　　brown,
Gave him the strength to run and romp and play,
　　And then she took the little clothes line down.

To-day I sat beside her bed, and she
　　Smiled the sweet smile of motherhood once
　　　　more.
"When I get up again," she said to me,
　　"I'll want a little clothes line by the door."

The Ballad of the Indifferent Whist Player

I am not much at the game,
　　Careless the things that I do;
Those whose approval I claim
　　When I attempt it, are few;
Bridge players look in dismay
　　After a hand I have played,
Always they icily say:
　　"Why did you lead me a spade?"

I, who am gentle and tame,
  Am scorned by a merciless crew;
I bear the brunt and the blame
  Whenever they mutter, "Down two!"
No matter what card I may play,
  No matter that whist's not my trade,
Always they sneeringly say:
  "Why did you lead me a spade?"

Matron, young maiden or dame,
  Brown eyes or gray eyes or blue,
Angrily treat me the same
  Recalling the cards that I drew.
Be it December or May,
  Ever she starts this tirade
With a look that's intended to slay:
  "Why did you lead me a spade?"

L'Envoi

Prince, when my soul flies away
  And my form in the cold ground is laid,
Let me rest where nobody will say:
  "Why did you lead me a spade?"

The Broken Wheel

We found the car beneath a tree.
" The steering knuckle broke," said he;
" The driver's dead; they say his wife
Will be an invalid for life.
I wonder how the man must feel
Who made that faulty steering wheel."

It seemed a curious thought, and I
Sat thinking, as the cars went by,
About the man who made the wheel
And shaped that knuckle out of steel;
I tried to visualize the scene—
The man, the steel and the machine.

Perhaps the workman never saw
An indication of the flaw;
Or, seeing it, he fancied it
Would not affect his work a bit,
And said: " It's good enough to go —
I'll pass it on. They'll never know."

" It's not exactly to my best
But it may pass the final test;
And should it break, no man can know
It was my hand that made it so.
The thing is faulty, but perhaps
We'll never hear it when it snaps."

Of course the workman couldn't see
The mangled car beneath the tree,
The dead man, and the tortured wife
Doomed to a cripple's chair for life—
His chief concern was getting by
The stern inspector's eager eye.

Perhaps he whistles on his way
Into the factory to-day
And doesn't know the ruin wrought
By just one minute's careless thought.
Yet human life is held at stake
By nearly all that toilers make.

The Tender Blossoms

"I will gather some flowers for our friend,"
    she said,
  So into the garden with her I went
And stood for awhile at the rose's bed
    As she stooped to her labor of sentiment

"Why not the full blown blossom there?
    Why do you leave it and pass it by?"
Those were the questions I asked of her.
    And she answered me: "It is soon to die."

" Here is a withered and blasted rose,
　　Better without it the plant would be ;
Cut it and mingle it now with those
　　You are taking away for your friend to see."

" Here is a peony stained and torn,
　　Take it and cling to your choicest bloom."
But she answered me with a look of scorn :
　　" These flowers are to brighten a sick friend's
　　　　room."

" Only the tenderest bud I'll take.
　　Never the withered and worn and old ;
Of my fairest flowers is the gift I make
　　By which my love for my friend is told."

" So, when the angels call," said I,
　　" And fold in their arms a little child,
Passing the old and the broken by,
　　Think of this and be reconciled.

" Always the tenderest buds they take,
　　Pure and lovely and undefiled.
When a gift of love unto God they'd make,
　　Always they come for a little child."

Questioning

You shall wonder as you meet
Drunkards reeling down the street,
Helpless cripples and the blind,
Human wrecks of every kind
Living on from day to day,
Why your loved one couldn't stay.

These are thoughts which always come
When the heart with grief is numb.
" Why," the anguished mother cries,
With the tears still in her eyes,
" Must my baby go away
And some sinful creature stay?"

Thus, rebellious in your grief,
You may falter in belief
And your blinded eyes will see
No just cause why this should be;
But the passing years will show
Wisely was it ordered so.

Hold your faith and bear the pain —
Questioning your God is vain.
None of us has power to know
Who should stay and who should go.
Hold this everlasting truth —
Heaven has need of lovely youth.

Think of this when you are tried:
If the wretched only died,
Then would death to us be sent
Always as a punishment?
But the passing from the earth
Is more beautiful than birth.

The Choir Boy

They put his spotless surplice on
  And tied his flowing tie,
And he was fair to look upon
  As he went singing by.
He sang the hymns with gentle grace,
  That little lad of nine,
For there was something in his face
  Which seemed almost divine.

His downcast eye was good to see,
  His brow was smooth and fair,
And no one dreamed that there could be
  A rascal plotting there;
Yet when all heads in prayer were bowed,
  God's gracious care to beg,
The boy next to him cried aloud:
  " Quit pinching o' my leg!"

A pious little child he seemed,
   An angel born to sing;
Beholding him, none ever dreamed
   He'd do a naughty thing;
Yet many a sudden " ouch! " proclaimed
   That he had smuggled in
For mischief-making, unashamed,
   A most disturbing pin.

And yet, I think, from high above,
   The Father looking down,
Knows everything he's thinking of
   And smiles when mortals frown,
For in the spotless surplice white
   Which is his mother's joy,
He knows he's not an angel bright,
   But just a healthy boy.

The Lay of the Troubled Golfer

His eye was wild and his face was taut with
     anger and hate and rage,
And the things he muttered were much too strong
     for the ink of the printed page.
I found him there when the dusk came down, in
     his golf clothes still was he,
And his clubs were strewn around his feet as he
     told his grief to me:
" I'd an easy five for a seventy-nine — in sight
     of the golden goal —
An easy five and I took an eight — an eight on
     the eighteenth hole!

" I've dreamed my dreams of the ' seventy men,'
     and I've worked year after year,
I have vowed I would stand with the chosen few
     ere the end of my golf career;
I've cherished the thought of a seventy score, and
     the days have come and gone
And I've never been close to the golden goal my
     heart was set upon.
But today I stood on the eighteenth tee and
     counted that score of mine,
And my pulses raced with the thrill of joy — I'd
     a five for a seventy-nine!

"I can kick the ball from the eighteenth tee and
　　　get this hole in five,
But I took the wood and I tried to cross that
　　　ditch with a mighty drive — "
Let us end the quotes, it is best for all to imagine
　　　his language rich,
But he topped that ball, as we often do, and the
　　　pill stopped in the ditch.
His third was short and his fourth was bad and
　　　his fifth was off the line,
And he took an eight on the eighteenth hole with
　　　a five for a seventy-nine.

I gathered his clubs and I took his arm and alone
　　　in the locker room
I left him sitting upon the bench, a picture of
　　　grief and gloom;
And the last man came and took his shower and
　　　hurried upon his way,
But still he sat with his head bowed down like
　　　one with a mind astray,
And he counted his score card o'er and o'er and
　　　muttered this doleful whine:
"I took an eight on the eighteenth hole, with a
　　　five for a seventy-nine!"

Shoes

I'll tell you it's a problem, when a youngster's
    nine years old,
To keep his feet in leather and to keep him
    heeled and soled;
Just about the time I fancy I've some money I
    can use,
His mother comes and tells me that he needs a
    pair of shoes.

Now I can wear a pair of shoes for several
    months or more,
But Bud, it seems, is working for the man who
    keeps the store,
And the rascal seems to fancy that his duty is
    to show
How fast a healthy, rugged boy can wreck a
    leather toe.

But shoes are made for romping in, for climbing
    and for fun,
For kicking bricks and empty cans, and I am
    not the one
To make him walk sedately in the way that
    grown-ups do —
There's time enough for that, I say, when all his
    boyhood's through.

So let him wreck them, heels and toes, and scuff
    their soles away,
I'll not begrudge the bill for shoes that I'm com-
    pelled to pay,
For I rejoice that it's my lot, when mother
    breaks the news,
To have a healthy, roguish boy who's always
    needing shoes.

Football

I'd rather fancied it would come, a healthy boy
    who's ten years old
Forecasts the things he'll want to do without his
    secrets being told;
And so last night when I got home and found
    his mother strangely still,
I guessed somehow that mother love had battled
    with a youngster's will.
" You'll have to settle it," said she; " there's noth-
    ing more that I can say,
The game of football's calling him and he insists
    he wants to play."

We've talked it over many a time; we've hoped
    he wouldn't choose the game,
And I suppose there's not a boy whose parents
    do not feel the same.
They dread, as we, the rugged sport; they won-
    der, too, just what they'll say

50

When son of theirs comes home, as ours, and
       begs to be allowed to play.
And now the question's up to me, a question
       that I can't evade,
But football is a manly game and I am glad he's
       not afraid.

He wants to play, he says to me; he knows the
       game is rough and grim,
But worse than hurt and broken bones is what
       his friends will think of him;
" They'd call me yellow," he explained, " if I
       stay out." Of all things here
There's nothing quite so hard to bear as is the
       heartless gibe or jeer,
And though I cannot spare him pain or hurt
       when tackles knock him flat,
Being his father, I've said " yes," because I choose
       to spare him that.

Partridge Time

When Pa came home last night he had a package
    in his hand;
" Now, Ma," said he, " I've something here
    which you will say is grand.
A friend of mine got home to-day from hunting
    in the woods,
He's been away a week or two, and got back with
    the goods.
He had a corking string of birds — I wish you
    could have seen 'em! "
" If you've brought any partridge home," said
    Ma, " you'll have to clean 'em."

" Now listen, Ma," said Pa to her, " these birds
    are mighty rare.
I know a lot of men who'd pay a heap to get a
    pair.
But it's against the law to sell this splendid sort
    of game,
And if you bought 'em you would have to use a
    different name.
It isn't every couple has a pair to eat between
    'em."
" If you got any partridge there," says Ma,
    " you'll have to clean 'em."

"Whenever kings want something fine, it's partridge that they eat,
And millionaires prefer 'em, too, to any sort of meat.
About us everywhere to-night are folks who'd think it fine
If on a brace of partridge they could just sit down to dine.
They've got a turkey skinned to death, they're sweeter than a chicken."
"If that's what you've brought home," says Ma, "you'll have to do the pickin'."

And then Pa took the paper off and showed Ma what he had.
"There, look at those two beauties! Don't they start you feelin' glad?
An' ain't your mouth a-waterin' to think how fine they'll be
When you've cooked 'em up for dinner, one for you an' one for me?"
But Ma just turned her nose up high, an' said, when she had seen 'em,
"You'll never live to eat 'em if you wait for me to clean 'em."

Stick to It

Stick to it, boy,
  Through the thick and the thin of it!
Work for the joy
  That is born of the din of it.
Failures beset you,
But don't let them fret you;
Dangers are lurking,
But just keep on working.
If it's worth while and you're sure of the right
      of it,
Stick to it, boy, and make a real fight of it!

Stick to it, lad,
  Be not frail and afraid of it;
Stand to the gad
  For the man to be made of it.
Deaf to the sneering
And blind to the jeering,
Willing to master
The present disaster,
Stick to it, lad, through the trial and test of it,
Patience and courage will give you the best of it.

Stick to it, youth,
    Be not sudden to fly from it;
This is the truth,
    Triumph may not far lie from it.
Dark is the morning
Before the sun's dawning,
Battered and sore of it
Bear a bit more of it,
Stick to it, even though blacker than ink it is,
Victory's nearer, perhaps, than you think it is!

Proud Father

There's a smile on the face of the mother to-day,
The furrows of pain have been scattered away,
Her eyes tell a story of wondrous delight
As she looks at the baby who came through the
        night.
It's plain she's as happy and proud as can be,
    But you ought to see me!

The nurse wears her cap in its jauntiest style,
And she says: "Oh, my dear, there's a baby
        worth while!
She's the pink of perfection, as sweet as a rose,
And I never have seen such a cute little nose."
Were it proper for nurses she'd dance in her glee,
    But you ought to see me!

Bud's eyes are ablaze with the glory of joy,
And he has forgotten he'd asked for a boy.
He stands by her crib and he touches her cheek
And would bring all the kids on the street for a
    peek.
Oh, the pride in his bearing is something to see,
  But you ought to see me!

You may guess that the heart of the mother is
    glad,
But for arrogant happiness gaze on the dad.
For the marvelous strut and the swagger of
    pride,
For the pomp of conceit and the smile satisfied,
For joy that's expressed in the highest degree,
  Take a good look at me!

The Mortgage and the Man

This is the tale of a mortgage and a dead man
    and his son,
A father who left to his only child a duty that
    must be done.
And the neighbors said as they gathered round
    in the neighbor's curious way:
" Too bad, too bad that he left his boy so heavy
    a debt to pay."

Day by day through the years that came, the
    mortgage held him fast —
Straight and true to his task he went, and he
    paid the debt at last;
And his arm grew strong and his eye kept bright,
    and although he never knew,
The thing that fashioned a man of him was the
    task he had to do.

Honor and fortune crowned his brow till the
    day he came to die,
But he said: " My boy shall never work against
    such odds as I.
I have planned his years, I have made them safe,
    I have paid his journey through."
And the boy looked out on a world wherein
    there was nothing for him to do.

His hands grew soft and his eyes went dull and
    his cheeks turned ashy pale,
For strength which isn't employed by day, with
    idleness grows stale.
"He is not the man that his father was," the
    neighbors often said,
"And better for him had he been left to work
    for his meat and bread."

Oh, the race dies out and the clan departs, and
    feeble grows the son
When they come at last to the dreadful day when
    all of the work is done.
For manhood dies on the roads of ease where
    the skies are ever blue,
And each of us needs, if we shall grow strong,
    some difficult thing to do.

The Scoutmaster

There isn't any pay for you, you serve without
    reward;
The boys who tramp the fields with you but little
    could afford;
And yet your pay is richer far than men who
    toil for gold,
For in a dozen different ways your service shall
    be told.

You'll read it in the faces of a troop of growing
    boys,
You'll read it in the pleasure of a dozen manly
    joys;
And down the distant future—you will surely
    read it then,
Emblazoned through the service of a band of
    loyal men.

Five years of willing labor and of brothering a
    troop;
Five years of trudging highways, with the Indian
    cry and whoop;
Five years of camp fires burning, not alone for
    pleasure's sake,
But the future generation which these boys are
    soon to make.

They have no gold to give you, but when age
    comes on to you
They'll give you back the splendid things you
    taught them how to do;
They'll give you rich contentment and a thrill
    of honest pride
And you'll see your nation prosper, and you'll
    all be satisfied.

The Way of a Wife

She wasn't hungry, so she said. A salad and a
    cup of tea
Was all she felt that she could eat, but it was
    different with me.
"I'm rather hungry," I replied: "if you don't
    mind, I think I'll take
Some oysters to begin with and a good old-
    fashioned sirloin steak."

Now wives are curious in this; to make the
    statement blunt and straight,
There's nothing tempts their appetites like food
    upon another's plate;
And when those oysters six appeared she looked
    at them and said to me,
"Just let me try one, will you, dear?" and right
    away she swallowed three.

On came the steak, and promptly she exclaimed:
    "Oh my, that looks so good!
I think I'd like a bit of it." The game is one I
    understood.
I cut her off a healthy piece and never whim-
    pered when she said:
"Now just a few potatoes, dear, and also let
    me share your bread."

She wasn't hungry! She'd refused the food I
    had been glad to buy,
But on the meal which came for me, I know she
    turned a hungry eye.
She never cares for much to eat, she's dainty in
    her choice, I'll state,
But she gets ravenous enough to eat whatever's
    on my plate.

Beneath the Dirt

He'd been delivering a load of coal, and a five-
    ton truck he steered;
He wasn't a pretty sight to see with his four
    days' growth of beard.
His clothes were such as a coal man wears, and
    the fine folks passing by
Would have scorned the touch of his dirty hands
    and the look in his weary eye.

He rattled and banged along the road, sick of his
    job, no doubt,
When in front of his truck, from a hidden spot,
    a dog and a child dashed out
And he couldn't stop, so he made one leap from
    the height of his driver's seat
And he caught the child with those dirty hands
    and swept her from the street.

Over his legs went the heavy wheels, and they
    picked him up for dead,
And the rich man's wife placed her sable coat
    as a pillow for his head.
And black as he was, the rich man said: "He
    shall travel home with me."
And he sat by his side in the limousine and was
    proud of his company.

You may walk in pride in your garments fine,
    you may judge by the things of show,
But what's deep in the breast of the man you
    scorn is something you cannot know.
And you'd kiss the hand of the dirtiest man that
    ever the world has known
If to save the life of the child you love, he had
    bravely risked his own.

The Out-Doors Man

He must come back a better man,
Beneath the summer bronze and tan,
Who turns his back on city strife
To neighbor with the trees;
He must be stronger for the fight
And see with clearer eye the right,
Who fares beneath the open sky
And welcomes every breeze.

The man who loves all living things
Enough to go where Nature flings
Her glories everywhere about,
And dwell with them awhile,
Must be, when he comes back once more,
A little better than before,
A little surer of his faith
And readier to smile.

He never can be wholly bad
Who seeks the sunshine and is glad
To hear a songbird's melody
Or wade a laughing stream;
Nor worse than when he went away
Will he return at close of day
Who's chummed with happy birds and trees
And taken time to dream.

A Book and a Pipe

Give me a book and my cozy chair and a pipe
    of old perique
And the wind may howl and I shall not care
    that the night is cold and bleak,
For I'll follow my friend of the printed page
    wherever he leads me on,
I'll follow him back to a vanished age and the
    joys of a life that's gone.

I'll stand with him on a brigantine with the
    salt wind in my face,
I'll hear him shout when the whale is seen and
    share in the stirring chase,
And I'll hear him say as the gulls fly by and
    round us overhead:
" Every bird up there with its ghastly cry is the
    soul of a sailor dead.

I'll go with him where the pole star gleams and
the arctic nights are long,
I'll go with him to his land of dreams away from
the surging throng,
I'll stand with him on the battle line where the
sky with flame turns red,
I'll follow this faithful friend of mine wherever
he wants to tread.

Oh, whether it be adventure grim or the calm of
a noble mind,
Or a sea to sail and a ship to trim or a pearl of
truth to find,
Grant me an hour in my easy chair and a pipe
full of old perique
And there's ever a friendly book up there that
can furnish the joy I seek.

Being Brave at Night

The other night 'bout two o'clock, or maybe it
    was three,
An elephant with shining tusks came chasing
    after me.
His trunk was wavin' in the air an' spoutin' jets
    of steam
An' he was out to eat me up, but still I didn't
    scream
Or let him see that I was scared — a better
    thought I had,
I just escaped from where I was and crawled
    in bed with dad.

One time there was a giant who was horrible
    to see,
He had three heads and twenty arms, an' he
    come after me
And red hot fire came from his mouths and
    every hand was red
And he declared he'd grind my bones and make
    them into bread.
But I was just too smart for him, I fooled him
    mighty bad,
Before his hands could collar me I crawled in
    bed with dad.

I ain't scared of nothing that comes pesterin'
     me at night.
Once I was chased by forty ghosts all shimmery
     an' white,
An' I just raced 'em round the room an' let 'em
     think maybe
I'd have to stop an' rest awhile, when they could
     capture me.
Then when they leapt onto my bed, Oh Gee!
     but they were mad
To find that I had slipped away an' crawled in
     bed with dad.

No giants, ghosts or elephants have dared to
     come in there
'Coz if they did he'd beat 'em up and chase 'em
     to their lair.
They just hang 'round the children's rooms an'
     snap an' snarl an' bite
An' laugh if they can make 'em yell for help
     with all their might,
But I don't ever yell out loud. I'm not that sort
     of lad,
I slip from out the covers and I crawl in bed
     with dad.

A Cup of Tea

Nellie made a cup of tea,
Made and poured it out for me,
And above the steaming brew
Smiled and asked me: "One or two?"
Saucily she tossed her head,
"Make it sweet for me," I said.

Two sweet lumps of sugar fell
Into that small china well,
But I knew the while I drained
Every drop the cup contained,
More than sugar in the tea
Made the beverage sweet for me.

This to her I tried to say
In that golden yesterday —
Life is like a cup of tea
Which Time poureth endlessly,
Brewed by trial's constant heat,
Needing love to make it sweet.

Then I caught her looking up,
And I held my dainty cup
Out to her and bravely said:
"Here is all that lies ahead,
Here is all my life to be —
Will you make it sweet for me?"

That was years ago, and now
There is silver in her brow;
We have sorrowed, we have smiled,
We've been hurt and reconciled —
But whatever had to be,
She has made it sweet for me.

The Inspiration of the Past

When melancholy rides the sky and fills
    The distance with her dust of gloom and
        doubt,
    And from despair there seems no gateway out;
When the cold blast of disappointment chills
The green young buds of hope and the once rosy
        hills
    Stand gaunt, forbidding battlements, too stout
For faltering strength to master, ere it kills
    Faith in high purpose, turn your face about.

Search the great past, the ages that have gone;
    Pause and reflect by some remembered grave;
At Valley Forge once more with Washington,
    Learn what it means to suffer and be brave.
Or stand with patient Lincoln and believe
That what is right, its purpose shall achieve.

Abe Lincoln

Bill and Jim drove into town on a pleasant
    summer day,
Puffed their pipes and talked of things in a
    friendly sort of way,
Talked of crops and politics, neighbors and the
    price of nails,
Then, as they were jogging on, passed a fellow
    splitting rails.
"Who's that yonder, Bill?" says Jim, "I don't
    seem to know his face."
"That's Abe Lincoln," answered Bill — "got a
    shabby sort of place."

Lawsuit going on one day, Bill and Jim had
    time to spare,
Dropped into the court awhile, found most all
    their neighbors there.
"Moonlight night," one witness said — pris-
    oner's chances mighty small,
Till his lawyer rose and proved there wasn't any
    moon at all.
"Who's defending him?" says Jim, "rather
    clever, I should say."
"That's Abe Lincoln," answered Bill, "homely
    as a bale of hay."

Politics was getting hot, meetings almost every
    night,
Orators from north and south talking loudly for
    the right.
Bill and Jim were always there cheering for their
    party's cause,
Then one time a chap got up talking morals more
    than laws.
" Who's that speaking now? " says Jim, " think
    I've seen his face before."
" That's Abe Lincoln," answered Bill, " shall we
    go or hear some more? "

Moral of it isn't much, greatness may be round
    about,
But when seen from day to day men are slow to
    find it out.
Those who saw him splitting rails, those who
    heard him plead a case
Passed him by with little thought, laughing at
    his homely face.
Those who neighbored with the boy, those who
    saw his summer tan,
Those who lived in Lincoln's time never really
    knew the man.

The Yellow Dog

It was a little yellow dog, a wistful thing to see,
A homely, skinny, battered pup, as dirty as could
    be;
His ribs were showing through his hide, his
    coat was thick with mud,
And yet the way he wagged his tail completely
    captured Bud.

He had been kicked from door to door and
    stoned upon his way,
"Begone!" was all he'd ever heard, 'twas all
    that folks would say;
And yet this miserable cur, forever doomed to
    roam,
Struck up a comradeship with Bud, who proudly
    brought him home.

I've never seen so poor a dog in all my stretch
    of years,
The burrs were thick upon his tail and thick
    upon his ears;
He'd had to fight his way through life and car-
    ried many a scar,
But still Bud brought him home and cried: "Say,
    can I keep him, Ma?"

I think the homeless terrier knows that age is
        harsh and stern,
And from the shabby things of life in scorn is
        quick to turn;
And when some scrubby yellow dog needs sym-
        pathy and joy,
He's certain of a friend in need, if he can find
        a boy.

The Fairy and the Robin

A fairy and a robin met
Beside a bed of mignonette.
The robin bowed and raised his hat,
And smiled a smile as wide as — that —
Then said: "Miss Fairy, I declare,
I'd kiss you, only I don't dare."

The fairy curtsied low and said:
"Your breast is such a lovely red,
And you are such a handsome thing,
And, oh, such pretty songs you sing —
I'd gladly kiss you now, but I
May only kiss a butterfly."

The robin spoke a silly word:
"I'm sorry I was born a bird!
Were I a fairy-man instead,

Then you and I might some day wed."
The fairy laughed and said: "My dear,
God had to have some robins here.

"Be glad you're what you are and sing
And cheer the people in the Spring.
I play with children as I'm told,
But you bring joy to young and old,
And it seems always strange to me
I'm one the old folks never see."

The robin spoke: "Perhaps it's best.
I'll sing my songs and show my breast
And be a robin, and you stay
And share in all the children's play.
God needs us both, so let us try
To do our duty — you and I."

How do I know they said these things?
I saw the robin spread his wings,
I saw the fairy standing up
Upon a golden buttercup,
I hid myself behind a wall
And listened close and heard it all.

Whooping Cough

There is a reason, I suppose, for everything
    which comes —
Why youngsters fall from apple trees and babies
    suck their thumbs;
And though I can't explain it all, when trouble
    comes I know
That since by Providence 'tis willed, it must be
    wiser so.
But knowing this, I still insist we'd all be better
    off
If little children could escape the dreaded whoop-
    ing cough.

I never see a red-faced child in spasms violent
But what I wonder why to babes such suffering
    is sent.
Though mumps and measles, chicken pox and
    scarlet fever, too,
Beset the lives of those I love, I still can see them
    through;
But terror seems to chill my blood the minute that
    I hear
That awful sign that someone's child with whoop-
    ing cough is near.

Old women say it has to be, but I grow pale as
     death
When I behold a boy or girl in anguish fight for
     breath.
They tell me not to be alarmed, but I'm not made
     of steel,
And every touch of agony the youngster has, I
     feel;
And could I run this world of ours, the first thing
     I'd cut off
From all the things which have to be, would be
     the whooping cough.

Over the Crib

Over the crib where the baby lies,
Countless beautiful visions rise
Which only the mothers and fathers see,
Pictures of laughter and joy and song
As the years come sweeping us all along.
Care seldom startles the happy eyes
Over the crib where the baby lies.

A wonderful baby lying there!
And strangers smile at the happy pair,
Proud and boastful, for all they see
Is the dimpled chin and the dimpled knee;

But never a little one comes to earth
That isn't a wonderful babe at birth,
And never a mother who doesn't see
Glorious visions of joy to be.

Over the crib where the baby lies,
Dreams of splendor and pride arise,
Deeds of valor and deeds of love
Hover about and shine above
The tiny form, and the future glows
With a thousand dreams which the mother
         knows,
And beauty dances before her eyes
Over the crib where the baby lies.

Yet we smile at her and we smile at him,
For we are old and our eyes are dim
And we have forgotten and don't recall
Yet world-wide over the mothers dream
The visions we saw when our babes were
         small,
And ever they see in a golden stream,
Wonderful joys in the by-and-by
Over the cribs where their babies lie.

Grass and Children

I used to want a lovely lawn, a level patch of
    green,
For I have marveled many times at those that I
    have seen,
And in my early dreams of youth the home that
    I should keep
Possessed a lawn of beauty rare, a velvet carpet
    deep,
But I have changed my mind since then — for
    then I didn't know
That where the feet of children run the grass
    can never grow.

Now I might own a lovely lawn, but I should
    have to say
To all the little ones about, " Go somewhere else
    to play! ",
And I should have to stretch a wire about my
    garden space
And make the home where gladness reigns, a
    most forbidding place.
By stopping all the merriment which now is ours
    to know,
In time, beyond the slightest doubt, the tender
    grass would grow.

But oh, I want the children near, and so I never
    say,
When they are romping around the home, " Go
    somewhere else to play! "
And though my lawn seems poorly kept, and
    many a spot is bare,
I'd rather see, than growing grass, the youngsters
    happy there.
I've put aside the dream I had in that far long
    ago —
I'd rather have a playground than a place for
    grass to grow.

The Hills of Faith

The hills are in the mist to-day,
Their purple robes are put away.
Like coast guards in their yellow coats
    They face the driving rain;
Like coast guards in their yellow coats,
Who watch the sea for ship-wrecked boats,
They watch the land for human craft
    In trouble on the plain.

The gray clouds rush among their peaks,
Some weakness there the storm-king seeks.
A frightened boulder breaks away
    And rolls into the glen;

A tree is crushed to earth again,
But staunch and brave the hills remain,
A symbol of unfaltering faith
    To all the hosts of men.

Time was the hills were tinged with gold,
About them seas of crimson rolled,
A gentle beauty graced their brows
    As delicate as May
Who comes with blossoms in her hair.
They laughed away the summer there,
But now sublimely stern they stand,
    Attired in somber gray.

Symbols of strength, unmoved they keep
Their place against the winds that sweep;
Defenders of our coast of faith,
    They signal to us all
That what is strong and best and true
Shall breast the gale and live it through
To greet the birth of spring again
    And hear the song bird's call.

Triumph

Back of every golden dream,
Every engine hissing steam,
Back of every hammer falling
And of every deed men dare;
Back of every tilt and fight
Is the coming home at night
To the loved ones who are waiting
In the victory to share.

When all is said and done
And the battle's lost or won,
It's the laughter of the children
And the mother's gentle smile,
It's the pride of those you know,
Good old friends who love you so,
That make the prize worth having
And the victory worth while.

'Tis not in success alone
That achievement's worth is known.
If we had no friends to cheer us
And no one at home to care;
If man's glory as a fighter
Did not make a few eyes brighter
He would cease to try for conquest
And would never do or dare.

Back of every man you'll find
Loving hearts who stay behind,
Watching, waiting, patient, loyal,
As he strives to meet the test,
And the thought which drives him daily
Is that they shall meet him gayly,
And shall glory in his triumph
On the day he does his best.

If It's Worth While

If it's worth while, then it's worth a few blows,
    Worth a few setbacks and worth a few bruises;
If it's worth while — and it is, I suppose —
    It's worth keeping on, though the first strug-
        gle loses.

If it's worth while, then it's worth a good fight,
    Worth a few bouts with the demon, Disaster,
Worth going after with courage and might,
    Worth keeping on till you've proved you are
        master.

If it's worth while, then it's worth a few pains,
    Worth a few heartaches and worth a few sor-
        rows,
Worth clinging fast to the hope that remains,
    Worth going on through the doubtful to-mor-
        rows.

Stand to the battle and see the test through,
    Pay all you have in endurance and might for
        it;
If it's worth while and a good thing to do,
    Then it is worth all it costs in the fight for it.

The Letter

The postman whistled down the street
And seemed to walk on lighter feet,
And as he stepped inside her gate
He knew he carried precious freight;
He knew that day he carried joy —
He had the letter from her boy.

Day after day he'd kept his pace
And seen her careworn, gentle face.
She watched for him to come and took
The papers with an anxious look,
But disappointment followed hope—
She missed the one glad envelope.

He stopped to chat with her awhile
And saw the sadness of her smile,
He fancied he could hear her sigh
The morning that he traveled by;
He knew that when to-morrow came
She would be waiting just the same.

The boy who was so far away
Could never hear her gently say:
"Well, have you brought good news to me?"

Her eager face he could not see,
Or note the lines of anxious care
As every day she waited there.

But when he wrote, on lighter feet
The happy postman walked the street.
" Well, here it is, at last," he'd shout,
" To end the worry and the doubt."
The robin on the maple limb
Began to sing: " She's heard from him."

Her eyes with joy began to glow,
The neighbors round her seemed to know
That with the postman at the door
Sweet peace had come to her once more.
When letters bring so much delight,
Why do the sons forget to write?

The Tower Clock

Day after day the clock in the tower
Strikes on its resonant bell, the hour.
Telling the throngs in the city block
Once again it's ten o'clock!
Day after day, and the crowds pass on,
Till they and another hour have gone.

I heard it first as an eager lad,
The largest clock which the city had,

And it rang the hour in the self-same way
That it rings it out for the town to-day,
And many who heard it then have gone,
Gone like the days that have journeyed on.

Mighty and many the throngs have grown,
Many the changes the town has known,
But the old clock still in its tower stands,
Telling the hour with its silent hands;
And the great pass by and they come no more,
But the bell still rings as it did of yore.

And I think to-day as I hear it ring
That the fame men crave is a fleeting thing.
Unchanged, unswayed by the pomps men praise,
The old clock high in its tower stays,
Sounding the hours for the great and low
As it sounded them in the long ago.

So when the throngs that are here pass by
And the pride of to-day in the dust shall lie,
When the new crowds come in their search for
        power,
The self-same clock in the self-same tower
Shall still ring out in the city block,
For them, as for us, it is ten o'clock.

The Busy Summer Cottage

Our friends have automobiles now. The sum-
 mer cottage where we went
To rest beside the water's blue in peace and in-
 dolent content
Is but an hour's swift ride away. So bright and
 early Sunday morn
Before the breakfast eggs are cooked, we hear
 the honking of the horn.

We must have bathing suits for ten, although
 our family numbers four;
Beds must be made for all who come, though
 father sleeps upon the floor;
Dishes and knives and forks and spoons are
 gathered in one huge display,
For we must be prepared to feed the visitors
 who come our way.

From Friday noon till Monday morn full many
 a weary trip I take,
Rowing the women and their babes upon the
 bosom of the lake;
And by that law which rules a host I'm at the
 mercy of the crew,
I must, until they say good-bye, do everything
 they wish to do.

The chef in yonder large hotel is not a busier
    man than I,
The fish for fifteen hungry mouths it is my duty
    now to fry,
And thus my glad vacation time from dawn to
    dusk is filled with chores,
For friends have made our resting spot the bus-
    iest place in all outdoors.

Good Enough

My son, beware of " good enough,"
It isn't made of sterling stuff;
It's something any man can do,
It marks the many from the few,
It has no merit to the eye,
It's something any man can buy,
Its name is but a sham and bluff,
For it is never " good enough."

With " good enough " the shirkers stop
In every factory and shop;
With " good enough " the failures rest
And lose to men who give their best;
With " good enough " the car breaks down
And men fall short of high renown.
My son, remember and be wise,
In " good enough " disaster lies.

With " good enough " have ships been wrecked,
The forward march of armies checked,
Great buildings burned and fortunes lost;
Nor can the world compute the cost
In life and money it has paid
Because at " good enough " men stayed.
Who stops at " good enough " shall find
Success has left him far behind.

There is no " good enough " that's short
Of what you can do and you ought.
The flaw which may escape the eye
And temporarily get by,
Shall weaken underneath the strain
And wreck the ship or car or train,
For this is true of men and stuff —
Only the best is " good enough."

My Goals

A little braver when the skies are gray,
　A little stronger when the road seems long,
A little more of patience through the day,
　And not so quick to magnify a wrong.

A little kinder, both of thought and deed,
　A little gentler with the old and weak,
Swifter to sense another's pressing need,
　And not so fast the hurtful phrase to speak.

These are my goals — not flung beyond my
　　power,
　Not dreams of glory, beautiful but vain,
Not the great heights where buds of genius
　　flower,
　But simple splendors which I ought to gain.

These I can do and be from day to day
　Along the humble pathway where I plod,
So that at last when I am called away
　I need not make apologies to God.

The Dreamer

The road lay straight before him, but the by-
paths smiled at him
And the scarlet poppies called him to the forests
cool and dim,
And the song birds' happy chorus seemed to lure
him further on;
'Twas a day of wondrous pleasure — but the day
was quickly gone.

He could not resist the laughter and the purling
of a brook
Any more than gray old sages can resist some
dusty book,
And though stern-faced duty bade him march
the highway straight ahead,
" The trees are better company than busy men,"
he said.

We wondered at his dreaming and his wander-
ings far astray,
But we were counting values by the gold and
silver way,
And sometimes as I saw him gazing idly at the
sky,
I fancied he had pleasures of a sort I couldn't
buy.

I fancy he saw something in the clouds above the
      trees
Which the gold and glory seeker passes by and
      never sees,
And I think he gathered something from the
      woods and running streams
Which is just as good as money to the man of
      many dreams.

Hot Mince Pie

I stood upon the coping of the tallest building
      known
And tried to walk that dangerous ledge, bare-
      footed and alone.
I started very bravely, then I turned to look be-
      hind
And saw a demon coming of the most ferocious
      kind;
He bade me get a move on, and I started in to
      run
And I slipped and lost my balance, and I knew
      that I was done.

I had a wild encounter with a mad and awful
      beast,
His eyes were bulged with malice, for he'd
      picked me for a feast.

I tried to scream, but couldn't.   Then he growled
 a fearful note
And gave one spring towards me and his fangs
 sank in my throat,
One gulp and it was over — it was much too
 black to see,
But I knew beyond all question that the end
 had come for me.

I tumbled from an aeroplane and looped and
 looped around,
And was twenty-seven minutes on my journey
 to the ground;
I bumped a dozen steeples on my perilous descent
And left as many flagstaffs either snapped in two
 or bent —
But when I woke, in terror, I discovered with
 a sigh
How much of real excitement lurks in mother's
 hot mince pie.

Morning Brigands

There may be happier times than this,
    But if there are I've never known them,
When youngsters jump in bed to kiss
    And wake the pa's and ma's who own them.
What if the sun be up or not,
    Another perfect day is dawning,
And is it not a happy lot
    With such delight to greet the morning?

Sometimes I hear them quit their bed
    And catch their bare-foot pitter-patter,
And other times they're at my head
    Before I know what is the matter.
Brigands to rob us of our sleep
    They come—their weapons love and laughter,
And though we're locked in slumber deep,
    They always get the joy they're after.

Some days there are when we would lie
    And dream our dreams a little longer,
Then " back to bed awhile," we cry —
    But oh, our love for them is stronger,
Yes, stronger than our wish to sleep
    And so we countermand the order
And let that pair of brigands leap
    With wild delight across love's border.

There may be happier times than this,
    But if there are I've never known them,
When youngsters jump in bed to kiss
    And wake the pa's and ma's who own them.
They miss a lot, the man and wife
    Who never feel those glad hands shake them,
Who rise by day to toil and strife,
    But have no little tots to wake them.

Grief's Only Master

Into the lives of all
The tears of sorrow fall.
Into the happiest hearts
Grief drives her darts;
No door however stout
Can shut Death's angel out.

Vain are the things we prize,
Treasure and pomp's disguise;
They cannot stay the tear
When the true griefs appear.
Where Death will strike to-day
Gold cannot bar the way.

There is no joy secure,
No peace that shall endure,
No smile that man shall keep.

God wills that he must weep,
And in his darkest hour
Vain is all earthly power.

What, then, should guard the gate?
How shall a man be great?
Through the dark days and long,
What power shall make him strong?
Wherein does courage lie,
Since all he loves must die?

When sorrow binds his hands,
Helpless the strong man stands.
One master only grief
Bows to, and that's belief —
Faith that he'll some day know
Why God hath willed it so!

Weaning the Baby

Her tears are very near to-day,
   There's sorrow in her eyes,
For they have ordered her away
   Whene'er the baby cries.
There's little beauty in the sun
   However fair the day be,
For now the mother has begun
   The weaning of the baby.

No more upon her gentle breast
   That little face may lie,
No more that little nose be pressed
   Against her food supply;
No more by night, no more by day,
   That wondrous pleasure may be —
This shadow falls across the way,
   The weaning of the baby.

Oh, you may smile, but mother sighs,
   And now the hours are sad.
She sees the look of pained surprise
   In eyes that once were glad,
And in her throat a lump comes up
   That's big enough to throttle,
Because her lovely babe must sup
   Her dinner from a bottle.

Now bottles can't sing lullabies
 When tender babies dine,
Or read the love in little eyes
 When eagerly they shine.
And so she sadly says to me:
 " I'll miss her fond caresses,
The cuddling ways which used to be,
 Her tugging at my dresses.

" I'll miss her cry for me at night
 And all her squeals of glee,
Her smile of welcome and delight
 When she discovered me;
I'll miss the tie that holds me near
 And long will every day be,
I'm sorry that the time is here
 For me to wean the baby."

The First Step

Last night she hurried out to say:
" The baby took a step to-day!"
A step alone! Those little feet
Walked out two waiting hands to greet;

Walked boldly out, and left the chair
Which little hands had clung to there,

A very glorious hint to make
Of many steps she soon will take.

At eve they hurried out to say:
" The baby took a step to-day ! "
What mattered letters, friendly calls,
And all the care which daily falls,
The news by 'phone, the gossip heard?
One thing important had occurred,
One big deed swept all else away:
The baby took a step to-day !

The baby took a step.   Ah, me !
The first of millions that will be !
Those little feet will walk and climb
And run along the road of Time;
They've started out, and where they'll go
'Tis not permitted us to know.
Out of her arms she turns away —
The baby took a step to-day !

Dear Lord, now hear me as I pray.
Our baby took a step to-day !
Grant that her little feet shall find
No cruel pathways or unkind.
Be Thou her guide through life, that she
May walk in safe security.
Let love and beauty light her way —
Our baby took a step to-day !

Failure

Failure is ceasing to try!
　'Tis accepting defeat
　And to all you may meet
Giving voice to a sigh;
'Tis in thinking it vain
　To attempt furthermore
And in bowing to pain
　When the muscles grow sore.

Failure is stepping aside
　From the brunt of the fray
　In a week-hearted way,
Being content to abide
In the shadows that fall,
　And in being afraid
Out of life, after all,
　Nothing's left to be made.

Failure is thinking despair,
　The forsaking of hope,
　And refusal to cope
With the day's round of care.
It's in heeding the cry,
　"All is lost!" and to stay
With defeat and not try
　For the happier day.

Baby Feet

Tell me, what is half so sweet
As a baby's tiny feet,
Pink and dainty as can be,
Like a coral from the sea?
Talk of jewels strung in rows,
Gaze upon those little toes,
Fairer than a diadem,
With the mother kissing them!

It is morning and she lies
Uttering her happy cries,
While her little hands reach out
For the feet that fly about.
Then I go to her and blow
Laughter out of every toe;
Hold her high and let her place
Tiny footprints on my face.

Little feet that do not know
Where the winding roadways go,
Little feet that never tire,
Feel the stones or trudge the mire,
Still too pink and still too small
To do anything but crawl,
Thinking all their wanderings fair,
Filled with wonders everywhere.

Little feet, so rich with charm,
May you never come to harm.
As I bend and proudly blow
Laughter out of every toe,
This I pray, that God above
Shall protect you with His love,
And shall guide those little feet
Safely down life's broader street.

A Fairy Story

Sit here on my knee, little girl, and I'll tell
    A story to you
    Of a fairy I knew
Who lived in a garden when I was a child.
She was lovely to see and whenever she smiled
The sunbeams came dancing around just to know
Whatever it was that was pleasing her so.

She lived in a poppy and used to peek out
    And shout: "Oh, Yoo-hoo!
    I've been waiting for you!"
And then I'd go over to her house and play
And she'd saddle a bee and we'd both ride away,
Or sometimes we'd take a most wonderful trip
With the sky for the sea and a cloud for our
    ship.

Oft my father and mother would look out and
     say:
       "The glad little elf
       Plays there all by himself,
And he comes in and tells us of things he has
     seen
And the marvelous places to which he has been;
He tells us of dining with princes and kings —
It's a curious boy who can think up such things."

Now this all occurred in the long years ago,
       And the fairy has fled,
       And the poppies are dead,
And never again may I ride on a bee,
Or sail on a cloud with the sky for the sea.
But that fairy has promised, when poppies are
     fair,
To come back again and to wait for you there.

Yes, you can go out when the skies are all blue
       And see what I've seen,
       And go where I've been.
You can have the fairies to lead you away,
To show you strange sights and to share in your
     play;
And the grown-ups may say that your fancies
     are wild,
But fairies are real to an innocent child.

"*Where's Mamma?*"

Comes in flying from the street:
    "Where's Mamma?"
Friend or stranger thus he'll greet:
    "Where's Mamma?"
Doesn't want to say hello,
Home from school or play he'll go
Straight to what he wants to know:
    "Where's Mamma?"

Many times a day he'll shout,
    "Where's Mamma?"
Seems afraid that she's gone out;
    "Where's Mamma?"
Is his first thought at the door -
She's the one he's looking for,
And he questions o'er and o'er,
    "Where's Mamma?"

Can't be happy till he knows:
    "Where's Mamma?"
So he begs us to disclose
    "Where's Mamma?"
And it often seems to me,
As I hear his anxious plea,
That no sweeter phrase can be:
    "Where's Mamma?"

Like to hear it day by day:
    "Where's Mamma?"
Loveliest phrase that lips can say:
    "Where's Mamma?"
And I pray as time shall flow,
And the long years come and go,
That he'll always want to know
    "Where's Mamma?"

The Boy and the Flag

I want my boy to love his home,
    His Mother, yes, and me:
I want him, wheresoe'er he'll roam,
    With us in thought to be.
I want him to love what is fine,
    Nor let his standards drag,
But, Oh! I want that boy of mine
    To love his country's flag!

I want him when he older grows
    To love all things of earth;
And Oh! I want him, when he knows,
    To choose the things of worth.

I want him to the heights to climb
　　Nor let ambition lag;
But, Oh! I want him all the time
　　To love his country's flag.

I want my boy to know the best,
　　I want him to be great;
I want him in Life's distant West,
　　Prepared for any fate.
I want him to be simple, too,
　　Though clever, ne'er to brag,
But, Oh! I want him, through and through,
　　To love his country's flag.

I want my boy to be a man,
　　And yet, in distant years,
I pray that he'll have eyes that can
　　Not quite keep back the tears
When, coming from some foreign shore
　　And alien scenes that fag,
Borne on its native breeze, once more
　　He sees his country's flag.

A Boy and His Stomach

What's the matter with you — ain't I always
    been your friend?
Ain't I been a pardner to you? All my pennies
    don't I spend
In gettin' nice things for you? Don't I give
    you lots of cake?
Say, stummick, what's the matter, that you had
    to go an' ache?

Why, I loaded you with good things; yesterday
    I gave you more
Potatoes, squash an' turkey than you'd ever had
    before.
I gave you nuts an' candy, pumpkin pie an'
    chocolate cake,
An' las' night when I got to bed you had to
    go an' ache.

Say, what's the matter with you — ain't you
    satisfied at all?
I gave you all you wanted, you was hard jes'
    like a ball,
An' you couldn't hold another bit of puddin',
    yet las' night
You ached mos' awful, stummick; that ain't
    treatin' me jes' right.

I've been a friend to you, I have, why ain't you
    a friend o' mine?
They gave me castor oil last night because you
    made me whine.
I'm awful sick this mornin' an' I'm feelin' mighty
    blue,
Because you don't appreciate the things I do for
    you.

Lullaby

The golden dreamboat's ready, all her silken sails
    are spread,
And the breeze is gently blowing to the fairy
    port of Bed,
And the fairy captain's waiting while the busy
    sandman flies
With the silver dust of slumber, closing every
    baby's eyes.

Oh, the night is rich with moonlight and the sea
    is calm with peace,
And the angels fly to guard you and their watch
    shall never cease,

And the fairies there await you; they have splen-
  did dreams to spin;
You shall hear them gayly singing as the dream-
  boat's putting in.

Like the ripple of the water does the dreamboat's
  whistle blow,
Only baby ears can catch it when it comes the
  time to go,
Only little ones may journey on so wonderful a
  ship,
And go drifting off to slumber with no care to
  mar the trip.

Oh, the little eyes are heavy but the little soul is
  light;
It shall never know a sorrow or a terror through
  the night.
And at last when dawn is breaking and the
  dreamboat's trip is o'er,
You shall wake to find the mother smiling over
  you once more.

The Man to Be

Some day the world will need a man of courage
    in a time of doubt,
And somewhere, as a little boy, that future hero
    plays about.
Within some humble home, no doubt, that instru-
    ment of greater things
Now climbs upon his father's knee or to his
    mother's garments clings
And when shall come that call for him to render
    service that is fine,
He that shall do God's mission here may be your
    little boy or mine.

Long years of preparation mark the pathway for
    the splendid souls,
And generations live and die and seem no nearer
    to their goals,
And yet the purpose of it all, the fleeting pleasure
    and the woe,
The laughter and the grief of life that all who
    come to earth must know
May be to pave the way for one — one man to
    serve the Will Divine
And it is possible that he may be your little boy
    or mine.

Some day the world will need a man! I stand
    beside his cot at night
And wonder if I'm teaching him, as best I can,
    to know the right.
I am the father of a boy — his life is mine to
    make or mar —
For he no better can become than what my daily
    teachings are;
There will be need for someone great — I dare
    not falter from the line —
The man that is to serve the world may be that
    little boy of mine.

Perhaps your boy or mine may not ascend the
    lofty heights of fame;
The orders for their births are hid. We know
    not why to earth they came;
Yet in some little bed to-night the great man of
    to-morrow sleeps
And only He who sent him here, the secret of
    His purpose keeps.
As fathers then our care is this — to keep in mind
    the Great Design —
The man the world shall need some day may be
    your little boy or mine.

The Old Wooden Tub

I like to get to thinking of the old days that are
　　gone,
When there were joys that never more the world
　　will look upon,
The days before inventors smoothed the little
　　cares away
And made, what seemed but luxuries then, the
　　joys of every day;
When bathrooms were exceptions, and we got
　　our weekly scrub
By standing in the middle of a little wooden
　　tub.

We had no rapid heaters, and no blazing gas to
　　burn,
We boiled the water on the stove, and each one
　　took his turn.
Sometimes to save expenses we would use one
　　tub for two;
The water brother Billy used for me would
　　also do,
Although an extra kettle I was granted, I admit,
On winter nights to freshen and to warm it up
　　a bit.

We carried water up the stairs in buckets and
    in pails,
And sometimes splashed it on our legs, and rent
    the air with wails,
But if the nights were very cold, by closing every
    door
We were allowed to take our bath upon the
    kitchen floor.
Beside the cheery stove we stood and gave our-
    selves a rub,
In comfort most luxurious in that old wooden
    tub.

But modern homes no more go through that joy-
    ous weekly fun,
And through the sitting rooms at night no half-
    dried children run;
No little flying forms go past, too swift to see
    their charms,
With shirts and underwear and things tucked
    underneath their arms;
The home's so full of luxury now, it's almost like
    a club,
I sometimes wish we could go back to that old
    wooden tub.

Understanding

Never seek too much to know
    Of another's plight.
Was his trouble or his woe
    Caused by faulty sight?
Was his folly all to blame
For his present hour of shame?
Stretch to him a helping hand,
Pity him and understand.

None so wise and none so sure,
    None so perfect strong
As to call himself secure
    From the price of wrong.
Hunger tappeth at the gate.
Let your word of counsel wait;
Share the food at your command,
Pity him and understand.

Sorely tempted, mortals fail
    Oft to keep the right,
Men at best are very frail.
    Many a sorry sight
By a happier chance had found
Footing firm on higher ground.
Seeing him on treacherous sand
Pity him and understand.

He who for another's aid
  Never has to plead,
Hungry, broken or afraid,
  Is fortunate, indeed!
Let your heart go out to them
Whom your reason would condemn,
Stretch to them a helping hand,
Pity them and understand.

"*Wait Till Your Pa Comes Home*"

"Wait till your Pa comes home!" Oh, dear!
What a dreadful threat for a boy to hear.
Yet never a boy of three or four
But has heard it a thousand times or more.
"Wait till your Pa comes home, my lad,
And see what you'll get for being bad.

"Wait till your Pa comes home, you scamp!
You've soiled the walls with your fingers damp,
You've tracked the floor with your muddy feet
And fought with the boy across the street;
You've torn your clothes and you look a sight!
But wait till your Pa comes home to-night."
Now since I'm the Pa of that daily threat
Which paints me as black as a thing of jet

I rise in protest right here to say
I won't be used in so fierce a way;
No child of mine in the evening gloom
Shall be afraid of my coming home.

I want him waiting for me at night
With eyes that glisten with real delight;
When it's right that punished my boy should be
I don't want the job postponed for me;
I want to come home to a round of joy
And not to frighten a little boy.

"Wait till your Pa comes home!" Oh, dear,
What a dreadful threat for a boy to hear.
Yet that is ever his Mother's way
Of saving herself from a bitter day;
And well she knows in the evening gloom
He won't be hurt when his Pa comes home.

Plea for Strength

Grant me the fighting spirit, grant me the rugged
heart—
Grant me the inner courage in battle to do my
part.
Whether the path be easy or thorny and rough
and long,
Let me press on to the evening, willing and brave
and strong.

Not from the cares that try me, would I be for-
ever free.
All that I ask is patience for whatever my task
may be;
Patience to wait the little brief while, till the
work is done,
And the needed strength, and the courage, for
the struggle that can be won.

Grant me the fighting spirit, and fashion me
stout of will,
Arouse in me that strange something that fear-
fulness cannot chill.
Let me not whimper at hardship! This is the
gift I ask:
Not ease and escape from trial, but strength for
the doubtful task.

Women Who Bait Fish Hooks

With rather dubious eyes I look
On women who can bait a hook,
And never squeal or never squirm
Impaling minnow or a worm.

A minnow, slippery and cold,
Seems such a slimy thing to hold,
That I've the ancient notion it's
A job to give a woman fits.

I know there's many a girl who can
Bait hooks as well as any man,
But just the same I seem to feel
That angle worms should make her squeal.

I do not criticise the kind
Of maid who man's work doesn't mind;
I'm just old fashioned and I look
Surprised to see one bait a hook.

Little Fishermen

A little ship goes out to sea
As soon as we have finished tea;
Off yonder where the big moon glows
This tiny little vessel goes,
But never grown-up eyes have seen
The ports to which this ship has been;
Upon the shore the old folks stand
Till morning brings it back to land.

In search of smiles this little ship
Each evening starts upon a trip;
Just smiles enough to last the day
Is it allowed to bring away;
So nightly to some golden shore
It must set out alone for more,
And sail the rippling sea for miles
Until the hold is full of smiles.

By gentle hands the sails are spread;
The stars are glistening overhead
And in that hour when tiny ships
Prepare to make their evening trips
The sea becomes a wondrous place,
As beautiful as mother's face;
And all the day's disturbing cries
Give way to soothing lullabies.

No clang of bell or warning shout
Is heard on shore when they put out;
The little vessels slip away
As silently as does the day.
And all night long on sands of gold
They cast their nets, and fill the hold
With smiles and joys beyond compare,
To cheer a world that's sad with care.

The Cookie-Lady

She is gentle, kind and fair,
And there's silver in her hair;
She has known the touch of sorrow,
But the smile of her is sweet;
And sometimes it seems to me
That her mission is to be
The gracious cookie-lady
To the youngsters of the street.

All the children in the block
Daily stand beside the crock,
Where she keeps the sugar cookies
That the little folks enjoy;
And no morning passes o'er
That a tapping at her door

Doesn't warn her of the visit
Of a certain little boy.

She has made him feel that he
Has a natural right to be
In her kitchen when she's baking
Pies and cakes and ginger bread;
And each night to me he brings
All the pretty, tender things
About little by-gone children
That the cookie-lady said.

Oh, dear cookie-lady sweet,
May you beautify our street
With your kind and gentle presence
Many more glad years, I pray;
May the skies be bright above you,
As you've taught our babes to love you;
You will scar their hearts with sorrow
If you ever go away.

Life is strange, and when I scan it,
I believe God tries to plan it,
So that where He sends his babies
In that neighborhood to dwell,
One of rare and gracious beauty
Shall abide, whose sweetest duty
Is to be the cookie-lady
That the children love so well.

Patience

To him who waits all things will come,
  But patience is not sitting down
  Upon the curbstones of the town
When skies are overcast and glum,
Nor is it watching day by day,
  Indifferent to the tasks at hand,
  Content in idleness to stand
Till something better comes your way.

The truly patient man is one
  Who, checked and hindered by the fates,
  Still bravely works the while he waits,
And holding fast unto his dream
  Though halted now, still plays the man
  And does whatever task he can,
However humble it may seem.

Day after day and week by week,
  Against the odds must patience fight,
  Clinging forever to the right.
'Tis not a virtue, pale and meek,
That merely sits beside the road
  And waits for luck to come along;
  But it's alive, alert and strong
And bravely bears a heavy load!

Temptation

If you were hungry in a wilderness
    And one should come and whisper in your ear:
"This way lies peace and comfort and success,"
    Could you still choose to keep your conscience
        clear?

If you were cornered and in deep despair
    And one should promise fortune for a wrong,
Would you sell all that you considered fair,
    Or keep the faith and try to get along?

Two years without a job he walked the streets,
    His children hungry, cold and thinly clad,
And then one day a chance to steal he meets.
    Could you have waited that long to go bad?

Little Girls

God made the little boys for fun, for rough and
    tumble times of play;
He made their little legs to run and race and
    scamper through the day.
He made them strong for climbing trees, he
    suited them for horns and drums,
And filled them full of revelries so they could be
    their father's chums.
But then He saw that gentle ways must also
    travel from above.
And so, through all our troubled days He sent
    us little girls to love.

He knew that earth would never do, unless a bit
    of Heaven it had.
Men needed eyes divinely blue to toil by day and
    still be glad.
A world where only men and boys made merry
    would in time grow stale,
And so He shared His Heavenly joys that faith
    in Him should never fail.
He sent us down a thousand charms, He decked
    our ways with golden curls
And laughing eyes and dimpled arms. He let us
    have His little girls.

They are the tenderest of His flowers, the little
    angels of His flock,
And we may keep and call them ours, until God's
    messenger shall knock.
They bring to us the gentleness and beauty that
    we sorely need;
They soothe us with each fond caress and
    strengthen us for every deed.
And happy should that mortal be whom God has
    trusted, through the years,
To guard a little girl and see that she is kept
    from pain and tears.

Dinner-Time

Tuggin' at your bottle.
    An' it's O, you're mighty sweet!
Just a bunch of dimples
    From your top-knot to your feet,
Lyin' there an' gooin'
    In the happiest sort o' way,
Like a rosebud peekin' at me
    In the early hours o' day;
Gloatin' over goodness
    That you know an' sense an' clutch,

An' smilin' at your daddy,
  Who loves you, O, so much!

Tuggin' at your bottle,
  As you nestle in your crib,
With your daddy grinnin' at you
  'Cause you've dribbled on your bib,
An' you gurgle an' you chortle
  Like a brook in early Spring;
An' you kick your pink feet gayly,
  An' I think you'd like to sing.
All you wanted was your dinner,
  Daddy knew it too, you bet!
An' the moment that you got it
  Then you ceased to fuss an' fret.

Tuggin' at your bottle,
  Not a care, excepting when
You lose the rubber nipple,
  But you find it soon again;
An' the gurglin' an' the gooin'
  An' the chortlin' start anew,
An' the kickin' an' the squirmin'
  Show the wondrous joy o' you.
But I'll bet you're not as happy
  At your dinner, little tot,
As the weather-beaten daddy
  Who is bendin' o'er your cot!

Castor Oil

I don't mind lickin's, now an' then,
An' I can even stand it when
My mother calls me in from play
To run some errand right away.
There's things 'bout bein' just a boy
That ain't all happiness an' joy,
But I suppose I've got to stand
My share o' trouble in this land,
An' I ain't kickin' much — but, say,
The worst of parents is that they
Don't realize just how they spoil
A feller's life with castor oil.

Of all the awful stuff, Gee Whiz!
That is the very worst there is.
An' every time if I complain,
Or say I've got a little pain,
There's nothing else that they can think
'Cept castor oil for me to drink.
I notice, though, when Pa is ill,
That he gets fixed up with a pill,
An' Pa don't handle Mother rough
An' make her swallow nasty stuff;
But when I've got a little ache,
It's castor oil I've got to take.

I don't mind goin' up to bed
Afore I get the chapter read;
I don't mind bein' scolded, too,
For lots of things I didn't do;
But, Gee! I hate it when they say,
"Come! Swallow this — an' right away!"
Let poets sing about the joy
It is to be a little boy,
I'll tell the truth about my case:
The poets here can have my place,
An' I will take their life of toil
If they will take my castor oil.

At Dawn

They come to my room at the break of the day,
With their faces all smiles and their minds full
    of play;
They come on their tip-toes and silently creep
To the edge of the bed where I'm lying asleep,
And then at a signal, on which they agree,
With a shout of delight they jump right onto me.
They lift up my eyelids and tickle my nose,
And scratch at my cheeks with their little pink
    toes;

And sometimes to give them a laugh and a scare
I snap and I growl like a cinnamon bear;
Then over I roll, and with three kids astride
I gallop away on their feather-bed ride.

I've thought it all over. Man's biggest mistake
Is in wanting to sleep when his babes are awake;
When they come to his room for that first bit of
    fun
He should make up his mind that his sleeping is
    done;
He should share in the laughter they bring to
    his side
And start off the day with that feather-bed ride.

Oh, they're fun at their breakfast and fun at
    their lunch;
Any hour of the day they're a glorious bunch!
When they're togged up for Sundays they're
    certainly fine,
And I'm glad in my heart I can call them all
    mine,
But I think that the time that I like them the best
Is that hour in the morning before they are
    dressed.

The Children

The children bring us laughter, and the children
    bring us tears;
They string our joys, like jewels bright, upon
    the thread of years;
They bring the bitterest cares we know, their
    mothers' sharpest pain,
Then smile our world to loveliness, like sunshine
    after rain.

The children make us what we are; the childless
    king is spurned;
The children send us to the hills where glories
    may be earned;
For them we pledge our lives to strife, for them
    do mothers fade,
And count in new-born loveliness their sacrifice
    repaid.

The children bring us back to God; in eyes that
    dance and shine
Men read from day to day the proof of love and
    power divine;
For them are fathers brave and good and mothers
    fair and true,
For them is every cherished dream and every
    deed we do.

For children are the furnace fires of life kept
blazing high;
For children on the battle fields are soldiers
pleased to die;
In every place where humans toil, in every dream
and plan,
The laughter of the children shapes the destiny
of man.

His Example

There are little eyes upon you, and they're watch-
ing night and day;
There are little ears that quickly take in every
word you say;
There are little hands all eager to do everything
you do,
And a little boy is dreaming of the day he'll
be like you.

You're the little fellow's idol, you're the wisest
of the wise;
In his little mind about you no suspicions ever
rise;

He believes in you devoutly, holds that all you
    say and do
He will say and do in your way when he's grown
    up just like you.

Oh, it sometimes makes me shudder when I hear
    my boy repeat
Some careless phrase I've uttered in the language
    of the street;
And it sets my heart to grieving when some little
    fault I see
And I know beyond all doubting that he picked
    it up from me.

There's a wide-eyed little fellow who believes
    you're always right,
And his ears are always open and he watches
    day and night;
You are setting an example every day in all
    you do
For the little boy who's waiting to grow up to
    be like you.

The Fun of Forgiving

Sometimes I'm almost glad to hear when I get
    home that they've been bad;
And though I try to look severe, within my heart
    I'm really glad
When mother sadly tells to me the list of awful
    things they've done,
Because when they come tearfully, forgiving
    them is so much fun.

I like to have them all alone, with no one near
    to hear or see,
Then as their little faults they own, I like to take
    them on my knee
And talk it over and pretend the whipping soon
    must be begun;
And then to kiss them at the end — forgiving
    them is so much fun.

Within the world there's no such charm as chil-
    dren penitent and sad,
Who put two soft and chubby arms around your
    neck, when they've been bad.
And as you view their trembling lips, away your
    temper starts to run,
And from your mind all anger slips — forgiving
    them is so much fun.

If there were nothing to forgive I wonder if
    we'd love them so;
If they were wise enough to live as grown-ups
    do, and always go
Along the pleasant path of right, with ne'er a
    fault from sun to sun,
A lot of joys we'd miss at night — forgiving
    them is so much fun.

The Right Family

With time our notions allus change,
An' years make old idees seem strange —
Take Mary there — time was when she
Thought one child made a family,
An' when our eldest, Jim, was born,
She used to say, both night an' morn':
" One little one to love an' keep,
To guard awake, an' watch asleep;
To bring up right an' lead him through
Life's path is all we ought to do."

Two years from then our Jennie came,
But Mary didn't talk the same;
" Now that's just right," she said to me,
" We've got the proper family —

A boy an' girl, God sure is good;
It seems as though He understood
That I've been hopin' every way
To have a little girl some day;
Sometimes I've prayed the whole night
    through —
One ain't enough; we needed two."

Then as the months went rollin' on,
One day the stork brought little John,
An' Mary smiled an' said to me;
"The proper family is three;
Two boys, a girl to romp an' play —
Jus' work enough to fill the day.
I never had enough to do,
The months that we had only two;
Three's jus' right, pa, we don't want more."
Still time went on an' we had four.

An' that was years ago, I vow,
An' we have six fine children now;
An' Mary's plumb forgot the day
She used to sit an' sweetly say
That one child was enough for her
To love an' give the proper care;
One, two or three or four or five —
Why, goodness gracious, sakes alive,
If God should send her ten to-night,
She'd vow her fam'ly was jus' right!

I Don't Want to Go to Bed

World wide over this is said:
"I don't want to go to bed."
Dads and mothers, far and near,
Every night this chorus hear;
Makes no difference where they are,
Here or off in Zanzibar,
In the igloos made of snow
Of the fur-clad Eskimo,
In the blistering torrid zone,
This one touch of nature's known;
In life's various tongues it's said:
"I don't want to go to bed!"

This has ever been the way
Of the youngsters at their play.
Laughter quickly dries their tears,
Trouble swiftly disappears,
Joy is everywhere about,
Here and there and in and out;
Yet when night comes on they cry
That so glad a day should die,
And they think that they will miss
Something more of precious bliss,
So shouts every curly-head:
"I don't want to go to bed!"

Age is glad to put away
All the burdens of the day,

Glad to lay the worries down,
Quit the noises of the town,
And in slumber end the care
That has met them here and there.
But the children do not know
Life is freighted down with woe;
They would run until they drop,
Hoping day would never stop,
Calling back when it has fled:
"I don't want to go to bed."

The World of Music

The world of music is to me
  An ancient country far away
Which I am not allowed to see,
  Beyond its borders I must stay.
Still, as a boy who looks at ships
  And pictures of some distant land,
The wish is ever on my lips
  That some day I may understand
And some day go at last to share
The ecstasy that must be there.

I hear them talk who know it well
  About the golden hours of song.
I listen as its people tell
  Of wood wind notes a half-tone wrong,
But as the orchestra begins
  A most majestic symphony
The magic of the violins
  No inner meaning brings to me.
I cannot pass the citadels
To tread the path where music dwells.

I envy them who walk its ways
  And claim the joys denied to me,
I know it is a realm ablaze
  With beauty I shall never see.
I'd like to walk its shores alone
  And feel my soul with rapture swept,
But I was fashioned deaf to tone,
  So at the outer wall I'm kept.
Friends freely pass within the gate
And leave me in the cold to wait.

Last Indian Summer Day

An Indian summer day was born
Within a cloud of mist at morn.
A calm, sweet infancy it knew,
And then the golden sun broke through,
Flood-lighting for its middle age
A crimsoned and empurpled stage.

The day itself knew naught of care,
It looked on beauty everywhere,
The walls of life appeared to be
Hung thick with ancient tapestry,
While at the edge of field and wood
Tall grenadiers in scarlet stood.

Men walked beneath a sky of blue
That Indian summer daytime through,
And in the splendor seemed to see
A hint of what this world could be.
Forgetful of their griefs, it seemed
The glory they beheld they dreamed.

Late in the afternoon a breeze
Rustled the garments of the trees,
Far in the West a cloud appeared,
Foreboding trouble as it neared.
Rain followed with the setting sun,
And bleak November had begun!

Plea for Courage

Would God would grant me grace today
One timely thought to think and say
   To one who gropes
   'Mid shattered hopes
And fancies all is lost and gone
To hearten him and cheer him **on.**

Would I could find amid the maze
Of words a simple line or phrase,
   Which I could say
   This very day
To one who walks his way in doubt
And draw his faltering spirit out.

"Let not your heart be troubled!" said
The Master, twenty centuries dead.
   And down the years
   Through care and tears
To Him, when hearts with anguish burned
The multitudes have bravely turned.

Hold fast and falter not today!
Before us lies the better way.
   The future waits
   Beyond the gates!
Step forth undaunted by despair,
Courage and faith can conquer care!

Up to the Ceiling

Up to the ceiling
And down to the floor,
Hear him now squealing
And calling for more.
Laughing and shouting,
"Away up!" he cries.
Who could be doubting
The love in his eyes.
Heigho! my baby!
And heigho! my son!
Up to the ceiling
Is wonderful fun.

Bigger than daddy
And bigger than mother;
Only a laddie,
But bigger than brother.
Laughing and crowing
And squirming and wriggling,
Cheeks fairly glowing,
Now cooing and giggling!
Down to the cellar,
Then quick as a dart
Up to the ceiling
Brings joy to the heart.

Gone is the hurry,
The anguish and sting,

The heartache and worry
That business cares bring;
Gone is the hustle,
The clamor for gold,
The rush and the bustle
The day's affairs hold.
Peace comes to the battered
Old heart of his dad,
When "up to the ceiling"
He plays with his lad.

Answering Him

"When shall I be a man?" he said,
As I was putting him to bed.
"How many years will have to be
Before Time makes a man of me?
And will I be a man when I
Am grown up big?" I heaved a sigh,
Because it called for careful thought
To give the answer that he sought.

And so I sat him on my knee,
And said to him: "A man you'll be
When you have learned that honor brings
More joy than all the crowns of kings;

That it is better to be true
To all who know and trust in you
Than all the gold of earth to gain
If winning it shall leave a stain.

" When you can fight for victory sweet,
Yet bravely swallow down defeat,
And cling to hope and keep the right,
Nor use deceit instead of might;
When you are kind and brave and clean,
And fair to all and never mean;
When there is good in all you plan,
That day, my boy, you'll be a man.

" Some of us learn this truth too late;
That years alone can't make us great;
That many who are three-score ten
Have fallen short of being men,
Because in selfishness they fought
And toiled without refining thought;
And whether wrong or whether right
They lived but for their own delight.

" When you have learned that you must hold
Your honor dearer far than gold;
That no ill-gotten wealth or fame
Can pay you for your tarnished name;
And when in all you say or do
Of others you're considerate, too,
Content to do the best you can
By such a creed, you'll be a man."

The Bumps and Bruises Doctor

I'm the bumps and bruises doctor;
  I'm the expert that they seek
When their rough and tumble playing
  Leaves a scar on leg or cheek.
I'm the rapid, certain curer
  For the wounds of every fall;
I'm the pain eradicator;
  I can always heal them all.

Bumps on little people's foreheads
  I can quickly smooth away;
I take splinters out of fingers
  Without very much delay.
Little sorrows I can banish
  With the magic of my touch;
I can fix a bruise that's dreadful
  So it isn't hurting much.

I'm the bumps and bruises doctor,
  And I answer every call,
And my fee is very simple,
  Just a kiss, and that is all.
And I'm sitting here and wishing
  In the years that are to be,
When they face life's real troubles,
  That they'll bring them all to me.

Always Saying "Don't!"

Folks are queer as they can be,
Always sayin' "don't" to me;
Don't do this an' don't do that.
Don't annoy or tease the cat,
Don't throw stones, or climb a tree,
Don't play in the road. Oh, Gee!
Seems like when I want to play
"Don't" is all that they can say.

If I start to have some fun,
Someone hollers, "Don't you run!"
If I want to go an' play
Mother says: "Don't go away."
Seems my life is filled clear through
With the things I mustn't do.
All the time I'm shouted at:
"No, no, Sonny, don't do that!"

Don't shout so an' make a noise,
Don't play with those naughty boys,
Don't eat candy, don't eat pie,
Don't you laugh and don't you cry,
Don't stand up and don't you fall,
Don't do anything at all.
Seems to me both night an' day
"Don't" is all that they can say.

When I'm older in my ways
An' have little boys to raise,
Bet I'll let 'em race an' run
An' not always spoil their fun;
I'll not tell 'em all along
Everything they like is wrong;
An' you bet your life I won't
All the time be sayin' " don't."

No Children!

No children in the house to play —
It must be hard to live that way!
I wonder what the people do
When night comes on and the work is through,
With no glad little folks to shout,
No eager feet to race about,
No youthful tongues to chatter on
About the joy that's been and gone?
The house might be a castle fine,
But what a lonely place to dine!

No children in the house at all,
No fingermarks upon the wall,

No corner where the toys are piled —
Sure indication of a child.
No little lips to breathe the prayer
That God shall keep you in His care,
No glad caress and welcome sweet
When night returns you to your street;
No little lips a kiss to give —
Oh, what a lonely way to live!

No children in the house! I fear
We could not stand it half a year.
What would we talk about at night,
Plan for and work with all our might,
Hold common dreams about and find
True union of heart and mind,
If we two had no greater care
Than what we both should eat and wear?
We never knew love's brightest flame
Until the day the baby came.

And now we could not get along
Without their laughter and their song.
Joy is not bottled on a shelf,
It cannot feed upon itself;
And even love, if it shall wear,
Must find its happiness in care;
Dull we'd become of mind and speech
Had we no little ones to teach.
No children in the house to play!
Oh, we could never live that way!

When There's Company for Tea

When there's company for tea
Things go mighty hard with me;
Got to sit an' wait an' wait
Till the last guest's cleaned his plate,
An' I mustn't ask Ma what
Kind of pie it is she's got,
Mustn't crunch my napkin up
Or dip cookies in my cup.

When there's company for tea
Home don't seem like home to me;
Got to wash my ears an' neck
Till they do not show a speck;
Got to brush my hair an' then
Got to change my waist again,
Then walk slowly down stairs an'
Try to be a gentleman.

When there's company for tea
Ma spends hours instructing me
How to eat an' what to say,
An' I can't go out to play
When I've finished, but must stay
Till Ma whispers: "Now you may!"
Sittin' still is not much fun
When you've got your supper done.

When there's company for tea,
Then the servant waits on me
Last instead of first, an' I
Mustn't talk when she comes by;
If the boys outside should call,
I don't answer 'em at all;
You'd never know that it was me
When there's company for tea.

The Good Little Boy

Once there was a boy who never
Tore his clothes, or hardly ever;
Never made his sister mad,
Never whipped fer bein' bad,
Never scolded by his Ma,
Never frowned at by his Pa,
Always fit fer folks to see,
Always good as good could be.

This good little boy from Heaven,
So I'm told, was only seven,
Yet he never shed real tears
When his mother scrubbed his ears,
An' at times when he was dressed
Fer a party, in his best,
He was careful of his shirt
Not to get it smeared with dirt.

Used to study late at night,
Learnin' how to read an' write;
When he played a baseball game,
Right away he always came
When his mother called him in.
An' he never made a din
But was quiet as a mouse
When they'd comp'ny in the house.

Liked to wash his hands an' face,
Liked to work around the place;
Never, when he'd tired of play,
Left his wagon in the way,
Or his bat an' ball around —
Put 'em where they could be found;
An' that good boy married Ma,
An' to-day he is my Pa.

The Finest Age

When he was only nine months old,
   And plump and round and pink of cheek,
A joy to tickle and to hold,
   Before he'd even learned to speak,
His gentle mother used to say:
   "It is too bad that he must grow.
If I could only have my way
   His baby ways we'd always know."

And then the year was turned, and he
   Began to toddle round the floor
And name the things that he could see
   And soil the dresses that he wore.
Then many a night she whispered low:
   "Our baby now is such a joy
I hate to think that he must grow
   To be a wild and heedless boy."

But on he went and sweeter grew,
   And then his mother, I recall,
Wished she could keep him always two,
   For that's the finest age of all.
She thought the self-same thing at three,
   And now that he is four, she sighs
To think he cannot always be
   The youngster with the laughing eyes.

Oh, little boy, my wish is not
   Always to keep you four years old.
Each night I stand beside your cot
   And think of what the years may hold;
And looking down on you I pray
   That when we've lost our baby small,
The mother of our man will say
   "This is the finest age of all."

My Paw Said So

Foxes can talk if you know how to listen,
    My Paw said so.
Owls have big eyes that sparkle an' glisten,
    My Paw said so.
Bears can turn flip-flaps an' climb ellum trees,
An' steal all the honey away from the bees,
An' they never mind winter becoz they don't
    freeze;
    My Paw said so.

Girls is a-scared of a snake, but boys ain't,
    My Paw said so.
They holler an' run; an' sometimes they faint,
    My Paw said so.
But boys would be 'shamed to be frightened
    that way
When all that the snake wants to do is to play:
You've got to believe every word that I say,
    My Paw said so.

Wolves ain't so bad if you treat 'em all right,
    My Paw said so.
They're as fond of a game as they are of a fight,
    My Paw said so.
An' all of the animals found in the wood
Ain't always ferocious. Most times they are
    good.

The trouble is mostly they're misunderstood,
    My Paw said so.

You can think what you like, but I stick to it when
    My Paw said so.
An' I'll keep right on sayin', again an' again,
    My Paw said so.
Maybe foxes don't talk to such people as you,
An' bears never show you the tricks they can do,
But I know that the stories I'm tellin' are true,
    My Paw said so.

A Boy and His Dad

A boy and his dad on a fishing-trip —
There is a glorious fellowship!
Father and son and the open sky
And the white clouds lazily drifting by,
And the laughing stream as it runs along
With the clicking reel like a martial song,
And the father teaching the youngster gay
How to land a fish in the sportsman's way.

I fancy I hear them talking there
In an open boat, and the speech is fair;

And the boy is learning the ways of men
From the finest man in his youthful ken.
Kings, to the youngster, cannot compare
With the gentle father who's with him there.
And the greatest mind of the human race
Not for one minute could take his place.

Which is happier, man or boy?
The soul of the father is steeped in joy,
For he's finding out, to his heart's delight,
That his son is fit for the future fight.
He is learning the glorious depths of him,
And the thoughts he thinks and his every whim,
And he shall discover, when night comes on,
How close he has grown to his little son.

A boy and his dad on a fishing-trip —
Oh, I envy them, as I see them there
Under the sky in the open air,
For out of the old, old long-ago
Come the summer days that I used to know,
When I learned life's truths from my father's
    lips
As I shared the joy of his fishing-trips —
Builders of life's companionship!

A Boy's Hope for the Future

I'd like to hunt for buffalo an' ride the western
    slope;
I'd like to be a cowboy an' make circles with a
    rope;
I'd like to be a trapper an' sit 'round a fire at
    night
An' hear the wolves an' catamounts a-growling
    at the light.
But buffalo an' catamounts I guess I'll never see,
Coz Pa says that he hopes to make a lawyer out
    of me.

I'd like to be an acrobat, performing in the air,
Pretending I was going to fall to give the folks
    a scare;
I'd like to balance on a pole an' dangle from my
    teeth
An' frighten all the little boys an' girls who sat
    beneath.
But Uncle John, he says he hopes for higher
    things than that,
An' I should have to run away to be an acrobat.

I'd like to be a circus clown an' run around the
    ring
An' wear a funny suit of clothes, an' laugh at
    everything;

I'd like to paint my face all white an' have a lot
    of fun,
But Ma says that she must be proud to say that
    I'm her son;
She wants to hold her head up high, as high as
    it can be,
An' she is hoping she can make a preacher out
    of me.

Couldn't Live Without You

You're just a little fellow with a lot of funny
    ways,
Just three-foot-six of mischief set with eyes that
    fairly blaze;
You're always up to something with those busy
    hands o' yours,
And you leave a trail o' ruin on the walls an' on
    the doors,
An' I wonder, as I watch you, an' your curious
    tricks I see,
Whatever is the reason that you mean so much
    to me.

You're just a chubby rascal with a grin upon
    your face,
Just seven years o' gladness, an' a hard an' try-
    ing case;
You think the world's your playground, an' in
    all you say an' do
You fancy everybody ought to bow an' scrape to
    you;
Dull care's a thing you laugh at just as though
    'twill never be,
So I wonder, little fellow, why you mean so much
    to me.

Now your face is smeared with candy or perhaps
    it's only dirt,
An' it's really most alarming how you tear your
    little shirt;
But I have to smile upon you, an' with all your
    wilful ways,
I'm certain that I need you 'round about me all
    my days;
Yes, I've got to have you with me for somehow
    it's come to be
That I couldn't live without you, for you're all
    the world to me.

Leader of the Gang

Seems only just a year ago that he was toddling
    round the place
In pretty little colored suits and with a pink
    and shining face.
I used to hold him in my arms to watch when
    our canary sang,
And now to-night he tells me that he's leader
    of his gang.

It seems but yesterday, I vow, that I with fear
    was almost dumb,
Living those dreadful hours of care waiting the
    time for him to come;
And I can still recall the thrill of that first cry
    of his which rang
Within our walls. And now that babe tells me
    he's leader of his gang.

Gone from our lives are all the joys which yes-
    terday we used to own;
The baby that we thought we had, out of the little
    home has flown,
And in his place another stands, whose garments
    in disorder hang,
A lad who now with pride proclaims that he's the
    leader of his gang.

And yet somehow I do not grieve for what it
    seems we may have lost;
To have so strong a boy as this, most cheerfully
    I pay the cost.
I find myself a sense of joy to comfort every
    little pang,
And pray that they shall find in him a worthy
    leader of the gang.

Lines for Doubters

I write these lines for doubting men:
    Of self-timidity beware.
One never knows the moment when
    A flash of pluck will banish care.
Hold fast and give no heed to fear;
    Battle the stream until you sink;
Failure is never quite so near
    As frightened people seem to think.

If now disaster sweeps away
    The little grain you thought to hold,
While still in health and strength you stay
    Your history's only partly told.
There still are left new goals to gain;
    'Tis only those who cease to strive
For whom no future hopes remain.
    Don't die while you are yet alive.

Grieve if you must a little while
   Oe'r what has happened, but return
Head high and brave and with a smile
   The lesson of your loss to learn.
Forget the past and face today
   With courage and with mind alert.
Who comes a victor from the fray
   Remembers not that he was hurt.

Give not your thoughts to bleak de-
   spair.
   Let failure never hold you down.
Out of the fearful swamps of care
   Strong men have struggled to renown.
What if the future dark appears?
   Fight to the last and don't give in;
Before you lies another year
   And somewhere is your chance to win.

What Home's Intended For

When the young folks gather 'round in the good
    old-fashioned way,
Singin' all the latest songs gathered from the
    newest play,
Or they start the phonograph an' shove the chairs
    back to the wall
An' hold a little party dance, I'm happiest of all.
Then I sorter settle back, plumb contented to the
    core,
An' I tell myself most proudly, that's what
    home's intended for.

When the laughter's gaily ringin' an' the room is
    filled with song,
I like to sit an' watch 'em, all that glad an' merry
    throng,
For the ragtime they are playin' on the old piano
    there
Beats any high-toned music where the bright
    lights shine an' glare,
An' the racket they are makin' stirs my pulses
    more and more,
So I whisper in my gladness: that's what home's
    intended for.

Then I smile an' say to Mother, let 'em move the
    chairs about,
Let 'em frolic in the parlor, let 'em shove the
    tables out,
Jus' so long as they are near us, jus' so long as
    they will stay
By the fireplace we are keepin', harm will never
    come their way,
An' you'll never hear me grumble at the bills that
    keep me poor,
It's the finest part o' livin' — that's what home's
    intended for.

Aw Gee Whiz!

Queerest little chap he is,
Always saying: " Aw Gee Whiz!"
Needing something from the store
That you've got to send him for
And you call him from his play,
Then it is you hear him say:
    " Aw Gee Whiz!"

Seems that most expressive phrase
Is a part of childhood days;
Call him in at supper time,
Hands and face all smeared with grime,
Send him up to wash, and he
Answers you disgustedly:
    " Aw Gee Whiz!"

When it's time to go to bed
And he'd rather play instead,
As you call him from the street,
He comes in with dragging feet,
Knowing that he has to go,
Then it is he mutters low:
    " Aw Gee Whiz!"

Makes no difference what you ask
Of him as a little task;
He has yet to learn that life
Crosses many a joy with strife,
So when duty mars his play,
Always we can hear him say:
    " Aw Gee Whiz!"

Story Telling

Most every night when they're in bed,
And both their little prayers have said,
They shout for me to come upstairs
And tell them tales of grizzly bears,
And Indians and gypsies bold,
And eagles with the claws that hold
A baby's weight, and fairy sprites
That roam the woods on starry nights.

And I must illustrate these tales,
Must imitate the northern gales
That toss the Indian's canoe,
And show the way he paddles, too.
If in the story comes a bear,
I have to pause and sniff the air
And show the way he climbs the trees
To steal the honey from the bees.

And then I buzz like angry bees
And sting him on his nose and knees
And howl in pain, till mother cries:
"That pair will never shut their eyes,
While all that noise up there you make;
You're simply keeping them awake."
And then they whisper: "Just one more,"
And once again I'm forced to roar.

New stories every night they ask,
And that is not an easy task;
I have to be so many things:
The frog that croaks, the lark that sings,
The cunning fox, the frightened hen;
But just last night they stumped me, when
They wanted me to twist and squirm
And imitate an angleworm.

At last they tumble off to sleep,
And softly from their room I creep
And brush and comb the shock of hair
I tossed about to be a bear.
Then mother says: "Well, I should say
You're just as much a child as they."
But you can bet I'll not resign
That story-telling job of mine.

The World and Bud

If we were all alike, what a dreadful world
'twould be!
No one would know which one was you or which
of us was me.
We'd never have a " Skinny " or a " Freckles "
or a " Fat,"
An' there wouldn't be a sissy boy to wear a
velvet hat;
An' we'd all of us be pitchers when we played
a baseball match,
For we'd never have a feller who'd have nerve
enough to catch.

If we were all alike an' looked an' thought the
same,
I wonder how'd they call us, 'cause there'd only
be one name.
An' there'd only be one flavor for our ice cream
sodas, too,
An' one color for a necktie an' I 'spose that
would be blue;
An' maybe we'd have mothers who were very
fond of curls,
An' they'd make us fellers wear our hair like
lovely little girls.

Sometimes I think it's funny when I hear some
    feller say
That he isn't fond of chocolate, when I eat it
    every day.
Or some other fellow doesn't like the books I
    like to read;
But I'm glad that we are different, yes, siree! I
    am indeed.
If everybody looked alike an' talked alike, Oh,
    Gee!
We'd never know which one was you or which
    of us was me.

Education

I think that I would rather teach a child
   The joys of kindness than long hours to spend
   Poring o'er multiple and dividend;
How differing natures may be reconciled
Rather than just how cost accounts are filed;
   How to live bravely to its end
   Rather than how one fortress to defend,
Or how gold coins once gathered can be piled.

There is an education of the mind
   Which all require and parents early start,
But there is training of a nobler kind
   And that's the education of the heart.
Lessons that are most difficult to give
Are faith and courage and the way to live.

To the Little Baby

You know your mother — that's plain as day,
But those wide blue eyes of you seem to say
When I bend over your crib: "Now who
Are you?"
It's little figure I cut, I know,
And faces trouble a baby so,
But I'm the gladdest of all the glad —
Your dad!

You're two months old, and you see us smile,
And I know you are wondering all the while
Whoever on earth can these people be
You see.
You've learned your mother; you know her well
When hunger rattles the dinner bell,
But somehow or other you cannot place
My face.

As yet, I'm but one of the passing throng,
The curious people who come along
And pause at your crib, and you seem to say
Each day:
"I know one voice that is sweet to hear,
I know her step when my mother's near,
I know her wonderful smile — but who
Are you?"

"You always come with the same old grin,
Your finger's rough when you tickle my chin,

But you run away when I start to cry,
And I
Don't understand when visitors call
Why you're so afraid they will let me fall.
You are the queerest of all the queer
Folks here!"

It's true that over your crib I stand
And tickle your chin with my rough old hand
And I run away when you start to cry,
But I
Have a right to my queer little funny ways,
To boast your worth and to sound your praise,
For I am the gladdest of all the glad —
Your dad.

Pretending Not to See

Sometimes at the table, when
He gets misbehavin', then
Mother calls across to me:
"Look at him, now! Don't you see
What he's doin', sprawlin' there!
Make him sit up in his chair.
Don't you see the messy way
That he's eating?" An' I say:
"No. He seems all right just now.
What's he doing anyhow?"

Mother placed him there by me,
An' she thinks I ought to see

Every time he breaks the laws
An' correct him, just because
There will come a time some day
When he mustn't act that way.
But I can't be all along
Scoldin' him for doin' wrong.
So if something goes astray,
I jus' look the other way.

Mother tells me now an' then
I'm the easiest o' men,
An' in dealin' with the lad
I will never see the bad
That he does, an' I suppose
Mother's right for Mother knows;
But I'd hate to feel that I'm
Here to scold him all the time.
Little faults might spoil the day,
So I look the other way.

Look the other way an' try
Not to let him catch my eye,
Knowin' all the time that he
Doesn't mean so bad to be;
Knowin', too, that now an' then
I am not the best o' men;
Hopin', too, the times I fall
That the Father of us all,
Lovin', watchin' over me,
Will pretend He doesn't see.

Creed

I would live this life so well
Strangers of me praise might
    tell.
Somehow I would like to be
Cherished here in memory,
Not as one whose skill was
    great;
Not as one who conquered
    fate;
Not as one who rose to fame,
Leaving a remembered name,
But as one who served some
    need
With a timely, kindly deed.

I would have my life be told
Not in glory or in gold,
Or in books which students
    read,
Giving name and date and
    deed
Of a dead man labeled great.
Let mine be the lesser fate.
Let me be to print unknown;
O'er my grave no towering
    stone.
'Tis sufficient at the end
To be mourned for as a friend.

Say of me I loved this earth,
Suffered sorrow, relished mirth;
Bravely tried to live and found
Friendships half the world
    around;
Say I did my best to share
Burdens others had to bear;
Seldom stayed to count the
    cost
Lest the chance to help be
    lost.
If of me this can be said,
Sweet my sleep when I am
    dead.

The Spoiler

With a twinkle in his eye
He'd come gayly walkin' by
An' he'd whistle to the children
    An' he'd beckon 'em to come,
Then he'd chuckle low an' say,
"Come along, I'm on my way,
An' it's I that need your company
    To buy a little gum."

When his merry call they'd hear,
All the children, far an' near,
Would come flyin' from the gardens
   Like the chickens after wheat;
When we'd shake our heads an' say:
"No, you mustn't go to-day!"
He'd beg to let him have 'em
   In a pack about his feet.

Oh, he spoiled 'em, one an' all;
There was not a youngster small
But was over-fed on candy
   An' was stuffed with lollypops,
An' I think his greatest joy
Was to get some girl or boy
An' bring 'em to their parents
   All besmeared by chocolate drops.

Now the children's hearts are sore
For he comes to them no more,
And no more to them he whistles
   And no more for them he stops;
But in Paradise, I think,
With his chuckle and his wink,
He is leading little angels
   To the heavenly candy shops.

Future Growth

He who doubts the future doubts the past
   And beaten is before the struggle starts.
   Tomorrow is the field for fighting hearts,
A scene unlighted now but wide and vast,
Where men in splendid roles shall soon be cast
   And boys today shall rise to noble parts.
   Many remember when men rode in carts
And fancied ten miles to the hour was moving
     fast.

Tomorrow holds adventure for us all,
   Where now we see but dimly skies shall clear.
No man can tell what next old fact shall fall
   Nor what discovery mark the coming year,
But from the past this truth we can recall:
   Growth and achievement mark men's journey
     here.

Wondering

I know so little. In a world so vast
I know so little of the ancient past.

That Caesar was a warrior, I know,
But not the curious twist that made him so.

In school I struggled with the books he penned
And was but little wiser at the end.

I cared not much just how his wars he fought,
But wondered why he thought the way he
    thought.

Brutus was kindly, so I've often read,
Yet he, too, wished the mighty Caesar dead.

How chanced that seed of hatred in his mind
That strength to stab an old friend he could find?

Nowhere appears a sage so wise to state
Why some men love what others truly hate.

Some crave great power; some coldly pass it by
To live more gently—and I wonder why.

The Light of Faith

When the dark days come and the clouds grow
      gray
All men must brave them as best they may,
   With never too much repining;
And bravest is he, when the shadows fall,
Who sees in the gloom of his darkened hall
   The light of his faith still shining.

In those lonely days when his heart shall ache
And it seems that soon shall his courage break,
   There is only one place to borrow;
One place to go for the strength he needs,
He must bind with faith every wound that bleeds,
   And cling to his faith through sorrow.

For truly forlorn is the man who weeps
When his dead lies buried in floral heaps
   And friends his path are lining;
And a pitiful creature he's doomed to be
If he cannot look through the gloom and see
   The light of his faith still shining.

Life

A little laughter, and a time for tears,
    A stretch of duty, and an hour for play—
'Tis thus we march life's journey through the years
    From baby curls to tresses thin and gray.

A friend or two whose faith in us remains;
    A roof where love has sheltered every dream,
Has counted all its losses and its gains—
    These make the fabric of life's noble scheme.

I saw a game played with a crowd of boys;
    Men gave them wire and string and nails and
        tin
And said: "A prize to him who best employs
    These useless things and brings his product in."

Then from those trivial bits grew ships a-sail—
    One lad the model of a castle made.
And there I saw us all, who win, who fail,
    Although 'twas but a game the youngsters
        played.

Life gives us bits of joys and bits of cares,
    And bids us fashion something as a whole.
We choose our own design, and if it bears
    The stamp of merit—God rewards the soul.

Constancy

When strange philosophers declare
The dismal doctrines of despair,
Walk round your garden and behold
The constancy of marigold.

Is it by chance from year to year
That blossoms fade and reappear?
That older than is history old
Are phlox and yellow marigold?

Is there a purpose to the plan
For garden flowers and not for man?
Do chrysalis and butterfly
Continue on and mortals die?

When order fails and spring no more
Brings the red robin to my door;
When stars run riot in the sky
I'll think that man was born to die.

While a Friend Undergoes an Operation

'Tis nine o'clock! How strange the day!
  This minute o'er him sleeping stands
  A surgeon calm, with skillful hands
To cut the painful part away.
  Now to his flesh the knife is laid
  And I am sitting here—afraid!

I know above his form they bend
  To make him well and strong again.
That ethered body is my friend,
  The kindliest and best of men.
Work quickly, surgeon, that I may
Put all these dreadful thoughts away.

Within that spotless room I know
  Precisely what it is they do.
The white-robed nurses come and go.
  The instruments I plainly view.
An hour to wait! 'Twill seem a year
Again till word from him I hear.

Now, troubled, at my desk I stay
  And put in feeble words the prayer
  That God my friend to me will spare
And help him through this painful day.
  Ring, telephone, your little bell
  And bring me word that all is well!

A Sense of Humor

"What shall I give him now?" said God.
"He has the strength with which to plod
The ways of life, the love of right,
The gift of song when the skies are bright.

"Wisdom is planted in his mind,
This man shall be both true and kind,
Earth's beauty shall delight his eyes
And to its glories he shall rise.

"He shall know right from wrong, and he
Defender of the faith shall be;
What more on him can I bestow
Before to earth I let him go?"

Then spake an angel standing near:
"Wisdom is not enough, I fear,
Master, for all that he must do—
Grant him a sense of humor, too.

"Grant him to smile at petty wrong,
The changing moods which sway the throng;
When cares annoy him, show him then
How laughable are angry men!"

Years after, when his strength was tasked,
"What keeps you patient?" he was asked,
"What keeps you brave who are so tried?"
"My sense of humor," he replied.

Old Man Green

Old Man Green, you've never heard of,
Papers never used a word of
Him or anything he did;
Seems as though his light was hid
Day by day from mortal eyes,
Wasn't clever, great or wise;
Just a carpenter who made
Odds and ends and liked his trade.

Old Man Green lived over there
In that humble cottage, where
Five plump babies came to bless
Those small rooms with happiness;
And as time went on they grew
Just as rich men's children do;
Three smart boys and two fine girls
With the prettiest of curls.

Old Man Green from day to day
Put up shelves to earn his pay,
Took the little that he made
Following faithfully his trade,
And somehow his wife and he
Managed it most carefully,
And five children, neat and clean,
Answered to the name of Green.

Old Man Green with saw and plane
Little from the world could gain,
But with that small sum he earned
Many things his children learned.
"Those Green boys," the teachers said,
"Have the stuff to get ahead.
Finest girls we've ever seen—
Little Kate and Mary Green."

This is all there is to tell,
Boys and girls are doing well;
Each with courage and with grace
Fills in life an honored place.
Old Man Green is dead and gone,
But his worth is shining on,
This his praise, if praise be needed,
As a father he succeeded.

Brothers All

We're brothers all, whate'er the place,
Brothers whether in rags or lace,
Brothers all, by the good Lord's grace.

Some may sit in a royal hall,
Some may dwell where the rooms are small,
But under the skin we are brothers all.

Some may toil 'neath the burning sun,
Some may dream where the waters run,
But we're brothers all when the day is done.

By the sun that shines and the rains that fall,
By the shadows flung on the garden wall,
By the good Lord's grace, we are brothers all.

By the hurt that comes and the falling tear,
By the common grief at the silent bier,
And the grave that awaits, we are brothers here.

Friendship

You do not need a score of men to laugh and sing
　　with you;
You can be rich in comradeship with just a friend
　　or two.
You do not need a monarch's smile to light your
　　way along;
Through weal or woe a friend or two will fill your
　　days with song.

So let the many go their way, and let the throng
　　pass by;
The crowd is but a fickle thing which hears not
　　when you sigh.
The multitude is quick to run in search of favorites
　　new,
And all that man can hold for grief is just a friend
　　or two.

When winds of failure start to blow, you'll find the
　　throng has gone—
The splendor of a brighter flame will always lure
　　them on;
But with the ashes of your dreams, and all you
　　hoped to do,
You'll find that all you really need is just a friend
　　or two.

You cannot know the multitude, however hard you
　　try:
It cannot sit about your hearth; it cannot hear you
　　sigh;

It cannot read the heart of you, or know the hurts
 you bear;
Its cheers are all for happy men and not for those
 in care.

So let the throng go on its way and let the crowd
 depart;
But one or two will keep the faith when you are
 sick at heart;
And rich you'll be, and comforted, when gray
 skies hide the blue,
If you can turn and share your grief with just a
 friend or two.

How and Why

Still as children asking why
Adults gaze upon the sky.

Still, as children, grownups seek
Reason for the comet's streak;

Still to sages baffling are
Sun and planet, moon and star.

On a garden's tiny space
Miracles are taking place.

And as children, Age explores
God's bewildering out-of-doors.

Questioning, till the day they die,
Life's great mystery—how and why?

Imagination

The dreamer sees the finished thing before the start
    is made;
He sees the roses pink and red beyond the rusty
    spade,
And all that bleak and barren spot which is so
    bare to see
Is but a place where very soon the marigolds will be.

Imagination carries him across the dusty years,
And what is dull and commonplace in radiant
    charm appears.
The little home that he will build where willows
    bend and bow
Is but the dreamer's paper sketch, but he can see
    it now.

He sees the little winding walk that slowly finds
    his door,
The chimney in its ivy dress, the children on the
    floor,
The staircase where they'll race and romp, the
    windows where will gleam
The light of peace and happiness—the house that's
    still a dream.

You see but weeds and rubbish there, and ugliness
    and grime,
But he can show you where there'll be a swing
    in summer time.

And he can show you where there'll be a fireplace
    rich with cheer,
Although you stand and shake your head and
    think the dreamer queer.

Imagination! This it is the dreamer has to-day;
He sees the beauty that shall be when time has
    cleared the way.
He reads the blueprint of his years, and he can
    plainly see
Beyond life's care and ugliness—the joy that is to
    be.

The Face on the Barroom Floor

(Modern Version)

He walked into the cocktail room, a figure gaunt
    and grim.
The ladies occupied the stools and left no room
    for him.
He doffed his hat and looked about. The bar-
    keep muttered: "Scram!"
"I want a drink," the stranger said. "A thirsty
    man I am.
Give me a shot of Bourbon, please. I'll take it in
    a cup."
"Out!" said the barkeep, "out with you! You
    can't drink standing up!"

"I've got a tale to tell," he said. The women gath-
    ered there
All turned to look upon the man, but no one left
    her chair.

"I know you think it strange," said he, "to see a
    man in here
Where all's so dainty and refined; but let me
    make it clear:
I used to be a happy man before we got repeal,
But now I never know what time I'll get my eve-
    ning meal.

"I loved a girl named Madelon and beautiful was
    she,
Before those Prohibition days her strongest
    drink was tea."
Some of the ladies laughed outright. A grandma,
    more refined,
Emptied her cocktail glass and said: "Let's hear
    what's on his mind."
"I've searched the town for Madelon. She's
    somewhere on the roam.
The children need their supper now, I want to
    take her home.

"I am an artist." From his coat a piece of chalk
    he fetched
And kneeling on the barroom floor a lovely face
    he sketched.
"There, that is Madelon!" he cried. The women
    turned to see.
"If she should drop in here tonight please send
    her home to me!"
He left the place without a drink. A lady fixed
    her hat
And said: "If I were Madelon I'd never stand
    for that!"

Crisis

In the crisis, right and wrong
   Make their bid for man;
Right insists that he be strong.
   Wrong has an easier plan.

Right may ask him patient to be,
   To suffer and toil and wait;
To stand to his task with bravery
   And battle the odds of fate.

Wrong may show him a simple trick,
   Seemingly safe and sure,
And forever after leave him sick
   With an ill he can never cure.

The crisis comes! In that moment tense
   On the choice man makes depends
Things of the gravest consequence,—
   Honor, and worth and friends.

Autumn

I want to come to autumn with the silver in my
    hair,
And maybe have the children stop to look at me
    and stare;
I'd like to reach October free from blemish or from
    taint,
As splendid as a maple tree which artists love to
    paint.

I'd like to come to autumn, with my life work fully
    done
And look a little like a tree that's gleaming in the
    sun;
I'd like to think that I at last could come through
    care and tears
And be as fair to look upon as every elm appears.

But when I reach October, full contented I shall be
If those with whom I've walked through life shall
    still have faith in me;
Nor shall I dread the winter's frost, when brain
    and body tire,
If I have made my life a thing which others can
    admire.

Prayer for the Home

Peace, unto this house, I pray,
Keep terror and despair away;
Shield it from evil and let sin
Never find lodging room within.
May never in these walls be heard
The hateful or accusing word.

Grant that its warm and mellow light
May be to all a beacon bright,
A flaming symbol that shall stir
The beating pulse of him or her
Who finds this door and seems to say,
"Here end the trials of the day."

Hold us together, gentle Lord,
Who sit about this humble board;
May we be spared the cruel fate
Of those whom hatreds separate;
Here let love bind us fast, that we
May know the joys of unity.

Lord, this humble house we'd keep
Sweet with play and calm with sleep.
Help us so that we may give
Beauty to the lives we live.
Let Thy love and let Thy grace
Shine upon our dwelling place.

Manhood

What is manhood, boasted much,
Something we can sense or touch?
Can it be a brilliant thing
Like a jewel in a ring?
Can a teller in a bank
Add it up and place its rank?
Can surveyors draw a line
Separating yours from mine,
Marking with their rigid arts
Where it ends and where it starts?

What is manhood? How and when
Comes this treasured thing to men?
When depleted is the store,
Can a rich man order more,
Or a poor man from his lot
Sell to him who has it not?
Can you save it, would you say,
For the far-off rainy day,
Spurning many a simple need
For one great and glorious deed?

What is manhood? Tell us, sage!
Printed letters on a page?
Victory wreaths or medals bright?
Any cornered beast will fight,

Any man who's trouble free
Very fair will seem to be.
So, I fancy, deeper lies
This rare gift which mortals prize:
'Tis the thought and not the deed,
'Tis the spirit, not the creed.

What is manhood, boasted much?
Nothing we can hold or touch.
'Tis for truth to battle on
When the last false friend is gone;
It is living, conscience clear,
Day by day and year by year,
Suffering loss and taking gain,
Letting neither leave a stain;
Being warrior, neighbor, friend,
Brave and patient to the end.

I Believe

I believe in friendship, and I believe in trees,
And I believe in hollyhocks a-swaying in the breeze,
And I believe in robins and roses white and red,
And rippling brooks and rivers and blue skies over-
  head,
And I believe in laughter, and I believe in love,
And I believe the daffodils believe in God above.

I am no unbeliever. I know that men are true,
I know the joy of summer time when skies above
  are blue,
I know there is no earthly power can shape a bud-
  ding rose,
Or bring a daisy into bloom; with all that wisdom
  knows
It could not fashion, if it would, the humblest
  blade of grass
Or stretch a living carpet where the weary travelers
  pass.

I believe in friendship, for I have found it good,
And I believe in kindly words, for I have under-
  stood;

My faith is founded on the years and all that I
    have seen,
Something of God I've looked upon no matter
    where I've been.
Within a swamp but yesterday a lily smiled at
    me
And only God could set it there to bloom for me
    to see.

Trees in Winter

All winter long the trees stand bare,
    The cold twigs rattle in the storm.
I see them black and silent there
    And wonder if their sleep is warm.

I wonder if they wake, as I,
    Sometimes half-startled by a dream,
Not knowing where they are, nor why
    So strange all things about them seem.

Does consciousness return to them
    For just an instant flash of time,
And do they see the leafless stem
    Trellised where roses used to climb?

For if they wake, how strange must seem
    The winter world they look upon,
With snow and ice on field and stream
    And all the birds of summer gone.

Things Work Out

Because it rains when we wish it wouldn't,
Because men do what they often shouldn't,
Because crops fail, and plans go wrong—
Some of us grumble all day long.
But somehow, in spite of the care and doubt,
It seems at the last that things work out.

Because we lose where we hoped to gain,
Because we suffer a little pain,
Because we must work when we'd like to play—
Some of us whimper along life's way.
But somehow, as day always follow the night,
Most of our troubles work out all right.

Because we cannot forever smile,
Because we must trudge in the dust awhile,
Because we think that the way is long—
Some of us whimper that life's all wrong.
But somehow we live and our sky grows bright,
And everything seems to work out all right.

So bend to your trouble and meet your care,
For the clouds must break, and the sky grow fair.
Let the rain come down, as it must and will,
But keep on working and hoping still.
For in spite of the grumblers who stand about,
Somehow, it seems, all things work out.

The Good World

The Lord must have liked us, I say when I see
The bloom of the rose and the green of the tree,
The flash of the wing of a bird flitting by,
The gold of the grain and the blue of the sky,
The clover below and the tall pines above—
Oh, there's something about us the good Lord must
    love.

The Lord must have liked us, I say when I stand
Where the waves like an army come into the land,
With the gulls riding high on the crest of the breeze
And the ducks flying north in their echelon V's,
The sun slipping down into liquefied gold—
Oh, it's then the great love of the Lord I behold.

The Lord must have liked us, I say at the dawn
When the diamonds of dew gleam and glow on
    the lawn,
And the birds from their throats pour the red wine
    of song
As if life held no burden of sorrow or wrong;
The Lord must have loved us, I whisper just then,
To give such a world to the children of men.

The Lord must have liked us, I say as I pass
The nest of a meadow lark deep in the grass,
Or hear in the distance the quail calling clear
And know that his mate and his babies are near;
Oh, I say to myself as His wonders I see,
The Lord loves us all or this never would be.

Envy

Time was when a king of the olden days,
  Disturbed by his fretful clan,
Sent ministers forth, both south and north,
  In search of a happy man.

"Go find me a man with his heart content,
  Who maketh no wish for more;
Let the search be had till you find one glad,
  One glad with his present store."

"You have health," said they, to a woodsman
    tanned,
  "And so have your children three;
You are truly blessed, for that gift is best"—
  "I would I were rich," said he.

"You have gold," they said, to a man of wealth,
  "You can buy what is ever sold."
"Yes," said he, "but I'd happier be
  With the strength of the woodsman bold."

Then they found them a man with a well-filled
    purse,
  And sturdy and strong was he,
But he said with a sigh: "No child have I,
  But the woodsman there has three."

They searched them high and they searched them
    low
  And back to the king they went,
And they said: "No man in this royal clan
  Sits down by his fire content.

"The woodsman sighs for the rich man's gold,
  And the rich man vows that he
Would give his wealth for the woodsman's health,
  Or even his children three.

"None thinketh himself by the good Lord blessed,
  But counteth his neighbor glad,
And is sure that he would happier be
  If the neighbor's joy he had."

There is none who knoweth life's joys complete,
  For so do God's blessings fall
That all are blessed as He deemeth best,
  But none may have them all.

Sunrise

To-day I saw the sun come up, like Neptune from
the sea,
I saw him light a cliff with gold and wake a dis-
tant tree;
I saw him shake his shaggy head and laugh the
night away
And toss unto a sleeping world another golden day.

The waves, which had been black and cold, came
in with silver crests,
I saw the sunbeams gently wake the song birds in
their nests.
The slow-retreating night slipped back, and strewn
on field and lawn,
On every blade of grass I saw the jewels of the
dawn.

Never was monarch ushered in with such a caval-
cade;
No hero bringing victory home has seen such wealth
displayed.
In honor of the coming day, the humblest plant and
tree
Stood on the curbstone of the world in radiant
livery.

Pageants of splendor man may plan with robes of
    burnished gold,
On horses from Arabia may prance the knights of
    old;
Heralds on silver horns may blow, and kings
    come riding in,
But I have seen God's pageantry—I've watched
    a day begin!

Hunger

I want to go fishing! somewhere on a stream
I want to give way to the longing to dream.
Away from the tumult of motor and mill
I want to be care-free; I want to be still!
I'm weary of doing things; weary of words
I want to be one with the blossoms and birds.

I want to push off from the river-kissed shore
Alone with my dreams and my fancies once more.
I am wearying of reading the books on my shelf
I want to be quiet and think for myself.
I've a feeling sometimes of huge things crushing
    me
And I want to go somewhere and set my soul
    free.

I want to go fishing! to sit all alone
Where only the purest of breezes are blown;
To visit in worlds that are different from ours,
The worlds of the insects, the song birds, the
    flowers;
To question the skies and the waters below
And be the glad youth that I was long long ago.

Love and a Friend

"What did you gather of worth and pride?"
  Said the Angel of the Lord.
"Little by skill," the soul replied
  "And nothing by the sword;
I lived the span of my years and died,
  And I gave when I could afford."

"You bring no more than you took away"
  Said the Angel, soft and low,
"Neither fame nor fortune marks your stay
  Of toil on the earth below;
And I fancy now you are going to say
  It wasn't worth while to go."

"I saw the light in my baby's eye
  And I felt her hand in mine;
I treasured her love as the days went by
  Though I builded no lasting sign;
Of my time on earth, I should say that I
  Had blessings nine times nine.

"And a friend I had who was tried and true
   Who shared in my bit of woe;
He wept whenever a grief I knew
   And smiled when the hurt would go,
And all that I suffered I'd brave anew
   Another such friend to know.

"Oh, it's little I gathered of earthly pride
   And it's little I did of worth;
But to sit again at my own fireside
   I'd pass through another birth."
"Love and a friend," the Angel replied,
   "Are the two great joys of earth."

A Thought

Were I as rich as Midas
   Or poor as Lazarus,
If love would walk beside us
   Together we'd discuss
A thousand lovely reasons
   For rapture and delight—
The ever-changing seasons,
   A wild duck's certain flight.

We'd sit the bright stars under
  And watch the moon arise,
And find it joy to wonder
  What lies beyond the skies;
We'd hear a blithe bird singing
  Its rhapsody of song,
And watch the rivers swinging
  Their seaward course along.

We'd hear the ocean booming
  Along the sandy shore,
And look at flowers, blooming
  Beside some humble door;
We'd gaze on green things growing
  And marvels everywhere
Beyond our little knowing
  And quite forget our care.

In spite of pain or duty,
  Or hearts that often ache,
We'd reap the joys of beauty
  Beyond man's power to make.
We'd find with love to guide us
  God's works miraculous,
Were I as rich as Midas
  Or poor as Lazarus.

Blessings

By the blue that bends above us,
By the smiling friends who love us,
By the laughter of a baby
  And the babbling of a brook;
By the glad Junes with their roses,
And each happy day which closes
With the prayers of little children
  Everywhere God turns to look,
We are blessed in countless ways
Through the number of our days.

By the hope which gilds to-morrow,
By the faith which sweetens sorrow,
By the beauty all around us
  When the dawn of day is fair;
By the health which God hath lent us
For the tasks for which he sent us,
We are richly compensated
  For the burdens we must bear;
And though tears of grief may fall,
God has blessed us, one and all.

By the glad smile of a neighbor,
By the joy of honest labor,
By the singing of the kettle
  And the home where we may rest;
By the true friend standing by us
Through the hours when burdens try us,
By uncounted little pleasures
  All our lives are richly blessed;
Never year nor day nor minute
But holds something lovely in it.

The Effort

When man has done his level best,
   I fancy God is satisfied.
He need not be in splendor dressed,
Known north and south and east and west,
   Nor tread the paths of pride;
If he is earnest in the test,
   God knows how hard he tried.

Not all the good men rise to fame,
   Nor all the kings are crowned.
Full many a long forgotten name
Has borne life's battle but to claim
   An unremembered mound.
And men from men have suffered blame
   When God no fault has found.

'Tis fine to do the splendid deed,
   'Tis sweet to reach the goal.
But oft the dreams of men may lead
Them past their strength, to fall and bleed,
   And failure signs the scroll.
But 'tis not said we must succeed
   To make the perfect soul.

When man has done his level best,
   I fancy God is satisfied.
Though night shall find him sore distressed,
Beset by cares, by men oppressed,
   His victory denied,
God knows how cruel was the test
   And just how hard he tried!

Advice

My boy, be easy with your friend.
To him be very glad to lend;
Make smooth his way whene'er you can;
Don't tell his faults to any man.
Spare him your censure; shut your eyes
To little flaws which may arise.
But in your search for fame or pelf,
Do not be easy with yourself.

For others have a gentle way;
Forgive their sins whene'er you may,
But with yourself be strict. Make sure
That fault of yours shall not endure.
See in yourself each trifling flaw,
And make yourself obey the law.
O'erlook the wrongs which others do,
But never blind yourself to you.

Although deceit might win your fight,
Compel your self to do what's right.
Of others' weakness never speak,
But do not let yourself be weak.
Have pity for the many woes
Which every man around you knows;
But when a trial comes to you,
Be glad that you can see it through.

Keep conscience always as your guide
And by its whisperings abide.
Be lenient and kind of heart;
Utter no speech which leaves a smart.
But always wheresoe'er you turn,
Remember, with yourself, be stern.
Be strict in all you say and do,
Not with your neighbors, but with you!

Friendship

To see the need nor pause to seek
  As one all-wise in right and wrong,
Why he has proved himself so weak
  Who had his moment to be strong;
To give, nor ever think to learn
What shall be given in return.

To hear a cry for aid and run
All haste from whence that summons came
To do what plainly must be done
  And bother not to fix the blame;
To serve the need and never pause
To know whose fault and what the cause.

To play the friend whene'er I can
  With all the power that I command,
Knowing the blow that fells a man
  Is quite enough to understand;
To see him down and lift him up,
Hungry and fill his plate and cup.

A Plea for Faith

O lad o' mine, O lad o' mine, be never coldly dumb
    to me!
Whatever care is on your heart, be ever quick
    to come to me.
Come with the truth upon your tongue, and have
    no fear or doubt of me—
I have such love for you, my lad, no hurt can drive
    it out of me.

O lad o' mine, O lad o' mine, your father God has
    made of me,
And shamed I'll be, to go to Him, if ever you're
    afraid of me.
I'll grieve to learn you've done a wrong, but 'twill
    be worse distress to me,
To find you've hid behind a lie and would not all
    confess to me.

O lad o' mine, O lad o' mine, you are the living part
    of me—
To find a stranger in my place would surely break
    the heart of me.
Keep faith in me; whate'er befalls, I'll stand and
    share the worst with you.
No friend shall be so true as I—but oh, I must
    be first with you.

As We Prayed

Often as we watched her there
From our lips there fell this prayer:
"God, give us the pain to bear!
Let us suffer in her place,
Take the anguish from her face,
Soothe her with Thy holy grace."

Then the angels came, and they
Took her lovely soul away
From the torture house of clay.
As we'd prayed, they brought release,
Smoothed her brow with gentle peace,
But our pain shall never cease.

Ours is now the hurt to bear,
Ours the anguish and despair,
Ours the agony to share!
When our hearts with grief were stirred,
Thus we prayed and thus were heard,
Shall we fail to keep our word?

Was our promise all in vain?
Would we call her back again
Just to spare ourselves the pain?
We are hurt, oh, that is true!
Desolate and lonely, too,
Suffering as we pledged to do.

Lovely now her life shall be
Safe through all eternity,
Always beautiful to see;
Now the pain is ours to know,
But we prayed to bear this blow
That she need not suffer so.

Heat

Oh, for gray skies again
And cooling rain!
Cold wind of the north
Come forth,
Make fresh and sweet
The city street!

But wind of the north find first
Not our best paths, but our worst!
Come to the dark abodes
Crowding the narrow roads.
The miseries abate
Of God's unfortunate.

Flutter that frayed, soiled lace
Now limp at the window place.
Caress the tired woman's brow
Whose child is so restless now.
Hear her utter such words as these:
"Thank God for this cooling breeze!"

Let neither pomp nor pride
Nor flattery turn you aside;
Nor wealth induce you to stay,
But hasten along your way
Until you have comforted first
The poor, whose need is the worst.

Wind of the north, make sweet
The pitiless, crowded street!

The Need

We were sittin' there, and smokin' of our pipes,
    discussin' things
Like taxes, votes for wimmin, an' the totterin'
    thrones of kings,
When he ups an' strokes his whiskers with his
    hand an' says to me:
"Changin' laws an' legislatures ain't, as fur as I
    can see,
Goin' to make this world much better, unless some-
    how we can
Find a way to make a better an' a finer sort o' man.

"The trouble ain't with statutes or with systems—
    not at all;
It's with humans jus' like we air an' their petty
    ways an' small.
We could stop our writin' law-books an' our regu-
    latin' rules
If a better sort of manhood was the product of
    our schools.
For the things that we air needin' isn't writin'
    from a pen
Or bigger guns to shoot with, but a bigger type of
    men.

"I reckon all these problems air jest ornery like
the weeds,
They grow in soil that oughta nourish only decent
deeds,
An' they waste our time an' fret us when, if we were
thinkin' straight
An' livin' right, they wouldn't be so terrible and
great.
A good horse needs no snaffle and a good man, I
opine,
Doesn't need a law to check him or to force him
into line.

"If we ever start in teachin' to our children, year
by year,
How to live with one another, there'll be less o'
trouble here.
If we'd teach 'em how to neighbor an' to walk
in honor's ways,
We could settle every problem which the mind o'
man can raise.
What we're needin' isn't systems or some regulatin'
plan
But a bigger an' a finer an' a truer type o' man."

The Mothers of the Ministers

The mothers of the ministers, how happy they
    must be,
For they have realized the dream my mother held
    for me!
They have the joy they hoped for, have the good
    for which they've prayed
And the wish that every mother of a baby boy
    has made.

I never see an acrobat go tumbling through the
    air,
But what I think some mother's little minister is
    there.
When Ty Cobb hits a homer and the crowd ap-
    plauds the "peach",
I wonder if his mother wouldn't rather hear him
    preach.

Above my little cradle, in the days of long ago,
A great cathedral hovered and the bells swung to
    and fro,
And every Sunday mother heard the chimes and
    seemed to see
The worshipers assembling there to listen unto me.

But, oh, I took to writing, for I was a willful lad,
And the minister she dreamed of was a joy she
    never had;
For my brothers took to business and I choose to
    serve the Press,
And I robbed my little mother of her dream of
    happiness.

Yet what if every mother had her fondest dream
    come true,
And every mother's son should do the work she'd
    have him do;
The world would teem with ministers, there'd be
    so many here
You couldn't get a plumber when the faucet's out
    of gear.

The Butterfly Discusses Evolution

"In a very recent age,"
Said a wise and serious sage
To a butterfly with wings of golden flame,
"You were not so fair to see,
You've a horrid ancestry,
From a crawling caterpillar stock you came.

"Now you proudly spread your wings
And you feed on dainty things,
You are beautiful to look at, but I shrug
My shoulders with disdain,
When I think how very plain
You must have been when you were but a slug."

Said the butterfly: "I know
In some distant long ago
As a caterpillar crawling on my way,
I was lowly as could be,
But what is that to you or me?
I am certainly a butterfly to-day!

"As a caterpillar slow
I could never guess or know
What my purpose was while crawling on the bough;
But I stretch my wings and fly,
And you surely can't deny
That I am a lovely butterfly right now!"

What Counts

It isn't the money you're making, it isn't the clothes
    you wear,
And it isn't the skill of your good right hand which
    makes folks really care.
It's the smile on your face and the light of your eye
    and the burdens that you bear.

Most any old man can tell you, most any old man
    at all,
Who has lived through all sorts of weather, winter
    and summer and fall,
That riches and fame are shadows that dance on
    the garden wall.

It's how do you live and neighbor, how do you work
    and play,
It's how do you say "good morning" to the people
    along the way,
And it's how do you face your troubles whenever
    your skies are gray.

It's you, from the dawn to nighttime; you when
   the day is fair,
You when the storm is raging—how do you face
   despair?
It is you that the world discovers, whatever the
   clothes you wear.

You to the end of the journey, kindly and brave
   and true,
The best and the worst of you gleaming in all
   that you say and do,
And the thing that counts isn't money, or glory
   or power, but *you!*

The Starlings

The martins all look down on them and treat
   them as their foes;
The wrens, I'm sure, consider them full-cousins
   to the crows,
And every song-bird 'round the place appears to
   look my way
As if he wonders just how long the starlings are
   to stay.

I'm told the starling family is a flock of ill-repute
That has a vicious history of stealing farmers'
   fruit.

They say the starlings all are tough and bully
    other birds
And in their conversation use a lot of ugly words.

I see them pecking at my lawn with gleaming
    yellow bills
And wonder just what purpose here the outlaw
    starling fills.
The blue birds live in dread of them and where
    the starlings stay
The lovely cardinals pack their goods and
    promptly go away.

The martins look at me as if I'd lost all sense of
    shame
To lease my grounds to such a crew, as if I were
    to blame.
The wrens in anger chirp at me; if matters don't
    improve
And I don't chase the starlings out they'll surely
    have to move.

Sermons We See

I'd rather see a sermon than hear one any day;
I'd rather one should walk with me than merely
   tell the way.
The eye's a better pupil and more willing than the
   ear,
Fine counsel is confusing, but example's always
   clear;
And the best of all the preachers are the men who
   live their creeds,
For to see good put in action is what everybody
   needs.

I soon can learn to do it if you'll let me see it done;
I can watch your hands in action, but your tongue
   too fast may run.
And the lecture you deliver may be very wise and
   true,
But I'd rather get my lessons by observing what
   you do;
For I might misunderstand you and the high advice
   you give,
But there's no misunderstanding how you act and
   how you live.

When I see a deed of kindness, I am eager to be
  kind.
When a weaker brother stumbles and a strong man
  stays behind
Just to see if he can help him, then the wish grows
  strong in me
To become as big and thoughtful as I know that
  friend to be.
And all travelers can witness that the best of guides
  to-day
Is not the one who tells them, but the one who
  shows the way.

One good man teaches many, men believe what
  they behold;
One deed of kindness noticed is worth forty that
  are told.
Who stands with men of honor learns to hold
  his honor dear,
For right living speaks a language which to every
  one is clear.
Though an able speaker charms me with his elo-
  quence, I say,
I'd rather see a sermon than to hear one, any day.

The Painter

When my hair is thin and silvered, an' my time
    of toil is through,
When I've many years behind me, an' ahead of
    me a few,
I shall want to sit, I reckon, sort of dreamin'
    in the sun,
An' recall the roads I've traveled an' the many
    things I've done.
An' I hope there'll be no picture that I'll hate
    to look upon
When the time to paint it better or to wipe it out
    is gone.

I hope there'll be no vision of a hasty word I've
    said
That has left a trail of sorrow, like a whip welt,
    sore an' red;
An' I hope my old age dreamin' will bring back no
    bitter scene
Of a time when I was selfish an' a time when I
    was mean;
When I'm gettin' old an' feeble, an' I'm far along
    life's way
I don't want to sit regrettin' any by-gone yester-
    day.

I'll admit the children boss me, I'll admit I often
smile
When I ought to frown upon 'em, but for such a
little while
They are naughty, romping youngsters, that I have
no heart to scold,
Age to me would be a torment an' a ghost-infested
night
If I'd ever hurt a baby, an' I could not make it
right.

I am painting now the picture that I'll some day
want to see,
I am filling in a canvas that will come back soon
to me.
An' though nothing great is on it, an' though
nothing there is fine,
I shall want to look it over when I'm old, an' call
it mine.
An' I do not dare to leave it, while the paint is
warm an' wet,
With a single thing upon it that I'll later on regret.

The Package of Seeds

I paid a dime for a package of seeds
    And the clerk tossed them out with a flip.
"We've got 'em assorted for every man's needs,"
    He said with a smile on his lip,
"Pansies and poppies and asters and peas!
Ten cents a package! And pick as you please!"

Now seeds are just dimes to the man in the store,
    And the dimes are the things that he needs;
And I've been to buy them in seasons before,
    But have thought of them merely as seeds;
But it flashed through my mind as I took them
        this time,
"You have purchased a miracle here for a dime!"

"You've a dime's worth of power which no man
        can create,
    You've a dime's worth of life in your hand!
You've a dime's worth of mystery, destiny, fate,
    Which the wisest cannot understand.
In this bright little package, now isn't it odd?
You've a dime's worth of something known only
        to God!"

These are seeds, but the plants and the blossoms
      are here
  With their petals of various hues;
In these little pellets, so dry and so queer,
  There is power which no chemist can fuse.
Here is one of God's miracles soon to unfold,
Thus for ten cents an ounce is Divinity sold!

No Escape

The dead man spoke no word,
  But wherever his killer went
Strangely a voice he heard—
  The voice of the man he'd sent
Crashing to death, unprayed,
As he told us—"I was afraid!

"I was afraid he knew my name.
  Afraid that the day might be
When somewhere he'd tell my shame
  And fasten a crime on me.
So just to get rid of him, I
Led him out to that place to die.

"I thought I could stop his tongue
  And get rid of his constant stare,
But I know now I was wrong,
  For he follows me everywhere.
The living forgive and forget,
But a dead man's wrongs are set!"

Kirby, the Rose Lover

I've been down to Kirby, down to Kirby and his
roses,
And his peonies and pansies and his countless
stock of posies,
And he never mentioned dollars, never talked about
his neighbors,
Never spoke a word of scandal or the hardship of
his labors.
But he led me through his gardens and, his eyes
with kindness glowing,
Like a father to his children, talked of living things
and growing.

We spent the day with blossoms, stood about and
talked them over,
Saw the orchards pink with beauty, and the mead-
ows white with clover.
And he taught me little secrets of the peonies
and roses,
As one mother to another all that she has learned
discloses,

Taught me how and when to plant them, how to
know wild shoots from true ones,
What to cherish of the old ones, what is worthy of
the new ones.

Oh, I don't know how to tell it, but I felt my soul
expanding,
Felt my vision growing wider as with Kirby I
was standing,
And I thought my little garden could be lovelier
and brighter,
That my roses might grow redder and my peonies
grow whiter,
And my life a little finer if I recognized my duty
And thought less of selfish profit and a little more
of beauty.

A Summer Day

Blue in the sky and green in the tree
And a bird singing anthems of gladness for me,
  A breeze soft and fair
  As a little girl's hair,
With nothing that's ugly or base anywhere;
  A world that's swept clean
  Of the doubtful and mean,
With nowhere a hint of the care that has been.

I stand at my gate with the sun in my face,
And I thank the good Lord for such beauty and
     grace.
  Time was, I declare
  When the snows drifted there,
And those boughs with their blossoms were ugly
     and bare.
  Now the sin and the wrong
  Of the cold days and long
Are lost in life's splendor of sunshine and song.

God makes it all right in good time, I believe,
We doubt when we're troubled, we doubt when we
     grieve;

Like a stark, barren tree
Looms the wrong which we see,
Hurt, anguish and care hide the splendor to be,
But at last from the pain
Rises beauty again,
And there's never a bough that has suffered in vain.

Perhaps at the last, 'neath a lovelier sun,
When the anguish and hurt of life's growing is done,
We may rise from our pain
Showing never a stain
Of the cares of the years which fell on us like rain;
When the soul is set free
All the flaws we now see
May be lost in the joy of the new life to be.

Grace at Evening

For all the beauties of the day,
The innocence of childhood's play,
For health and strength and laughter sweet,
Dear Lord, our thanks we now repeat.

For this our daily gift of food
We offer now our gratitude,
For all the blessings we have known
Our debt of gratefulness we own.

Here at the table now we pray,
Keep us together down the way;
May this, our family circle, be
Held fast by love and unity.

Grant, when the shades of night shall fall,
Sweet be the dreams of one and all;
And when another day shall break
Unto Thy service may we wake.

GRANDPA'S WALKING STICK

My grandpa once was very sick
And now he's got a walking stick,
Coz one of his legs, as he says to me,
Isn't quite so good as it used to be;
And he can't run and he daresen't kick
Coz he'd fall if he hadn't his walking stick.

When my grandpa comes to our house to stay
I like to carry his stick away,
And put it in places where he can't see,
Then he can't get up to come after me.
And he shouts out loud: "Hey! Everyone!
Who knows where my other leg has gone?

"I had it here by my chair and now
It's disappeared from its place somehow.
I'll bet this little Miss Mischief here
Knows something about it, she looks so queer.
Was it you, who carried my leg away?"
"Maybe 'twas eat by a bear," I say.

Then he can't get up and he can't move round
Till I come and tell him his leg is found.
The bear didn't swallow it after all,
He must have got frightened and let it fall.
Then my grandpa laughs till his sides are sore,
And we hippety-hop to the candy store.

IN THE GARDEN

I sometimes get weary of people, and weary of
    being polite;
I sometimes grow tired of the dull man, and some-
    times am bored by the bright.
And then when my nerves are a-tingle I walk in
    the yard that is ours,
And I thank the good Lord for the comfort of
    songbirds and blue skies and flowers.

I never grow tired of the martens which circle about
    overhead;
I never grow weary of robins—there is nothing
    about them I dread.
I smile when I see them returning, I sigh when at
    last they depart,
And perhaps it's because they are never vindictive,
    or petty, or smart.

And the trees don't expect to be talked to. I can lie
    there and dream in the shade,
And not have to think up an answer to some dreary
    question that's made.
So I often slip into my garden when I'm weary of
    hearing things said,
And thank the good Lord for my roses and trees
    and the birds overhead.

CONTENTMENT

Money and fame and health alone
Are not enough for a man to own;
For healthy men are heard to sigh
And men of wealth go frowning by,
And one with fame may play his part
With a troubled mind and a heavy heart.
If these three treasures no joy possess,
How shall a man find happiness?

Health comes first in the famous three,
But cripples can smile, as we all must see;
Fame is sweet, as we all must own,
But the happiest hearts are not widely known.
Money is good, when it's truly earned,
But peace with fortune is not concerned,
For the bravest and loveliest souls we know
Have little of silver and gold to show.

Yet there must be a way to the goal we seek,
A path to peace for the strong and weak,
And it must be open for all to fare,
In spite of life's sorrows and days of care.
For those who have suffered the most the while
Look out on the world with the tenderest smile,
And those who have little of wealth to boast
Are often the ones that we love the most.

So I fancy the joy which men strive to win
Is born of something which lies within,
A strain of courage no care can break,
A love for beauty no thief can take—
For they are the happiest souls of earth
Who gather the treasures of gentle worth—
The pride of neighbors, the faith of friends
And a mind at peace when the sun descends.

AGE

How strange is age, that season of decay
   Which all men dread yet strongly hope to gain,
   And all men wish their loved ones to attain.
We pity those whose strength has slipped away.
The tired old people, done with work and play,
   Once more as children, keep the window pane
   And watch the world's swift moving human train
Bearing the freightage of the busy day.

Not to grow old, in youth a man must die.
   The price of age is fading sound and sight
And wrinkled foreheads and the sitting by
   While younger hearts press forward in the fight.
We know that age puts out ambition's fire,
Yet to grow old is every man's desire.

THE INN-KEEPER MAKES EXCUSES

"Oh, if only I had known!"
  Said the keeper of the inn.
"But no hint to me was shown,
  And I didn't let them in.

"Yes, a star gleamed overhead,
  But I couldn't read the skies,
And I'd given every bed
  To the very rich and wise.

"And she was so poorly clad,
  And he hadn't much to say!
But no room for them I had,
  So I ordered them away.

"She seemed tired, and it was late
  And they begged so hard, that I
Feeling sorry for her state,
  In the stable let them lie.

"Had I turned some rich man out
  Just to make a place for them,
'Twould have killed, beyond a doubt,
  All my trade at Bethlehem.

"Then there came the wise men three
  To the stable, with the morn,
Who announced they'd come to see
  The great King who had been born.

"And they brought Him gifts of myrrh,
  Costly frankincense and gold,
And a great light shone on her
  In the stable, bleak and cold.

"All my patrons now are dead
  And forgotten, but to-day
All the world to peace is led
  By the ones I sent away.

"It was my unlucky fate
  To be born that Inn to own,
Against Christ I shut my gate—
  Oh, if only I had known!"

THE MOTHER TELLS HER STORY

When first I met your father, it was at a wedding,
　　dears,
And he wore a high white collar which stretched
　　up to his ears,
He was thin and short and nervous, and his dress
　　suit didn't fit,
And I didn't like the way he dressed his hair a little
　　bit.
It was parted in the middle and it lopped across his
　　brow—
And I never dreamed that evening I'd be married
　　to him now.

I knew a dozen fellows who were handsomer than
　　he,
And all of them were richer, and they thought a
　　lot of me;
They brought me flowers and candy each time they
　　came to call—
So this meeting with your father didn't mean much
　　after all.
And besides his ways annoyed me—I'd have told
　　him if I dared
That I didn't like his manner and the *vulgar way
　　he stared.*

Well, next Sunday after dinner he came up to call
    on me
And stayed so long that Grandma then invited him
    for tea.
After that he came so often that your Grandpa used
    to say:
"That skinny gawk is driving all the healthy stock
    away!"
But somehow I'd grown to like him, and I marveled
    that I could,
For he never tried to kiss me—though I often wished
    he would.

Now that's all there is to tell you—by next June I
    was his bride,
But before that I had made him part his hair upon
    the side,
And I'd made him change his collars, and I'd slicked
    him up a lot—
For I taught him what he should do, and the things
    which he should not.
But don't tell him that I've told you. That's the way I
    met your dad.
Would I do the same thing over? Well, he hasn't
    been so bad!

FATHER GIVES HIS VERSION

Well, you see, I met your mother at a wedding, long
    ago,
And though I was four-and-twenty, up to then I
    didn't know
That in all our busy city, which I'd traveled up and
    down,
There was such a lovely creature, with such lustrous
    eyes of brown.
But the minute that I saw her I just stared and
    stared and stared,
And right then I would have hugged her and kissed
    her—if I'd dared!

She was acting as the bridesmaid, I was best man
    for the groom,
And of course the bride was lovely, but the loveliest
    in the room
Wasn't just then getting married—'twas my thought
    as I stood there—
For I couldn't keep from staring at your mother, I
    declare,
And I couldn't keep from thinking, as we knelt there,
    side by side,
There must be another wedding, and then she must
    be my bride.

Well, the wedding party scattered, bride and groom
    and guests and all,
But I asked that lovely bridesmaid if she'd let me
    come to call.
Well, she blushed and gave permission, and when
    Sunday evening came
I bought a box of candy, with a very famous name,
And I went up there to see her, and her Pa and Ma
    were there,
And I wanted *so* to kiss her—but of course I didn't
    dare.

Now that's how I met your mother—and 'twas
    twenty years ago,
And there was another wedding—just the one I'd
    longed to know,
For one lovely Sunday evening, when I went up
    there to call,
I caught her up and kissed her, as we lingered in
    the hall,
And we planned right then to marry—it was love
    that made me bold—
Now that's how I met your mother—but don't tell
    her that I told.

A PRAYER

Grant me, O Lord, this day to see
The need this world may have for me;
    To play the friend
    Unto the end;
To bear my burden and to keep
My courage, though the way be steep.

Grant me, O Lord, to set aside
The petty things of selfish pride;
    To toil without
    Too much of doubt;
To meet what comes of good or ill
And be a gracious neighbor, still.

Grant me, O Lord, to face the rain
And not too bitterly complain;
    Nor let a joy
    My calm destroy;
But teach me so to live that I
Can brother with each passer-by.

THE DEAD OAK TREE

An oak tree died the other day
  Despite my constant care;
Now men must carry it away
  And leave my garden bare.

It came to leaf in early spring.
  To live 'twas guaranteed;
Man is so vain and proud a thing,
  He vaunted God, indeed.

For how can mortal guarantee
  The breath of life, and say
That he can keep within a tree
  What God may take away?

It cannot be that man can sense,
  As do the sun and rain,
What living trees experience
  Of loneliness and pain.

I think they never heard it sigh,
  Nor ever dreamed a tree ·
Could, broken-hearted, pine and die,
  Who wrote that guarantee.

WHAT A MAN LIKES

This is what a man likes: a blue sky and a stream,
The lily pads off yonder and the shore with gold
    agleam,
The west wind gently blowing for then the fishing's
    sure—
A friend to share the glory and a bass to take the
    lure.

This is what a man likes: a day away from things,
A day where dreams are golden and malice never
    stings,
A friend to read his heart to, who'll keep the tale
    secure,
A reel that's running freely and a bass to take the
    lure.

This is what a man likes: a chance to test his skill,
The hazard of disaster and a struggle's surging
    thrill,
The joy of honest hunger and hardships to endure,
The gulls to fly above him and a bass to take the
    lure.

This is what a man likes: a friend to share his boat,
The freedom of the open, an old and shabby coat.
For all the aches of failure, 'tis here he finds a
    cure—
A haunt God made for fishing, and a bass to take the
    lure.

BOYHOOD MEMORY

It used to be fun in the good old days to rise at
    the dawn of day
And dig for worms for a fishing trip. It used to
    be fun, I say,
For I'll swear that a robin who hovered near
    knew just what we were about,
Since he flew to the ground when the earth was
    turned and begged us to toss one out.
Yes, it used to be fun to go fishing then, but
    Time has rewritten my terms
Of what pleasure is, and I never get up to dig
    for a can of worms.

We'd sit on a dock and we'd swing our legs all
    day in the blazing sun,
And a few small fish on a piece of string was our
    ultimate dream of fun.
Then digging for worms was an easy task, but I
    tried it a year ago
And the earth seemed hard as a city street where
    the streams of traffic flow.
And I'd lost the knack of clutching a thing that
    wriggles and twists and squirms,
So I said to myself: "You will never again go
    digging at dawn for worms."

I stuck to the task till my hands grew sore, I
    labored and toiled and wrought,
But the worms were scarce and no robins came,
    and it wasn't the fun I thought.
But a small boy said as we walked away: "I'm
    wondering, Uncle Ed,
When there's so much pleasure in getting up,
    how can old folks stay in bed?"
I could only answer him this: "My lad, all ex-
    perience confirms
The dreadful fact that there comes a time when
    it's labor to dig for worms."

LIKE CALLS TO LIKE

If you walk as a friend you will find a friend
    wherever you choose to fare,
If you go with mirth to a far strange land you
    will find that mirth is there.
For the strangest part of this queer old world is
    that like will join with like,
And who walks with love for his fellowmen an
    answering love will strike.

Here each of us builds his little world, and chooses
 its people, too;
Though millions trample the face of earth, each
 life touches but the few.
And the joy you'll find as you venture forth your
 fortune or fame to make,
Lies not in some stranger's power to say, for it's
 all in the joy you take.

If you walk in honor then honest men will meet
 you along the way,
But if you be false you will find men false, wher-
 ever you chance to stray.
For good breeds good and the bad breeds bad; we
 are met by the traits we show.
Love will find a friend at the stranger's door where
 hate would find a foe.

For each of us builds the world he knows, which
 only himself can spoil,
And an hour of hate or an hour of shame can ruin
 a life of toil.
And though to the farthermost ends of earth your
 duty may bid you fare
If you walk with truth in your heart as a friend,
 you will find friends waiting there.

MARBLES AND MONEY

Ed and John were little boys in the long ago,
Playing marbles day by day, just like boys you know.
Ed was clever, so was John. Ed one difference
     bore—
Winning marbles when he played made him wish
     for more.
Heavier grew his little sack, still on winning bent—
Ed had more than he could use, but was not content.

John played marbles now and then, never lost them
     all;
Had enough to join the game when the boys would
     call,
Played at baseball, climbed the trees, loved the birds,
     and knew
Many a thrill of doing things Ed would never do.
Kept his marbles in a sack smaller far than Ed's;
Hadn't more than fifty mibs, blues and whites and
     reds.

"John," said Ed one day to him, still on marbles
     bent,
"I've a thousand in my sacks, but I'm not content.
Just how many now have you?" Answered John,
     "A few.
Fifty marbles, I should say, but I've more than
     you."

"More than I?" said Ed, surprised, "surely that
    can't be!"
"Yes," said John, "I've more than you—I've all I
    want, you see."

Rich man, piling wealth on wealth, catch John's
    point of view!
Who has all he wants to-day is richer far than you.

THE OLD PROSPECTOR TALKS

Gold is found in the hills, and then
Carried back to the haunts of men.
And two of us came in the early days
To pan the streams for the dirt that pays.

And we stuck it out for a time, till he
Got sick of the game which enchanted me.
And he went back to the town one day
To get his gold in an easier way.

He quit these hills and he left me cold
To scramble with men for his bit of gold.
Now some like walls and roofs and rooms,
But I like mountains where thunder booms,

And skies and trees and the open plains
Where a man must work for the bit he gains.

So I've stayed right here and I've dreamed my dreams
And smoked my pipe by these running streams,

And kept my cabin up here alone,
With all this beauty to call my own.
I've taken my gold with pick and pan
And sent it back to be stained by man.

I've wrestled with rocks and streams for mine
And made my friendships with fir and pine.
Now the world down there may think me odd,
But maybe I won't seem queer to God.

UP AND DOWN THE LANES OF LOVE

Up and down the lanes of love,
With the bright blue skies above,
And the grass beneath our feet,
Oh, so green and Oh, so sweet!
There we wandered, boy and girl,
Sun-kissed was each golden curl;
Hand in hand we used to stray,
Hide-and-seek we used to play;
Just a pair of kids were we,
Laughing, loving, trouble free.

Up and down the lanes of love
With the same blue skies above,

Next we wandered, bride and groom,
With the roses all in bloom;
Arm in arm we strolled along,
Life was then a merry song,
Laughing, dancing as we went,
Lovers, cheerful and content;
No one else, we thought, could be
Quite so happy as were we.

Up and down the lanes of love,
Dark and gray the skies above;
Hushed the song-birds' merry tune,
Withered every rose of June.
Grief was ours to bear that day,
All our smiles had passed away;
Sorrow we must bear together,
Love must have its rainy weather,
Keeping still our faith in God,
As the lanes of love we trod.

Up and down the lanes of love,
Still the skies are bright above.
Feeble now we go our way,
Time has turned our hair to gray;
Rain and sunshine, joy and woe,
Both of us have come to know.
All of life's experience
Has been given us to sense;
Still our hearts keep perfect tune
As they did in days of June.

THE OLD HAT

To-day as I was starting out,
The lady that I write about
Stood at the door as if to chat,
Then handed me an old-time hat,
A bonnet I had worn, I know,
The first time several years ago;
"Now get this cleaned," she said to me,
"And just as good as new 'twill be."

I chuckled as I carried down
That old fedora, rusty brown.
I chuckled, living that scene o'er,
The good wife standing at the door,
As earnest as a wife can be,
Handing that worn-out lid to me,
And saying: "Have this cleaned, my dear,
'Twill serve you for another year."

Let's twist the scene around and see
What would occur if I should be
Prompted to try a trick like that
And hand to her an ancient hat,
A bonnet of a vintage rare,
Saying: "It's good enough to wear
Just have this blocked and cleaned, my dear,
'Twill serve you for another year."

I fancy then the fur would fly
If such a trick I dared to try.
She'd wither me with looks of scorn
And spoil another autumn morn.
But let it drop. A man and wife
Have different views of hats and life,
And meekly to the Greek I went
And had it cleaned—and she's content.

ENRICHED

Looking back, it seems to me
All the griefs which had to be
Left me, when the pain was o'er,
Richer than I'd been before;
And by every hurt and blow
Suffered in the Long-ago,
I can face the world to-day
In a bigger, kindlier way.

Pleasure doesn't make the man,
Life requires a sterner plan.
He who never knows a care
Never learns what he can bear;
He who never sheds a tear
Never lives through days of fear,
Has no courage he can show
When the winds of winter blow.

When the nights were dark and bleak
And in vain I'd strive to seek
Reasons for my bitter grief,
When I faltered in belief,
Little did I think or know
I should find it better so;
But to-day I've come to see
What those sorrows meant to me.

I am richer by the tears
I have shed in earlier years;
I am happier each morn
For the burdens I have borne;
And for what awaits me yet,
By the trials I have met,
I am stronger, for I know
What it means to bear a blow.

YOUTH AND THE WORLD

There is many a battle that's yet to be won,
There is many a glorious deed to be done.
The world is still young! For the youth at its door
There are tasks some shall do never dreamed of
    before.
It is not an old world, worn and wrinkled and gray,
It's a world that is being reborn every day.

The old hearts are settled and fixed and they'll do
Nothing that's daring or brilliant or new.
Their days of adventure have long since gone by,
They have finished their tasks and they're waiting
     to die;
But the youngsters who stand at the world's open
     door
Have much to achieve never dreamed of before.

On the well-traveled lanes of the land and the sea
Every day will the crowds of humanity be.
On the streets which are paved and the avenues
     known
Are the people who care not to venture alone.
But the young heart and stout sees the goal that's
     afar,
And dares to set out where the strange dangers are.

What's not possible now shall be possible when
Some young heart and brave shows the way to all
     men.
Youth shall remake the world. What is best of
     to-day
Shall to-morrow to something that's better give way.
So, come you young fellows to life, with a will,
While you work and you dream the world cannot
     stand still.

MY AUNT'S BONNET

They say life's simple—but I don't know.
Who can tell where a word will go?
Or how many hopes will rise and fall
With the weakest brick in the cellar wall?
Or how many hearts will break and bleed
As the result of one careless deed?
Why, my old Aunt's bonnet caused more dismay
Than a thousand suns could shine away.

She wore it high through her top-knot pinned,
A perfect kite for a heavy wind,
But the hat would stick though a gale might blow
If she found the place where the pins should go.
One Sunday morning she dressed in haste,
She hadn't a minute which she could waste,
She'd be late for church. Now the tale begins,
She didn't take care with those bonnet pins.

Oh, the wind it howled, and the wind it blew,
And away from her head that bonnet flew!
It swirled up straight to select its course,
First brushing the ears of the deacon's horse;
With a leap he scampered away in fright
And scattered the children, left and right.
A stranger grabbed for the horse's head,
But stumbled and fractured his own instead.

After the bonnet a small boy ran,
Knocked over a woman, and tripped a man.
The deacon's daughter married the chap
Who rescued her from the swaying trap,
And she lived to regret it later on.
In all that town there abided none
Whose life wasn't changed on that dreadful day
When my old Aunt's bonnet was blown away.

Some were crippled, and some went mad,
Some turned saintly, and some turned bad,
Birth and marriage and death and pain
Were all swept down in that bonnet's train.
Wives quarreled with husbands! I can't relate
The endless tricks which were played by fate.
There are folk to-day who had not been born
Had my Aunt stayed home on that Sunday morn.

THE JOY OF GETTING HOME

The joy of getting home again
  Is the sweetest thrill I know.
Though travelers by ship or train
  Are smiling when they go,
The eye is never quite so bright,
  The smile so wide and true,
As when they pass the last home light
  And all their wandering's through.

Oh, I have journeyed down to sea
  And traveled far by rail,
But naught was quite so fair to me
  As that last homeward trail.
Oh, nothing was in London town,
  Or Paris gay, or Rome
With all its splendor and renown,
  So good to see as home.

'Tis good to take these lovely trips,
  'Tis good to get away,
There's pleasure found on sailing ships,
  But travel as you may
You'll learn as most of us have learned,
  Wherever you may roam,
You're happiest when your face is turned
  Toward the lights of home.

SHE WOULDN'T GO TO BED

Once there was a little girl who wouldn't go to bed,
Wanted to sit up all night. That is what she said.
So her pa and ma and nurse said they didn't care,
Went to bed themselves and left her sitting in her
    chair,
Left her downstairs all alone, turned out every light,
All except the one where she was sitting up all night.

Soon the house got, oh, so still and shadowy and
    queer!
This little girl who wouldn't sleep began to say:
    "Oh, dear,
I wish they hadn't gone upstairs and left me all
    alone!
I wish the wind would go away and stop that awful
    moan!
I wish the shutters wouldn't bang! I wish I hadn't
    said
I'd rather stay up all the night and never go to
    bed!"

The rocking chair dropped off to sleep, the books
    upon the shelves
Looked just as though they'd gone to bed and
    covered up themselves.
Her dolls and tea things lost their charm and grew
    too tired to play

And nothing looked as bright to her as it had look'd
    by day.
She heard the great clock ticking and she fancied
    that it said:
"It's time that little girls like you were safely tucked
    in bed."

Then up the stairs she scampered just as fast as she
    could race
And, oh, it felt so good once more to feel her
    mother's face!
And, oh, it felt so good to feel her arms and kiss her
    cheek
And snuggle down beside her and to hear her daddy
    speak!
And now I ought to tell you when the moon shines
    overhead,
I know one lovely little girl who's glad to go to bed.

SAID THE CARPENTER TO ME

"What this house is going to be,"
Said the carpenter to me,
"From the plan I cannot see.
With my hammer, saw and plane,
I can build it to remain,
Long to buffet wind and rain.

"Square the room, and strong the roof,
I can make it weather-proof,
True below and fair aloof;
But I cannot guarantee
That this house shall lovely be,
Filled with joy and sorrow-free.

"Shall these rooms with peace be filled?
Here shall anger's voice be stilled?
They must say for whom I build.
When at last I go away,
Here shall all that's tender stay?
Those who come to dwell must say.

"I have finished. Staunch the place,
Now it needs the touch of grace,

Needs a mother's smiling face,
Needs the living spirit here,
Growing lovelier year by year,
Ere this house shall glow with cheer.

"I have tried to build it well—
But shall beauty truly dwell
'Neath this roof? The years must tell.
By the tenderness displayed,
By the brave souls, unafraid,
Must this home at last be made."

THE MISERY OF CHEATING

He cheated just a little and his comrade never
    knew.
  He won a little silver cup to place upon a shelf,
And someone made a pretty speech and called
    him "sportsman true,"
  Which only seemed to make him more dis-
    gusted with himself.

He took a sly advantage when nobody else could
    see.
  He thought he would be proud to own that
    little trinket cheap,

He thought he would be happy to achieve that
    victory,
    But when he went to bed that night he found
      he couldn't sleep.

The cup stood on his mantel shelf, but every time
    he turned
    It seemed to whisper to him: "You're a liar
      and a cheat!
I'm the token of a triumph which you know you
    haven't earned.
    I'm the symbol of a victory you know you can't
      repeat."

At last he took that cup away and hid it out of
    sight.
    He couldn't bear to see it sneer upon his man-
      tel shelf.
He'd fooled a dozen people for a bit of metal
    bright,
    But when he got it home he found he couldn't
      fool himself.

HIS PHILOSOPHY

"I'm not a philosopher, bearded and gray,"
  Said he unto me.
"I'm simple of speech and I'm plain in my way,
  Which is easy to see.
I don't know the whys and the wherefores and
    whences,
What life really is and just how it commences,
But I do know the living encounter expenses.

"With high-sounding language I cannot compete,
  But some things I've learned.
I know that the money for house rent and meat
  Must always be earned.
And whether the man be day-toiler or scholar,
If his need be for coal or a tie for his collar
He must either have credit, or dig up the dollar.

"I know that I live and shall live till I die,
  And I don't have to read
Deep volumes to tell me as time hurries by
  There is much I shall need.
My problem is this: in foul weather or sunny,
My children will frequently want bread and honey
And the grocer who sells them will ask for the money.

"So having to live on the earth day by day,
  Along with the rest,
The problem's not which is the easiest way,
  But which is the best.
My philosophy's this: to look after my fences,
To think of the future before it commences
And to work for an income to meet life's expenses."

THE NEW CAR

I had an old, tired car,
  Worn with long years of travel,
A bus with many a scar
  And stained with pitch and gravel,
And all within our city
Upon the wreck took pity.

Nothing could harm it more,
  Long since was gone its splendor,
And all who looked it o'er
  With it were, oh, so tender!
Truck drivers passing there
Watched out for it with care.

And then I turned it in
  And bought a shiny new one.
Glistened its side of tin.

I'd picked a Royal blue one.
A lady in her car
Gave it its first day's jar.

I left it on the street
  In all its regal splendor,
A boy, delivering meat,
  Crumpled the forward fender.
The next day it was struck
By one who drove a truck.

Safe is the man who wears
  His face well-trimmed with plaster,
Safe seems the car that bears
  The scars of grim disaster.
But all the reckless crew
Pick on the car that's new.

THE MIND

The mind is that mysterious thing
Which makes the toiler and the king.
It is the realm of thought where dwells
The nursery rhymes the father tells.
It is the source of all that gives
High color to the life he lives.
It starts the smile or shapes the frown,
It lifts man up or holds him down.
It marks the happy singing lad,
It marks the neighbor kind and glad,
And world wide over this we find—
A man is fashioned by his mind.

How strange it is that what we see
And seem to cherish tenderly
Is not the outward garb of clay,
For all are formed the self-same way.
Not in the hands and legs and cheeks,
Not in the common voice which speaks,
Lies man's identity on earth—
All these come with the gift of birth.
But love and friendship and delight
Lie in a world that's hid from sight.
The mind of all is master still
To fashion them for good or ill.

So men and women here are wrought
By this strange hidden power of thought,
And each becomes in life the thing
The mind has long been fashioning.
Man's body moves and eats and drinks
And but reflects the thoughts he thinks.
His every action leaves behind
Merely the prompting of his mind.
Bad men have arms and legs and eyes.
That which we cherish or despise
And shapes each individual soul
Is wholly in the mind's control.

LOSER AND VICTOR

He was beaten from the start,
Beaten by his doubting heart,
And he had a ready ear
For the busy tongue of fear,
And he had a timid mind
Unto fretfulness inclined,
Filled with many reasons why
It was vain for him to try.

Given a task he'd shake his head,
"Can't do that!" he often said,
"Times are hard and none will stay,
Listening to the words I say.

It is futile now to try.
People simply will not buy!"
Thus he walked the streets of trade,
Both discouraged and afraid.

But another kind of man
Thought this way: "Perhaps I can!
If I will supply the pluck,
Fortune may provide the luck.
If I have the grit to try,
There are people who may buy;
Anyhow, I'll not submit
To defeat before I'm hit."

One was beaten from the start,
Beaten by his doubting heart,
Beaten when he gave his ear
To the busy tongue of fear.
But another with his chance
Seized the moment to advance,
And came happy home at night
Just because he dared to fight.

OUR HOUSE

I like to see a lovely lawn
Bediamoned with dew at dawn,
But mine is often trampled bare,
Because the youngsters gather there.

I like a spotless house and clean
Where many a touch of grace is seen,
But mine is often tossed about
By youngsters racing in and out.

I like a quiet house at night
Where I may sit to read and write,
But my peace flies before the tones
Of three brass throated saxophones.

My books to tumult are resigned,
In vain my furniture is shined,
My lawn is bare, my flowers fall,
Youth rides triumphant over all.

I love the grass, I love the rose,
And every living thing that grows.
I love the books I ponder o'er,
But oh, I love the children more!

And so unto myself I say:
Be mine the house where youngsters play.

Oh, little girl, oh, healthy boy,
Be mine the house which you enjoy!

HONEST PEOPLE

Life is queer and people move
Curiously along its groove.
Strange things happen now and then—
Women fair and busy men,
Led by pleasure, want or greed,
Startle us with many a deed.
Up they rise or down they fall,
Life's a puzzle to us all,
But when all is sifted out
Honor calmly walks about.

Neither wealth nor pomp nor fame
Can withstand the touch of shame.
None so clever to elude
Nature's laws of drink or food,
None so smart that he can break
Nature's laws for pleasure's sake.
Life, with all its curious turns,
Soon the shrewd observer learns,
Howsoe'er his battles cease,
Leaves the honest man in peace.

Life is queer, but gentle ways
Win the world's unstinted praise,
Sin and shame and vice are here,
Taking toll from year to year;
But the brave heart and the true
Need not fear what they may do,
And the clean of heart and hand
All these terrors can withstand;
For when all is sifted out
Honor calmly walks about.

THE FIRST EASTER

Dead they left Him in the tomb
And the impenetrable gloom,
Rolled the great stone to the door,
Dead, they thought, forevermore.

Then came Mary Magdalene
Weeping to that bitter scene,
And she found, to her dismay,
That the stone was rolled away.

Cometh Peter then and John,
Him they'd loved to look upon,
And they found His linen there
Left within the sepulchre.

"They have taken Him away!"
Mary cried that Easter Day.
Low, she heard a voice behind:
"Whom is it you seek to find?"

"Tell me where He is!" she cried,
"Him they scourged and crucified.
Here we left Him with the dead!"
"Mary! Mary!" Jesus said.

So by Mary Magdalene
First the risen Christ was seen,
And from every heart that day
Doubt's great stone was rolled away.

THE LITTLE HOME

The little house is not too small
To shelter friends who come to call.
Though low the roof and small its space
It holds the Lord's abounding grace,
And every simple room may be
Endowed with happy memory.

The little house, severely plain,
A wealth of beauty may contain.
Within it those who dwell may find
High faith which makes for peace of mind,
And that sweet understanding which
Can make the poorest cottage rich.

The little house can hold all things
From which the soul's contentment springs.
'Tis not too small for love to grow,
For all the joys that mortals know,
For mirth and song and that delight
Which makes the humblest dwelling bright.

A BANK OF LILACS

I have a bank of lilacs near my door,
  A bank that never fails when May returns;
Its lovely dividends grow more and more,
  And more and more my gratitude it earns.
The humblest twig is freighted now with bloom
  Of purple petals, beautiful to see,
Exquisite tapestry from nature's loom
  Which every year the lilacs promise me.

Poor troubled men, perplexed and fretted much,
　Build governments their peace to guarantee;
They spoil the things their blundering fingers
　　　touch,
　Striving for goals they can but dimly see.
Beyond their power great promises they make,
　And sorrow follows every failing plan,
But lilacs never falter here or break—
　They always keep their promises to man.

Beside my door a bank of lilacs now
　In needle point of purple stands arrayed.
Though cold the spring has seemed to us, some-
　　　how
　The promised dividends are being paid.
The air is sweet with fragrance once again.
　Now to the bloom comes back the hungry
　　　bee—
A glow of beauty lights my window pane—
　My lilac bank has kept its pledge to me.

THE MISSING MAN

There was a man I once knew well,
Who had no stocks and bonds to sell;
  No subdivided acres which
  In seven years would make me rich;
No sets of books to fill my mind
With knowledge of the deeper kind;
No self-improvement courses in
The mystery of how to win.
Whene'er he called it was to say:
"Well, how are all your folks to-day?"

I wonder where this man has flown?
I wish he'd make his presence known.
  Whene'er he came to visit me,
  He asked no gift for charity,
He never asked me to subscribe
To funds to feed an Indian tribe,
Or carry on deep sea research
Or lift the mortgage on his church.
  Whene'er he called it was to chat
  In fellowship of this and that.

I watch to see him pass my door,
But unto me he comes no more,
  For every caller now I find
  Has dotted lines he wishes signed.
Oh, good old friend! I fancy you

Suspect that I have work to do,
And that is why you stay away,
But come again to me, I pray,
    That I may say: "Well, after all,
    One man still pays a friendly call."

FOR FISH AND BIRDS

For fish and birds I make this plea,
May they be here long after me,
May those who follow hear the call
Of old Bob White in spring and fall;
And may they share the joy that's mine
When there's a bass upon the line.

I found the world a wondrous place.
A cold wind blowing in my face
Has brought the wild ducks in from sea;
God grant the day shall never be
When youth upon November's shore
Shall see the mallards come no more!

I found the world a garden spot.
God grant the desolating shot
And barbed hook shall not destroy
Some future generation's joy!
Too barren were the earth for words
If gone were all the fish and birds.

Fancy an age that sees no more
The mallards winging into shore;
Fancy a youth with all his dreams
That finds no fish within the streams.
Our world with life is wondrous fair,
God grant we do not strip it bare!

MY LIFE

I have a life I can't escape,
　A life that's mine to mold and shape,
Some things I lack of strength and skill,
　I blunder much and fumble; still
I can in my own way design
　What is to be this life of mine.

It is not mine to say how much
　Of gold and silver I shall clutch,
What heights of glory I shall climb,
　What splendid deeds achieve in time;
Lacking the genius of the great
　The lesser tasks may be my fate.

But I can say what I shall be,
What in my life the world shall see;
Can mold my thoughts and actions here

To what is fine or what is drear.
Though small my skill, I can elect
To keep or lose my self-respect.

No man can kindlier be than I,
No man can more detest a lie,
I can be just as clean and true
As any gifted genius, who
Rises to earthly heights of fame
And wins at last the world's acclaim.

I can be friendly, blithe of heart,
Can build or tear my life apart,
Can happy-natured smile along
And shrug my shoulders at a wrong.
I only choose what is to be
This life which symbolizes me.

MERIT AND THE THRONG

A thousand men filed in by day
To work and later draw their pay;
A thousand men with hopes and dreams,
Ambitions, visions, plans and schemes.
And in the line a youth who said:
"What chance have I to get ahead?
In such a throng, can any tell
Whether or not I labor well?"

Yet merit is so rare a trait
That once it enters by the gate,
Although 'tis mingled with the throng,
The news of it is passed along.
A workman sees a willing boy,
And talks about his find with joy;
A foreman hears the word, and seeks
The lad of whom another speaks.

So up the line the news is passed,
And to the chief it comes at last.
A willing ear to praise he lends,
Then for that eager boy he sends
And gives him little tasks to do
To learn if all that's said be true.
Among the throng the lad is one
He keeps a watchful eye upon.

Oh, youngster, walking with the throng,
Although to-day the road seems long,
Remember that it lies with you
To say what kind of work you'll do.
If you are only passing fair
The chief will never know you're there,
But if you've merit, have no doubt,
The chief will quickly find it out.

THE WASTER

Oh, the days I've wasted, the days I've had to spend
And tossed away to serve a whim, as if they'd have
no end.
Old Father Time can tell you that I'm a wayward
son,
I've had a dozen fortunes and gone through every
one.

I should have turned the grindstone when steel
required an edge,
But summer birds were singing upon my window
ledge.
I should have strung together small words to make
a rhyme,
But summer is for playing and work for winter-
time.

They tell me time is money, and well I know that's
    true,
But who would be a rich man when skies above are
    blue?
And I have turned from toiling a game of golf to
    shoot,
And what its cost in silver I wouldn't dare compute.

A slave to fame and fortune I have no wish to be,
There are a thousand splendors on earth I want to
    see.
A dreamer and a waster I've laughed my way along
Indifferent to fortune, but tempted by a song.

CHECKING THE DAY

I had a full day in my purse
    When I arose, and now it's gone!
I wonder if I can rehearse
    The squandered hours, one by one,
And count the minutes as I do
    The pennies and the dimes I've spent.
I've had a day, once bright and new,
    But, oh, for what few things it went!

There were twelve hours when I began,
    Good hours worth sixty minutes each,
Yet some of them so swiftly ran
    I had no time for thought or speech.

Eight of them to my task I gave,
  Glad that it did not ask for more.
Part of the day I tried to save,
  But now I cannot say what for.

An hour I spent for idle chat,
  Gossip and scandal I confess;
No better off am I for that,
  Would I had talked a little less.
I watched steel workers bolt a beam,
  What time that cost I don't recall.
How very short the minutes seem
  When they are spent on trifles small.

Quite empty is my purse to-night
  Which held at dawn a twelve-hour day,
For all of it has taken flight—
  Part wisely spent, part thrown away.
I did my task and earned its gain,
  But checking deeds with what they cost,
Two missing hours I can't explain,
  They must be charged away as lost.

ON CHURCH BUILDING

God builds no churches! By His plan,
That labor has been left to man.
No spires miraculously rise,
No little mission from the skies
Falls on a bleak and barren place
To be a source of strength and grace.
The humblest church demands its price
In human toil and sacrifice.

Men call the church the House of God,
Towards which the toil stained pilgrims plod
In search of strength and rest and hope,
As blindly through life's mists they grope,
And there God dwells, but it is man
Who builds that house and draws its plan;
Pays for the mortar and the stone
That none need seek for God alone.

There is no church but what proclaims
The gifts of countless generous names.
Ages before us spires were raised
'Neath which Almighty God was praised
As proof that He was then, as now.
Those sacred altars, where men bow
Their heads in prayer and sorrow lifts
Its heavy weight, are Christian gifts!

The humblest spire in mortal ken,
Where God abides, was built by men.
And if the church is still to grow,
Is still the light of hope to throw
Across the valleys of despair,
Men still must build God's house of prayer.
God sends no churches from the skies,
Out of our hearts must they arise!

A FEW NEW TEETH

The dentist tinkered day by day,
  With wax and sticky gum;
He built a model out of clay
  And shaped it with his thumb.
He made the man a lovely plate,
  With three teeth in a row,
And bars of gold to keep them straight,
  Then said: "They'll never show.

"Go forth," the dentist told the man,
  "As proud as you can be.
Those teeth are perfect. No one can
  Tell they were bought from me.
Why I, by whom the work was wrought,
  The truth had never known.
Were you a stranger I'd have thought
  Those teeth were all your own."

While going out he bumped a miss.
  "Excuthe me pleathe," he said.
The lady smiled to hear him hiss—
  His cheeks went flaming red.
He met a friend upon the street,
  Who joined him for a walk
And said: "Let's go where we can eat,
  And have a quiet talk."

"I'd rather walk," the man exclaimed.
  "Leth thtay upon the threet,
For with you I thould be athamed
  Thum tholid food to eat."
"New teeth?" the friend remarked, and low
  The troubled man said: "Yeth!
My dentith thwore you'd never know.
  However did you guetth?"

THE OLD SAILOR TALKS

There was action in the old days when I learned to
love the sea,
There was beauty in the canvas which your turbines
can't replace.
Oh, the liner is a lady! But she's not the girl for me,
For she's business-like and snappy and there's
hardness in her face,
And I like to see my woman wear a little bit of lace.

There was poetry in sailing when the seas were
running free,
There was music in the rigging when the wind
began to blow,
But the liner, she is haughty, and she's not the girl
for me,
She walks away from humble ships who try to say
"hello!"
And I like to have my woman sort o' friendly, don't
you know.

It's all business now, in sailing, as I think you will
agree,
With arrivals and departures just as regular as bed.
Oh, the liner is a lady! But she's not the girl for me,
She always shows about the same each time the
log is read,
And I'd rather have a woman with some nonsense
in her head.

EQUIPMENT

Figure it out for yourself, my lad,
You've all that the greatest of men have had,
Two arms, two hands, two legs, two eyes,
And a brain to use if you would be wise.
With this equipment they all began,
So start for the top and say, "I can."

Look them over, the wise and great,
They take their food from a common plate,
And similar knives and forks they use,
With similar laces they tie their shoes,
The world considers them brave and smart,
But you've all they had when they made their start.

You can triumph and come to skill,
You can be great if you only will.
You're well equipped for what fight you choose,
You have legs and arms and a brain to use,
And the man who has risen great deeds to do,
Began his life with no more than you.

You are the handicap you must face,
You are the one who must choose your place,
You must say where you want to go,
How much you will study the truth to know.
God has equipped you for life, but He
Lets you decide what you want to be.

Courage must come from the soul within,
The man must furnish the will to win.
So figure it out for yourself, my lad,
You were born with all that the great have had,
With your equipment they all began.
Get hold of yourself, and say: "I can."

AUNT JANE WORRIED

Aunt Jane was one of the worrying kind,
Early and late with a troubled mind
Fearing the worst, in her chair she sat
Grieving herself over this and that.

Aunt Jane's particular stock in trade
Was things of which she could be afraid.
There wasn't a horror of which she'd read
That ever escaped from her shaking head.

Murder, robbery, death at sea,
Troubled and frightened her terribly.
Every possible evil which may occur
Was a terrible thing which might happen to her.

She feared death by trolleys, and death by fire,
Nothing but bad news came by wire,
And the curious thing about my Aunt Jane
Is all that she gathered from life was pain.

It never occurred to her once to think
That thousands of steamers at sea don't sink.
By a horrible fate was her life accurst,
She was doomed forever to fear the worst.

Never she looked to receive the best,
Always by gloom was her mind impressed;
And at last death ended life's frightful round,
But not once was she murdered, or robbed, or
    drowned.

THE GENTLE MAN

His life was gentle, and his mind
The little splendors seemed to find.
  The baser side of life he saw,
  But from the blemish and the flaw
He turned, as if he understood
That none of us is wholly good.

He lived as one who seemed to know
That as the swift days come and go
 Clouds blanket skies that should be fair,
 Rain is encountered everywhere,
And so o'er every human form
Must blow at times the bitter storm.

As one who loves a garden, he
Walked round the world its charms to see.
 Not only by the rose he stayed,
 The tiniest violet in the shade
On his devotion could depend,
To great and low he played the friend.

And as the gardener seems to give
More care to plants which fight to live
 So he, with tenderer regard,
 Befriended those whose tasks were hard.
Thus dealing gently, he became
More than a high and haughty name.

This was his wealth, that good and bad
Of him some happy memory had.
 This was his fame, that high and low
 Their love for him were proud to show.
This his success, that at the end
Men mourned the passing of a friend.

DREAMS

One broken dream is not the end of dreaming,
　　One shattered hope is not the end of all,
Beyond the storm and tempest stars are gleaming,
　　Still build your castles, though your castles fall.

Though many dreams come tumbling in disaster,
　　And pain and heartache meet us down the years,
Still keep your faith, your dreams and hopes to
　　　　master
　　And seek to find the lesson of your tears.

Not all is as it should be!　See how littered
　　With sorry wreckage is life's restless stream.
Some dreams are vain, but be you not embittered
　　And never cry that you have ceased to dream!

"I DIDN'T THINK AND I FORGOT"

The weakest excuses of all the lot
Are: "I didn't think" and "I forgot."
Worn and weary and haggard and pale,
They follow the path of the men who fail—
In thread-bare raiment from place to place
They've dogged the steps of the human race.
In most of the blunders which men have made
This pitiful pair a part have played.

A man cries out on disaster's brink:
"I should have stopped but I didn't think!"
Was the barn door locked last night? 'Twas not.
And somebody mutters: "Oh, I forgot!"
Since Adam and Eve and the world began,
This pair have followed the trail of man.
The commonest phrases in printer's ink
Are "I forgot" and "I didn't think."

Yet man will think if a pleasure calls,
And there isn't a doubt that he recalls
The promise another has made to him;
And a boy will think that he wants to swim,
And the chances are that he won't forget
That he mustn't come home with his hair all wet.
It's strange, but duty is all I find
That ever escapes from a failure's mind.

Search the burdens which men must bear
And you'll find the tracks of this precious pair.
With needless trouble this world they've filled,
And who can measure the tears they've spilled?
"I forgot" has wrecked ship and train,
"I didn't think" has caused endless pain,
And God must smile, as He sees us sink,
At our "I forgot" and "I didn't think."

GIANT STORIES

One time I told a giant tale before she went to bed,
But now when evening comes I tell her fairy tales
      instead,
  "A story shouldn't frighten her,
  It really ought to brighten her,
You should have been ashamed to talk of giants,"
      Mother said.

This giant had an ugly face with whiskers just like
      wire,
He lived upon a mountain top, and kept a blazing
      fire
  And so one night I chaptered him.
  And told her how they captured him—
A story not just suitable when little girls retire.

For in the night she woke and shrieked and shouted
      loud for me.
And what the trouble was, of course, I hurried in
      to see,
  "The giant came in here!" she said,
  "His ugly face was near," she said,
An awful dream, which Mother says should never,
      never be.

So fairy tales at night I tell, of pretty hills and dales,
Of dances up and down the hills and on the blossomy
      trails.
  I know I mustn't frighten her,
  And so I try to brighten her,
But strange to say that little miss still begs for giant
      tales!

THE HARD JOB

It's good to do the hard job, for it's good to play the
man,
For the hard job strengthens courage which the
easy never can,
And the hard job, when it's over, gives the man a
broader smile—
For it brings the joy of knowing that he's done a
thing worth while.

Oh, stand you to your hard job with the will to see
it through,
Be glad that you can face it and be glad it's yours
to do;
It is when the task is mighty and the outcome deep
in doubt,
The richest joys are waiting for the man who'll work
it out.

Beyond the gloom of failure lies the glory to be
won,
When the hard job is accomplished and the doubtful
task is done;
For it's manhood in the making and its courage put
to test—
So buckle to the hard job—it's your chance to do
your best.

SEA-DREAMS

I never see a gallant ship go steaming out to sea,
But what a little boy who was comes running back
    to me,
A little chap I thought was dead or lost forevermore,
Who used to watch the ships go out and long to quit
    the shore.

He followed them to India, to China and Japan,
He told the flying sea gulls that he'd be a sailor-man.
"Some day," he said, "I'll own a ship and sail to
    Singapore,
And maybe bring a parrot back, or two or three or
    four."

And often when he went to bed, this little boy would
    lie
And fancy that the ceiling was a wide and starry sky;
The ocean was beneath him, and as happy as could be
He was master of a vessel that was putting out to sea.

But something happened to the lad, and now he is no
    more,
For in his place there is a man who never leaves the
    shore;
I often think of him as dead, but back he comes to me
Whene'er I see a gallant ship go steaming out to sea.

TEAM WORK

It's all very well to have courage and skill
　And it's fine to be counted a star,
But the single deed with its touch of thrill
　Doesn't tell us the man you are;
For there's no lone hand in the game we play,
　We must work to a bigger scheme,
And the thing that counts in the world to-day
　Is, How do you pull with the team?

They may sound your praise and call you great,
　They may single you out for fame,
But you must work with your running mate
　Or you'll never win the game;
Oh, never the work of life is done
　By the man with a selfish dream,
For the battle is lost or the battle is won
　By the spirit of the team.

You may think it fine to be praised for skill,
　But a greater thing to do
Is to set your mind and set your will
　On the goal that's just in view;
It's helping your fellowman to score
　When his chances hopeless seem;
It's forgetting self till the game is o'er
　And fighting for the team.

HAD YOUTH BEEN WILLING TO LISTEN

If youth had been willing to listen
  To all that its grandfathers told,
If the gray-bearded sage by the weight of his age
  Had been able attention to hold,
We'd be reading by candles and heating with wood,
And where we were then we'd have certainly stood.

If youth had been willing to listen
  To the warnings and hints of the wise,
Had it taken as true all the best which they knew,
  And believed that no higher we'd rise,
The windows of sick rooms would still be kept shut
And we'd still use a cobweb to bandage a cut.

If youth had been willing to listen,
  Had it clung to the best of the past,
With oxen right now we'd be struggling to plough
  And thinking a horse travels fast.
We'd have stood where we were beyond question
    or doubt
If some pestilent germ hadn't wiped us all out.

So, although I am gray at the temples,
  And settled and fixed in my ways,
I wouldn't hold youth to the limits of truth
  That I learned in my brief yesterdays.
And I say to myself as they come and they go:
"Those kids may find something this age doesn't
    know."

STUDY THE RULES

Oh, whether it's business or whether it's sport,
   Study the rules.
Know every one of them, long and the short.
   Study the rules.
Know what you may do, and what you may not.
Know what your rights are. 'Twill help you a lot
In the critical times when the battle is hot.
   Study the rules.

Life's not a scramble, and sport's not a mess.
   Study the rules.
Nothing is left to haphazard or guess.
   Study the rules.
Know what's a foul blow, and what is a fair;
Know all the penalties recognized there;
Know what to go for, and what to beware.
   Study the rules.

Nature has fixed for us definite laws.
   Study the rules!
Every effect is the child of a cause.
   Study the rules.
Nature has penalties she will inflict,
When it comes to enforcing them nature is strict.
Her eyes are wide open. She never is tricked.
   Study the rules.

Play to your best in the game as it's played.
    Study the rules.
Know how a fair reputation is made.
    Study the rules.
Sport has a standard, and life has a plan—
Don't go at them blindly; learn all that you can—
Know all that is asked and required of a man.
    Study the rules!

THE BATTERED DREAM SHIP

Oh, once I sent a ship to sea, and Hope was on
        her bow,
But Time has brought her back to me and Wis-
        dom's painted now;
Yes, Time has brought me many things and some
        of them were good,
And some of them were failure's stings I little
        understood.

When Hope set forth the dream was fair, the sea
        was calm and blue,
I knew men met with storms out there and had to
        ride them through;
But still I dreamed my ship would ride and weather
        every blow,
For Hope flings many a truth aside which Wisdom
        comes to know.

The storms have come with bitter cold, I've prayed
      unto the Lord,
I've had false cargoes in the hold and thrown them
      overboard;
I've trimmed my sails to meet the gale, I've cut my
      journey short;
With battered hulk and tattered sail at last I've
      come to port.

'Tis not enough to hope and dream, for storms will
      surely rise,
However smooth the sea may seem, 'tis there dis-
      aster lies;
And I have learned from time and stress, that those
      who ride the wave
And come at last to happiness must suffer and be
      brave.

THE HOME TOWN

It doesn't matter much be its buildings great or
    small,
The home town, the home town is the best town,
    after all.
The cities of the millions have the sun and stars
    above,
But they lack the friendly faces of the few you've
    learned to love,
And with all their pomp of riches and with all their
    teeming throngs,
The heart of man is rooted in the town where he
    belongs.

There are places good to visit, there are cities fair
    to see,
There are haunts of charm and beauty where at
    times it's good to be,
But the humblest little hamlet sings a melody to
    some,
And no matter where they travel it is calling them
    to come;
Though cities rise to greatness and are gay with
    gaudy dress,
There is something in the home town which no other
    towns possess.
The home town has a treasure which the distance
    cannot gain,

It is there the hearts are kindest, there the gentlest
    friends remain;
It is there a mystic something seems to permeate
    the air
To set the weary wanderer to wishing he were
    there;
And be it great or humble, it still holds mankind
    in thrall,
For the home town, the home town, is the best town
    after all.

BENEATH THE STARS

Beneath the stars at night when all was clear,
    We sat and talked and wondered how and when
    The truth first broke within the sight of men;
What was it set them dreaming, thinking here;
Led them to hope and struggle year by year,
    To turn their backs upon the cave man's den;
    See order here and beauty's charm and then
Discover God where all seemed bleak and drear.

"They must have felt within themselves," one said,
"The spark eternal and the fire divine;
They must have heard God whispering overhead
    On nights like this with every star ashine."
And all agreed that man began to rise
When first he sensed the splendor of the skies.

PERILS OF A PUBLIC SPEAKER

A public speaker's lot is not an easy one to bear,
There's many a slip twixt thought and lip which
      takes him unaware,
For the ablest chap will meet a trap he never
      dreamed was there.

From year to year uncounted queer and startling
      things have sprung
All unforeseen, where I have been, to trip my halt-
      ing tongue;
I've stood in state, compelled to wait, while parents
      spanked their young.

But last July, I'll vow that I met my extremest fate,
In church I stood, with all the good, a moment to
      orate,
With one brave swoop I looped the loop with their
      collection plate.

I did not know it stood below and just within my
      reach,
My only thought was what I ought to mention in
      my speech.
I flicked my hand. You understand, that gesture
      was a peach!

Direct and straight I caught that plate beneath its
     velvet chin,
The nickels flew as nickels do, the dimes went roll-
     ing in
The furnace pipe. Oh, cruel swipe, which started
     such a din!

That goodly coin went down to join perdition's
     blazing coals,
While much concerned I stood and learned how far
     a quarter rolls.
I lost the speech, designed to reach those panting,
     thirsty souls.

With one fell crash, I knocked that cash right back
     from whence it came;
The parson sighed, the warden cried, my cheeks
     grew red with shame.
The children fought for dimes. They thought it
     was a scrambling game.

At times I've had some moments sad, some cruel
     pranks of fate,
But never quite so grim a plight, I venture now to
     state,
As when in church, from off its perch, I knocked
     that money plate.

A HINT

My son, when plans have gone astray
  And careless blunders bring
The crash which spoils your hopeful day
  Or failure's bitter sting,
Remember, as you face despair,
The dullest fool knows how to swear.

When things go wrong, as oft they will,
  Don't let your passions go;
Remember signs of temper ill
  The dullest mind can show.
It's proof of neither strength nor brains
To whine too loudly at your pains.

An idiot can curse and swear,
  A dolt can rave and shriek,
But oft it calls for courage rare
  No angry word to speak.
Fools are proficiently profane.
Who would stay cool must have a brain.

POSSESSION

The woods and fields and trees are ours
With all their lavish wealth of flowers;
The stars at night which brightly shine,
The morning sun, are yours and mine;
And added to such joys as these
We stand possessors of the breeze.

Who calls us poor, because we lack
The nation's printed yellow-back,
Is only partly right.   We share
God's mercy with the millionaire.
No more of beauty can he see
Than that which smiles at you and me.

We own the earth for all our time.
Wherever summer roses climb
For us to gaze on, they are ours.
Where'er a snow-capped mountain towers
We've but to turn our heads to say,
That splendid thing is ours to-day.

To us the blue of Heaven belongs.
Ours are the wild birds' merry songs.
Silver and gold are scarce, but oh,
What countless charms the days bestow!
And here, right at our humble doors,
Of splendor we have endless stores.

THE ORGANIST

"I played so badly," said the organist,
  "I'm thankful but a few
Came here to-night through all the fog and mist
  To hear me through.

"My fingers seemed to fumble with the keys
  As if they, too, were proud
And would not bend a little, just to please
  So small and poor a crowd."

And saying this, he left the cold, dim hall;
  But one there was who stayed,
Still lingering, as if trying to recall
  Some melody he'd played.

"How glorious it was!" she said to me.
  "What matters rain,
When one by music can uplifted be
  Above all pain?"

And so I set this down in hope that he
  May learn and smile,
Finding that work, which poor he deemed to be,
  Was still worth while.

DEATH, THE COLLECTOR

Death, the collector, came to him and said:
"I want the payment for your drink and bread!
I want the price which tenants all must pay
For having occupied a house of clay.
This is a bill which cannot be denied."
"Please call another time," the man replied.

"I'm sorry, but to-day I'm not prepared.
I really thought your master little cared
How long this lease of mine on earth should run.
I've planned some work which still is far from done.
There's still a hill or two I wish to climb;
Come back, collector, at some other time."

"I've heard that story countless times before,"
Said the collector, standing at the door.
"You say you want more time! Well, Mr. Man,
Give me the date precisely, if you can.
Suppose I grant you five years more or ten,
Are you quite sure that you'll be ready then?

"When will your work be finished? Can you say
At fifty with a smile you'll go away?
At sixty shall I call? and will you then
Be glad to quit the fellowship of men?
Ah no, my friend, only the Master knows
The day and hour life's mortgage to foreclose!"

SUMMER

Bees are in the blossoms,
  Birds are on the wing,
Roses climb, and summertime
  Is kissing every thing.
Little pansy faces
  Wink and smile at me,
And far and near there's not a tear
  That human eye can see.

There's beauty in the garden,
  There's beauty in the sky,
The stately phlox and hollyhocks
  Have put their sorrows by.
The gentle breath of summer
  Has blown the cares away;
All nature sings, for morning brings
  Another lovely day.

Yet some are blind to beauty
  And some are deaf to song;
The troubled brow is heard to vow
  That all the world is wrong.
And some display their sorrow,
  And some bewail their woe
And some men sigh that love must die
  And summertime must go.

Yet some there are who blossom
  Like roses in the sun,
Who dare to climb in summertime
  When all their care is done.
They hide 'neath smiles of beauty
  The sorrows they have borne,
They seem content that God hath sent
  Another lovely morn.

THE CYNIC

In all this world of loveliness there lies
Some blemish to attract the cynic's eyes;
The rose of June is born of ache and hurt;
The cynic says: "Its roots are in the dirt."

A little child comes racing down the street;
The cynic says: " 'Twill grow to be a cheat."
Ground for a hospital a rich man buys;
The cynic jeers: "It pays to advertise."

Honor is doubted, mercy a mistake.
The marriage vow is only made to break;
The cheerful neighbor is a grinning fool,
And only idiots live by law and rule.

Yet youth goes blithely singing on its way,
And men and women brave the heat of day,
Finding life's beauty worth its cost in tears;
And joy exists, despite the cynic's sneers.

WHO GETS THE WATCH AND CHAIN

I've sat upon his left, and I
    Have sat upon his right,
I've heard him sob, I've heard him sigh
    On many a banquet night.
Oh, we're a sentimental crew,
    The fact is very plain,
I'll prove it by the fellow who
    Receives the watch and chain.

He may appear a man severe,
    But let the speech begin,
And you can see the falling tear
    And mark the trembling chin.
He tries to speak, but seldom can,
    A fog obscures his brain,
I'm always sorry for the man
    Who gets the watch and chain.

I've sat where I could hear his heart
   In mortal anguish thump,
I've watched the grateful tear drops start,
   I've seen that awful lump
Come rising in his throat, and I
   Have wondered at his pain,
Why must the fellow always cry
   Who gets the watch and chain?

Man likes to pose as harsh and stern,
   But underneath his vest
Most of us some day come to learn
   He's easily distressed.
When he is honored by his clan
   His tears will fall like rain,
Grief always overcomes the man
   Who gets the watch and chain.

HER AWFUL BROTHER

Who teaches little Janet slang,
And trains those lips to say: "Gol Dang!"?
   Her awful brother!
Who whispers wise cracks in her ear
When none to stop his pranks is near?
   Her awful brother!

Who thinks up things for her to say
To shock her grandma day by day?
 Her awful brother!
Who laughs to hear her cry: "Oh, heck!"
Or "be your age!" And "wash your neck!"
 Her awful brother!

When friends have happened in for tea,
Who knows she'll mutter loud: "Oh gee!"
 Her awful brother!
Who likes to have his sister rough,
And fills her head with dreadful stuff?
 Her awful brother!

And yet, despite his love of mirth,
Who thinks that child the best on earth?
 That awful brother!
And who is it of whom she'll boast
And tell you that she loves the most?
 That awful brother!

THE FOOL

I'm the sort of a fool that will pull up a chair,
And then let a child come and rumple his hair,
And climb on his stomach and wiggle about,
Go through his pockets and empty them out,
And say when such mischievous rompings are done:
"Well, wasn't it fun?"

I'm the sort of a fool that will settle to read
A book, or a paper, a tract, or a screed,
And then let a blue-eyed and plump little maid,
Who of nobody living seems ever afraid,
Come right up and snatch what I'm reading away
Shouting: "Come, let us play!"

I'm the sort of a fool that will calmly sit by,
While a cute little finger is poked in his eye,
And a cute little foot kicks him square in the front
So hard that the neighbors are shocked at his grunt,
And then say with a grin when the fooling is done,
"Well, wasn't it fun!"

THE YOUNG DOCTOR

They said he was a doctor six or seven months
    ago,
They gave him a diploma he could frame and
    proudly show,
And they said: "Go out and practice and just show
    'em what you know."

Now I've never been a doctor, but a lot of them
    I've met,
And that first year, so they tell me, is a year they
    won't forget—
With the practice slow in growing, and the mus-
    tache slower yet.

So I chuckled when I saw him, and his curious
    mustache,
And I chuckled when I heard him sob about his
    lack of cash,
And the scarcity of people with the measles or a
    rash.

"I've a very fine diploma," he explained, "upon a
    peg,
But if something doesn't happen I shall soon be
    forced to beg;
It's a lonely business waiting for some fool to break
    his leg."

The older doctors listened to his dismal tale of
    woe,
And a flood of reminiscence then it seemed began
    to flow—
They had all been youthful doctors in the distant
    long ago.

They had all sat down and waited through that
    terrifying year,
With their skill and knowledge ready for a promis-
    ing career;
They'd all grown those first mustaches so that
    older they'd appear.

I still see that youthful doctor with the sadness in
    his eye,
Sitting bravely in his office while the sick world
    travels by—
When that first poor patient finds him, Oh, I hope
    he doesn't die!

THE YOUNGER GENERATION

This younger generation seems
　　To mock at all our preaching;
To want to build its house of dreams
　　Without our wiser teaching.

It looks at us with cool disdain
　　And scorns the hints we're giving.
We've lived, of course, but all in vain;
　　What do we know of living?

We are the kill-joys of the place
　　Who cry: "Beware of strangers.
Sin lurks behind the smiling face.
　　The streets are full of dangers."

So, poor old fogies that we are,
　　We sit with fingers drumming,
The pale, despairing Pa and Ma
　　Who dread what next is coming.

Ah, well! one time at counsel wise
　　We sneered in youth's elation;
We scorned the old who would advise
　　To seek our own salvation.

So why should we grow sorely vexed,
  Or trouble seek to borrow?
They'll be the kill-joys of the next
  Glad age which starts to-morrow.

The good advice they're heeding not
  They'll very soon be giving,
And hear *their* children wonder what
  They know of life and living.

PRAYER FOR A LITTLE GIRL

Dear Lord, our little baby bless
And fill her life with happiness.
Protect her through the coming years
And keep her lovely eyes from tears;
Keep her from pain and let her stay
As perfect as she is to-day.

Dear Lord, watch over her, lest she
Shall catch some ugly fault from me;
Guard her from selfishness and pride,
From anger at some whim denied.
And as the swift years come and go,
Grant that still lovelier she may grow.

Dear Lord, we ask, keep pure her mind,
Grant that no hasty thought may find
Lodgment therein, but from above
Send her the wisdom of Thy love.
May there be nothing base or vile
The joy of knowledge to defile.

Dear Lord, this for our babe we ask,
The strength and courage for her task,
Keep her from sin, and let her be
Always as radiant to see,
As beautiful and blithe and gay,
As perfect as she is to-day.

COUNTING THE BABIES

How many babies have you?
Well, really we've more than a few!
We've little Miss Laughter
And little Miss Pout,
And then there is little
Miss Scamperabout;
I never have counted them, good, bad and fair,
For the number is constantly changing I swear.

We've babies too many to tell,
We've little Miss Arrogant Belle,
We've little Miss Mischief
And little Miss Bold,

We've little Miss Whimper
And little Miss Scold.
And little Miss Hunger, who gets in the way,
Begging for cookies each hour of the day.

You'd not see them all in a week,
There's the bashful and little Miss Meek.
We've little Miss Blue Eyes
And little Miss Don't,
And that dreadful and
Troublesome little Miss Won't!
And the one that's as grasping as misers can be,
I refer to our little Miss Give It To Me!

I wish all their names that I knew,
There's little Miss Take Off Her Shoe.
There's little Miss Tippy-toe,
Little Miss Clutch,
Little Miss Sticky-thumbs,
Ruining much,
We've little Miss Drowsy, but need I keep on?
We've every known baby, and yet we've but one!

THE FUTURE

'Tis well enough to brag and boast,
But men who really do the most
   Sit very still.
They're very conscious all the time
To-morrow they will have to climb
   Another hill.
Nor all the little dreams come true
Make up for deeds they want to do.

Achievement is a pleasant thing,
But there's no end to conquering,
   And wise men see
That what is done, however fair,
Cannot in any way compare
   With what's to be.
And wise men's thoughts are ever turned
On secrets that are still unlearned.

I praise my skillful surgeon's hand.
"So much you've come to understand,"
   To him I say.
And then he smiles and whispers low;
"The things I really want to know
   Lie far away.
You think I've learned a lot, but oh,
There is so much I do not know!"

There is no conquest all complete;
No stopping place for human feet;
  No final goal.
Onward and upward men ascend
And none of us shall see the end
  Of glory's scroll.
But small and trivial is the past,
It is the future which is vast!

MEN OF SCIENCE

While ordinary mortals play
And laugh and dance the hours away,
The men of science, hid from sight,
Toil at their problems through the night
Within a laboratory room
Seeking to bring a thought to bloom.

We laugh and jest and eat and sleep,
The paths we tread are rutted deep,
The little tasks we're hired to face
Are known to all and commonplace,
But men of science fare alone
Into the future's great unknown.

From ceaseless toil at last there springs
One of the world's astounding things,
Proved beyond doubt and fit for fools
To place within their kits and tools,
And this becomes our common text:
"What will mankind discover next?"

We are the waiters of the world,
Debtors to every test tube curled;
The pale dependents on the few
Who bring to birth the glorious new.
Ours is to wonder while we live
What next the scientists will give.

A MOTHER FINDS REST

And now she dwells where neither doubt nor fear
   May find her breast;
No crying child may now disturb her here
   Or break her rest.

Ended the ache of living. Here she lies
   In wondrous peace.
God left a smile about her lovely eyes
   With her release.

How oft we fretted her or caused her pain,
  We cannot say.
Long hours she watched beside the window pane
  With us away.

Her sleep we broke with whimpering and sighs
  When we were ill.
Nor thought it much to rouse her with our cries,
  As children will.

But now we suffer so, and vainly call
  For her to come.
Her feet will never tread again the hall,
  Her lips are dumb.

Love had no more sweet service to provide,
  But this we know,
She'll watch for us upon the other side,
  Who tried her so.

IN TIME OF TRIAL

Oh, I have fared through laughter 'neath skies of
    summer blue!
And many an hour of mirth and joy I've danced
    and scampered through,
But, Lord, when joy was mine to know, I gave no
    thought to you.

I've had my days of pleasure and I've had my gold
    to spend,
But when my purse was plump and full I thought
    'twould never end,
And when I had no care to face I didn't need a
    friend.

I've whistled down the summer wind, I've sung a
    merry tune.
We never think of winter's snow when we are deep
    in June,
And no one dreams when pleasure calls that it will
    go so soon.

But, Lord, the skies are gray to-day and I am deep
    in care,
And I have need for help and strength my weight
    of grief to bear,
And so, like many an erring son, I turn to Thee in
    prayer.

BIRD NESTS

What a wonder world it is
  For a little girl of five
At the June time of the year,
  And so good to be alive,
With the meadows to explore,
  Seeking bird nests near and far,
And a dad of forty-four
  Who can show her where they are!

Every evening after tea
  We go wandering about
To the nests which we have found,
  Where the little birds are out.
And we tiptoe hand in hand
  To a certain lovely crest
Where delightedly we stand
  At a killdeer's curious nest.

And a meadow-lark we know
  With five babies of her own!
What a wonder world it is,
  And what miracles are shown!

She can scarcely stay for tea—
  How she bolts her pudding through,
With so much she wants to see
  And so much she wants to do!

So we hurry out of doors
  And excitedly we race
To the mother meadow lark
  And the killdeer's secret place.
And we talk of God Who made
  All the birds and trees and flowers,
And we whisper, half afraid:
  "What a wonder world is ours."

CANTERBURY BELLS

I stand and look about to-day
  And something plainly tells
The gardens are expecting May
  And Canterbury Bells.

I cannot hear the slightest sound,
  But somehow I can feel
A certain bustling underground
  That's very near and real.

Strange mysteries are going on
  Within the damp and gloom;
In worlds I cannot look upon
  The roses plan to bloom.

But I can only guess their plans
  And wait and watch them toil,
Convinced a greater work than man's
  Goes on below the soil.

The power of God I feel and see
  In every bud that swells,
In blossoms on the apple tree
  And Canterbury Bells.

TO A LITTLE GIRL

Little girl, just half-past three,
Take this little rhyme from me,
All the joy that gold can bring,
All the songs the birds can sing,
All this world can hold to give
Grown-up men the while they live,
Hath not half the charm of you
And the lovely things you do.

Little girl, just half-past three,
When God sent you down to me
Oft I wonder, did He know
Fortune's power would dwindle so?
Did He know that I should find
Such a curious change of mind,
And should some day come to see
Just how trivial pomp can be?

Little girl, just half-past three,
Lost are dreams that used to be.
Now the things I thought worth while
Could not buy your lovely smile,
And I would not give you up
For the golden plate and cup
And the crown a king may boast.
In my life you're uppermost.

Little girl, just half-past three,
This is what you mean to me,
More than all that money buys,
More than any selfish prize,
More than fortune, more than fame,
And I learned this when you came.
Other fathers know it, too.
Nothing matters more than you.

THE COMMON DOG

One time there was a common dog who envied
      nobler breeds,
He noticed that their coats were smooth and free
      from burrs and seeds;
He saw them held in ladies' laps and following
      rich men's heels,
And learned they had good beds at night and most
      delicious meals.
And so he vowed unto himself that constantly he'd
      strive
To make himself as smooth and sleek as any dog
      alive.

And outwardly he turned the trick; he found a
      rich man's door
Who took him in and let him sleep upon his velvet
      floor.
He fed him well and brushed his coat; his tail to
      wag would start
To hear his master speak of him as a noble dog and
      smart;
But having come to luxury and fought that battle
      through
He thought he then could do the things that com-
      mon canines do.

And so he ran away at night and roamed the alleys,
    where
The dirty homeless dogs are found, and soiled his
    glossy hair.
And torn and tattered he'd return to everyone's
    disgust,
Until the rich man's wife declared; "Get rid of
    him you must!
This dog is just a common cur, as everyone must
    know,
He wasn't bred for luxury." And so they let him
    go.

Well, men at times work tricks like that, as every-
    where appears;
To get to walk with millionaires they'll work and
    slave for years,
And when at last their fortune comes, they fling
    the barriers down
And chase the pleasures which belong to the com-
    monest folks in town.
Then men and women everywhere disgusted turn
    and say:
"He wasn't bred for luxury or he wouldn't act that
    way."

NIGHT

When night comes down
To the busy town
  And the toilers stir no more,
Then who knows which
Is the poor or rich
  Of the day which went before?

When dreams sweep in
Through the traffic's din
  For the weary minds of men,
Though we all can say
Who is rich by day,
  Who can name us the rich man then?

It is only awake
The proud may take
  Much joy from the stuff they own,
For the night may keep
Her gifts of sleep
  For the humblest mortal known.

By day held fast
To creed and caste
  Men are sinner and saint and clown,
But who can tell
Where the glad hearts dwell
  When the dreams come drifting down?

TWILIGHT

There come to me a few glad moments, when
  The busy day is ended, and I stray
Into the garden, shut away from men
  And all their tasks and all the sports they play.

The birds are homing for the coming night,
  The air is still and peaceful and serene,
But there's a beauty in the fading light
  Which at the noon of day is seldom seen.

Pansies and poppies, peonies and phlox,
  All with a long day's toil complete to view!
Trees which have stood perennial storms and shocks,
  Old as the world, yet always young and new.

I walk among them where the shadows fall,
  And seem to feel in touch with things divine;
Who knows, but I am brother to them all,
  Brother to bluebell, rose and columbine?

TO THE JUNE BRIDE

The groom is at the altar, and the organ's playing
low,
Young and old, your friends are waiting, they are
sitting row by row.
Now your girlhood's all behind you, in a few brief
minutes more
You'll be wife to him who's waiting, through the
years that lie before.

Oh, I say it not to daunt you, but to strengthen you
for fate,
In the distance for your coming many heavy trials
wait.
Whoso enters into marriage takes a very solemn
vow
To be faithful to the other when the days are not
as now.

Arm in arm you'll walk together through the lane of
many years,
Side by side you'll reap life's pleasures, side by side
you'll shed your tears;

'Tis a long road you'll be faring, for I've jour-
neyed half the way,
But if love and faith sustain you you will tri-
umph, come what may.

There's the happy time of marriage, but to every
man and wife
Also come the hurts and sorrows and the bitter-
ness of life;
For by these your faith is tested, 'tis by these
your love shall grow,
And my prayer is love shall guide you whereso-
ever you shall go.

A DOG

'Tis pity not to have a dog,
  For at the long day's end
The man or boy will know the joy
  Of welcome from a friend.
And whether he be rich or poor
  Or much or little bring,
The dog will mark his step and bark
  As if he were a king.

Though gossips whisper now and then
  Of faults they plainly see,
And some may sneer, from year to year
  My dog stays true to me.

He's glad to follow where I go,
  And though I win or fail
His love for me he'll let me see
  By wagging of his tail.

Now if I were to list the friends
  Of mine in smiles and tears
Who through and through are staunch
      and true
  And constant down the years,
In spite of all my many faults
  Which critics catalog
Deserving blame, I'd have to name
  My ever-faithful dog.

'Tis pity not to have a dog,
  Whatever be his breed,
For dogs possess a faithfulness
  Which humans sadly need.
And whether skies be blue or gray,
  Good luck or ill attend
Man's toil by day, a dog will stay
  His ever-constant friend.

THE HOME

Write it down that here I labored,
Here I sang and laughed and neighbored;
Here's the sum of all my story,
Here's my fortune and my glory;
These four walls and friendly door
Mark the goal I struggled for.
Never mind its present worth,
Here's one hundred feet of earth
Where the passer-by can see
Every dream which came to me.

Write it down: my life uncloses
Here among these budding roses;
In this patch of lawn I've tended,
Here is all I've counted splendid;
Here's the goal that's held me true
To the tasks I've had to do.
Here for all the world to scan
Is my secret thought and plan;
Through the long years gone·before,
This is what I struggled for.

Write it down, when I have perished:
Here is everything I've cherished;
That these walls should glow with beauty
Spurred my lagging soul to duty;
That there should be gladness here

Kept me toiling, year by year.
Here in phlox and marigold
Is my every purpose told;
Every thought and every act
Were to keep this home intact.

THE WILD FLOWERS

Men cover the earth with brick and stone
    But the violets steal away
To the shady places but little known
To be found by some one who walks alone
    In the calm of a summer day.

And the ferns move out to some distant spot
    Where the earth is cool and sweet;
With trees and song birds they cast their lot,
Let men build cities, they like them not,
    Nor the ceaseless tramp of feet.

The wild flowers sneer at man's buildings great
    And flee from the city's hum;
Away from turmoil and pride and hate
They live and bud and blossom, and wait
    For the few friends who may come.

THE CHILDREN KNOW

Old folks see the tulips red
Growing in my garden bed;
Childhood with a clearer sight
Peeps into the blossoms bright,
And upon a silver chair
Sees a fairy sitting there.

Old folks walk my garden round
With an air that's most profound,
Seeing here and there a weed,
Noting blossoms gone to seed;
Little Janet, though, can tell
Visitors where goblins dwell.

Age which knows so much **can see**
All the dead limbs on the tree,
Every blemish round the place;
Janet, with a happier face,
Has a thousand charms to show,
Charms which only children know.

Ready for Promotion

There's going to be a vacancy above you later on;
Some day you'll find the foreman or the superin-
tendent gone,
And are you growing big enough, when this shall
be the case,
To quit the post you're holding now and step into
his place?

You do the work you have to do with ease from
day to day,
But are you getting ready to deserve the larger
pay?
If there should come a vacancy with bigger tasks
to do,
Could you step in and fill the place if it were offered
you?

To-morrow's not so far away, nor is the goal you
seek;
To-day you should be training for the work you'll
do next week.
The bigger job is just ahead, each day new changes
brings—
Suppose that post were vacant now, could you take
charge of things?

It's not enough to know enough to hold your
    place to-day;
It's not enough to do enough to earn your weekly
    pay;
Some day there'll be a vacáncy with greater tasks
    to do—
Will you be ready for the place when it shall fall
    to you?

THE TRAMP

This is what he said: In all his life
    He'd done no useful thing;
Had idled, dodging children and a wife,
    And all the care they bring.

He thought that school was prison as a boy,
    And when he'd older grown
He had no gifts men wanted to employ,
    So off he trudged alone.

He'd never fretted; never shed a tear
    Beside a loved one's bed.
He'd never watched all night, heart-sick with
    fear,
    Or buried any dead.

He'd walked away from all that offered care
    This simple fact to find,
That those who would be happy here must share
    The woes of all mankind.

The Singer's Revenge

It was a singer of renown who did a desperate
  thing,
For all who asked him out to dine requested him
  to sing.
This imposition on his art they couldn't seem to see.
For friendship's sake they thought he ought to work
  without a fee.

And so he planned a dinner, too, of fish and fowl
  and wine,
And asked his friends of high degree to come with
  him to dine.
His banker and his tailor came, his doctor, too,
  was there,
Likewise a leading plumber who'd become a mil-
  lionaire.

The singer fed his guests and smiled, a gracious
  host was he;
With every course he ladled out delicious flattery,
And when at last the meal was done, he tossed
  his man a wink,
"Good friends," said he, "I've artists here you'll
  all enjoy, I think.

"I've trousers needing buttons, Mr. Tailor, if you
  please,
Will you oblige us all to-night by sewing some on
  these?

I've several pairs all handy-by, now let your needle
jerk;
My guests will be delighted to behold you as you
work.

"Now, doctor, just a moment, pray, I cannot sing
a note;
I asked you here because I thought you'd like to
spray my throat;
I know that during business hours for this you
charge a fee,
But surely you'll be glad to serve my friends, to-
night, and me?"

The plumber then was asked if he would mend a
pipe or two;
A very simple thing, of course, to urge a friend
to do;
But reddest grew the banker's face and reddest grew
his neck,
Requested in his dinner clothes to cash a good
sized check.

His guests astounded looked at him. Said they:
"We are surprised!
To ask us here to work for you is surely ill-advised.
'Tis most improper, impolite!" The singer shrieked
in glee:
"My friends, I've only treated you as you have
treated me."

Myself

I have to live with myself, and so
I want to be fit for myself to know;
I want to be able as days go by
Always to look myself straight in the eye;
I dont want to stand with the setting sun
And hate myself for the things I've done.

I don't want to keep on a closet shelf
A lot of secrets about myself,
And fool myself as I come and go
Into thinking that nobody else will know
The kind of a man I really am;
I don't want to dress myself up in sham.

I want to go out with my head erect,
I want to deserve all men's respect;
But here in the struggle for fame and pelf,
I want to be able to like myself.
I don't want to think as I come and go
That I'm bluster and bluff and empty show.

I never can hide myself from me,
I see what others may never see,
I know what others may never know,
I never can fool myself—and so,
Whatever happens, I want to be
Self-respecting and conscience free.

Pain

Were pain more difficult to give,
　And easier to cure,
Then happier all men would live—
　With less they must endure.

But, oh, the careless word can smite
　A blow no scar reveals,
And man can cause by just a slight
　A wound which never heals.

Devotion naught can separate
　Is difficult to gain,
So swiftly grow the seeds of hate
　And bitterness and pain.

And one with but a scornful glance
　Can change a friend to foe,
And not recall the circumstance
　Wherein he dealt the blow.

How strange a world, where frown and word
　To hurt and maim are sure,
And pain, so easily incurred,
　Remains so hard to cure!

When Janet Goes to Bed

When little Janet goes to bed
  We seem to heave a sigh,
At last the paper may be read
  And all the toys put by.
Now may we settle down and hear
  The things the others say
A lovely sense of calm seems near
  When Janet's tucked away.

When Janet's up and on her feet
  The home's at her command.
For one so innocent and sweet
  She rules with tyrant hand.
If I have something to relate
  Of what's been done and said,
I find it always best to wait
  Till Janet goes to bed.

Now should I sit me down to read,
  Or lie me down to rest,
She'll keep at me until I heed
  Her latest strange request.
And have I several tasks to do
  By which I earn our bread,
I never hope to see them through
  Till Janet goes to bed.

Ah, well, this roguish little lass
    Too soon will older grow;
Too soon these days of joy will pass
    And calm be ours to know.
So let her romp and let her shout—
    The coming years I dread
When we shall sit alone, without
    A child to put to bed.

Sunset

Some days die, as some men,
Softly and peacefully, and then
Others with pain-wracked twisted forms
Go to their graves 'mid gales and storms,
And knowing only skies of gray
And the wind's weird wail they pass away.

I watched the death of yesterday.
Golden the couch on which it lay.
Imperial purple edged a cloud
As if it were a monarch's shroud,
And there was neither pain nor fright
To mar the silence of the night.

Beauty and glory watched beside
The old day's bed until it died.
Troops robed in scarlet seemed to stay
To bear the noble corpse away,
Then hooded dusk with footsteps slow
Lighted night's candles, row by row.

Lord, for my loved ones, this I pray:
Sweet be the sunset of their day!
May beauty grace their lives, and when
Thou call'st their spirits home again
May trails of glory round them sweep
As silently they fall asleep.

A Mocking Bird in Florida

A mocking bird in Florida at dawn begins to sing.
He floods my room with melody and sets me won-
dering
Can waking up to toil again be such a happy thing?

Incessant is his silver call. "Get up!" he seems to
trill,
"The sun is at the ocean's edge and soon your room
will fill.
Get up! Get up! Get up!" he cries. I mutter:
"Oh, be still!"

Oh, little silver throated bird, I cannot sing as you,
But when at last I quit my bed I've many tasks
to do,
And it may be that I shall grieve before the day
is through.

And I am sick with weariness and tired are my
eyes;
The happiest man on earth is he who long in slum-
ber lies,
And yet with joy you sing to me: "The dawn is
in the skies."

I fancy you are right and yet so oft I've waked
    to weep,
So oft I've risen but to lose the joys I'd longed to
    keep,
That grumblingly I quit my bed and say fare-
    well to sleep.

But, happy-hearted mocking bird that sings the
    morning in,
So much of happiness is here for human hearts
    to win
That we should be as glad as you to see the day
    begin.

Hand in Hand

All the way to age we'll go
  Hand in hand together;
All the way to brows of snow
  Through every sort of weather.
Rain or shine, blue sky or gray,
  Joy and sorrow sharing
Hand in hand along the way
  We'll go bravely faring.

All the way to sunset land
  We'll walk down together
Side by side and hand in hand
  Held by Cupid's tether.
Once we danced in early May
  Steps we'll long remember;
So we'll trip the miles away
  Even to December.

Let the years go fleeting by!
  Gray old age shall find us
Still recalling smile and sigh
  Long since left behind us.
And though feeble we may grow,
  Worn by wind and weather,
All the way to Age we'll go
  Hand in hand together.

Barabbas

Barabbas, convicted of murder; Barabbas, the
    ne'er-do-well,
Awaiting the death of a felon, sat in his prison
    cell,
Already his cross was fashioned—at dawn they
    would nail him high;
When down through the dingy cell house there
    came to his ears a cry:

"Barabbas! Barabbas! Barabbas! Barabbas whose
    hands are red!
Take you the lowly Nazarene's and spare us his
    life instead."
And a sickened and frightened Pilate who dared
    not their pleas deny
Released to the mob Barabbas and ordered the
    Christ to die.

They saved him with shout and tumult, Barabbas
    with hands unclean,
Barabbas, of evil doing, who knew not the Naza-
    rene,
Was saved by a sudden fancy, turned loose and
    not knowing why—
Sent back to the street and the gutter, alone and
    unloved, to die.

In the gloom of that gray Good Friday the Sav-
  iour they crucified,
And the mad throng stood about Him and
  mocked till the hour He died;
They knew not what they were doing, but Pilate,
  pale and afraid,
Stood at the window watching, regretting the
  choice they'd made!

Money

Does money bring men gladness?
    Yes, at times!
It also brings men sadness
    And to crimes.

Earned well it is a pleasure,
    None denies;
But in the love of treasure
    Danger lies.

Who grasps for it in blindness,
    Foul or fair,
Sells out to bleak unkindness
    And despair.

By money friends are parted;
    Hatred sown;
For money, marble-hearted,
    Men have grown.

Money's important. All require it
    Till life is o'er,
But it destroys men who desire it
    And nothing more.

William Comes Courting

William comes a-courting,
  And smiles his best on me;
His happiest behavior
  Is offered me to see,
His eyes are bright with smiling,
  He speaks a glad hello,
And asks me how I'm feeling,
  As if he cared to know.

When William comes a-courting
  He stands, with courteous air,
Until I say: "Be seated,"
  And offer him a chair.
He asks about my business
  And talks of all the news.
When William comes a-courting
  I think he'd shine my shoes.

When William comes a-courting
  It's plain as plain can be,
Although he wants my daughter
  He's also courting me.
And I just sit and chuckle
  To watch this hopeful lad,
For years ago, just like him,
  I worked on Nellie's dad.

Missed

"It's not his money I miss," she said,
"For I've all that he had, now he lies dead.
But his gold won't buy me the tender word
That over and over from him I've heard.
Gold will buy me a great hall chair,
But it won't put his hat and his top coat there.

"I used to laugh at his farewell kiss,
Not thinking that was the thing I'd miss,
And I used to scold at his careless ways—
Now all that lies in my yesterdays
And I'd give his gold, could I see once more
His paper strewn on the parlor floor.

"The garden he loved will bloom in spring,
And over it all will the martins swing,
The flowers will smile as they've always done,
And I shall gather them, one by one,
But the thing I'll miss, is the muddy pair
Of gardening shoes which he used to wear."

The Padre

The kindly padre in his gown
Goes daily walking up and down.
The little boys with whom he chats
With reverence remove their hats,
And also reverence to show
The little girls all curtsey low,
While grown up folks like you and me
Wish more like his our lives could be.

"Aha," says he, with twinkling eye,
"I would not change you, though I try.
You should be good, and oft I pray
The Lord to take your sins away;
But Oh I love you, good and bad;
I love the mischief in the lad;
I love the merry hearts of you
In spite of all the wrong you do.

"Oh, were it not that I am bound
To sing the mass in vestments gowned,
And held by solemn orders here
To walk the narrow paths severe,
The boy in me on many a day
Would break the laws he should obey,
But I am what I am, you see,
Because it is my job to be.

" 'Tis very cold, this life I lead,
And heavy are the books I read,
And many, many are the woes
Which people unto me disclose;
But still I think that most of them
The Lord above will not condemn.
And I believe He'll love them, too,
In spite of all the bad they do."

Fathers and Little Girls

My father thinks that I ought to be the brightest
    child in school;
That I should remember what's six times six and
    never forget a rule.
And he says if only I'd stop to think of the word
    that I have to spell
I'd get a "hundred" every time, but I never do
    quite that well.
He shakes his head and he says to me: "Well, I
    certainly think it queer
That a bright little girl like you would make such
    blunders as I see here."

My father's sure that I ought to be the best little
    child they've got.
He says I possess the ability—but somehow or
    other I'm not.

For I'm always thinking of fairy tales and witch-
    es that ride on sticks,
And I just can't bother to keep in mind the an-
    swer to six times six.
If you were dreaming of something else I think
    it would trouble you
To be jumped to your feet to name right off the
    capital of Peru.

My father thinks that I ought to be at the very
    top of my class,
And he shakes his head when I say to him: "I'll
    be glad if I only pass."
But fathers are very much all alike, for the other
    girls say to me
Their daddies are sure if they'd only try at the
    top of the room they'd be.
And maybe the whole world's much alike and all
    little girls alive
Have trouble remembering six times six and
    guess it is thirty-five.

The Second-hand Shop

There's a little old man in a little old shop
That is cluttered with things from the cellar to top.
There is something of everything scattered about,
But whatever you want, he can ferret it out.
"Now just wait a minute," he says with a grin,
"I'll find what you're after. It's somewhere within."

This second-hand store of this little old man
I drop in to visit whenever I can,
For he in himself is a lovely antique,
And there's something about him so gentle and
    meek
That, just like the trinkets he sells, it appears
He has taken on charm with the dust of the years.

I chuckle to see him go shuffling around
Till the treasure he seeks in the rubbish is found,
And I fancy sometimes, as I sit there and chat
In that jumble of things, that man's mind is like
    that.
It's a second-hand shop filled with good stuff and
    cheap,
Gathered down through the years and all tossed in
    a heap.

Man gathers the good and the bad as he goes;
What he has, where it is, it is he only knows.
The stranger who sees but the rags and the
    bones,
Looks in without finding the good thoughts he
    owns;
But buried beneath all the rubbish that's vile,
May be fancies and dreams that are very worth
    while.

Heat

Cloudless sky and pitiless sun
And acres of harrowing to be done;
All day long that the corn may grow
The farmer toils in it, row by row.
The south breeze blows across dunes of sand
Great waves of heat from a burning land.

Hour after hour in the blazing sun
The reapers work till the harvest's done;
Like molten gold seems the ripened grain
Where the land breeze blows, but all in vain,
For heat, like fire, is a pitiless thing
Which mocks at man and his suffering.

In the open fields where the wheat is laid
A man must work without cooling shade,
And I often think as I pass him by,
As the sun beats down from a cloudless sky,
How little we know of the pain that's borne
For the bread we eat and our yellow corn.

Genius

A skylark in a by-gone day
   Mounted the sky
Singing its long familiar lay,
   And passing by
Went men and women up and down
   With hearts unstirred.
Theirs was the business of the town—
   But Shelley heard.

The air had borne those liquid notes
   For ages long;
From countless million golden throats
   Had poured that song,
And still the people sold and bought
   And toiled for fame.
'Tis but a bird that sings, they thought,
   Till Shelley came.

Enraptured by that lovely thing
   And touched with pain,
With every nerve set quivering
   Like leaves in rain,
He stood the while the twilight rang
   With chords divine,
And caught the song the skylark sang
   In deathless line.

Who knows what beauty and what grace
   Are hidden still,
Buried among the commonplace
   Of mart and mill,
Waiting with patience through the years,
   As did the lark,
Until the genius appears
   Their charms to mark?

Books

Upon my shelf they stand in rows,
   A city-full of human souls,
   Sages, philosophers and drolls—
Good friends that everybody knows.
   The drunkard shoulders with the saint;
   The great are neighboring with the quaint
And they will greet me one and all
At any hour I care to call.

There's Dickens with his humble crew
   That has no end of joy to give.
   With all his people I can live
By moving just a foot or two.

Or should I choose to sail the sea,
  Stevenson there will pilot me,
While jovial, lovable Mark Twain
Waits patiently my call again.

Sometimes a friend drops in and looks
  My little sitting room around
  And, in a manner most profound,
Remarks: "Your shelves are lined with books!"
  "Not books," I say, "but people wise
  And men to cling to or despise.
Vast peopled cities, calm and still;
For me to visit when I will."

Life Goes On

Life goes on. No end appears
To its laughter and its tears.
Wise men die, but just as wise
Men tomorrow will arise.
All that is will still go on
After we who toil are gone.

Life unaltered keeps its pace;
There's a man for every place.

Every day sees death and birth,
Marriage, melody and mirth.
While the great sun lights the sky
Men will toil as you and I.

Rain and sunshine, joy and care,
All who come to earth will share.
What we've known of pain and woe
Those who follow us shall know;
And in gardens much like ours
Still will bloom the self-same flowers.

Men will wonder, just as we,
What beyond this earth can be.
Never will the mind of man
Solve the Great Creator's plan.
Puzzle o'er it as they will,
Life will stay a mystery still.

His Grandpa

Who thinks that we are too severe?
　　His Grandpa.
Who thinks the modern doctors queer?
　　His Grandpa.
Who takes him walking down the street,
　And shows him off to all they meet,
And buys him stuff he shouldn't eat?
　　His Grandpa.

Who will not let the youngster cry?
　　His Grandpa.
Who slips him candy on the sly?
　　His Grandpa.
Who scoffs at every law we make
　To save him from the tummy ache,
And fills him full of chocolate cake?
　　His Grandpa.

Who thinks that we are silly fools?
　　His Grandpa.
Who mocks all hygienic rules?
　　His Grandpa.
Who laughs at all his wilful ways,
　And thinks him cute when he displays
His temper to the public gaze?
　　His Grandpa.

And yet who was it once was stern?
His Grandpa.
Who made his son obedience learn?
His Grandpa.
Who was it once pronounced the word,
Which now he says is most absurd,
That children should be seen, not heard?
His Grandpa.

The Poor Man

"I am a poor man," said a friend to me.
"I have to work so hard to earn my bread."
But he had praised the blue sky overhead
And smiled my patch of zinnias to see;
He was familiar with each vine and tree.
He quoted lines from poets he had read;
Knew Shelley, Browning and what Shake-
speare said,
And cherished dreams of what his son would be.

He spoke of beauty in a tender voice.
He told me pretty memories of his wife;
How never once regretted she her choice,
And all she did to ease his path of life.
"Just poor of purse," said I, "but rich in mind
And owning treasures of the nobler kind."

Santa Passes

Well, it was a Merry Christmas, of that fact there
is no doubt;
The little house proclaims it for the toys are strewn
about.
From the break of day till bedtime there was laugh-
ter in the place,
But I fancied that I noticed something curious in
her face.
In the midst of the excitement there would come
a wistful pause,
And I somehow have the notion that's the last of
Santa Claus.

Down the years we've had him with us; every
Merry Christmas day
Santa Claus has paid his visit in the good old-
fashioned way.
For when Buddy rose to boyhood, little Janet came
along,
But I somehow have the notion she suspects there's
something wrong;
For I thought that I detected in her conduct, now
and then,
A break in her devotion to the jolliest of men.

She hung her little stocking by the fireplace as of
old,
And she gave a cheer for Santa, but it lacked the
ring of gold,

And though Christmas day was merry, I began to
    realize
That our lovely little baby now is growing very
    wise;
And I can't help feeling saddened and regretful,
    just because
I am sure our house last Christmas saw the end
    of Santa Claus.

How to Be Cheerful

How to be cheerful, do you say,
When the wind is cold and the skies are gray?
How to be cheerful? Just one way:
Forget yourself for awhile today.

Never mind self and your irksome cares.
Somebody else greater burden bears.
Stretch out a helping hand and play
The friend to all who may chance your way.

You'll never be cheerful sitting there
Sorrowing over the hurts you bear,
For never a joyous hour is known
By the man who thinks of himself alone.

How to be cheerful? Scatter cheer;
Share your life with your neighbors here;
Encourage the weary and comfort the sad
And you'll find more joy than you've ever had.

Baby Letters

Oh you may have your letters with the line, *"find
check enclosed,"*
And you may smile at letters which agree as you've
proposed.
A friendly note is good to get; the mail's so full
of things
That one can hardly over-praise the joy the post-
man brings,
But when you're far away from home, the letter
best of all
Is filled with hugs and kisses in a youngster's
awkward scrawl.

The President once wrote to me; his letter's in a
frame,
I've kept a few epistles sent to me by men of
fame,
I've smiled to read the merry news which kindly
hands have penned,
But to the final hour of life of letters there's no
end,
Except to those entrancing notes your babe sits
down to scrawl
With penciled hugs and kisses, and I count them
best of all.

You only get of them a few. With time's swift
passing flight,

In but another year or two, she'll write as others
  write,
But now the mother guides her hand: "I love you,
  daddy dear!"
Sums up the news she tries to tell in letters quaint
  and queer,
And always printed boldly at the bottom of the
  sheet
Is a line of hugs and kisses just to make the letter
  sweet.

Time takes the joys we have away and newer joys
  bestows—
The lovely little bud of May, June blossoms as a
  rose;
The charms of childhood wisdom steals new love-
  liness to give,
And so these childish messages have little time to
  live,
But of the letters humans pen the happiest are
  those
With hugs and kisses scrawled below—as every
  father knows.

Every Boy's Chance

The night school swings its doors for all;
    Near-by the libraries are.
Who will, has knowledge at his call,
    Nor need he travel far.
Not much for wisdom need he pay,
    However poor the lad,
He has a better chance to-day
    Than Lincoln ever had.

However lowly born he seems,
    A richer child is he
Than Lincoln, with his youthful dreams,
    Who read beneath a tree.
However poor the circumstance
    Which hedges him around,
Life offers him a better chance
    Than Abraham Lincoln found.

Oh, boy, if courage you possess,
    And have the will to learn,
No one can keep you from success,
    From book to book you'll turn.
No library shelf to you is barred,
    No school denied to you,
Your battle cannot be as hard
    As that which Lincoln knew.

Who has the will to understand,
  Will find wise teachers near;
The poorest urchin in the land
  Has but himself to fear,
For 'spite of humble circumstance
  And fate and fortune sad,
To-day gives boys a better chance
  Than Lincoln ever had.

Because He Stayed Humble

Because he loved the poor of purse
  And gave his hand to them,
The rich and proud who scorned the crowd
  Were prompted to condemn.
Because he often stopped to speak
  With people poorly clad
And sought to ease their miseries,
  The wise men thought him mad.

Because by purple robes and gold
  He was not much impressed,
But daily taught this simple thought
  That brotherhood is best,

The men who fancied wisdom lies
   Alone in ancient lores,
With faces grim looked down on him
   And drove him from their doors.

Because he knew and understood
   The heartaches of the throng
And with them walked and freely talked
Great statesmen thought him wrong.
Because he said the joys of life
   And all that makes it good,
And peace at night were a common right,
   He died, misunderstood.

Because he chose to play the friend
   To those whose need was great
And liked to share a poor man's care
   He won a monarch's hate.
And still men worship pomp and power
   And thrust the meek aside,
Nor ever guess what friendliness
   Is lost through petty pride.

Suggestions for Men

She ordered her lunch, and then as she sat
At the table she took off her little blue hat,
Held up a mirror, as wide as a book,
And sideways and frontways proceeded to look;
She picked up a comb and she tossed back her hair,
She pulled it out here and she tucked it in there.
As I watched her I said to myself: "There's a
  hunch!
That's something to do while you're waiting for
  lunch!"

From a tube she squeezed stuff on her pink finger
  tips
And calmly proceeded to varnish her lips;
She penciled her eyebrows an ebony black,
And I wondered what else she could have in that
  sack;
She tinted her cheeks till they beggared the rose,
And the maid brought her food as she powdered
  her nose.
"Now there is a first-class idea," thought I,
"If the girls can do that why should men be so
  shy?"

Why doesn't somebody get out for a man
A neat little package, with soap in a can,
A razor, a brush and a looking-glass small,
So neat that his pocket could carry it all?

This is one of the sayings the classics produce,
"The sauce for the gander is sauce for the goose."
After ordering lunch, precious time could be
    saved
If, while waiting, he got out his razor and shaved.

Why not copy the women? 'Twould be no dis-
    grace
For a man to be openly kind to his face.
With a neat pocket outfit like this I suggest,
Man could always contrive to appear at his best.
At noon time, on street cars, with moments to
    spare,
At the dentist's, while waiting his turn in the
    chair,
Or while dummy at bridge, unconcernedly grave,
He could take off his necktie and collar and shave.

Christmas Day

I wonder on that Christmas night
    How many passers-by
Beheld that strange and lustrous light
    In Bethlehem's patch of sky?
We know how the shepherds chanced to be
    Unto the stable sent,
But did that star some rich man see
    And wonder what it meant?

They've told us of the crowded inn
　　And of the laughter gay;
But was there none who entered in
　　On that first Christmas Day
To say he'd seen a wondrous sight
　　And bear the news to them
That God had hung a beacon light
　　High over Bethlehem?

Of all the throng that hurried by
　　Did no one lift his eyes
To read the glory of the sky?
　　Were all so worldly-wise
That God should bid the angels sing,
　　Upon that midnight clear,
An anthem to the new-born King
　　And only shepherds hear?

I wonder is it still the same?
　　Are we beyond His reach?
Have we, pursuing wealth and fame,
　　Grown deaf to gentler speech?
Should such a strange thing come to be
　　And angel choirs appear,
Would only watchful shepherds see
　　And thoughtful shepherds hear?

Dandelions

At dandelions men may scoff
  And fight them as they will,
But if they ever drive them off
  A lovely thing they'll kill.

I hope I'll never live to see
  The dandelions' doom,
For what would days of springtime be
  Without that yellow bloom?

I battle with them day by day,
  I sometimes rise at dawn
To drive the golden heads away
  That dot my patch of lawn.

I often think of them as weeds
  Whose roots are strong and stout,
And caring for my garden's needs
  I coldly pull them out.

But I should hate to see them go
  From field and countryside;
It would not be the spring we know
  If dandelions died.

The Human Body

By scientists, both wise and old,
The human body, I've been told,
Which weighs about one-forty-five
And is what mortals call alive
Is made of water, nitrogen,
Carbon, sulphur, iron and then
Potassium, sodium, iodine,
Magnesium, trace of fluorine
Chlorine, calcium, phosphorus—
Alike in monarchs as in us.

They've analyzed our flesh and bone,
To them precisely now is known
How much of this, how much of that
Combine to make us lean and fat.
The lovely maiden, fair to see,
Is water, mostly, just like me,
Plus so much carbon, iron and all
Those chemicals I won't recall.
'Tis proved, this stuff we all possess—
No one has more; no one has less.

Well, as they've measured, dump them in
A great retort of glass or tin
And stew them well and stir them round
And see if man you can compound.

I fancy you could mix for weeks
And never get two rosy cheeks,
Or from the batter you prepare
Produce a maiden young and fair,
Or anything that eats or drinks
Or laughs or sighs or sings or thinks.

I do not doubt this curious list
But think some properties were missed.
To me the human body seems
To be composed of fancies, dreams,
High courage, tenderness and skill,
Ambition, wisdom, strength of will,
Love, pity, mirth and all the arts
And these not given in equal parts.
And thus we differ, you from me,
Who share the self-same chemistry.

Hot Dog

'Twas two o'clock when he came in, and rising in
    my bed,
"Where have you been till such an hour?" to him I
    sadly said.
"Oh, she was hungry," he replied. "She had a sand-
    wich yen,
And so we hopped into the car to find a hot dog
    den."
"And did you find one?" I inquired. "Of course I
    did," said he,
"There's one just twenty miles away—an Indian
    tepee!"

There was no harm in such a trip; so do our customs
    change,
That youngsters view with no concern what older
    minds think strange.
This hot dog craze is modern stuff; the car is at
    the door,
And when a girl wants frankfurters, what's twenty
    miles or more?
Distance and time are different now, and taste has
    altered, too;
When girls in our day hungry were, a hot dog
    wouldn't do.

We took the trolley home at night; no motor cars
    had we.
Who stayed till after midnight knew an angry
    dad he'd see.
But, is it fair to judge them now by standards
    long outworn?
The modern girls, it seems, like food their moth-
    ers viewed with scorn.
Though twenty miles seem far to us, it's just a
    hop to them
Who yearn for hot dog sandwiches at two o'clock
    A. M.

This Man Culbertson

For eight and twenty years we've shared
    The summers fair and winter blizzards,
The ins and outs, the hopes and doubts,
    The chicken livers, wings and gizzards.
We've kept serenely on our way,
    Despite the cares which came to fret us,
And so to her I smile and say:
    "Why now let Culbertson upset us?"

I've done full many a foolish thing,
  But far apart we've never wandered.
No angry word from her I've heard
  About the money I have squandered.
Adown the years until today
  We've shared whate'er the Lord would let us,
And so to her I smiling say:
  "Why now let Culbertson upset us?"

What if my two-bid now and then
  Is made without sufficient holding?
I could rehearse faults so much worse
  She's borne and never thought of scolding.
We've lived through many a troubled day
  And never let grim hatred get us,
And so to her I smiling say:
  "Why now let Culbertson upset us?"

We've never met this teacher chap.
  I'm sure that he has never seen us.
'Tis not his looks; it's just his books
  And system which have come between us.
As one we've stood when skies were gray,
  As one we've thought when trouble tried us,
And so to her I smiling say:
  "Why now let Culbertson divide us?"

Relatives

Relatives are people who
Bring little presents in to you.
They're more like friends who come to call,
Except you've got to learn them all
An' know their names, so you won't miss
When mother asks you: "Now, who's this?"

I've got two grandmas, an' I know
Them both becoz they love me so.
I know my grandpas, when they come
They bring me chocolate bars and gum.
You see how well I'm getting on—
I also know my Uncle John.

Although I'm only half-past three,
My daddy says, it's good for me
To know so much. I never miss
The right name when they say: "Who's this?"
It would be awful not to know
Your Aunt Irene and Auntie Flo.

It isn't often I forget.
I don't know all my cousins yet
Or what a cousin is at all,
But daddy says when you are small
It proves that you are very smart
If you know half your folks by heart.

Awakening

Oh, I wanted to be pampered and I wanted to be
 petted;
I thought that Life should run to me with comfort
 when I fretted,
And so I used to wail for joys I had no means of
 buying,
But Life went on about its work and never heard
 me crying.

I used to fly in tantrums when some pleasure was
 denied me;
I fancied everyone was wrong who raised a voice
 to chide me.
I thought that Life should run to me with pretty
 things to show me,
But Life went on about its work and never seemed
 to know me.

I know not how the thought began nor why so long
 it lasted;
I wanted cake and pie to eat while others bravely
 fasted;
I wanted easy tasks to do, high pay without the
 labor,
But Life, I noticed, passed me by to visit with my
 neighbor.

Then suddenly I faced about—stopped my sense-
less whining.
Took disappointment with a grin and loss with-
out repining;
I found that woes were everywhere and some
would surely strike me;
I strapped my burdens on my back—and Life be-
gan to like me.

Care

Through every life there runs the thread of care
That winds and twists itself about the years;
High place or low, it everywhere appears.
Not long can man walk pleasure's thoroughfare,
Upon his shoulders burdens he must bear,
Know doubt and disappointment, failure's
fears,
And, soon or late, pale sorrow's bitter tears,
For Time from these no favorite will spare.

Nor wealth nor place nor power can keep away
The common griefs which Age insists upon;
Man must have faith and courage to be gay.
The joy he seeks is bravely to be won.
Who reads the book of life may be assured
The happiest hearts have many an ache endured.

The Eighteenth Hole

The eighteenth hole and the evening gloam,
The end is near and I'm getting home!
The club house looms in the twilight shade,
Where the boys will ask me with whom I played,
And just what sort of a score I made.

It's the eighteenth hole and the game is done;
What matters it now have I lost or won?
In many a pit and trap I've been,
I've had the thrill of a contest keen,
But I'm coming home with my record clean.

The best and worst of the sport I've had—
Some shots were good and a few were bad.
I made mistakes which I couldn't mend,
I've lost many a hole but never a friend,
And now I've come where the fairways end.

Lord, when I come to the eighteenth hole
And my last putt drops, as I homeward stroll,
May I be met at the club house door
By the boys who have all holed out before,
And be welcomed there though I failed to score!

When I Was Being Rushed

The boy has gone to college and we're lonely as
    can be,
But his letters bring a lot of joy to mother and
    to me.
"I'm being rushed," he tells us. "I had breakfast
    yesterday
With the Upsi Epsa Etas, and I dined with Ex Owe
    Jay!
As I strolled along the campus came a senior up to
    me,
And he whispered: 'Sunday ev'ning come and sup
    with A. B. C.' "

Oh, the college that I went to was the big world's
    ceaseless grind,
And the letters of our youngster bring those early
    days to mind;
With a chuckle I recall them, and the things men
    said and did
As they welcomed into business just another eager
    kid.
At the tricks they played upon me in my ignorance
    I blushed,
It was all so very different when I was being rushed.

For a left-hand wrench they sent me, for a round
    square I was chased;
I was called to look at type lice and a spray of ink
    I faced;

It was: "Hey, there! Get a move on! Run these
    proofs to Brown and Black;
Stop at Coats and Suits for copy and be sure you
    hurry back!"
In that school of harsh experience oft my cheeks
    with shame were flushed,
But I learned what legs were made for when I was
    being rushed.

Those old days gave us no emblems we could pin
    upon our vests,
But they did initiate us, and they gave us all the
    tests;
And much like these college "rushings" when at
    last probation ends
In the ranks of those we've worked with we have
    found our lifetime friends;
So I chuckle, recollecting all the type I've cleaned
    and brushed,
Saying: "Mother, as a youngster, there's no doubt
    that I was rushed."

I'm No Milliner

Some men, encountering women fair,
Can see the brilliants in their hair
And note their gowns and later tell
If they became them very well,
Or were they pink or gray or blue
Or biege or any other hue,
But I have never learned to care
Or notice what the ladies wear.

To save my life I can't recall
Were Mabel's earrings large or small,
Or later dare to make a guess
Concerning Jennie's hat or dress;
I never by a woman stand
To count the jewels on her hand,
Or look some lovely lady o'er
And think: "I've seen that gown before!"

How oft to me has Nellie said:
"In all the years that we've been wed,
Not once have you remarked upon
The hat or gown that I had on,
Or raised your eyes above your book
To say: 'My dear, how nice you look!'
Women wear beautiful attire
For men to notice and admire."

Last night as she came tripping down
I thought to speak about her gown.
"My dear," I said, "I like your dress,
It adds unto your loveliness.
In all my life I've never seen
So beautiful a shade of green."
"Good heavens!" she cried, in accents cold,
"This thing is nearly two years old!"

Song of Consolation for Poor Golfers

Golf is an art, a timely knack
Which few possess and many lack.
Nor all the tutoring with the clubs
Can fashion experts out of dubs.
　　　So cease to frown
　　　And write it down
If hook or slice your trouble be,
　　　In all you know
　　　Of golfing woe
You've always excellent company.

Though Mussolini may be great,
He cannot drive a golf ball straight.
And I will bet that England's king
Has never learned the golfing swing.

So for the dubs
Of all the clubs
This one consoling line I pen,
Who's born so weak
That he must peek,
Looks up with countless gentlemen.

In vain it is to curse and rage.
The game has baffled many a sage
And many an eloquent divine
Can't keep a golf ball on the line.
Tough brassie lies
Perplex the wise,
So when you err with game at stake
Part with your pelf
Then tell yourself
Few great men ninety ever break.

Absent

I sometimes think of them as here
Or very near,
Who have from this world gone away
Sometimes by day
I fancy Marjorie appears,
Despite the absence all these years,
To smile away my doubts and fears.

And sometimes comes the father, too.
The look I knew
So long ago of gentle grace
Upon his face
Shines out as clear
As when we walked together here,
And I am sure he's standing near.

The old friends, one by one, return,
As if to learn
The gossip of the passing day.
In some strange way
In fancy I can see them there
Beside the bookcase or the stair,
Or in an old, familiar chair.

It is not given to us to know
Just where they go,

Or is Heaven near or far away
No man can say;
But there are times I seem to hear
Them whispering softly in my ear:
"Don't worry. We are very near."

Golf After Many Years

For nine and twenty years they've said:
"Be sure you do not lift your head,
Then let your club-head follow through!"
Still something else I try to do.

For nine and twenty years I've known
The club-head must be outward thrown
To drive a golf ball straight and true.
Still something else I try to do.

For nine and twenty years the pro
Has told me what I surely know.
In his advice there's nothing new,
Still something else I try to do.

For nine and twenty years, the swing
I've known is just a simple thing.
Compact, precise, and timely, too;
Still something else I try to do.

And Billy Phelps, who plays with me,
Agrees that very shortly we
Shall celebrate, beside some cup,
Our thirty years of looking up!

Old John

He knew the flowers by name, and though a man
was he,
Blood-brother to the daffodil and rose he seemed
to be.
He'd lived his life among them, and when spring
is in the air,
There'll be sorrow in the garden for Old John will
not be there.

From dawn to dusk he labored through the years
among the flowers,
And I'm sure he lived a richer and a happier life
than ours,
For his face was calm and placid, and he never
seemed to care
For the glory that is business or the crown that
skill might wear.

All his waking time was given to forget-me-nots
and phlox,
To his peonies and pansies, and his sturdy holly-
hocks;
And I've watched him many a summer bending over
bloomy beds,
Just as tender as a mother stroking little curly
heads.

Now the Lord has called him yonder, and the
    spring is coming on,
And the tulips and the jonquils will be asking:
    "Where is John?"
And I'm wondering what the roses and forget-
    me-nots will say
When the word is passed among them that "Old
    John" has gone away.

Friendly Greetings

Once in an old time picture book
My father called on me to look
Upon a miser counting gold
Within his hovel bleak and cold.
A little chest of brass-bound wood
Upon the floor beside him stood.
The room was bare and he appeared
As ragged as his untrimmed beard,
A creature most forlorn and sad,
Counting the dearest friends he had.

'Tis strange that picture I should find
Still fresh and vivid in my mind,
And after all the years recall
That miser of my boyhood small.

Yet suddenly I seem to be
Counting my friends the same as he
And gloating (yes, the term is right)
Not over coins of metal bright
But over stacks of Christmas cards
Which brought us love and kind regards.

Here for a happy hour or more
I've run these Christmas greetings o'er.
Each one a friend, who, far or near,
Has sent to me a line of cheer.
Behold the stack! I'll swear it seems
Beyond a miser's wildest dreams.
Again I gloat: "Friends, everywhere!"
And still not one that I can spare,
Here in this lovely tinseled heap
Are riches that I hope to keep.

Evolution of the Flapper

The flapper of yesterday worried her mother,
And worried her grandma and worried her brother;
Her dress was outrageous; her conduct seemed bold;
And she was the constant despair of the old,
And they oft sat together as grown-ups will do
To wonder "whatever that child's coming to!"

To-day as I strolled on a bungalow street
This young woman in question I happened to meet;
She was pushing a little pink carriage wherein
A baby was nestled tucked up to the chin,
And she lifted a blanket and gave me a peep
At the cute little rascal that lay there asleep.

She urged me to look at his dear little nose;
She forced me to gaze on his fingers and toes;
She talked of his feedings, and pinching his cheek
She boasted the pound he had gained in a week,
And said, in the way that all fond mothers do:
"He never gets cross and he sleeps the night
   through!"

I thought as I left her, the frivolous day,
Like everything else, comes and hurries away.
The oldsters may think that the world's gone to pot;
That virtues they've preached are wiped out, but
   they're not;
For the best of our customs and manners survive
And they all get old-fashioned when babies arrive.

Perfection

Bright and beautiful and gay
Twenty roses in bouquet,
Twenty roses, pink and white!
Where could be a prettier sight?
But an expert shook his head,
"Just one perfect bloom," he said.

"Most of these have suffered pain,
Borne the wind and felt the rain,
Struggled for existence, and
If a rose you understand
Closely scan them; you will see
Flaws and faults that shouldn't be.

"Here's the only perfect bloom
Of the twenty in the room,
See the petals, note the stem—
Just as God intended them;
All the rest, though fair to see,
Fail the finished rose to be."

"Since," thought I, "the perfect rose
Only very seldom grows,
Is it any wonder, then,
In this teeming world of men,
Swayed and torn by storms of care,
Perfect souls are very rare?"

The Fish That Gets Away

Some mourn the fish that gets away
  And boast his size and weight;
They stop their friends at night to say
  How sorry was their fate.
Almost unto the net they'd brought
  This beauty superfine;
It seemed to them they had him caught
  And then he snapped the line.

Oh, yes, they had some fish to show
  For all the time they'd spent;
Some luck they'd been allowed to know,
  But they were not content.
The ones they'd caught seemed rather small
  When put upon display,
And could not be compared at all
  With that which got away.

He broke but once where sunbeams dance
  Upon the waters blue,
And though at him they'd but a glance
  His weight and size they knew.
Not one in all their splendid catch,
  Which came to them that day,
For beauty could begin to match
  The fish which got away.

Perhaps against us one and all
   Could lie the self-same charge:
The joys we catch seem very small,
   The ones we lose seem large;
We pass our many blessings by
   As though no worth had they,
And dolefully we magnify
   The joy that gets away.

Bethlehem

No doubt they thought in Bethlehem
The world would never hear of them.
They had an inn where sometimes stayed
The wandering caravans of trade,
And near it was a stable kept
Wherein at night the cattle slept;
But lost to splendor and renown,
Theirs was a little wayside town.

One night a man and woman worn
Asked to be sheltered till the morn.
The keeper of the inn replied:
"My every room is occupied.

There is no space that I can spare."
The man said: "We must rest somewhere.
What of the stable, yonder, sir?
There I can make a bed for her."

"Yes," said the keeper, "go ahead!
Toss down some straw and make a bed."
No doubt he was surprised at morn
To hear a baby had been born,
And shepherds wandering from afar,
Guided to Bethlehem by a star,
Had come that little Child to see,
As if important He could be.

The caravans of trade moved on,
The great officials soon were gone.
Nor did it once occur to them
That fame had come to Bethlehem.
The poor innkeeper never knew
He should be long remembered, too,
Because on that first Christmas morn
'Twas in his stable Christ was born.

Dreamland

Oh, there is a land which no grown-up may see,
  Though he's sure it is wondrously fair;
It's the country where blossoms the sugar-plum tree,
  And the fairies are sentinels there;
It's the marvelous realm where the lakes and the
    streams
  Are liquefied silver and gold,
The place where the little ones go in their dreams,
  And it's barred to the weary and old.

They won't let us stern-faced old cross patches in
  With our terrible burden of cares,
For the place would be spoiled should we ever begin
  To tamper with Dreamland's affairs.
It's enough for the day we should fret and should
    scold
  And hold them so fast to the right,
Without letting parents and grandparents old
  Follow after the children at night.

So when evening slips down over city and town
  To Dreamland the little ones go,

Where there's no one to scold them and no one
    to frown
    And no one to cry to them: "No."
There all through the nighttime with fairies they
    play,
    And picnic 'neath sugar-plum trees—
In that wonderful realm till the break of the day
    The children may do as they please.

A Wish

If I could have my wish it would not be for
    wealth or fame at all,
But a firmer grip on fellowship and all joys great
    and small,
And I'd like to know as I come and go much
    more of this world we share,
With a wiser mind I could always find some joy
    in the task I bear.

If I could have my wish it would not be for a
    strong man's power,
But a mind so filled with love 'twere thrilled by
    the sight of a bird or flower,

And a heart so deep it could safely keep all good
   things warm within
So that I could turn with delight to learn what
   each new day ushered in.

If I could have my wish it would not be for some
   glittering prize,
But a faith so strong it could walk along wher-
   ever my pathway lies.
My best I'd give to each hour I live and whether
   in peace or strife
I should like to stay to my final day aglow with
   the joy of life.

Sharing

We who have wept together know what it means
   to love.
We who have suffered sorrow, strewn roses a
   mound above,
And knelt on the ground together to whisper a
   common prayer
With trembling lips and hearts aching know what
   it means to share.

Time was when we danced together and laughed
    as the days went by.
Month after month we romped through with
    never a tear in her eye.
We fancied we loved each other, but little of life
    we knew.
And I was a jesting comrade with only my work
    to do.

Then suddenly sorrow found us. Out there by a
    tiny grave
We learned what it means to be tender and just
    what it means to be brave.
We learned that love deepens and strengthens by
    hurts it is asked to bear,
And out of our common heartache we learned
    what it means to share.

On Going Out

The women folks look up at me
And cry: "You are not fit to see!
That coat needs brushing, and your tie
Is old and worn and all awry
And very shabby is your hat;
Surely you won't go out like that!"

They're fretted by the speck of dirt
Which seems to settle on my shirt,
And should the collar band be worn,
Or show a spot that's frayed and torn,
They'll give the ultimatum flat:
"Now you're not going out like that!"

How easily they dust the coat
And trim the muffler round my throat!
How lightly they apply the touch
Of neatness which I need so much,
That outwardly at least I'll be
What women folks call "fit to see."

Lord, when it comes my time to die,
Let not my spirit be awry;
Grant me the time, the while I live,
To ask forgiveness and forgive,
That this old soul of mine may be,
On its arrival, "fit to see!"

Let some one come to me who knows
Where every little blemish shows
And say: "This bit of wrong, repair!
Brush off those dusty signs of care!"
And with the same old friendly pat,
Make sure I don't go out like that!

Trained At Last

When mother thinks we ought to go
To see a moving picture show
Though I've a book I'd like to read
I put the volume down with speed.

When mother says: "We ought to do
Your old arm chair in navy blue."
Though I am rather fond of red
I promptly vote for blue, instead,

When mother looks across at me
And says: "My dear, take no more tea!"
Though much I'd like a second cup
I promptly give the notion up.

When I've rebelled as now and then
I have like all the stubborn men
And let my will run free and strong
My judgment usually was wrong.

Now for the second piece of pie
I've ceased to ask when mother's nigh
And reconciled to growing old
I've learned to do just as I'm told.

Forever

Forever is a long time, the life of moon and stars,
A longer life than churches know, or prison gates
and bars,
And I have vowed to love her, forever and a day,
A vow that knows no changing or crumbling or
decay.

Forever is a long time, the life of sea and tide,
No calendar can mark it, no seasons can divide;
It has no bitter ending—let life bring what it may,
My love must last forever, forever and a day.

Though buildings fall in ruins and earthly splendors
fade;
Though death shall separate us, still stands the
vow I made;
Though fashions change and fancies sweep all
charms we know away,
Our love must last forever, forever and a day.

The Vaster Future

It is so little after all,
  The cheer of yesterday is stilled.
So quickly do night's curtains fall
  Upon the day with splendors filled,
That ere we realize it comes
The sound of morning's stirring drums.

What was is done. To live too long
  With things accomplished is to die.
To-day needs men of purpose strong
  To brave the tasks it will supply.
So small and trivial seems the past—
It is the future that is vast.

What though you conquered yesterday?
  Death has not come to end your tale.
New tasks confront you down the way
  And are you not afraid to fail?
The rose which blossoms once, must bear
New blooms to-morrow, just as fair.

There is a never-silenced call
  For courage in the hearts of men,
Success comes and night's shadows fall,
  But one must rise to work again.
The thing accomplished merely leads
The way to more and greater deeds.

Keeping and Spending

These I would have him spend:
   Silver and gold,
Serving some useful end,
Playing the man and friend
   'Till he grows old.

Thus let him give away
   All that I leave,
Spending as best he may,
Comforting, day by day
   Hearts when they grieve.

But this I'd have him keep
   Down to the last,
Faith when the road is steep,
Faith when his eyes must weep,
   Holding it fast.

Silver and gold are naught,
   Those he may spend,
But howsoever wrought,
God grant the faith I taught
   Be his to the end.

The High Peaks of Pride

Life gives us two or three sweet thrills we like to
talk about.
The memory of the first home run fades not entirely
out.
To every man comes soon or late one rapturous
hour of fame
When satisfaction with himself is his to boast and
claim.

That night the lovely maiden blushes red and whis-
pers: "Yes,"
He walks the world on airy feet aglow with hap-
piness,
And there's no doubt that he is proud and boastful,
I may say,
With every right to strut a bit upon his wedding
day.

The next event which stirs his blood and fills his
soul with joy
Is when the doctor says to him: "All's well, and
it's a boy!"
Or let it be a little girl, the thrill is just the same,
There is a pride in fatherhood which nothing else
can claim.

These three high peaks of perfect bliss already I
    have known,
And now the graybeards say to me one other I
    shall own.
"You'll boast as ne'er before," they say, "and
    strut the way we do
The day your son or daughter makes a grandpa
    out of you."

The Brighter Side

Though life has its trouble and life has its care
    And often its dark days of sorrow,
There is always the hope that the sky will be
      fair
    And the heart will be happy tomorrow.
There is always the light of a goal just ahead,
    A glimpse of the dream we're pursuing,
In spite of the difficult pathway we tread
    There is much it is good to be doing.

Time empties the purse of the pennies of youth,
    The heart of its innocent laughter,
But gives in return just a few grains of truth
    And the promise of more to come after.

There's never a new day lived out to the end,
   However life's tempests may pitch us,
But what with a triumph, a joy, or a friend
   The swift, fleeting hours may enrich us.

There is so much to do and there's so much to
      see
   In spite of the troubles that fret us;
So much to wait for and so much to be
   If only the future will let us—
That life with its burdens and life with its tears
   And its heart burning touches of sadness
Still lures us all on to the end of our years
   With its friendships, its loves and its gladness.

Worn Out

They left me home to "mind" her and I smiled at
    such a task,
To mind a lovely three-year-old's a job that I
    should ask.
Thought I: "I'll let her romp about, and sit be-
    neath a tree,
And smoke my pipe and read a book, as happy as
    can be."

And now the day is over, and at last she's safe in
    bed,
But, oh, my feet are weary by the strenuous pace
    she led!
My nerves are all a-tingle and my muscles stiff
    and sore—
There's too much steam in three-year-olds for a
    man of forty-four!

I chased her through the garden, and I chased her
    down the street,
And little girls of three glad years have wings
    upon their feet.
I thought I had her anchored at a sand box, full
    content,
But when I sat me down to read, away Miss Mis-
    chief went.

I rescued her from water, and I rescued her from
fire,
I took her from a fence or two all tangled with
the wire;
I hadn't any notion there was so much mischief
round
As in the day I minded her that little lady found.

But now the day is over, and now I'm nearly
dead,
And now I hear her crying: "I don't want to go
to bed!"
And I have learned a lesson which I didn't know
before:
There's too much steam in three-year-olds for a
man of forty-four.

Tale of a Brooch

A little woman found a brooch upon the street one
    day;
It looked to her like jewelry the 10-cent stores dis-
    play.
She took it home to pin her waist while out to
    wash she went,
And day by day that trinket gleamed as o'er the
    tub she bent;
But no one stopped to notice it. No mistress at the
    door
Would cast a second glance at things the washer-
    woman wore.

"It is a pretty brooch," she thought. "I'll wear it
    while I may,
Then give it to my daughter on her graduation day.
It's rather sad to look at now; I've lost a pearl or
    two,
But I can pay a jeweler to make it good as new."
So when the happy time arrived she asked a man
    the cost
Of two small pearls which would replace the ones
    that she had lost.

The jeweler the trinket took and gravely looked it
    o'er.
Said he: "Wait just a moment, please; I fear 'twill
    cost you more

Than you expect. These pearls are rare." She
trembled at his speech.
"For gems like this we'll have to charge two thou-
sand dollars each.
This is a most expensive brooch, exquisite, charm-
ing, quaint!"
The washerwoman heard no more. She'd fallen in
a faint.

To find that brooch police had searched the city up
and down,
And all the time it glistened on a woman's ging-
ham gown,
And all the time it glistened as she toiled some floor
to scrub
Or shed its rays of loveliness above the steaming
tub.
But like this washerwoman, countless folks, year in,
year out,
Perhaps are blessed with riches they have never
learned about.

Questions for the Boy

Boy, if a mountain you should see
   Crusted with jewels thick,
And you were told that you were free
   Each day a gem to pick
And bear away the precious stone,
Henceforth to be your very own,
Would you return with spade and sack,
Or on such fortune turn your back?

Suppose by him who watched it there
   'Twas very plainly told
That each could take what he could bear
   Of silver and of gold,
But must himself alone obtain
And carry what his strength could gain,
Would you begrudge the labor which
Promised in time to make you rich?

Well, college is a mountain steep,
   With jewels richly set;
And who shall venture there may keep
   Whate'er he wills to get.
But he himself must dig it out,
Unaided carry it about,
And to that mountain come alone
To make the knowledge there his own.

Who toils for truth shall find it there—
  'Tis ever on display,
And none who watches you shall care
  How much you take away.
The gems are stored on ledge and shelf,
But you must earn them for yourself;
'Tis yours to choose and yours to say
What riches you will bear away.

Man's Seven Photographic Ages

First he's welcomed to the earth—
"Mother to a son gives birth!"

Pictured he will next appear
Among "the babies of the year!"

Then ('tis every school boy's dream):
"Valued member of the team!"

Soon this double-column spread:
"College graduate to wed."

Follows this at forty-five:
"Heads a charitable drive!"

Now this text his cut requires:
"Prominent business man retires!"

Final picture! Sadly say:
"Well-known man died yesterday!"

Little Miss Curious

Little Miss Curious, Little Miss Pry,
Little Miss What's That and Little Miss Why,
Little Miss Tell Me and Little Miss How,
Would I could settle your problems right now,
But wait for the answers. They'll come in their
  turn,
And some of the things you must grow up to learn.

Little Miss Question Box, flooring me flat,
Wanting to know all of this and of that.
If when we're naughty God sees and is sad,
Why does He let little children be bad?
Why can't the angels who brought me to you
Bring me a cute little girl baby, too?

What makes the whiskers come out on your chin?
Grandma has teeth she takes out and puts in,
How did she get them, and why does she need
Glasses whenever she sits down to read?
Little Miss Busy Tongue, I can't explain
Half of the problems which trouble your brain.

Little Miss Curious, Little Miss Pry,
Little Miss What's That, and Little Miss Why,
Come with your questions and wide-open eyes,
I'll do my best, though I'm not very wise,
For even I wonder, as onward I go,
And am puzzled by things I am too young to know.

The Little Old Woman

There was a little woman whose hands were worn
and red,
And long ago the beauty of her youthful days had
fled,
For she had suffered sorrow, and she had suffered
pain,
But after these had left her she learned to smile
again,
And out she'd come with cookies for the children
on the street
Till it seemed where'er she wandered there were
young ones round her feet.

She hadn't any money; she was never gayly dressed;
She had a shawl and bonnet which she called her
Sunday best.
And if you gave her something, in a little while
you'd see
Some other person strutting in that bit of finery,
And she'd give this explanation if you asked the
reason why:
"I thought she ought to have it. She's so much
worse off than I."

No one ever seemed to notice that her hands were
coarse and red;
That she wasn't good to look at no one ever heard
it said,

And the smartest of her neighbors, who appeared
    to know it all,
Never spoke a word in censure of her bonnet or
    her shawl.
So I take this truth for granted: that a sweet and
    tender smile
And a heart so brave and kindly never do go out
    of style.

Friends Old and New

Here's to the old friends true
Who share in all we do
And have learned all our ways
Through many yesterdays.
Theirs are the hearts that share
All that we meet of care;
Theirs are the eyes that see,
Though grave our faults may be,
The good that lies below.
That's why we love them so!

But here's to the happy day
When comes across our way
A new friend, blithe and bold,
To join the faithful old.
Glad is the sheltering door
To welcome in one more.
Brighter the fireplace where
We draw another chair,
But happiest, at day's end,
Are we to gain a friend.

The Master

They seldom show Him with a smile.
  Always His face is sad to see,
  As if a jest could never be
Nor He be merry for a while.
The kindly humor that could pat
  The brows of boys He chanced to see
  And say: "Let children come to me!"
No brush has ever pictured that!

The man who loved a little child
  And walked the common ways of men,
  Though troubled often, now and then
With those about Him surely smiled.
I fancy as I read His word
  I hear Him chuckling, soft and sweet,
  Telling to Mary, at His feet,
Some curious thing He'd seen or heard.

He must have had a twinkling eye,
  Which danced at times with gentle mirth,
  So greatly to be loved on earth,
So bravely on the cross to die.

Small Service

Time makes the little service great,
  Two thousand years ago and more
The Master saw a widow pause
And give her little to the cause,
  And still men tell the story o'er.

The measure of the kindly deed
  Is not its present worth or size,
The word of cheer one stops to speak
May lift unto the mountain peak
  The youth the desert terrifies.

One may himself a failure seem,
  And yet perhaps some trivial gift
His heart has prompted him to make
Unselfishly, for friendship's sake,
  Another from the depths may lift.

Lives have been changed in moments rare
  Along the pathways mortals plod;
Unseen and little understood
Are many ways of doing good
  And many ways of serving God.

The Struggle

Not in the goal attained or task complete,
  Or in the glittering prize,
  Contentment lies,
But in the struggle and the battle heat,
The pressing onward against sure defeat,
  The matching wit with wit,
  Hitting and being hit.

Men long to rest, but resting long to fight;
  Men stand to pain
  An end to gain,
But only the very old can take delight
From comfort, never broken day or night.
  Victors are fain
  To risk defeat again.

Contentment's in the doubting and the deed,
  Not in the triumph won,
  But in the keeping on,
'Tis in the hurt of open wounds which bleed,
The turmoil and the planning to succeed.
  Once rested, man would go
  New pains to know.

The long pursuit, the scheming and the fears,
    The need for skill
    And strength of will
And all the hardships of the building years,
Take on true glory, when their end appears.
    Men at their tranquil time
    Long for new hills to climb.

The Price

Into the court he came. Beyond a doubt
    A thief—convicted by a jury of his peers!
So from the world the law must shut him out
    For fifteen years.

Thieves prey on men and women. Therefore they
    With their own outcast kind must dwell,
Marching in step and robed in garments gray,
    A number and a cell!

Nor spring, nor summer, nor the autumn rich,
    Nor the white glory of the winter's snow
Brings any difference to the dull round which
    Is theirs to know.

There must be safety for the lawful throng.
    But still whene'er a thief is led away
I pity him the bitter price of wrong
    Good men ask him to pay.

The Statue

We stood before a marble bust
   That critics called the perfect thing,
Defying time and care and rust,
   Once treasured by an ancient king,
A beauty and a joy forever
Which suffers pain and sorrow never.

The tranquil features never change,
   The smile is frozen on the face;
In all the years I think it strange
   That grief has never left one trace
Upon those cheeks, or gentle pity
Made lovelier those glances pretty.

Anger the marble cannot know,
   For stone is heartless, dull and cold;
It smiles alike on friend and foe,
   Stays young the while the world grows old;
Should it become a vile man's treasure
That face would never show displeasure.

Rather I'd know the living joy
   Of eyes that weep and cheeks that fade,
The charms which time and care destroy,
   Than beauty so superbly made,
Excelling any marble splendor
Are living spirits, warm and tender.

Nine Years Old

At nine a little girl begins
To beg her pa and ma for twins
Or if we can't arrange for two,
Another baby boy will do,
Or if we can afford the price
A little girl is sometimes nice,
But anyhow she often weeps
Because no babies come for "keeps."

At nine a little girl will shout
When older people are about
And rush into the room pell-mell
Her day's adventurings to tell.
Though older tongues may talking be
She'll pay no heed to them, for she
Has something marvelous to state
Which positively cannot wait.

Nor look, nor shaking head, nor frown,
Can tone that nine-year spirit down;
So filled her world is with delight
She finds no time to be polite,
Where everything is bright and new,
So much there is for her to do,
That she forgets our good advice
And all our talk of being nice.

At nine years old a little girl
Has hair that will not stay in curl,
And legs so bruised and scratched that she
Is oft a sorry sight to see.
Her strength has just begun to flower,
She's into mischief every hour—
A victim of the awkward stage,
And yet it is a lovely age.

Thinking Over a Dull Day

"A dull and dreary day!" I said
As I was tumbling into bed.
And then in those few moments ere
Sleep came to close the mind to care
I thought a small voice asked of me:
"Did you this morning's sunrise see?
I wonder if by chance you heard
The lovely music of a bird,
A crimson cardinal on high
Who sang to you as you went by?

"Across the street with news to tell
There walked a man that you know well
Who tried his best to catch your eye
But all unseen you passed him by.
So buried in yourself were you
And all the tasks you had to do

From dawn until the even-fall
No joyous sight can you recall.
And yet about you everywhere
Was much to balance toil and care.

"Had you but walked with eyesight keen
A thousand charms you might have seen
Which never, as you journeyed on,
You stayed or turned to gaze upon.
Where'er you went today occurred
Much that you neither saw nor heard;
Scenes that had thrilled you through and
    through
Had you not been so wrapped in you.
Life offers flowers you failed to cull,
The day was bright, but you were dull."

Table-Cloths

Some people, when they sit to eat,
Prefer to see the table neat.
They want the linen spotless white,
The glasses dazzling in the light,
The silverware in trim array.
But, as for me, I often say
Give me glad childhood's table-cloth
Well stained with jelly, milk and broth.

Not long in peace could I abide
In houses cold with pomp and pride,
Or dwell where dignity commands
Precision's care from little hands.
I much prefer the happier place
Illumined by a smiling face,
The dining-room, where soon I know
A glass of milk will over go.

Be mine the room with laughter filled
Where no one frets o'er what is spilled.
For what are table-cloths that they
Should drive all merriment away
And why think accidents a crime,
Especially at dinner-time.
They gather sorrow for their pains
Who make too much of jelly stains.

I should not like always to dine
Where silverware and glasses shine
And linen white outlasts the meal;
Too sad and lonely should I feel.
In table-cloths I take no pride,
I want the children at my side.
My joy is in those splotches red
When jelly dances from the bread.

Old Age

I used to think that growing old was reckoned
  just in years,
But who can name the very date when weariness
  appears?
I find no stated time when man, obedient to a
  law,
Must settle in an easy chair and from the world
  withdraw.
Old Age is rather curious, or so it seems to me.
I know old men at forty and young men at sev-
  enty-three.

I'm done with counting life by years or temples
  turning gray.
No man is old who wakes with joy to greet an-
  other day.

What if the body cannot dance with youth's elastic spring?
There's many a vibrant interest to which the mind can cling.
'Tis in the spirit Age must dwell, or this would never be:
I know old men at forty and young men at seventy-three.

Some men keep all their friendships warm, and welcome friendships new,
They have no time to sit and mourn the things they used to do.
This changing world they greet with joy and never bow to fate;
On every fresh adventure they set out with hearts elate.
From chilling fear and bitter dread they keep their spirits free
While some seem old at forty they stay young at seventy-three.

So much to do, so much to learn, so much in which to share!
With twinkling eyes and minds alert some brave both time and care.
And this I've learned from other men, that only they are old
Who think with something that has passed the tale of life is told.

For Age is not alone of time, or we should never
    see
Men old and bent at forty and men young at
    seventy-three.

Brotherhood

"Am I my brother's keeper?" answered Cain
When questioned of his brother Abel, slain,
And since such record keepings first began
This phrase has lingered on the lips of man.
Still is it heard: "Oh, is it mine to care
What miseries my brother has to bear?
Lord, is it not enough that I must see
That I have food and all is well with me?"

Suppose a plague should fall upon the town,
Would it not trouble men of great renown
To learn that on some little near-by street
Were those, perhaps, they once had scorned to
    meet
Sore-stricken with the malady? And would
They not unite with all the neighborhood
To win to health and happiness again
The very humblest of their fellow-men?

Within their brother's health they'd seek their
    own,
To them his daily progress would be known.
They'd watch the sick and suffering and share
Their misery lest the pain be theirs to bear.
For what harms one another may destroy.
Not in our own but in another's joy
Lies common welfare. Brothers are we all!
Where one man stumbles every one may fall.

Possession

When they're very, very good
And are doing as they should,
When the youngsters are polite,
Never wrong and always right,
And this very oft occurs—
Mother speaks of them as "hers."

When the parson comes for tea
Should he take them on his knee
And a blessing, soft and low,
On their little heads bestow,
In those few brief, fleeting hours,
Mother speaks of them as "ours."

But if little girl and lad
Have been very, very bad,
Have their tempers been displayed,
Have they boldly disobeyed,
Then when I come home to dine
Mother speaks of them as "mine."

How to Be a Captain

"I'd like to be the captain of a ship that sails the
    sea;
I'd like to wear that uniform," a youngster said
    to me.
Said I: "Let's ask the captain what a youngster
    has to do
Who wants to be the master of a vessel and its
    crew."
So up we went to see him, with this question on
    our lips:
"What is it captains have to do before they get their
    ships?"

There was a twinkle in his eye as unto us he said:
"Well, first I tugged at anchor chains until my hands
    were red;
I scrubbed the decks and learned the ropes and
    trundled bales below;
I washed the dishes for the cook, but that was
    years ago;
I carried slops and polished brass—when I was
    young like you.
There wasn't anything about the ship I didn't do.

"I stokered and I learned to oil, and in a year or
    two
They let me take my trick at wheel which I had
    longed to do,

And well I mind the happy lump which came into
   my throat
The day they made me Number One of the Number
   Seven boat.
I served as petty officer for several years or more
And by and by as second mate a uniform I wore.

"And when I'd learned a little more—I don't recall
   the date—
My captain recommended me to be the vessel's mate.
So when you see a captain in his braided uniform
It means that he's been tried below, and tried above
   in storm.
He's had many years of service in the crow's nest
   and the hold,
And worked his way through grease and dirt to get
   that braid of gold."

Gift Givers

Six of us gathered together; we were eager to honor
    a friend.
For something of gold or of silver we were willing
    our money to spend.
We were anxious to give him a token, a watch or a
    pin or a ring,
As a permanent symbol of friendship, but no one
    could think of a thing
Which he needed or said that he wanted; no gift
    which our love could supply,
Which already his purse hadn't purchased, and bet-
    ter than that we might buy.

A dinner? He dines on the finest! A watch? He
    now carries the best!
Already we knew him provided with all that our
    minds could suggest,
So we gave up the thought of a token, and sent him
    a feebly drawn scroll
As a mark of our lasting affection which his chil-
    dren might some day unroll;
But I couldn't help thinking that evening the hap-
    piest mortals who live
Are those who have left to their friendships just
    something or other to give.

The joy or surprise and the gladness of owning
    a gift from a friend
Are thrills which can never be purchased though
    millions a rich man may spend.
And there is a rapture in giving which friendship
    is eager to know,
For love and affection seek ever some token of
    worth to bestow.
Though all men are toiling for riches, may it
    never be said while I live
That I furnished my life so completely that
    friends could find nothing to give.

Autumn

Splash of scarlet, splash of gold,
Mornings touched with autumn's cold,
Weary fields beneath the sun
Resting with their labor done.
Scythe and sickle put away.
Night is longer now than day.

Later now the sun to rise.
Gone are birds and butterflies.
Just a few brave blossoms stay,
Relicts of their kindred gay
Still with courage carrying on
'Till their strength is wholly gone.

Neither field nor forest taints
Nature's purpose with complaints.
Chilled by frost unto the heart
Silently the flowers depart.
Stand the trees, like warriors bold
Dressed in scarlet and in gold.

Nothing sad or tearful here
At the twilight of the year.
These October mornings glow
Just as if they seem to know
Past all doubt and questioning
Life is an eternal thing.

Eyes

Eyes are different, some can see
Leaf and bud on many a tree,
Some discover, here and there,
Tiny little lines of care
Stamped on faces white and wan
Others never look upon.

Some, whatever they behold,
Merely see its cost in gold.
Theirs are advantageous eyes,
Shrewd, and sharp, and cold, and wise,
Seeing only things which may
Serve their own concerns some day.

Some have eyes which sweep about
Finding little follies out.
They can readily detect
Clothes which are not quite correct,
But they never seem to find
Rich endowments of the mind.

From the self-same point of view
Some see more than others do;
What is beautiful to one
Others never look upon;
And I wonder can it be
Life is merely what we see.

Envy

I wonder if the poppy shows
The slightest envy of the rose?

Or if the pansy wastes its time
Regretting that it cannot climb?

Do blossoms of a yellow hue
Complain because they are not blue?

Do birds which God designed to sing
Envy the wild ducks' fleeter wing?

And does the sparrow sadly mourn
Because he was not goldfinch born?

I cannot say, but fancy not.
Each seems contented with his lot.

'Tis only man who thinks that he
Some other man would rather be.

Brothering with Jonah

Jonah was swallowed by a whale,
So runs the ancient Bible tale,
And later cast upon the shore
To face the tasks of life once more.

How many, many times I've smiled
To hear this story as a child,
This ancient epic of the sea,
And wondered could it really be.

Yet I, like Jonah, have been swayed
From duty's pathway, much afraid,
And swallowed by strange notions, too,
Seeking an easier task to do.

I've been gulped whole by fancies weird!
I have been lost and reappeared
Once more to find my duty plain;
To laugh with men and work again.

Perhaps false teachings swallow men
Later to cast them out again—
At least that's how I read the tale
Concerning Jonah and the whale.

The Drowning Swallow

I stood beside the water's brink
And watched a struggling swallow sink.
It fluttered round and round, in vain
Attempts to climb the air again.
I wondered by what sad mistake
That bird was prisoner of the lake,
Or what sad chance had plunged it down
In such a helpless way to drown.

Gifted with skill and strength to fly
It could have darted through the sky;
On land had it but chanced to be
It could have found a sheltering tree,
But soon its little strength was spent
In seas for which it wasn't meant.
By wind and water thus assailed,
Out of its element it failed.

Oh, helpless bird, thought I, like thee
Men also drown in failure's sea;
By chance or fate, they, too, are thrown
Into deep elements, not their own,
And there they struggle, but to die,
And   sometimes never knowing why;
But had they found their place on earth
They might have liked to prove their worth.

Creation

I never see a butterfly
  Or hear a singing bird,
But what in some strange manner I
  Am very deeply stirred.

Who first conceived the tender wings
  On which it seeks the rose?
Has human thought such lovely things
  To fashion and disclose?

O singing bird upon a tree!
  Has ever human mind
Contrived to solve the mystery
  Of how you were designed?

Man writes his loftiest thoughts in words,
  And builds with brick and stone.
But dreams of butterflies and birds
  Belong to God alone.

Faith

These are the best that our fortunes can bring to us:
  Gardens of summer and friendships to cherish,
Now and then wild birds that sweetly will sing
    to us,
  Now and then loveliness, quickly to perish.

High-born or lowly, life takes little note of us;
  Life has no pride in our arrogant glory;
Never it turns for the wail or the gloat of us;
  We are a part, not the whole of its story.

Brightly the sun shines on saint and on sinner;
  Be what we will, it is all of our choosing.
Men may give prizes of gold to the winner,
  But life has no thought for our gaining or losing.

Fatten our purses and still we must sorrow,
  Still must our pillars of pleasure be shaken,
Still shall the frosts find our gardens to-morrow,
  Still from our sides shall our loved ones be taken.

Only our faith has composure to bring to us
  Faith, which is friend to the great and the lowly;
Ever it gleams, as the blossoms of spring to us,
  Lighting life's purpose and making it holy.

Garden in Autumn

My garden wears a weary look
  Like one who toils no more
But drowses o'er the Holy Book
  Before his cottage door.

The best of beauty lies behind,
  The last rich bloom has gone;
To what is past it seems inclined
  To-day to ponder on.

A few brief days of life remain,
  And so my garden seems
To sense that further toil is vain
  And vain are further dreams.

An air of contemplation lies
  Upon each plant and tree;
I fancy that at times it sighs
  For joys that used to be.

So like the tired old man who knows
  The strength for deeds is gone,
My garden waits with sweet repose
  The change that's coming on.

I fancy that I hear it say:
  "The end is coming soon;
But I with tulips once was gay,
  And roses owned in June."

If You Would Please Me

If you would please me when I've passed away
   Let not your grief embitter you. Be brave;
   Turn with full courage from my mounded grave
And smile upon the children at their play;
Let them make merry in their usual way;
   Do not with sorrow those young lives enslave
   Or steal from them the fleeting joys they crave;
Let not your grieving spoil their happy day.

Live on as you have lived these many years,
   Still let your soul be gentle and be kind—
I never liked to see those eyes in tears!
   Weep not too much that you must stay behind;
Share in the lives of others as you'd share,
If God had willed it still to leave me there.

Personality

You may know just as much as the other man
    knows,
You may go just as far as the other man goes,
You may be just as strong, just as clever, as true,
Yet somehow or other he wins over you.
And you cannot see why this difference should be,
When you know in your heart you're as able as he.

The difference is not in the things which you know,
It is not in the skill or the force of your blow,
It is not in the work you are able to do,
It's in the personality labeled as "you."
The thing you don't see is the manner which he
Always at his best makes the effort to be.

He is keen and alert, with a light in his eye,
And a smile and a word for all men who pass by.
He wins their affection and values it, too;
He makes his life stand out, and just so could you.
But you scowl and you sigh and when strangers are
    nigh,
There's no warmth in your grip and no light in
    your eye.

It is not what you know which will carry you far,
It's not what you can do, but it is what you are.
Improve your mind? Yes, with books on the
shelf,
But give time and thought to improving yourself.
Make the effort and plan to be that sort of man
That the world loves to honor whenever it can.

Golfers

A golfer is a man who thinks
Exquisite is the putt which sinks,
And goeth home with heart elate
When drives of his were far and straight.

A golfer is a mortal mad
A mashie shot makes sad or glad,
Who counts that day well-spent when he
Scores the four one-shot holes in three.

Lions and dogs and cats reveal
Contentment when they've had a meal;
But golfers, to be happy men,
Must make a "birdie" now and then.

Dinner and dress and fame are not
Enough to grace a golfer's lot.
Granted all these, he'll dismal look
If he should either slice or hook.

Golfers are people who will bear
Life's ordinary round of care
Without complaint, and whimper sadly
Because they play a game so badly.

Memory

And if I shall remember
  The tulips of the spring,
The Christmas each December,
  The songs the children sing,
Their bits of merry laughter
  Which meant so much to me,
That's all in that hereafter
  I'd keep in memory.

I do not ask to go there
  With boastful tales to tell
I'd like to have them know there
  This life I've loved so well.
I would recall a few things
  My eyes rejoiced to see,
The tender and the true things
  Which brightened life for me.

And shall I wake from sleeping
  To face eternity
But these I would be keeping
  Of earthly memory,
But these I would remember:
  The songs the children sing,
The Christmas each December,
  The tulips in the spring.

Peace

Some have found it in a garden, some have found
    it on a stream,
For the peace of true contentment is the depth of
    every dream;
Some have found it on the hill tops, and the search
    is ages old,
But no man has ever found it in a selfish strife for
    gold.

Oh, 'tis plain what men are after as they scramble
    with the throng,
'Tis the hope of every toiler through the weary days
    and long,
'Tis the hope of every sailor standing duty far at
    sea:
The peace which follows labor in the days that are
    to be.

There are countless ways to win it; some have
    found it in a child,
Some have come to it through sorrow, when their
    hearts were reconciled;
But whichever way you wander and whichever
    choice you make
You must leave a touch of beauty for the happiness
    you take.

You will never rest contented if you serve your-
    self alone;
From your comrades, from your neighbors, comes
    the peace that you would own;
It is born of love and friendship, in a thousand
    ways 'tis told,
But no man has ever found it in a selfish strife
    for gold.

Beauty in Bleak Surroundings

Six tulips blossomed in a row.
Not many, as tulips often grow,
And later, as sped the month of May,
A peony clump bore blossoms gay.
Scarce thirty feet of lawn was seen,
Yet what there was from weeds was clean.
And through the summer bits of phlox
Vied with geraniums in a box,
Adding their color and their grace
To what had been a dreary place.

There is no doubt that garden small
Seemed scarce worth mentioning at all,
But when elsewhere you turned your eye
And only bleak neglect could spy,
When end to end upon that street
Your gaze but ugliness could meet,
That peony gay, those tulips few,
That tiny lawn loomed large to view
And told a culture and a care
Which lived undaunted by despair.

Men and Grass

Some blades of grass are tall,
  Some rich with green,
Some seem so very small,
  Some harsh and mean.

Stand close and you may see
  The patches of despair;
The difference in degree
  Of wealth that's there.

Stand off at dusk or dawn,
  And every single blade
Blends to a velvet lawn
  That life has made.

The cutter comes and mows
  The rich blade and the tall;
No favorite he knows,
  He levels one and all.

So with the world of men:
  Stand close and shame we see,
Plainly we notice then
  The difference in degree.

But from the distance viewed,
　Even as lawns grow fair,
The great, the low, the rude
　A lovely grace may wear.

And death, the cutter, mows
　Alike the great and small.
No favorite he knows;
　He levels one and all.

When a Baby Comes

When a little babe is born
　Changed is all the mighty earth.
Still the sun will rise at morn,
　But that miracle of birth
Brings another life to share
All the world's increasing care.

With that first sweet, plaintive cry
　There is ushered in one more
Who in all the years gone by
　Earth has never known before.
And that little tiny thing
May bear gifts none else could bring.

Not alone unto the few
   Dear and close are changes brought,
There are countless strangers who
   Must give time and care and thought
To the life that's just begun
Till their own last hour is run.

And it may be as the years
   Swing their rapid course away
And the proper time appears
   All the world shall hail the day
Sounding cymbal, drum and horn,
When that little babe was born.

Christmas Eve

Tomorrow morn she'll wake to see
The trinkets on her Christmas tree,
And find beside her little bed,
Where tenderly and soft of tread
Old Santa Claus has walked to leave
The toys that she might still believe.

Her stocking by the chimney place
Gives to the room a touch of grace
More beautiful than works of art
And velvet draperies can impart.
Here is a symbol of a trust
Richer than wisdom thick with dust.

I see it through the half-swung door,
And smile to think long years before
I, too, on Christmas Eve was young
And eagerly a stocking hung
Beside the chimney just as she,
Ere knowledge stole my faith from me.

Upstairs about her bed there seems
The peace of childhood's lovely dreams,
And I, grown old, almost forget
The truths with which I am beset.
Upon this blessed Christmas Eve
I, too, in Santa Claus believe.

The Golden Chance

There is in life this golden chance
  For every valiant soul,
The unpenned poem or romance—
  The undiscovered goal.

Beyond the sum of all we know
  And all that man has done,
Life holds a never-ending row
  Of glories to be won.

Still waits the canvas for the paint,
  The paper for the pen;
Still searches Faith to find a saint
  Among the ranks of men.

Though man, it seems, has traveled far
  Along achievement's way,
His conquests and his triumphs are
  But splendors for a day.

In all that is of paint and print,
  And marvels which we see,
Life gives us but the faintest hint
  Of splendors yet to be.

On still untraveled roads of fame
  The feet of men shall climb,
Far nobler goals than ours to claim
  From the rich lap of time.

Unreckoned genius yet unborn
  Undreamed of deeds shall do.
Night ends the old. With every morn
  Life bids us start the new.

Heart Courageous

There's a little old lady who lives down the way
Who has never a word of her sorrows to say.
She has buried her husband, her children and
    friends,
Still bravely her gay little garden she tends,
And bravely she smiles as if never a care
Or the anguish of sorrows had silvered her hair.

One morning as downcast I wandered along,
Because some little plan of my own had gone
    wrong,
She noticed my frown as I came to her gate
And asked me my burden of trouble to state.
"Oh, I know how you feel," she replied with a
    smile,
"But don't bear a grudge, for it isn't worth
    while!"

I thought of her sorrows and stood there ashamed
To think that my own petty trouble I'd named.
She passed me a rosebud to pin on my coat,
And I couldn't say thanks for the lump in my
    throat.
She patted my arm and she said to me there:
"Remember we all have some burdens to bear.'
Dear, brave little lady, thought I, as I left,
Of all who have loved you, so swiftly bereft,
Yet smiling and cheerful and hiding your woe
'Neath a manner so gentle that no one may know
Should I be the last of my circle to stay,
God grant me such faith as I've seen you display

Spirit

I know not whether middle age can fight again
    to win.
'Tis possible that youth alone can stand the bat-
    tle's din.
Perhaps man's courage fades with time and fifty
    is too late
To have to start a second bout with all the odds
    of fate.
But this I know: that man is lost, though young
    or old he be,
Who says: "I'm sure it's vain to try; that task's
    too hard for me."

Perhaps from silvered brows they turn and ask
    for younger men;
Perhaps to men of middle age they give no
    chance again.
But long ago was failure known, and history
    appears
An endless tale of men who rose to fame when
    old in years.
One fact of life is sure and 'tis the weakling
    soonest dies,
And in the dust that man must stay who will
    not try to rise.

Too old to start anew? Ah, no! While health
    and will remain,
Time locks no door against the man who wants
    to start again!
Though some from thinning brows may turn, by
    history is it told,
Full many a fortune has been won by men the
    world called old.
'Tis not our years that cut us down, but fear and
    failing will,
And who has spirit for the fight may live to con-
    quer still.

The Lesson

When you have found the sweetness of your
    sorrow,
In some far-off to-morrow,
Out of your heart
Pain will depart
And leave a lovely beauty you shall cherish,
A beauty that shall never fade nor perish.

Though this dark day your heart is sick with
    grieving
And torn with disbelieving;
Though now you weep,
Across the deep
Tempestuous sea of sorrow lies a shore
Where peace shall soothe your soul forevermore.

There you shall wake to find the pain departed,
And braver-hearted
You'll go your way,
From day to day,
And smile once more, and turn unto your labor,
To all mankind a gentler friend and neighbor.

The Street

Oh, who can tell what feet shall fare the roadway
    with the morning,
What grief turn the corner there without a word
    of warning,
What burden weary age shall bear, what danger
    youth be scorning?

For up and down the road they tramp, the fleeting
    joys and sorrows,
Which never find a resting camp. 'Tis only man
    who borrows
The oil from pleasure's shining lamp against his
    dark to-morrows.

Death called last week across the way. Near-by
    there was a wedding.
A babe was born but yesterday. All history is
    treading
This little street whereon we stay, and all that
    man is dreading.

Whatever be the street or lane, it knows the
    world's full story
Of happiness and cruel pain, birth, marriage, old
    age hoary,
And all that years of life contain from failure up
    to glory.

Keep Your Dreams

Keep your dreams—they're richer far
Than the facts discovered are.

Do not seek all things to touch;
Do not want to know too much.

Growing old, still play the child;
Keep some glory undefiled.

What if clouds are mist and air?
Still see ships sailing there.

What would life be if we knew
Only those things which are true?

If the things of bad and good
Were by all men understood,

Nature's hills and brooks and springs
Would be catalogued as things.

Keep your dreams, for in them lies
Joy denied to men grown wise.

Still build castles in the air!
Still see white ships sailing there!

Still have something to pursue,
Something which you wish you knew.

William Howard Taft

I shall come some day to your grave
In Arlington, and at my side,
Shall be the boy I hope to save
From all the shams of foolish pride.

And standing there, to him I'll say:
"This great, courageous soul remained
Against the perils of the day
Gentle, and kindly and unstained.

"Power from his charm could not detract,
With sympathy his life was sweet,
He never did one scornful act
To snatch a triumph from defeat.

"Men loved him best who knew him best,
In him the poorest found a friend;
By every spiritual test
His life was noble to the end.

"Here sleeps a strong man who was kind,
A great soul who had time for mirth,
Who rose, but would not leave behind
The simple beauties of the earth."

Suspenders

One pair of suspenders was all he owned,
And day by day through the year he groaned:
"Oh, for suspenders enough to wear!
Too long I've done with a single pair
Give me suspenders, I beg of you,
I care not whether they're red or blue
Or green or black or embroidered stuff,
I want suspenders, and want enough;
Lucky the man to whom fortune grants
A pair for each separate pair of pants."

Christmas came and his thanks to win
His friends and relatives brought them in:
Suspenders, satin and linen and silk,
Suspenders white as the whitest milk,
Suspenders yellow and red and blue,
Dress suspenders, initialed, too;
Purple, ochre and sepia shades,
Fancy, medium and common grades
Rubber and canvas and frail and strong
Fell like rain on him all day long.

It seems that his cousins and uncles and aunts
Remembered each separate pair of pants;
Suspenders from England, suspenders from Spain
Fell on him all day long like rain.

He piled them high and he piled them wide,
But still came more he must take inside,
And he groaned at night and he said: "I swear
I've suspenders enough for a troop to wear,
And I wish to heaven that these folks had known
Two pairs of trousers are all I own!"

Rich or Poor

The use of money marks the man.
   The wrong is not in having gold;
All men should gather what they can
   In other ways is failure told.

The sin lies not in growing rich
   But in forgetfulness of pain
And all the bitter suffering which
   Beset the men who poor remain.

No virtue lies in poverty,
   Poor men may be as vile or worse
And fail God's purpose utterly
   As those who may be rich of purse.

Within the sphere where we may dwell
   The test is not of yellow gain,
But do we use our talents well?
   Does sympathy in us remain?

'Tis not the role that makes the priest,
   'Tis not the purse that makes the man.
The proof of greatest and of least
   Is: Does he do the best he can?

The Home at Peace

Here is a little world where children play
  And just a few red roses greet July;
  Above it smiles God's stretch of summer sky;
Here laughter rings to mark the close of day;
There is no greater splendor far away.
  Here slumber comes with all her dream supply,
  And friendship visits as the days go by;
Here love and faith keep bitterness at bay.
Should up this walk come wealth or smiling fame,
  Some little treasures might be added here,
But life itself would still remain the same:
  Love is no sweeter in a larger sphere.
This little world of ours wherein we live
Holds now the richest joys which life can give.

Friendly

Heigho, for the man with a smile on his face
　　And a couple of wrinkles of care,
And an eye that can twinkle, in spite of his place
　　Or the troubles he happens to bear.
He may not be rich and he may not be wise,
　　He may not be cultured and clean,
But you know from his grin and the look in his eyes
　　There is nothing about him that's mean.

There's a jest on his lips if it's laughter you need,
　　And there's pity, if pity you lack,
You know there is brotherly love in his creed,
　　You are sure he won't stab in the back.
It may be you never have seen him before,
　　But you feel he is kindly and true;
And you're never afraid when he comes to your door
　　That a wrong he is plotting to do.

There are millions of him the world over I'd say,
　　Men patient and happy and fair,
You can meet them by night and can meet them by
　　　day
　　No matter what raiment they wear,
And you know by the light in their eyes and the grin
　　Which they flash as they see you come near,
That their hearts are wide open to welcome you in
　　And there's nothing about them to fear.

The Choice

And one man said:
"All hope is dead
  And I wish that I were, too!
For rough is the way
And the skies are gray
  And I can't get work to do.
I've lost the things which I thought were mine,
And it's now no use for the sun to shine."

In similar straits,
Betrayed by the fates
  And stripped of his worldly gear,
Another man said:
"Well, I'm far from dead,
  And I don't want to die this year!
There's a lot proved false which I thought was true,
But I want to be here when the sun breaks through."

All men must choose
Of these opposite views,
  And it's easy enough to fail,
If you're willing to quit
You can argue for it
  With a truly deplorable tale,
But always the difficult thing to do
Is to stick to a problem and see it through.

Destiny

Who knows what lies behind us all
  That we who live to-day
Might train a rose along a wall
  And see our children play?

We cannot mark each deed or thought
  In some long vanished year
By which the present earth was wrought
  For us to labor here.

But all we find along our way
  To times by-gone we owe,
The world is as it is to-day,
  Because men made it so.

And since to-day must be the sum
  Of all that was before,
Our lives may hold what is to come
  When we shall be no more.

Blindly perforce the road we tread,
  And cope with good and ill
That one a thousand years ahead
  His little place may fill.

So strangely is God's purpose planned,
   That none of us can see
Into the great uncharted land
   Which men call destiny.

Now we are here and know not why,
   The end, no man can say;
The answer to our lives may lie
   Long centuries away.

He Never Saw His Father

I never saw my father. I am like him, people say.
I was just a little baby at the time he passed
   away.
But my mother talked about him. Oft her eyes
   were wet with tears
And I came to understand him with the passing
   of the years.
Oh, we've had our share of trouble, but my one
   regret must be
That I couldn't thank my father for the things
   he did for me.

He knew about my coming and he knew the hurt
   and strife
And the cares and disappointments that are in-
   cident to life.
So my schooling he provided, and my holidays
   were glad,
For there always was a present bought by money
   left by dad.

Thus I grew older, wiser, I began to sense and
see,
Though I never knew my father, he was very
near to me.

But I couldn't go to thank him for his tender love
and care
And I mentioned this to my mother and she said:
"I'm sure a prayer
Would be carried to him promptly. But an even
better way
Of remembering your father is to be from day to
day
The sort of man he dreamed of in the tasks you
have to do.
It wasn't thanks he looked for, but he wanted
pride in you."

Now above our little table for a moment's prayer
we lean
To thank the Heavenly Father of us all Whom
none has seen.
Though the world is filled with trouble and we
trudge a rugged road,
We have all known countless blessings which
His bounty has bestowed.
Though our grateful prayers may reach Him, it
may be that all He asks
Is that we shall stand with courage and devotion
to our tasks.

Sailor Heritage

An uncle, long time dead and gone,
  Would often say to me:
"My boy, as long as you live on
  You'll dream about the sea.
And ships with masts and many ropes,
  Whene'er they cross your view,
Will always rouse long-buried hopes,
  There's sailor blood in you!"

I do not know the name of him
  In our ancestral line,
Who sometime back in ages dim
  Went sailing o'er the brine;
But part of him must dwell in me,
  Still pulsing hale and strong,
For when a ship puts out to sea
  I ache to go along.

The land has kept me for its own
  For all these many years,
For sailor's work too old I've grown,
  Still, when a ship appears,
I stand and watch it as it moves
  On lake or far-flung sea,
And feel that yearning strange, which proves
  The sailor blood in me.

A Christmas Bit

If I were Santa Claus this year
  I'd change his methods for the day;
I'd give to all the children here
  But there are things I'd take away.

I'd enter every home to steal,
  With giving I'd not be content.
I'd find the heart-aches men conceal
  And take them with me when I went.

I'd rob the invalid of pain;
  I'd steal the poor man's weight of care;
I'd take the prisoner's ball and chain
  And every crime which sent him there.

I'd take the mother's fears away,
  The doubts which often fret the wise—
And all should wake on Christmas Day
  With happy hearts and shining eyes.

For old and young this is my prayer:
  God bless us all this Christmas Day
And give us strength our tasks to bear,
  And take our bitter griefs away!

Courage

This is courage: to remain
Brave and patient under pain;
Cool and calm and firm to stay
In the presence of dismay;
Not to flinch when foes attack,
Even though you're beaten back;
Still to cling to what is right,
When the wrong possesses might.

This is courage: to be true
To the best men see in you;
To remember, tempest-tossed,
Not to whimper, "All is lost!"
But to battle to the end
While you still have strength to spend;
Not to cry that hope is gone
While you've life to carry on.

This is courage: to endure
Hurt and loss you cannot cure;
Patiently and undismayed,
Facing life still unafraid;
Glad to live and glad to take
Bravely for your children's sake,
Burdens they would have to bear
If you fled and ceased to care.

The Happy Toad

As I was walking down the road
I met an ugly, grinning toad,
Who squatted in the shade and said:
"I never wish that I were dead.
Wherever I may chance to stray
I find rich food along the way;
I have no dreams I can't fulfill;
I owe no other toad a bill;
In slimy places I abide,
But with them I am satisfied.
My little children I forsook
As tadpoles in a nearby brook;
I know not where they are nor care.
I have no burdens I must bear.
At night I never lie awake.
My bitterest enemy is the snake.
I have no taxes, no beliefs,
No cares, ambitions, hopes or griefs;
No clothes to buy, no cash to lose,
No tools that I must learn to use.
I sing no dirges, tell no jokes.
I'm just a jumping toad who croaks.
Contented, placid, happy I
Shall be until the day I die."

*　　*　　*　　*

Yet, as I trudged along the road,
I thought, "Who wants to be a toad?"

The Birch Tree

Out of a jutting rock, wind blown,
A birch tree braves the world alone.
A crevice in the granite first
Captured the seed; a wave immersed
That tiny embryo. The sun
Warmed it and thus was life begun.

Scant food the passing breezes give
And yet that tree contrives to live!
Cruel the clutch of granite gray,
Yet the brave roots from day to day
Into the great stone deeper creep,
A surer hold on life to keep.

Twisted and bent some limbs appear,
But still undaunted year by year
Those roots in cheerless channels sunk
Courageously support' the trunk
And green against the lake and sky,
A birch tree catches every eye!

Man thinks he knows what nature wills.
But much he plants the winter kills,
While far away from human care
And on a cliff by storms swept bare,
Denied the commonest of needs,
A birch tree silently succeeds!

At Her Wedding

I came across 'em, by the stair,
Those two old women simpering there,
Sniffling, as if they both had colds,
And were a pair of nine-year olds.
"What's wrong," said I, "and why these tears?
You've thought about this day for years,
And now it's come, why cry this way?
Remember, it's her wedding day!"

"I know," said Aunt Eliza, "I
Know very well I shouldn't cry,
But—" here the other aunt began,
"You can't explain it to a man,
Nor can you possibly reveal
The dreadful things we women feel.
Men think a wedding should be gay,
And so they never cry this way!"

"Oh, bawl your heads off!" I replied,
"I'm on my way to kiss the bride,"
And left that funny red-nosed pair
Still sorrowfully sniffling there,
But at her door, I seemed to note
A curious tightening round my throat,
And had to stop, to my surprise,
To wipe some tear drops from my eyes.

Because He Lived

Because he lived, next door a child
To see him coming often smiled,
And thought him her devoted friend
Who gladly gave her coins to spend.

Because he lived, a neighbor knew
A clump of tall delphiniums blue
And oriental poppies red
He'd given for a garden bed.

Because he lived, a man in need
Was grateful for a kindly deed
And ever after tried to be
As thoughtful and as fine as he.

Because he lived, ne'er great or proud
Or known to all the motley crowd,
A few there were whose tents were pitched
Near his who found their lives enriched.

Washington

Privations grim were his to bear
  Long hours of doubt were his to face.
With faith sublime and courage rare,
  Goalward he set his face.

Some heroes on full-tide are swept
  To glory and the chance they seek,
But Washington, at slow pace, crept
  Uncheered from week to week.

His was the genius of despair,
  The courage of the bitter doubt.
He saw men faltering everywhere
  But kept his own heart stout.

Had Washington by sufferings keen
  And envy's rancor been dismayed
Men's right to freedom might have been
  A century more delayed.

Plant A Garden

If your purse no longer bulges and you've lost your
    golden treasure,
If at times you think you're lonely and have hungry
    grown for pleasure,
Don't sit by your hearth and grumble, don't let
    mind and spirit harden.
If it's thrills of joy you wish for, get to work and
    plant a garden!

If it's drama that you sigh for, plant a garden and
    you'll get it.
You will know the thrill of battle fighting foes that
    will beset it.
If you long for entertainment and for pageantry
    most glowing,
Plant a garden, and this summer spend your time
    with green things growing.

If it's comradeship you sigh for, learn the fellow-
    ship of daisies.
You will come to know your neighbor by the blos-
    soms that he raises;
If you'd get away from boredom and find new
    delights to look for,
Learn the joy of budding pansies which you've kept
    a special nook for.

If you ever think of dying and you fear to wake
    to-morrow,
Plant a garden! It will cure you of your melan-
    cholic sorrow.
Once you've learned to know the peonies, pe-
    tunias and roses,
You will find that every morning some new hap-
    piness discloses.

Royal Welcome

The weary man comes home at eve
A royal welcome to receive.
For always at his humble gate
His roguish, bright-eyed children wait,
And ere a greeting he can speak
An honest kiss is on his cheek.

His features may be drawn and soiled;
His hands give proof that he has toiled;
But monarch at his castle door
From those he loves can get no more
Of tenderous and welcome sweet
Than is the worker's lot to meet.

His little garden, bright and gay,
Receives him at the close of day,
And every bud and bloom appear
Exultant as he wanders near,
While somewhere near a happy wren
With song receives him home again.

Thrice blest the man whose arm stays strong
For toil, although the day be long.
Sweet tastes the food his strength provides,
Love decks the house where he abides,
And when he turns from duty grim
A royal welcome waits for him.

The Bread Line

They stood in line and shivered and the man in the
    middle said:
"Tell me the way to do it. Do I ask them for soup
    and bread?
Will they question my name and address?" The
    two of them looked him o'er
And one of them spoke up quickly: "Have you
    never been here before?"

"Never," the poor man answered. The man in the
    front turned round,
"You've always been used to comfort! Now the
    pain of the poor you've found."
And the man just behind said: "Easy! Don't jibe
    at him any more.
The bread line is cruel business if you've never
    been there before.

"You and I know no better; we've always worn
    clothing thin.
We've always been poor and lowly; we can stand
    in the line and grin,
We are used to this bitter business—but here at
    this kitchen door
Let's help him to get his breakfast—he's never been
    here before!"

The Temptress

As I went walking down the way I met a pretty
   miss,
Who boldly looked at me and said: "A lovely day
   is this!"
Her hair was of a golden brown, her eyes a spar-
   kling blue.
I proudly doffed my hat to her and answered,
   "Howdy-do!"

She placed her graceful hand in mine and turned
   to go my way.
Said I: "I have no time to flirt; I've work to do
   to-day,
I think you'd better run back home." With sadness
   dropped her chin.
"We'll pass the drug store soon," said she. "I
   thought you'd take me in."

"Oh, no," said I, "that wouldn't do. The hour is
   growing late
And I am on my way to town to keep a business
   date.
Besides, to make it very plain, no time for girls
   have I!"
At such a cold rebuff from me the maid began to
   cry.

Now, though I've been a married man for six-
and-twenty years,
I haven't learned in all that time to cope with
woman's tears.
And so I let that temptress fair, who's scarcely
seven years old,
Escort me to the pharmacy where ice cream cones
are sold.

Thought While Shaving

As I was shaving, in the glass
Across my face there seemed to pass
The frown of yesterday which made
My little child of me afraid.
And something whispered: "Take a view
At what ill temper does to you.

"Day after day in manner grave
You stand before this glass to shave
And can you quite contented be
With that complacent face you see?
I wonder does it cross your mind
Just how you look when you're unkind?

"Suppose you speak a cruel word,
And many times has that occurred,
Can you your face reflected here
Behold with heart and conscience clear?
Can you still smile and stay serene
When you've been selfish, false or mean?

"Does it not bother you to know
That as the mornings come and go
Before this glass upon your shelf
You'll have to stand and see yourself?
Take care of what you are and do
That you may proudly look at you."

At the School Exercises

The fathers and the mothers on a certain happy
    day
Are called to watch their children in a pretty little
    play;
And the tired old faces glisten with the glory of a
    smile,
For everything the youngsters do seems very much
    worth while.
The cares are all forgotten and their hearts with
    rapture beat
As the little sons and daughters dance about on
    nimble feet.

On the day of graduation weary eyes aglow with
    pride,
Every sign of disappointment bravely seem to put
    aside.
One would never guess to see them all the labor of
    the weeks
To teach that boy the verses which he now so proud-
    ly speaks.
In that hour of young achievement triumph hides
    each fault and scar,
And the fathers and the mothers of their cares
    forgetful are.

It may be we shall discover when life's last long
    shadows fall
We shall go as little children to the Father of us
    all,
And in spite of every folly and the sins to which
    we've turned
He shall smile upon us proudly for the lessons
    we have learned.
By some little deed accomplished we may please
    Him at the last,
And repay the loving Father for our failures of
    the past.

Questions

Are we wrong in all our teaching
That triumph lies in summit reaching;
That all enjoyment earthly lies
In being proud and shrewd and wise;
That to be rich is to be glad
Since little else from life is had?

Should we not pen a different story
Concerning human peace and glory?
Should we not to our children tell
That true success is serving well;
That all life's happiness depends
Less on wealth and more on friends?

Should we not make a little clearer
The fact that happiness lies nearer
Than youth may early guess or know
For all of us on earth below;
That countless pleasures close at hand
Are strewn at every one's command?

Should we not teach them less to grumble
At modest means and dwelling humble;
That fellowship with woods and seas
Possesses endless power to please;
That doing well and staying true
Will gladden them a lifetime through?

Starting Out

They're planning to get married, and I'm rather glad
    they are,
Although the road ahead to-day seems difficult and
    far.
They've very little money, and I'm rather pleased
    at that.
They'll know the joy of striving in an inexpensive
    flat.

They're launching out together with high hopes and
    courage great.
They'd dreamed of having riches, but they've chosen
    not to wait,
And they're starting out with little—just his salary
    every week—
And they'll have to save and struggle now for every
    gain they seek.

Their bills will give them trouble, and they'll sigh
    for things in vain.
She's going to do the cooking, and I fancy 'twill
    be plain.
He'll help her in the kitchen and he'll dry the dishes,
    too,
And learn a lot of duties that he never thought he'd
    do.

But every chair they purchase will be laden with
   delight;
Every trinket toiled and saved for will with joy
   be doubly bright.
So I'm not the least bit sorry, but am positively
   glad,
For they'll know the fun of striving which their
   dads and mothers had.

The Ant World

As I was playing golf today
   Across a patch of grass I trod
   And something strange upon the sod
Caused me in wonderment to stay.
Ant hills of earth in little mounds,
   Resembling pyramids of old,
   The story of a region told
Where ceaseless energy abounds.

I'd seen them many times before,
   But curiously then thought I
   A world beneath my feet must lie,
A world which men cannot explore.

These busy creatures tug and strain
  And daily scurry to and fro,
  Tunnelling the mighty earth below,
Not thinking all their toil is vain.

Man goes about his tasks and games
  And knows his world and its affairs,
  Its pleasures and its daily cares.
His goal his whole attention claims.
But here's the ant world fraught with strife
  Building its pyramids of sand,
  And if we could but understand,
Sharing the mystery of life.

Joseph of Arimathea

Joseph of Arimathea had lived out his long career,
Growing by counseling wisely, wealthier, year by
    year.
He was known as a righteous rich man, gentle and
    kind and true,
But history seldom lingers to tell us what such men
    do.

Joseph of Arimathea in the gloom of a Friday night
Visited Pontius Pilate—the envoy of Roman might.
"There was a man named Jesus nailed to a cross
    to-day,"
Said he, "and I ask permission to care for his
    lifeless clay.

"Little I know about him, but I've heard that his
    life was clean.
I am told that because of his teachings men hated
    this Nazarene.
Those who are called his apostles still fear what
    the mob may do,
So I ask your august permission to care for a
    fellow Jew."

And Pilate who trusted Joseph and honored him,
    promptly said:

"I will give you a guard of soldiers. Go now and
    bury the dead."
Thus strangely is history fashioned. From one
    kindly deed there came
To the rich man of Arimathea eternal glory and
    fame.

To a Baby

Just a little bunch of gladness,
    Just a little pack of glee!
In this world no hint of sadness
    Or of trouble can you see.
Life is feasting; life is laughter,
    And a tickling of the chin.
Never mind what follows after,
    Drain your bottle now and grin.

Lovely baby, shake your rattle
    As I'm bending over you.
There'll be time enough for battle
    And the things which grownups do.
There'll be time enough to hurry
    After things you want to win,
Time enough for care and worry—
    Drain your bottle now and grin.

Oh, it's good to hear you cooing
  At the breaking of the day;
Good to look at you reviewing
  All the folks who come your way;
Good to see you know your mother
  As she brings your bottle in,
And your father and your brother,
  And it's good to see you grin,

The Dog

I like a dog at my feet when I read,
Whatever his size or whatever his
    breed.
A dog now and then that will muzzle
    my hand
As though I were the greatest of men in
    the land,
And trying to tell me it's pleasant to be
On such intimate terms with a fellow
    like me.

I like a dog at my side when I eat.
I like to give him a bit of my meat;
And though mother objects and insists
    it is bad
To let dogs in the dining room, still I am
    glad

To behold him stretched out on the floor
by my chair.
It's cheering to see such a faithful friend
there.

A dog leads a curious life at the best.
By the wag of his tail is his pleasure
expressed.
He pays a high tribute to man when he
stays
True to his friend to the end of his
days.
And I wonder sometimes if it happens
to be
That dogs pay no heed to the faults
which men see.

Should I prove a failure; should I stoop
to wrong;
Be weak at a time when I should have
been strong,
Should I lose my money, the gossips
would sneer
And fill with my blundering many an
ear,
But still, as I opened my door, I should
see
My dog wag his tail with a welcome for
me.

The Lovely Smile

The little lady old and gray
  Still had a lovely smile for all,
And many a cheery word to say
  When people came to call.

And if you stopped beside her gate
  In summer, autumn or the spring,
Your coat lapel she'd decorate
  With some gay bit of blossoming.

We thought of her as always gay
  And lovely as a sunny morn,
Who smiled our bitterness away,
  And yet herself no care had borne.

She showed no scar of injuries old
  And never mentioned hurts she'd known.
She listened to the woes we told;
  Deep hidden kept her own.

Yet out of sorrow's bitterest hours,
  And out of heartache and distress,
The little lady raised her flowers
  And earned that smile of loveliness.

What's in It for Me?

We fancied he'd share in our cause. Instead,
"There is nothing in it for me!" he said.
He passed up pity and play and mirth
And counted his time to the penny's worth.
Ask for his help, and this would be
His answer: "What is there in it for me?"

Nothing it meant if you said: "In this
Perhaps is friendship you'll some day miss.
Here is a task that won't pay in gold,
But will leave you prouder when you grow old.
Though nothing for this will your purse collect,
It will pay you richly in self-respect."

"What is there in it for me?" he said.
We mentioned pride, but he shook his head.
"The joy of giving," he flicked his hand—
That he never could understand.
And he found when life's last far bend was turned
That money was all he had ever earned.

The Carver

I sing of the old-fashioned carver who gracefully
    wielded his blade,
Who sat in his place with a grin on his face and
    was deaf to the comment we made;
He had learned every joint of a chicken, a turkey,
    a partridge, or goose,
And he sat there or stood as a gentleman should as
    he cleverly whittled them loose.
Oh, there was an artist worth watching, a master
    performer was he;
But the age has grown smart, and that glorious art
    is a joy that no longer we see.

My grandfather taught to my father the knack of
    dissecting a hen,
He made him recite where was dark meat and light
    again and again and again.
He trained him to sharpen his knife on the steel, and
    to flourish his blade in the air,
He shouted: "Alack! You do nothing but hack,
    when you ought to be slicing with care."
'Twas a gentleman's boast as he sat at a roast that
    he skillfully handled his knife;
And until a boy knew where the second joint grew
    he wasn't thought ready for life.

Now they whittle the meat in the kitchen, and
    bring it piled up on a plate;
Be it roast beef or ham, or a turkey or lamb, it
    is passed in the ready-carved state.
And nobody jests with the carver, and nobody
    praises his art;
There are grown men to-day who unblushingly
    say they can't get a drum stick apart,
But something has gone from the dinner, how-
    ever expensive its cost,
That we viewed with delight in the age taken
    flight, ere the fine art of carving was lost.

Missed Opportunities

Some walk so thickly wrapped in self
    And all their petty care
They never see a blossoming tree
    And wholly unaware
Of cardinal or throstle song
They trudge their dreary way along.

So muffled up in sordid things
    And hopes for gain are they
They never know that violets grow
    A few short miles away,
And never guess the deep woods hold
Entrancing pleasures manifold.

They hear the clink of coin 'gainst coin,
  Tall buildings cold they see,
But miss the mirth which floods the earth,
  As if joy couldn't be,
And never hear along the way
The curious speeches strangers say.

Who stays within the narrow rut
  Carved deep by strife and care
Will travel far where roses are
  And never know they're there.
For self is like a prison wall
Which makes the world seem harsh and small.

Love of Beauty

The love of beauty once possessed
   Outlives the sordid dust and grime,
And holds its dwelling in the breast
   Against the ravages of time.

And this is why a woman wan
   And grayed and beaten by defeat,
From day to day will struggle on
   To keep an ugly dwelling neat.

Day after weary day will see
   Her battling with the dirt and dust,
Fighting the filth of poverty
   Because her nobler nature must.

So fond of beauty humans are
   That often in a squalid room
A woman fills with stones a jar
   And brings a lily bulb to bloom.

Fear

The great god Fear grinned back at me:
"I am the foe men never see,
The hurt they never feel," said he.

"I am the wrong they never bear,
The poison they themselves prepare.
I am the shadow on the stair.

"I have no voice and yet I speak;
No strength and yet I blanch the cheek
And leave the strongest mortals weak.

"I am the blackguard man befriends,
Heeds most, feeds, cherishes, attends
And 'gainst all counsel wise defends.

"I fire no gun, I make no cry,
No lodging place in fact have I,
Yet I'm the countless deaths men die.

"Mine is a humor ghastly grim,
The lamp of reason I can dim,
Though I am nothing but a whim.

"I am man's cruelest, bitterest foe,
Yet past his door I could not go,
Had he the wit to tell me; 'No'."

The Layman

Leave it to the ministers, and soon the church will
   die;
Leave it to the women folk; the young will pass
   it by;
For the church is all that lifts us from the coarse
   and selfish mob,
And the church that is to prosper needs the layman
   on the job.

Now, a layman has his business, and a layman has
   his joys;
But he also has the training of his little girls and
   boys;
And I wonder how he'd like it if there were no
   churches here
And he had to raise his children in a godless atmos-
   phere.

It's the church's special function to uphold the
   finer things,
To teach the way of living from which all that's
   noble springs;
But the minister can't do it single-handed and alone,
For the laymen of the country are the church's
   corner-stone.

When you see a church that's empty, though its
  doors are open wide,
It is not the church that's dying; it's the laymen
  who have died;
For it's not by song or sermon that the church's
  work is done;
It's the laymen of the country who for God must
  carry on.

The Passing Year—1933

Soon must the old year die. Already
Upon its legs it grows a bit unsteady;
Its face turns paler and 'tis very clear
Not longer will it be among us here.
With each December death cuts off a
  year.

With each December death the old year
  smothers
And bears it to the past with all the
  others,
And whether it brought joy to earth or
  woe,
Was sorrow-laden or was good to know,
Like all its fellows it is doomed to go.

This was a year of struggle and of trial,
Of heartache, loss and care and self-
  denial,
Yet we may learn before our journey's
  end
That it is best harsh judgment to sus-
  pend.
Who treats us worst may be our truest
  friend.

We'll cheer the new, but there'll be little
  sighing
To mark the passing of the year now
  dying,
But some day looking backward we may
  find,
When we have left our troubles far
  behind,
Old Thirty-three at heart was not un-
  kind.

Grace at Table

When I was but a little lad, not more than eight
    or nine,
The mother had a table prayer she taught us line
    by line.
With all the family gathered round, heads bowed
    and hands in place
We'd sit in solemn silence until one of us said
    grace.

"Be present at our table, Lord," her favorite grace
    began.
"Be here and everywhere adored," the little couplet
    ran.
"These creatures bless and grant that we—" I hear
    it now as then—
"May feast in Paradise with Thee!" and all would
    say, *"Amen."*

Day in and out through weal and woe, high gain or
    common-place,
At every meal our heads we bowed throughout this
    simple grace.
"Be present at our table, Lord!" From all that has
    occurred
And all the joy that we have known—I'm sure He
    must have heard.

Landlord and Tenant

The landlord wouldn't paint the place
  Or keep it in repair,
Yet at the window panes was lace,
  Though every board was bare,
And those who passed it by could trace
  The tenant's tender care.

And those who passed it by could see
  A blossoming plant or two.
Despite the tenant's poverty
  A little garden grew,
Lovely and gay and orderly
  The blazing summer through.

The landlord Life at times seems cold
  And deaf to every plea,
Yet to our dreams we still can hold,
  Courageous we can be
And 'round the place plant marigold
  For passers-by to see.

We, too, with faith, can plant a rose
  Where all is bleak and bare
And fashion pretty furbelows
  For windows of despair,
And work, till our poor dwelling shows
  A tenant's tender care.

The Martins

The Martins are peculiar and whimsical at best,
They're very charming tenants if with you they
    choose to nest,
But though the house you build for them may per-
    fect seem to be
You cannot coax them into it if something wrong
    they see.

I do not know precisely what the Martins ask from
    men;
I only know they like a house with rooms for eight
    or ten,
And it must stand above the ground full fourteen
    feet or more
With unimpeded space about for them to wheel and
    soar.

The neighborhood must suit their choice; the gar-
    dens must be neat,
Nor will they stay to raise their young along a
    noisy street,
And many a man has built a house their fellowship
    to win
Which for some cause, to him unknown, they would
    not enter in.

The scouts come on in early spring to look the
    houses o'er,

And if they do not like the place you'll see their
    charms no more,
But should the home their fancies suit, within a
    day or two
The Martins will arrive to spend the summer-
    time with you.

Advice to Young Lovers

When I was courting Nellie, eight and twenty
    years ago,
My best side to her father I believed it wise to
    show.
Although she was my objective, in an artful way
    I knew
It would be to my advantage could I win her
    father, too.
So to please him, walking homeward, for we
    didn't have a car,
I would drop into a drug store for a good ten-
    cent cigar.

Being young, I had the notion that a present for
    her dad
Would delight Miss Nellie's parent and would
    also make her glad;
But I later on discovered not all sweetness filled
    the cup,
For at times as late as midnight he would still
    be sitting up.

And though I was bent on wooing, all my fond-
est hopes he'd mar
By remaining calmly with us till he'd smoked
that good cigar.

Oh, the hours I sat and watched him, wishing he
would go to bed,
As he puffed that clear Havana and not hearing
half he said.
Oft I'd say: "Smoke this tomorrow." He'd re-
ply, with wrinkled brow,
"Since it isn't quite my bedtime, I believe I'll
light it now."
And instead of courting Nellie I would have to
sit and stare
At her father blowing smoke rings from his an-
cient easy chair.

So, young men who go a-wooing, bear this help-
ful thought in mind,
It will be to your advantage to her father to be
kind.
But though good cigars may please him, if the
hour be growing late,
Keep your present in your pocket or you'll have
to sit and wait
Just as I did, wasting moments—and how pre-
cious few they are—
Till the daddy of your sweetheart puffs away
your good cigar.

Incident

There was a lonely woman in a cottage. Day by
day
Alone she walked her garden round to pass the time
away.
Alone she brewed her cup of tea. At nine o'clock
at night
Alone she walked from room to room to lock the
windows tight.

She heard the neighbors laughing, but she never
turned to see,
Nor raised her head nor took a step to share their
revelry.
Her hair was thin and silvered and her face was
lined with care.
And only little children ever found a welcome there.

For them she fashioned cookies to resemble polar
bears
And sugar dates and walnut cakes and other sweet
affairs,
And every little boy or girl who passed her
threshold o'er
Could eat her stock of goodies till they couldn't
swallow more.

She paid no heed to grown-ups, and the neighbors
  wondered why.
Alone she chose to keep her house; alone she chose
  to die.
The men folk thought her crazy, and the women
  often stood
And wondered who had wronged her, but the chil-
  dren thought her good.

We never learned her story. All alone one night
  she died
And when the children missed her, men were called
  to break inside.
They found her lying on the floor, her voice forever
  stilled,
And in the room the cookie jar, which she had just
  re-filled.

About Children

Little children ought to be
    Seen and seldom heard.
If at dinner time or tea
    Such a thing occurred,
I should promptly make a plea
    For a merry word.

If they waited until they
    First were spoken to,
As the grown-ups often say
    Little ones should do,
I should ask them right away,
    "Children, how are you?"

I don't want them sitting there
    Solemn as can be,
Each one rigid in his chair;
    If I want to see
Images and statues rare
    Art museums are free.

Little children should be seen
    And not heard by day!
Who could by a thought so mean
    Lead the world astray?
What a grouch he must have been
    Such a thing to say!

Beauty

The busy world has time and space
For posey and bits of lace,

For paintings, star dust, silver streams,
And things as fanciful as dreams.

Not all in nature men behold
Is sternly practical and cold,

For countless lovely things she weaves
For which no purpose man perceives.

At times she seems to draw apart
Merely to make a work of art,

Or brighten with her labors rare
Places which otherwise were bare.

So in the busy life of man
Which reason wholly seems to plan,

The self-same impulse bids him take
The time to work for beauty's sake,

And count as his supreme success,
Trifles of dainty loveliness.

Linen and Lace

A linen man from Syria has pretty wares to sell,
Embroidered things and lacy things which women
love so well.
He brings them in a mighty grip held fast with
leather stout,
And any wife will have to buy if once he gets them
out.

A banquet cloth from Italy he spreads across his
knee;
"Oh, madam, here's a bargain that's as cheap as
cheap can be!
And here is lace from Normandy that's truly very
fine;
While here I have a damask cloth of marvelous de-
sign!"

To me, they're merely table spreads and napkins he
displays.
I cannot see why women sit so long at them to gaze;
But, oh, the wily linen man has speech at his com-
mand,
Concerning lovely luncheon sets which ladies un-
derstand.

I have expensive habits of my own, I must con-
    fess;
I've often looked at costly books and hungered
    to possess.
I've bought them when I shouldn't, so I under-
    stand her case.
Her weakness is for pretty things of linen and of
    lace.

"Move We Adjourn"

When I'm weary of argument wordy
    And tired of continuous debate,
When the speaker like some hurdy gurdy,
    Which carries on early and late,
Keeps up a monotonous bellow
    On lessons I don't want to learn,
'Tis then I give cheers for the fellow
    Who rises and moves to adjourn.

There are motions to lay on the table,
    There are motions for this and for that,
And I stick just as long as I'm able
    And hark to the chatterer's chat,
I stand for the rising thanks motion
    For the one who has done a good turn,
But my friend is the chap with the notion
    To get up and move to adjourn.

There are some who like papers and speeches,
  And open discussions of things,
The heights some new orator reaches,
  The lesson and message he brings.
But each his own fancy must cling to,
  What one chooses others may spurn,
So this simple tribute I sing to
  The brother who moves to adjourn!

Wisdom

This is wisdom, maids and men:
Knowing what to say and when.

Speech is common; thought is rare;
Wise men choose their words with care.

Artists with the master touch
Never use one phrase too much.

Jesus, preaching on the Mount,
Made His every sentence count.

Lincoln's Gettysburg address
Needs not one word more nor less.

This is wisdom, maids and men:
Knowing what to say and when.

Sleeping Child

I like to tiptoe round her when she's lying fast
    asleep
And straighten out the covers where she's kicked
    them in a heap,
And when I find her sprawling kitty-corner on the
    bed
I find it fun to set aright that lovely sleepy-head.

Oh, whether late or early I'm retiring for the night,
I slip into her bedroom just to see that she's all
    right;
I stand and gaze upon her and I chuckle when I see
Her feet are on the pillow where her little head
    should be.

She's grown so very lively that she can't stay still
    at all.
The moment that she drops asleep she starts right
    in to crawl
And sometimes, like a wooly dog, as comfy as you
    please,
I've found her lost in dreamland with her head be-
    tween her knees.

Oh, I have tasks that weary me, and tasks that I
    detest.

The mother's always calling me to work when I
    would rest,
But straightening out a little girl who's sleeping
    wrong-end to,
I'd call the happiest task on earth a father has
    to do.

Gift of Life

Not much from this great world
    I ask
Beyond the strength to do my
    task.
It is enough that I may be
On hand to see a blossoming
    tree
And hear a songbird, now and
    then,
Singing his hymns of joy to
    men.

Books on a shelf; a ruddy fire,
A restful nook whene'er I tire;
Laughter of children at their
    play,
Outside a little garden gay,
Where all the blazing summer
    through
Comes into bloom some splen-
    dor new.

I do not ask that life shall be
Forever care and sorrow free,
Nor that some distant morning I
Shall not awake to grieve and
    sigh.
I ask but faith to stand before
Whate'er the future has in store.

Let me be one whose courage
    springs
From all the countless little
    things
Of joy and beauty which
    abound
Wherever man may look around.
Let me exult in peace or strife
That I have had the gift of
    life.

The Business of an Uncle

It's the business of an uncle, which I've frequently
  expressed,
To buy the toys and candies which the youngsters
  like the best,
And although the dads and mothers must at times
  some joys refuse,
An uncle's proper function is to give 'em what they
  choose.

It may be a mother's duty now and then to mutter,
  "No";
And a wise and proper father should not every
  sweet bestow,
But with nephews and with nieces every uncle worth
  his salt
Should disdain all such restrictions and be generous
  to a fault.

Now I know the uncle business, in these very pros-
  perous times.
He should always, on his visits, take a pocketful of
  dimes,
And of course if there is something which the par-
  ents have denied,
It's an uncle's job to buy it just to keep them sat-
  isfied.

It's the duty of the parents to be strict and very
  stern,
And to teach those little rascals all the lessons
  they must learn,
But an uncle's job is different. He's another sort
  of man,
And the business of an uncle is to spoil 'em if he
  can.

For a Friendly Hearth

We would not have you go elsewhere
  When heart and mind and body tire
Beneath life's load of grief and care
  To seek a friendlier fire.

Tap at our door! A welcome waits
  As warm as are the logs aglow.
The buffetings of all the fates
  We understand and know.

Come here! For you a chair is kept.
  Unburden here your troubled mind.
Perhaps for all the tears you've wept
  Some comfort we can find.

Come from the sunshine or the storm!
  Come whether skies be gray or blue!
This hearth with sympathy is warm,
  Our hearts have room for you.

Garden Experience

It was difficult to work with; it was stubborn yel-
　　low clay,
So we dug it from the garden and threw it all away,
And we bought a load of top soil, very rich and
　　very black,
Which with scarcely any effort, would with blos-
　　soms pay us back.

Yellow clay is dull to work with and it bakes be-
　　neath the sun
And the man who has to fight it knows his work
　　seems never done.
So we threw it in the alley, for impatient folks are
　　we,
And we wanted flowers in summer without such a
　　costly fee.

But our roses failed to flourish and we saw them
　　pine and die,
And we called upon a gardener who knew to tell us
　　why.
He looked the bushes over in his wise and kindly
　　way
And said: "If you want roses what you need is
　　yellow clay."

In our ignorance we'd fancied only richer soils
    were good.
That the heavy clay held virtue we had never
    understood.
It had seemed so dull and stubborn that we found
    to our dismay
We had had the stuff for roses, but had thrown
    it all away.

Time

Old Father Time is not annoyed
Because some city is destroyed.
If he would have a city there
Some day the damage he'll repair.
Should man cut down his forests wild
To such a loss he's reconciled
For in a thousand years or so
He'll watch another forest grow.

Old Father Time is not disturbed
Because some trivial whim is curbed.
Complacently from day to day
And silently he goes his way
For while men's brains and bodies tire
Struggling to win what they desire
Old patient Father Time can spend
A million years to gain his end.

'Tis only man who has to haste
Because he has no day to waste,
He wants his temple spires to rise
Before death comes to close his eyes;
The grain of truth he finds appears
The rich achievement of his years,
But Father Time can wait to see
The wonders that are yet to be.

Man battles in his little role
To build a pathway to his goal,
But change and storm and stress combine
To batter down his structures fine
While Father Time holds out to youth
An undiscovered grain of truth
And seems to know, beyond a doubt
Some day some lad will find it out.

The Tinsmith Goes Above

"What did you do?" asked the Lord, and the travel-
    ing tinsmith said:
"I used to mend old pots and pans to earn my daily
    bread.
And you can't get rich at that, for it's little the poor
    can pay
For closing a gap in a kettle's side, and the rich just
    send you away.

"Lord, I hadn't much chance on earth, for I traveled
    the humble streets
Where none but the needy and common folks a trav-
    eling tinsmith meets.
Perhaps I am all to blame, but I haven't the right
    to ask
A place up here with the great and wise for doing
    so small a task."

And the good Lord smiled and said: "I have so
    devised my plans
That a place in Heaven may at last be won by a
    mender of pots and pans.
And all that I care to know and all that I'd have
    you tell
Is, when you were given a kettle to mend, are you
    sure that you did it well?"

Circus Memories

Oh, never comes the circus with its wonders into
town
But I recall a little boy who longed to be a clown,
And high above the heads of all an acrobat I see
That little lad of long ago was hopeful he would be.

No care had he for words that rhyme. A more en-
trancing thing
Was jumping on and off a horse within a sawdust
ring.
And all the verses ever penned he'd gladly trade
back then
To be the spangled hero in the roaring lions' den.

There was a riding lady in a fluffy skirt of pink
Who might have lured this little boy away from
printer's ink,
But destiny or fortune or the fates (or was it dad?)
Contrived to change the life-work of this circus
dreaming lad.

He would not now retrace his steps. Through eyes
now growing dim
He sees an acrobat's career would not have done for
him.
But still when bands are playing and the circus bark-
ers shout
A little boy of fifty-one walks wide-eyed round
about.

Autumn Scene

Upon the hills the giant trees with color were ablaze,
Like smoke from smouldering embers rose the late
    October haze.
All silent and magnificent I fancied I could see
The Master Artist touching up some solitary tree,
But the glory of the landscape was a flash of crim-
    son flame
At the bottom of the picture where the painter signs
    his name.

Now I cannot speak the language of the men who
    paint and draw,
And with technical precision can't describe the scene
    I saw.
All I know is that a picture was unrolled for me to
    see,
And the high lights and the shadows seemed just
    what they ought to be,
But that gorgeous burst of color in the foreground
    caught my eye,
And I knew it made the landscape, though I couldn't
    say just why.

It struck me as peculiar, where an earthly painter
    signs,
The Master Artist splashed His name in tangled
    shrubs and vines.

And as I stepped up closer I discovered and was
glad
He had given that touch of splendor to the poor-
est stuff He had.
To the common things in summer which man
scarcely sees at all
He had given the place of honor and the glory
of the fall.

Growth

Life is but growth, at first in
strength and size,
Until at last is physical prime
attained.
But there's a growth that's never
wholly gained:
An inner struggle always to be
wise,
To see things earthly with clearer
eye;
Braver to be when flesh is
sorely pained;
A growth in spirit, constant and
ingrained
Which all the scars and hurts of
life defy.

Bodies grow old and furrowed
with the years
And show the marks of all that
lies behind,
But souls that have experienced
much grow kind
And gather understanding from
their tears.
Wiser in life, with tenderness
they view
As did the Master, much that
mortals do.

Those First Long Trousers

We went together, just as though
Together we must share the blow;
Though she alone had gone before,
We went together to the store
And watched him proudly try them on,
And then our little boy was gone.
Our little knickerbockered lad
Came out a youth, in trousers clad!

The smiling clerk said: "Fine!" but, oh,
Our stab of pain he couldn't know.
Perhaps he truly thought it strange
That mother didn't like the change
And felt that something in her died
The minute that he stepped inside
That little dressing room alone,
But well I understood that moan.

She knew that never more he'd be
The little boy upon her knee,
The laughing, loving, roguish child
Whose kisses on her cheek were piled.
She knew what change was taking place
Within that narrow dressing space.
Her child went in beyond a doubt,
But soon a man was coming out.

The clerk said: "Fine!" but well I knew
The mother held a different view.
The little lad she'd loved was gone,
There stood a youth with trousers on;
A youth with shoulders broad and square,
A youth who had a jaunty air,
And when we left that clothing store
We had a little boy no more.

Nellie

After seven and twenty years,
Nellie lovely still appears,
And I sometimes sit and wonder,
As her smiling eyes I see,
How she's managed to contrive
Such vexations to survive
As were bound to be her portion
Living all that time with me.

Such a restless thing am I
That a patient saint I'd try.
Half forgetful, half impulsive,
I've rushed headlong on my way,
That I marvel that her face
Shows of fretfulness no trace,
And she welcomes me with smiling
At the ending of the day.

Oh, we've had our ups and downs
And our hours of sighs and frowns,
And we've had our share of sorrow,
When the pair of us have wept,
But the strength of her has stayed
My frail nature, when afraid
I looked out upon the future
And the seas were tempest-swept.

Now I look at her, and she
Is as lovely as can be,
And I glory in her beauty
As I did long years ago;
And I'm grateful and I'm glad
That so fair a wife I've had,
Who could live the years so bravely,
But I marvel that it's so!

Hello, Tulips

Hello, tulips, don't you know
Stocks to-day are very low?
You appear so bright and glad,
Don't you know that trade is bad?
You are just as fair to see
As you were in times when we
Rolled in money. Tell me how
You can look so happy now?

Hello, tulips, white and red,
Gleaming in the garden bed,
Can it be you haven't heard
All the grief which has occurred?
Don't you see the saddened eye
Of the human passer-by?
By his frowning, can't you tell
Things have not been going well?

Hello, tulips, in the sun
You are lovely, every one.
But I wonder why don't you
Wear a sad expression, too?
Can it be you fail to see
Things aren't what they used to be?
This old world is all upset,
Why don't you begin to fret?

And they answered me: "Hello.
Nothing's altered that we know,
Warm the sun, and sweet the rain,
Summer skies are blue again,
Birds are singing and we nod
Grateful tulip prayers to God.
Only mortals fret and strive.
We are glad to be alive."

The Home Serene

A home where quarrels never rise
  And bitterness is never known,
This is the dream of all the wise,
  The joy that all men long to own.

A home where faith and love abide
  And lovely laughter oft is heard;
This is the deepest source of pride
  By which the hearts of men are stirred.

A home where anger has no place
  And hatreds never pass the door,
Where never enters dark disgrace;
  The greatest man can gain no more.

A home where dwells contentment sweet
  In spite of grief and loss and pain,
To lose this is to know defeat,
  To win it is success to gain.

Indebted

The interest on the mortgage on the house is over-
due.
The grocer's writing letters threatening us that he
will sue.
The plumber wants his money for a washer for a
tap.
The Damsel Shoppe is dunning us for sister's eve-
ning wrap,
But the thing that worries mother till her face is
wreathed in frowns,
Is the fact that we're indebted for a dinner to the
Browns.

We haven't paid the doctor since the market went
to smash.
The man who runs the laundry writes to say he
needs some cash.
I owe the tailor something and I hate to catch his
eye;
I always look the other way until he's traveled by;
But the thing that worries mother isn't money that
she lacks,
But the fact that we're indebted for a dinner to the
Blacks.

It is not for me to quarrel with the women and their
ways;

They've a certain code of honor and from it no
  one strays.
Men may think their worries greater, but the so-
  cial laws are stern,
And the dinner you've accepted is the meal you
  must return.
So I sympathize with mother as she lies awake o'
  nights,
Since for weeks we've been indebted for a dinner
  to the Whites.

The Joyous Gifts

A book to read, an easy chair,
A garden when the days are fair,
A friend or two life's path to share.

A game to play, a task to do,
A goal to strive for and pursue,
Sweet sleep to last the whole night through.

Such wisdom as will man befit
To sit with learned sage and wit,
Discussing life and holy writ.

Some judgment as to right and wrong,
The sense to value mirth and song,
With these the humblest man is strong.

With these the humblest man can find
His path with countless pleasures lined:
Contentment, pride and peace of mind.

The Little Country Drug Store

Liniments for horses,
  Medicines for cows;
Oils to rub on women folk
  To soothe their aching brows.
Little country drug store,
  Not like those in town,
Where is heard the rustle
  Of many a silken gown.

Remedies in bottles
  For bruises, hurts and sprains,
Panaceas commended
  For human aches and pains.
Tonics for the poultry
  When hens refuse to lay
Put out where city druggists
  Have perfumes on display.

Cures for every ailment
  To which the flesh is heir;
For mothers in the country
  Have little time to spare.
And so the village drug store
  A hundred needs supplies,
Including soothing syrups
  Whene'er the baby cries.

The city drug store glistens
  With countless pretty things,
And all the trifling trinkets
  Which love of beauty brings,
But still the country drug store
  By every inch of space
Proclaims the cares and problems
  The wives of farmers face.

I Laugh at Gold

I laugh at gold! It cannot buy
  A line of Shakespeare ready-made to quote.
A man must on the page set mind and eye
  Before one phrase can issue from his throat.

I laugh at gold! It cannot tell
  Its proud possessor why the sun's eclipse,
Nor teach him how to write his letters well,
  Nor check the faulty sentence on his lips.

I laugh at gold! It cannot hire
  Wisdom to serve when problems grave arise.
Fools may be rich, but still their need is dire
  When comes the great occasion to be wise.

The Everlasting Flowers

The everlasting flower is grown
In many a garden. Springtime sown
It blossoms in the early fall
And has no fear of death at all.

Its pink and yellow petals feel
Like highly lacquered flakes of steel
Which, if you run your finger round,
Produce a strange metallic sound.

These everlasting flowers defy
The death that other blossoms die.
Stuck in an urn the winter through
They hold their shape and color, too.

They gather dust like statues old
And rattle when the wind blows cold,
Till tired of seeing them about
At last the housewife throws them out.

True charms are delicately made.
The loveliest blossoms soonest fade;
We pass blooms everlasting by
To cherish those we know must die.

Trophies

There's a moose head in the hall,
And a dead fish on the wall,
And a stuffed owl on the mantelpiece,
And birds in a shining case.
There's an antlered deer upstairs,
And a mounted fox which shares
With a partridge prone at its wily feet
A nice mahogany base.

There's a maid each morn who must
Go round the rooms to dust,
And day by day on her weary face
There is ever a dismal scowl,
And this is the song she sings:
"Dead deers are dreadful things!
And I hate fish on a shining board
And the wings of a mounted owl!

"Oh, if ever a man I wed,
May he care for books instead
Of moose and mountain goats and deer
And ducks in a glassy dome;
May his hobby be postage stamps
Instead of the Northern camps,
For I've had my fill of dusting things
Which a hunting man brings home."

Gift from Heaven

(A husband is a gift from Heaven to woman, says a
prominent sociologist.—*News item.*)

Does your gift from Heaven give you all the money
    that you need?
Does he bring men home for dinner when but two
    you'd planned to feed?
Does your gift from Heaven always do exactly as
    he should?
Does he hang up his pajamas or just leave them
    where he stood?
As a husband have you thought him in his manners
    rather slack?
Well, he's now your gift from Heaven! Would you
    like to send him back?

Does your gift from Heaven, lady, stay out rather
    late at night?
Does he grumble in the morning if the coffee isn't
    right?
Does he whistle while he's shaving? Does he toss
    his things about?
When you make a bid at contract does he always
    take you out?
Does he frequently annoy you by the silly things
    he'll do?
Then remember, little lady, he was Heaven's gift
    to you.

A scientist has told us that he thoroughly believes
A husband is a present which from Heaven the
    wife receives,
And I know the men will hail him as a friend, but
    I shall fear
To quote my Heavenly rating for I know she'll
    say, "My dear,
You may be a gift from somewhere, but you can't
    be Heaven sent,
The professor's made an error—'twas the other
    place he meant."

The Cynic and the Doll

"Ah," the scoffing cynic said,
    "You thought your doll a lovely thing.
You took it in your arms to bed
    And fancied it worth cherishing.
But now it's broken, child, and you
    Shed tears above it in despair.
This is a foolish thing you do.
    There's merely wax and sawdust there."

Said one unto the weeping child
    Who knew the truth as well as he:
"Come, little one, be reconciled!
    Perhaps your doll can mended be.
Forget the sawdust you have seen.
    Forget this grim and dreadful truth.
Such tragedies as this have been
    An everlasting part of youth.

"So keep your love of dolls, my dear,
　And cherish them the while you may.
You'll find with every passing year
　That many a joy must go away.
Cling fast to beauty though it fades
　And press your playthings to your heart.
When reason cold your mind invades
　Then much that's tender must depart.

"So treasure wax and sawdust things
　Which warm the soul and glad the eye.
Heed not the cynic's mutterings
　Who coldly reasons how and why.
'Tis well to love the good and true,
　But keep your dreams and fancies here
And never grow so wise that you
　Are left with naught to do but sneer."

Weariness

God set him in a garden fair
  Where tulips bloomed each spring;
About him always everywhere
  Was many a lovely thing,
With miracle and mystery
  His every day was filled,
And yet he only seemed to see
  The structures mortals build.

He knew the stars were overhead,
  But seldom raised his eyes,
The paths of life he chose to tread,
  A stranger to the skies.
From youth to manhood, then to age,
  He plunged his spirit deep
In figures on the ledger page,
  Correct accountants keep.

He never learned the names of flowers,
  Or birds or friendly trees,
In all his busy wakeful hours
  He never heard the breeze
Enticing him with bits of song
  To let a day go by
To watch a brooklet race along
  Or gaze upon the sky.

God set him in a garden fair
  With countless splendors strewn,
But all he saw while walking there
  Was stone some man had hewn,
And all he talked was loss and gain
  And cold commercial strife—
Which makes it easy to explain
  How tired he grew of life.

One of My Faults

Oh, so much better I would be
If only I'd the power to see
My neckwear, handkerchiefs and hose
Which lie beneath my very nose.

Could I discover right off hand
My shirt studs in my dressing stand
Or find my shoes of white and tan
It would improve me as a man.

If I were not foredoomed to shout:
"Hey, mother! I've looked all about.
My white belt's nowhere to be found!"
I'd be all right to have around.

But up the stairway Nellie flies
In answer to my frantic cries
And finds the things I want to wear
Precisely where she said they were.

Prisoner at the Bar

And the judge said: "What! no money to pay
In your hour of need
A lawyer to plead
Your case to-day?
And you come to the bar
Just as you are,
Poor and alone, with no friend to nudge
The solemn sides of the powerful judge
And ask as a personal favor that you
Be spared the punishment justly due?
Well, be not afraid!
Let your case be laid
Here before me. Though poor you are
And alone you must stand at the judgment bar
With the best and the worst of you known, my son,
I'll forgive you most of the wrong you've done."

If these lines you've read
You may think them odd,
But the man was dead
And the judge was God.

The Apple Vendor

The apple man upon the corner worries me a lot.
I wonder if he sells enough to pay his rent or not;
I wonder if he lives alone, or has he children small,
And just how many apples he must sell to feed
    them all.

It's no concern of mine, of course; I've never
    learned his name,
I don't know where he goes to, nor from whence
    the fellow came,
And yet I never see him on the corner with his box
But I wonder how he stands it in those worn-out
    shoes and socks.

I wonder as I pass him what misfortune cut him
    down
And left him selling apples on some corner of the
    town;
And if his wife is grateful for the little that he
    gives,
And what he does on Sunday and just where it is
    he lives.

I wonder who his friends are, and is he what he
    seems,

Or a man of high ambitions in the wreckage of
his dreams?
And has he wasted chances or done everything
he could?
And a thousand other questions which I wish I
understood.

The Inner Charm

And should another come my way,
    Younger and prettier of face,
Still unenchanted I should say
    She lacks your tenderness and grace.

What if her hair were thin spun gold?
    Her eyes as blue as Heaven is blue?
Her dazzling charms would leave me cold.
    She would not have the soul of you.

Others are fair. I answer "Yes,
    But love is not alone of eye,
And there's a spirit loveliness
    Exterior charms cannot supply."

There is a beauty much too deep
    For age or cruel care to find,
Outlasting all the storms that sweep,
    And that is loveliness of mind.

Gladiolas

Call them gladiolas! That's how mother knew them!
  Never mind the Latin name—it's not half as
    pretty.
Gladiolas! Everybody in the country grew them
  Thinking they were just the same to people in
    the city.

Came an aunt to visit us one summer time and she
  Had a lot of wisdom and took every chance to
    share it;
Tried to teach us children how to say: "gladioli!"
  Mother wouldn't learn it 'cause she simply
    couldn't bear it.

Call them gladiolas! That is what they'll always be
  To folks who really love 'em and whose natures
    never harden;
People who remember to pronounce "gladioli"
  Maybe aren't familiar with the friendships of a
    garden.

The Wayward

Sometimes into the finest group there slips
  The plunderer and the cheat
Who, with a sullen look upon his lips,
  Mocks good men he may meet.

And those who well their high employments bear
  Are sick with hurt and shame,
That one who has no thought for them must share
  Their calling and their fame.

High-minded men forever here must face
  With shame's hot burning cheek
The deeds of those who find with them a place—
  The traitorous and the weak.

To every family come the ones who fail—
  The strange, black sheep—
And only God knows why they are so frail
  And how their fellows weep!

Victim of Fear

He feared so much the growing old
  And poverty's grim curse
That he refused to let the gold
  Escape his tight-locked purse
And let his youth turn gray with mould—
  A tragedy much worse!

He robbed his middle-age of all
  That makes a lifetime sweet
And walked, with fortune at his call,
  A poor man down the street,
Fearing that when the shadows fall
  Such poverty he'd meet.

In giving he found no delight.
  With fortune at his side
He thought with failing strength and sight
  He'd need what coins provide.
He lived a poor life that he might
  Be rich the day he died.